≋ *The Policy Puzzle*

≋ THE POLICY PUZZLE

FINDING SOLUTIONS IN THE DIVERSE AMERICAN SYSTEM

Donald T. Wells
West Georgia College

Chris R. Hamilton
Western Kentucky University

PRENTICE HALL, UPPER SADDLE RIVER, NEW JERSEY 07458

Library of Congress Cataloging-in-Publication Data

WELLS, DONALD T.
   The policy puzzle: finding solutions in the diverse American
system/Donald T. Wells, Chris R. Hamilton.
      p.   cm.
   Includes bibliographical references and index.
   ISBN 0-13-300088-5
   1. United States—Politics and Government.   2. Policy sciences
I. Hamilton, Christopher.   II. Title.
JK271.W378   1995
320′.6—dc20   95-25290
                                                              CIP

Editorial/production supervision, interior design,
   and electronic page makeup: Kari Callaghan Mazzola
Acquisitions editor: Mike Bickerstaff
Editorial assistant: Anita Castro
Cover design: Tom Nery
Buyer: Bob Anderson

 © 1996 by Prentice-Hall, Inc.
Simon & Schuster/A Viacom Company
Upper Saddle River, New Jersey 07458

Printed in the United States of America
10   9   8   7   6   5   4   3   2   1

ISBN 0-13-300088-5

PRENTICE-HALL INTERNATIONAL (UK) LIMITED, *London*
PRENTICE-HALL OF AUSTRALIA PTY. LIMITED, *Sydney*
PRENTICE-HALL CANADA INC., *Toronto*
PRENTICE-HALL HISPANOAMERICANA, S.A., *Mexico*
PRENTICE-HALL OF INDIA PRIVATE LIMITED, *New Delhi*
PRENTICE-HALL OF JAPAN, INC., *Tokyo*
SIMON & SCHUSTER ASIA PTE. LTD., *Singapore*
EDITORA PRENTICE-HALL DO BRASIL, LTDA., *Rio de Janeiro*

≋ CONTENTS

Preface   xi

Chapter 1

Understanding Public Policies: Policy Issues and Government's Search for Solutions   1

What to Do for Baby Catherine   1

What's in Most Policy Textbooks—and What's in This One   4

The Basics of Public Policy   5

What Is "Public Policy"?   6

The New Dimensions of Public Problems   9

The Real Value of Comparisons with Other Countries and Localities   12

Policy Change and Stalemate in the Federal System   13

Why Do We Have Policy Cycles?   14

The Enduring Policy Issues   16

Critical Policy Choices in America Today   18

Who Has Clout: Policy and Political Power   19

Intergovernmental Policy Clout   20

Democratic Control over Policy   20

Chapter 2

Policy Change in the Twentieth Century 21

A Look at the Early Twentieth Century 21

The Rise of Modern Problems, and How Government
Got Involved 23

The Evolution of Governmental Responsibilities
in the Mid-Twentieth Century 27

Changes During and Immediately after World War II 30

Changes in the Postwar Years 31

Changes from the Late 1950s to the 1990s 33

The New Map of Responsibilities in the 1990s 36

Chapter 3

*The Limits of Imagination: How Policy Myths
and Cultures Affect What Americans Think
and Do about Public Problems* 40

Policy Myths and Cultures and Their Effects 40

Information Pollution: The Growth of Disinformation 43

The Four Major American Policy Cultures 48

General American Policy Myths 49

American Political Ideologies 60

Summary 64

Chapter 4

*The American Tapestry: The Diversity of Federalist
and Regional Policy Cultures* 65

Federalist Policy Cultures 65

Regional Policy Cultures 68

Summary 84

Chapter 5

The Intergovernmental Playing Fields of Policy 85

What Is the Role of Policy Structures? 86

The Policy Map: The Eight Patterns in the American Federal System 91

Legislatures: Mirrors of Subjurisdictional Interests 93

Executives: The System's Personification and Pseudo-Manager 97

Bureaucracy: Gatekeeper of Government Action Channels 98

Courts: The Political Arbitration Councils 101

Patterns of Interaction among Governments 102

The Interstate Structure: In the Thicket of Governments 105

Policy Structures: More Than Boxes on Organizational Charts 110

Chapter 6

Environmental Policy: Necessity versus Denial 112

A Cauldron of Contaminants: The Critical Issues 113

The Ozone Layer: Planet Earth's Sunscreen 115

Global Warming: A Greenhouse for Planet Earth 117

Acid Rain: Singing in the Rain Is Not What It Used to Be 121

Chemical Waste: Societies Use a Lot and Waste a Lot 122

Ambient Quality: The Air We Breathe and the Water We Drink 126

Where Are We Now? Policy Response to the Critical Choices 129

American Response in a Multinational Context 129

American Unilateral Policy Response 131

Unscrambling the Puzzle: How We Got to Where We Are 137

Chapter 7

Economic Policy: Policies and Choices for Prosperity 144

The Scope of Government Economic Activity: Competing Visions 145

Is a National American Industrial Policy Possible? 147

What Does the National Debt Really Mean? 149

The Balanced Budget Amendment Rides Again:
Uncertain Change, Uncertain Effects   152

The Domestic Economic Policies of Governments   155

Dilemmas and Critical Choices in Economic Policy   175

Chapter 8

Education Policy: A Nation at Risk   180

Four Recurring Issues   180

Education for Whom?   181

What Type of Institutions Should Deliver Education?   182

Who Administrates the Schools?   183

Who Is Accountable?   184

Policy Responses to the Critical Choices in Education   185

Education toward Disciplined Intelligence
versus Disciplined Skills   186

The Mix of Public and Private Institutions   187

The Limits of Local Administrative Control   190

The Accountability Movement   192

State Education Reforms   196

Feasible Policies for Education   197

Chapter 9

Code Blue for Health Care: America's Medical Crisis   202

The Drumbeat of Disinformation: The Killing
of Health Care Reform 1994   202

The Economic Giant: The American Medical System   204

The Context of Medical Systems Worldwide   205

How the Great American Cultural Tale about Medicine
Limits the Debate   207

Five Expert Pictures of the Health Care Problem   209

The Common Element: Cost, Cost, Cost   212

Code Blue Response: Proposed Solutions
to Health Care Problems   222

Combining Managed Care and Public Health: The Clinton Plan   229

The Medical Monopolism Picture: Restoring True Competition   235

The Historical Evidence of Monopolism   236

An Outline for a Politically Feasible Health Care Reform   243

The Final Frontier: How the States Are Taking Over   244

Summary   249

Chapter 10

Issues and Ethics at the Extremes of Life: Abortion and Euthanasia   251

Abortion: A Never-Ending Battle   252

Conflicting Values of Pro-Choice versus Pro-Life Advocates   258

The Drift toward Balanced Stakes Abortion   260

Euthanasia: Choosing How and When to Leave   265

Case Studies of Near-Death Choices   268

Policy Solutions for Euthanasia and Abortion Dilemmas   277

Chapter 11

How to Fit the Puzzle Pieces Together: Rethinking Feasible Solutions   279

The State of the System at the Beginning
of the Twenty-First Century   280

The National Government: Policy Gridlock
and Relative Failure   280

The Spread of Solutions across Levels of the Federal System   287

State and Local Governments: Policy Momentum
and Relative Success   289

Why the Shift from the National Level: Gridlock versus Activism   294

Important Lessons from Our Friends: The Recovery
of Democratic Community   302

Appendix A
Technical Distinctions of Regions   306

Appendix B
A Research Note on the Euthanasia Case Studies   308

Bibliography   310

Index   327

≋ PREFACE

THE RICHNESS OF THE AMERICAN POLICY SCENE

This book presents the rich, diverse American policy scene. We have tried to portray its vast richness, to be faithful to its true diversity. We know this is a difficult goal, one that political science has not tried hard enough to fulfill.

What do we mean by richness? Literature now portrays life in America with a sense of richness and realism. There is a new American writer movement that is striving for a sensitivity, a comprehensiveness, and a sustained reach in portraying the diverse experiences of Americans. William Least Heat Moon, for instance, writes sensitively about the uplifting spirit and tradition in the mysterious Flint Hills of Kansas in *Prairy Erth* (1992). David Lamb portrays the spirited, optimistic, and admirable lives of millions in the vast stretches of nonurban America in *A Sense of Place: Listening to Americans* (1994). Such clear-eyed prophets and poets can be heard by one who listens, their voices rising above the cacophony of cynicism, negativism, and shallow caricatures that pass today as discussion about our society. Sadly, political science has succumbed somewhat to the virus of one-line, one-idea caricature. The public policy area of political science has suffered a kind of myopia and has not been fully faithful to the richness of our vast American federal democracy.

We wrote this book because we have been mightily concerned that the true richness of Americans' efforts to resolve their problems among themselves—as good a definition of public policy as there is—has been getting lost in political science and the media. In public policy studies, we have observed, with growing pain and some alarm, a creeping loss of the American variety. Our policy history, diversity of region and village, experimentation, failure (and yes, success) are all too often overlooked. We have sensed this loss in students, textbooks, and policy theories. We sense it in the policy journals, in the scholarship, and in the growing characterization of policy and life as "economic."

There was an age when political and policy information was informed by a sense of our diverse culture, our history, and grass roots real-world practice. That was the era of V. O. Key, Jr. (*Southern Politics*, 1949). Key and an entire generation of political scientists got their feet dirty through the 1950s exploring American politics out on the street, where it was practiced. They then wrote the richness of what they found into the bones of American political science. That sense is fading. In the giant forge that was the 1960s and 1970s an attention to American policies was born, and we named it "policy studies." But after the earlier generation of scholars, this academic stripling grew up and came to depict the American policy experience with a different language: the technical talk of empirical theories, behavioralism, and now economics. The street, the plains, the mountain regions—and the individuals who lived and struggled there to resolve problems among themselves—somehow got lost in this new-age theoretical wilderness.

No one can capture the true picture of diversity and richness in the American policy experience. But we can adjust ourselves to *look* at it. To do so, we need to be a bit more like the clear-eyed literary poets and prophets. We need a heightened awareness of policy history, various cultures and practices, regional differences, local experimentation, success, and failure. Above all, we need a better sense of how the possibilities are working out in the American federal democracy.

THE PURPOSES AND AUDIENCES OF THE BOOK

This book was written with multiple audiences fixed clearly in our minds. For beginning students and for undergraduate majors, we strove to write in clear, engaging English. In the first half of the book we lay out our sense of the richness of the American policy scene, something we believe both students and scholars need.

The first chapter clearly lays out multiple concepts of public policies, to enable us to examine the vast diversity of "doing policies" and the options available to us as we try to resolve problems in the federal democracy. Chapters 2 to 5 move through increasingly higher levels of explanation. Here we explain American policy history and the distinctive ways of thinking about and acting on American policies. We look at what feeds and limits our imaginations about how we ought to "do policies" as we examine our major policy styles, mythologies, and the variety of regional differences. Chapter 5 explains the true richness of public policies as being intergovernmental in America. By this point, the more advanced student and the scholar will recognize the method in our madness in steadily adding higher levels of explanation. In doing so, we aim both to instruct and to step beyond the boundaries of the current dominant approaches to public policy evaluation. And by trying to retain clear and engaging English, we hope to carry both the beginning student and the scholar into the realm of the richness of American policy. In the last part of the book we aim for a decent level of sophistication in analyzing and recommending alternatives for some of the critical problems Americans are trying to resolve.

In other words, the last half of the book allows us, in baseball lingo, to "really deliver the heat." From Chapters 6 to 11 we use our approach to analyze and describe policy problems in detail, focusing on the national, state, and local levels. Most important, we use this approach to explore alternative solutions, describing problems and policies in the critical areas of economic development, environmental regulation, education reform, health care reform and regulation, and the major cultural and ethical battles over abortion and euthanasia.

"The heat" in those chapters seeks to explain state and local efforts to resolve problems, not just national attempts. In the end, we attempt to deliver three things. We hope first to deliver a wider view of American problems and policy solutions that is faithful to the richness of our history, regionalism, cultural styles, and limits. Second, we strive to see the transnational forces in our midst, the possibilities of solutions from abroad, and the intergovernmental solutions that we are struggling to create. Finally, we strive to use this wider view to diagnose problems and prescribe some of the better alternatives that Americans have worked out in the real practice of the American federal democracy.

NOTES TO SCHOLARS

American policy scholars need to think carefully about the richness of the American policy scene, and about how to return to it. This book represents a fledgling attempt to make such a return. There are several features about the landscape of the vast policy scene we wish to note.

The public policy subfield in political science is a bit like a resolute turtle that has traversed a long distance, only to end up high-centered on a mound of sand. This is so because the current analysis of policy is too segmented into somewhat narrow images. The richness and diversity of the policy scene in the American intergovernmental system are too often overlooked. The urge toward *reductionism* is possibly the root of this narrowing policy myopia. One cause may be the scarcity of research resources. But a more important cause seems to be the research agendas of the "invisible colleges" of research colleagues that dominate the journals. At bottom, the guiding concepts of research are too national, economic, institutional, or political in nature. In the etymology of political science, we pay too much attention to the middle of the political system and public policy, and too little to Easton and others' historic conception of what lies at both ends of the system: namely, culture, setting, styles, and environmental forces at one end, and the vast creativity in innovation and implementation at state and local levels at the "outcome end" of the political system.

Boiling theory down to practice, this means that one cannot simply neglect the differences in society and politics across our land. We especially cannot ignore the regional and intergovernmental patterns and the distinctions between the activities of people *inside* governments, people working *with* governments, and people acting in voluntary associations and agencies *instead of* governments as they work to resolve our problems. These policy realms make up the real policy scene in America. Scholars have not done a good job of researching this real-world policy context. For some twenty years, research concepts about the "official middle" of the political process have instead dominated policy research. The "research modes" of interest groups or legislative process, implementation, bureaucratic policymaking, cost–benefit calculation, organization development, economic rationality, and even evaluation research are among the dominant idealizations of public policies. Together they segment and obscure our wider vision of America, for the richness of the policy scene cannot be perceived mainly in the official and bureaucratic middle.

We need to return to the richness of the American policy scene, or we run the risk of presenting nearly as much a caricature of American policy choice and practice as does the increasingly histrionic mass media.

The neglect of the richness is ultimately a failure to focus on the correct concepts in research and writing, which tap into the diversity of our federal democracy. For instance, public policies today are not merely national, or "rational," as research so often assumes, but are also a stubborn blend of the subnational, intergovernmental, and cultural. The best illustrations of this are the state and local policies virtually taking over economic development in the United States (Chapter 7). In addition, policies do not diffuse only from top officials to other top officials, as is generally the idea of research; they diffuse more through bureaucratic networks, from region to region, and through the media and the cultural and specialist "information networks." An example of this is the health care reform among the states (Chapter 9). Also, policies are not merely "economic" in motive or nature; they are probably even more motivated and infused by cultural, religious, stylistic, and diverse motives and values, as illustrated by the education reforms of the states (Chapter 8). Finally, policies do not stem only from elected or judicial institutions or from interest groups, as most scholarship implies (see Chapter 10). Policies also spring from reactive and creative bureaucratic networks, both in and out of government. Within governments, perhaps environmental innovations illustrate this best (Chapter 6). The spread of euthanasia practices among medical professionals (Chapter 10) and the mushrooming voluntarism in states and localities illustrate the vast public policy diffusion largely outside of government. And perhaps most of all, policies stem from deeply entrenched policy beliefs, derived ultimately from differences in regions and cultures (see especially Chapters 2, 4, and 11). It is this type of richness that needs to be emphasized if we are to fully understand American policies. This is what we seek to explore in this book.

We wish to thank Nicole Signoretti of Prentice Hall, who did a wondrous service for us in obtaining reviews, which we used in reworking the book, and we would like to thank the following reviewers: Midiad Kraft, *University of Wisconsin*; Patricia K. Freeman, *University of Tennessee*; and John F. Whitney, Jr. We also stand in admiration of the editorial-production wizardry of Kari Callaghan Mazzola.

Finally, for Chris Hamilton, I am indebted to two unusual personalities. One is Professor Mike Harder, retired, of the University of Kansas. In his distinguished career, Professor Harder inspired me and hundreds of others to think carefully about the real practice of politics and bureaucracy at the state and local levels. The other is my mother, a spirited Catholic visionary and feminist before her time. She raised me—on the windswept plains of Kansas—to look up at the shimmering stars and wonder about things.

Donald T. Wells
Chris R. Hamilton

≋ THE POLICY PUZZLE

 CHAPTER **1**

*U*NDERSTANDING *P*UBLIC *P*OLICIES

POLICY ISSUES AND GOVERNMENT'S SEARCH FOR SOLUTIONS

What to Do for Baby Catherine

As the fall leaves were turning brilliant, Baby Catherine had her first birthday. The party was fun, the presents were bright and cheery, and she had a great time diving into her birthday cake, covering herself, her family, and friends with sticky pieces. Behind the happy events, however, were some difficult family circumstances and some even more difficult American policy problems which Baby Catherine could not know about. Her father, in his forties, had been unemployed for three months. He had a great deal of managerial business experience but no college degree, and he found it difficult to compete in the job market with younger men with college degrees. Also, like many others, he was haunted by the fear of a deepening recession. Catherine's mother had spent years raising two children and had quit her medical records job in a doctor's office in order to pursue a degree in accounting at the local university.

The various problems the family faced were compounded by Baby Catherine's medical problem. At twelve months she had had an intestinal hernia—a condition easy to fix but still potentially very threatening. Her family, like 38 million other Americans, had no adequate health insurance. Her father, like 20 percent of the working population, had no health insurance available at his previous job. Her mother, a college student, found that the university offered students no health insurance plans. Even if her mother dropped out of school to return to work, the family practice doctor who had been her employer offered no health insurance plan for her employees. Such a plan was too expensive, and the doctor had to pay off huge medical school loans and the costs of starting up a practice.

It was estimated that Baby Catherine, if she entered the hospital for a simple one-day surgery and a two-day stay, would run up a bill close to $15,000. Actually her parents were fortunate in living in a part of the country where medical costs were lower than in big cities and certain other regions. Otherwise the bill could easily be as high as $25,000.

Catherine's mother was an astute person. She knew what great risks the family faced from potentially catastrophic medical bills, even for simple problems, and so she had tried to find private health insurance. She found out that policies "adequate enough" to cover most major expenses were too expensive. On the other hand, policies that were affordable had huge deductibles, requiring thousands of dollars out-of-pocket before the policy "kicked in." She settled for the "cheap" but inadequate coverage—at about $100 per month it was all the family could afford.

The problem was that this affordable insurance policy would cover only about half the bill. The family didn't have half of $15,000 lying around in a cookie jar. There were no rich and willing relatives and no way to acquire adequate health insurance. So behind the images of the birthday cake lay a very disturbing problem: How can Baby Catherine's parents ensure that she receive necessary medical treatment?

To fully understand this case, you must look at it also from the point of view of the hospital. Hospitals these days are frequently in a financial bind. In 1989 and 1990 thirteen inner-city Chicago hospitals closed their doors as a result of financial difficulties. The financial condition of most hospitals is such that they simply cannot let large bills go unpaid. They usually have procedures to screen out patients who cannot pay or who have inadequate insurance. Local hospitals and physicians are reluctant to treat cases like Baby Catherine unless state laws force treatment for immediately life-threatening circumstances. What was the family to do? What would happen to Baby Catherine?

Here enters public policy. As the family searched for options, they heard of the government program called Medicaid, which was designed in the 1960s to provide emergency medical assistance to those too poor to afford it. Unfortunately for the parents, Medicaid was a favorite program in the 1980s and 1990s for budget cuts and eligibility restrictions. Soon the family learned that neither parent was personally eligible for Medicaid. Then the question became this: Would the benefits be available to Baby Catherine? Even if she qualified, however, Medicaid procedures and forms were such that there would be a waiting period of six weeks to two months before they knew if Baby Catherine would be eligible for the aid. Yet she needed medical attention immediately. So what are the parents' options? Here enters the first thought experiment.

Read through the thought experiment in Box 1.1 and develop some constructive solutions for the medical care crisis in the United States. Searching for feasible solutions is hard work, but the effort is worth while. Throughout the text we will be presenting other such thought experiments on the critical choices or dilemmas Americans face as we enter the twenty-first century.

The issues with which public policy presents us are vexing and have no easy solutions. For example, who is "at fault"—if fault is to be found—for the lack of programs to treat health problems such as those faced by Baby Catherine? Does it make sense to search for blame in partisan politics? Is it the fault of the Democrats, who the Republicans claim want to tax and spend on programs that don't really treat the problems that people actually have? Is it the Republicans, who the Democrats claim have been meat-axing social programs for at least twenty years in order to transfer those monies to favored pork barrel programs of the rich? Does it make more sense to skip these partisan arguments and search for "blame" in the bureaucracy and its stringent regulations of a program like Medicaid? As you can see, the really tricky question is: Where do we look to start to understand the system and to find the solutions to the problems of American public policy?

1.1   ***SEARCHING FOR SOLUTIONS***

1. What are the reforms we need for the hundreds of thousands of people like Baby Catherine each year who need medical attention but can't afford it?

2. In 1980 Americans spent $202 billion for health care. In 1990 it was $606 billion and it is estimated to soar to over $1.5 trillion by the year 2000. This is equal to over $5,800 per year for every person in the country. What are we to do with a health care system that rises in cost approximately 1 percent a month and that increasingly sees larger percentages of the American population stranded without health care insurance?

3. Suppose you are a U.S. senator. How is this problem supposed to be balanced with other needs in the budget crisis situation and recession of the early 1990s, when massive government deficits each year total at least $200 billion? Do you raise taxes to pay for problems like these or do you cut more programs and more people out of benefits that might affect their health or welfare?

4. We have an essentially private health care system, yet over 38 million persons had no health insurance coverage in 1990, and this number is certain to rise sharply in coming years. With severe "gaps and costs" like this in our health system how do we ensure that either private coverage or public programs can be made to work? That is, how do we give the Baby Catherines of America the help they need without excessive waste or cost?

WHAT'S IN MOST POLICY TEXTBOOKS—AND WHAT'S IN THIS ONE

The majority of research and textbooks about public policies are written from some theoretical standpoint developed in political science. In general, the policy system and its problems are presented from a "Washington looking down" point of view, or a national policy perspective. From that point of view public policy is typically explained in two ways. First, it is described as if it happens only between Congress, the presidency, and the national bureaucracy. A second approach describes how policies develop through phases over time, "filtering down" to local levels. Other points of view about public policy have stressed such things as theories of different types of policies, different means of policy choice (political, economic), or how public policy looks from or is provided by state and local governments (as in Henig 1985).

Some presentations of public policy concentrate on its subtlety. This view explains how policy problems are often paradoxical or difficult to define, and how we must recognize the unexpected consequences of decisions made by officials (Stone 1988). Certainly, for example, the series of financial catastrophes was an unexpected consequence of the deregulating of savings and loans in the 1980s to allow them to make speculative investments as their bigger-brother banks had done for decades (Pizzo, Fricker, and Muolo 1989). The colossal mismanagement of investments by a handful of savings and loans in different parts of the country sank the national finance and banking system into an unprecedented debt, by some estimates equal to $1.4 trillion after all costs are figured. Nobody expected that result from deregulation. One goal of the study of public policy should be at least to alert people to anticipate and hopefully prevent such developments.

This book presents public policies in America from angles that have been rather neglected. It sees policy problems and solutions from the grass roots. One general approach is to look at policies from both practical and analytical angles. It describes policies and problems and tries to stimulate thinking about potential solutions. For example, Chapter 2 describes the history of public problems and policies in the twentieth century, and Chapter 3 explains the typical American styles of public policy. Both topics are extremely important for a proper understanding of our problems and what we do about them, but they are seldom considered. Chapter 5 describes the American intergovernmental or federal system of policies, also vital but often overlooked. The middle chapters describe the details of key areas of public policies, such as economic development, health care and medical ethics policies and problems, environmental policy, and education. These chapters explore solutions to these troublesome problems, partly by looking at solutions that have been developed in the various states, or even abroad. Thus the book's central theme might be described as explaining the typically American public policy system, the key areas of policy concern, and the history, record, and possibilities of solution in the American federal democracy.

The point of view of the book is therefore established from two basic hard-nosed perspectives that can help us define what policy problems are, understand the ways of the policy system, and search for solutions that fit into those ways.

The first hard-nosed perspective is the *intergovernmental or federal picture of public policy*. Virtually everybody in political science recognizes that public policy is intergovernmental: Policies made in Washington, such as hospital cost-control regulations, have to be filtered through a massively complex maze of national-to-local governments, bureaucrats, interest groups, and social forces in the federal system. Only after this filtering do they affect somebody like Baby Catherine, determining whether or how she gets the treatment she needs. Most scholars pay homage to the idea that American public policy is "processed" through a kind of "intergovernmental meat grinder," but this book highlights what happens to these policies at the different levels of the intergovernmental system, and emphasizes the intergovernmental record of success, failure, and possibility of solutions.

The second hard-nosed perspective behind this book is the street-level or average American experience of public policy. Chapters 2, 3, and 4 have this slant, describing *the history and the typical American styles of public policies*, as well as the practical ways these yield different results for people in various regions of the country.

THE BASICS OF PUBLIC POLICY

Public policy is what governments do or avoid doing to and for people on behalf of public or private interests. It has deep and far-reaching effects on our lives. The study of public policy is very exciting, sometimes deeply disturbing, and is certainly deeply paradoxical. It is important at this point to get some sense of what government policy means to us as individuals. To do so, try another thought experiment (see Box 1.2).

1.2	

SEEING THE IMPORTANCE OF POLICIES

Imagine a typical college student, if there is such a person. How does the government affect that individual in an ordinary day? Think of what Jane College is likely to do first as she wakes in the morning. She probably will turn on the light in her room. Behind that simple fact lie many government activities. Let's identify a few. Certainly the electricity was provided by a public utility. These are companies that enjoy a monopoly granted by the government in exchange for submitting to regulation of their operation and rates. The wiring that carried the electricity to the light was manufactured in plants subject to numerous safety, environmental, and other regulations. Imagine in what other ways government may be involved in the simple act of Jane's turning the light on. Then follow Jane through the actions of getting ready for school. How is government involved? How does she get to school? How is that affected by government? What about her experiences at school? After school? After the day is through, what is the last thing that Jane will do at night? Probably she is back to that bedroom light and we've come full-circle.

As you can see from Jane's first action in the morning to her last one at night, government policy affects her in direct, specific, and even personal ways. Actually we should also point out that government affects Jane while she is sleeping. For example, there are fire protection regulations on the content of her mattress and pillow. She also has police and fire protection. When you really try to identify all the ways the government affects the average person in an average day, the list is a very long one indeed. Now that you have the personalized effects of policy clearly in mind, let's look in greater detail at the basics of public policies.

WHAT IS "PUBLIC POLICY"?

The word *policy* is often used in ordinary conversation. Your professor might have said, for example, that it is her policy to give a midterm exam. Or you may have heard a fellow student at the student union building say it is her policy never to get too involved on the first date. So what is policy? What makes a policy public as opposed to private? Political science analysts are not agreed on a common definition of public policy. As you read over the definitions in Box 1.3, keep in mind that your understanding will grow as you continue to think about public policy. The definitions are merely a starting point. Our definition is a practical one: A public policy is what governments do or avoid doing to or for people on behalf of public or private interests.

| 1.3 | *PUBLIC POLICY: WHAT THE EXPERTS SAY* |

Public policy is whatever governments chose to do or not to do. (Dye 1987, p. 1)

Government policies are courses of action made up of a series of *decisions*, discrete choices (including the choice not to act), over a period of time. (Rushefsky 1990, pp. 1–2)

Public policy is the sum of the activities of government, whether directly or through agents, as it has influence on the lives of citizens. (Peters 1986, p. 1)

The term *public policy* always refers to the actions of government and the intentions that determine those actions. (Cochran et al. 1990, p. 2)

> There is no *grand unified theory of public policy*. We can make a useful start toward understanding American public policy by considering such matters as these: Who is involved in policy formation? On what kinds of issues, under what conditions, and to what effect? And how do policy problems develop? (Anderson, Brady, and Bullock 1978, p. 7)
>
> Comparative public policy is the study of how, why, and to what effect different governments pursue particular courses of action or inaction. (Heidenheimer, Heclo, and Adams 1983, pp. 2–3).
>
> Public policy can readily be viewed as the output of a political system that comprises *individuals* who come together in *small groups* within the framework of *organizations* characterized by hierarchy, division of labor, and specialization. (Lynn 1987, p. 14)
>
> Public policies [are] the *expressed interests* of government actors relative to a public problem and the activities related to those intentions. (Dubnick and Bardes 1983, p. 8)

In our definition, as in most, public policies have five common elements. First, public policies involve *governmental authority* in several ways. For one, they can be under the direct development and influence of government. An example is surely the action of armed forces on the battlefield, something not much under the immediate influence of private business managers, but rather of military commanders. Another imprint of government is that it can give policies public legitimacy even if its actions are partly on behalf of narrow or private interests. An example is the development of a new weapon by a private contractor for the Defense Department.

The policy authority structure in the United States is intergovernmental, with eight distinct patterns occurring among approximately 80,000 governments. Within these eight patterns of federalism, specific government institutions provide the context within which private agents and political forces are played out. In Chapter 5 we explain how public policies are inherently intergovernmental and how they are guided by the eight patterns of federalism. This structure also means that responsibility for specific policies is more or less located at one level or another of the federal system.

A second aspect of public policy in all definitions is that policies develop through the *action or inaction of government*. Governments build schools, construct roads, vaccinate children, inspect meat packing plants, fight wars, make peace, and take tens of thousands of other actions. Governments also act by choosing *not* to do something (although these actions are not as visible). This is the well-known concept of a *nondecision* (Bacharach and Baratz 1970), that is, a deliberate government choice to *not* do something, to suppress a concern in order to prevent it from becoming an issue, or perhaps to prevent action. For example, many have long held that the government has helped cover up facts about President Kennedy's assassination in 1963 (Lifton 1980).

Another important example of a nondecision is the "choice" in our political system not to impose competency qualifications on the President. For example, we do not require presidents to take seminars on international relations or even to take instruction from former presidents, even though these measures might lead to vital improvements in the presidency. U.S. local governments also seem to have a knack for suppressing concerns and preventing them from becoming issues. Think of the frustration of citizens who become concerned about an issue only to find that it is difficult to get anyone to listen to them. And governments sometimes more actively prevent actions from being taken. For example, a supervisor in a meat-packing plant can order inspectors to look the other way rather than conscientiously perform their jobs. Although these government non-decisions are difficult to see, there is almost a limitless range of them, and their effects are hard to exaggerate. So whether they are positive actions or nondecisions, public policies are deliberate activities engaged in by governments.

Third, all public policies carry *purposes and intentions*. Like all choices, public policies are based on values, opinions, prejudices, biases, and all the other elements that make up the complex process of humans choosing to do or not do something. Public policies are "culturally driven." In the United States, issues become public policies only as they are guided by certain constraints and cultural forces. Americans understand and act on policy in typical ways on the basis of culturally determined belief systems (see Chapter 3).

A fourth aspect of all public policies is they have *outcomes or effects on people and society*. Policy outcomes are important because they affect the lives of individuals in direct, personal, and continuous ways. This fact gives rise to many complex questions: Who wins and who loses as a result of public policies? Can public policies be structured in such a way that everyone wins? If so, policies are a *positive sum game*, even if different people get different levels of benefits. Until recently many analysts have seen public policy as a *zero sum game* (this point of view is taken mainly from economics). That is, there are winners and losers, and usually it is assumed that the size of gains for one party is equal to the size of losses for someone else. This idea that society has only limited resources that are divided among winners and losers—in the concept of trade-off—has come into serious question in recent years (Stone 1988, Chapters 2–5). It is highly questionable, for example, that there must be a trade-off of lost jobs against strengthened environmental programs (we will examine this issue in a later chapter).

Analysts have pointed out many other important and more complex aspects about public policies than the simple idea of winning and losing. For example, most public policies are paradoxes in one way or another (Stone 1988). They can be looked at from a variety of stances. Starting with the old idea of whether a glass is half full or half empty, Deborah Stone has pointed out that policies are paradoxes more often than not. An example is the policy paradox of surrogate mothers. Is signing a contract to be a surrogate mother simply agreeing to a fee for a service, or is it something more emotionally loaded, like selling babies? Or is it both? As Stone argues, public policies are often several things at once because of the different values people attach to or read into policies. Consider how differently abortion is seen, for another example. To the anti-abortion side abortion is simply "murder," while the opposite side views it as "a woman's basic freedom." Thus public policy is not simply the idea of winners and losers; there are many other issues involved.

Stone and others have argued with great success that public policies have many meanings to people, many unexpected consequences, and many aspects of "winning and losing" about them. Public policies are closely tied not so much to "actual benefits or beneficiaries" but to what people think about public policy. In other words, public policy is partly what people *think* they are getting, what they *think* is good or bad, evil or desirable, and so on. As a result, the "soft side" of public policy—such as popular symbols like the flag, "family values," and the like—usually is much more important to people than rational gains or losses. We will explore later the American styles of public policy.

A fifth common element in all definitions of public policies is that they are *problem oriented*. Most people tend to think about public policy this way. In other words, a public policy can be a governmental response to a perceived need or a public demand. For example, suppose a city has a problem with drug trafficking in a certain area of town. In response to that problem, the police might adopt a policy of intensifying police patrols in that area.

Dubnick and Bardes (1983) remind us that public policies can also *generate* problems. An example is the idea of *unexpected consequences*. As an analogy, medical research has identified a group of ailments known as iatrogenic disorders, which are illnesses induced unintentionally by a physician who is diagnosing and treating another illness. Medical colleges now offer courses in iatrogenic disorders. Public policy analysts should be more sensitive to government actions that generate such unintended domino-effect problems or unexpected consequences.

In some cases governments are sensitive to unexpected consequences. In mobilizing the National Guard units during the Iraq invasion crisis in the fall of 1990, the American government tried to be sensitive to the disruptions that mobilizing would cause to communities, guard members' families, and their professions. In other cases, however, governments are insensitive to the iatrogenic type "disorders" caused by public policies. For years the federal government has encouraged the production of tobacco, which has been virtually proven to be a carcinogenic, as well as a life-threatening practice in a variety of other ways. Whether they generate problems or solve problems, public policies are problem oriented.

THE NEW DIMENSIONS OF PUBLIC PROBLEMS

The social problems that public policies are intended to treat are not entirely what they were in the past. In the last fifty years these problems have taken on some entirely new features. The unintended or iatrogenic aspects of policies are one set of new complications. But the most important new complications of policy problems are described by the terms *international, intergenerational*, and *intergovernmental*. We will discuss the first two below and the third in the next section.

Public policy within the United States commonly shows *international* influences on a much larger scale today than in earlier periods. This is so because of the powerful interdependent and global forces of the mid-twentieth century (see the classic by Keohane and Nye 1977; Kegley and Wittkopf 1989). Thus it is common today to speak of the international economy's effects on local jobs and even local governments. For instance, the skyrocketing oil and energy prices of 1990 were a result of the Iraqi invasion of Kuwait and the Gulf crisis. On another level, Ford Motor Company described the Ford Escort as the great "American" car, although it was made up of parts from over sixty countries! For all practical purposes, the Escort was simply assembled in the United States. Also the dramatic changes in the Soviet Bloc countries have brought into sharp focus both the international character of policy problems inside individual countries, and the necessity of multinational efforts to help those countries find solutions. We also need to recognize that the international effects on American problems do not stop at the national level. Bayliss Manning developed the concept of "intermestic affairs" to illustrate this point (Manning 1977). In her analysis of economic policy, Manning found that a disruption of economic activity, say trade flows between two nations, can cause hardship in particular *local* areas. The increased hardship would produce an intensified political reaction at the local level, which would then filter up through the intergovernmental system. In brief, international affairs increasingly affect local policy, and local policy can filter up to affect national and even international affairs.

Now try another thought experiment to think of the ways that international forces can affect the community in which you live. Imagine how your community can respond to something like the rise in oil prices in order to affect the national level of government and policy. How can forces from your local community percolate up to affect international relations?

The point is that it is impossible today to understand the domestic policy of the United States or even of local governments as isolated from the global community. Consideration of most policies and problems, to be realistic, must include international factors. Unfortunately, public policy studies in general have only recently begun to appreciate the international forces behind public policy. Also, U.S. policymakers have usually not considered policy solutions worked out overseas as possibilities for the United States. Later we will examine some policy solutions from other countries that might successfully apply to American critical public problems.

The second kind of newer complication of public policy is *intergenerational*. Intergenerational aspects of policies continue on in time to affect future generations. Ancient peoples were often sensitive, maybe more so than we are, to the intergenerational consequences of policy. For example, the Bible records these words: "For I the Lord, thy God, am a jealous God visiting the iniquity of the fathers to the third and fourth generation..." (Exodus 20:5). This quote points out that even in the time of Moses and the Ten Commandments, leaders wanted people to see how their actions today (the fathers) would have intergenerational consequences for the lives and social fabric of the Hebrew people (the children). Of course important changes were made in this view before the twentieth century. One line of thought coming out of the European Renaissance led to the modern emphasis on the creative potential and the accountability of the individual for actions. Outside of religious history, this view developed over time to find expression in the extreme individualism of American society. In the past century and a half, sensitivity in America to the intergenerational consequences of action was weakened seriously as a result of this individualism as well as consumerism and other factors (see, for example, the arguments of the famed economist and critic Thorstein Veblen).

Select a policy problem of interest to you, and try to pick out the intergenerational elements or consequences in it. For example, let us consider again the policy of the American government to support and encourage the production of tobacco. In the twentieth century, which has exhibited the most extreme individualism, it has until recently been assumed that the health threat associated with an individual's smoking affected only that individual (the Surgeon General's 1989 report states that 400,000 Americans die from breathing their own smoke each year). However, since the 1960s, research on passive smoke inhalation has shown that a health threat occurs also to individuals who are near the smoker. By some estimates 50,000 die each year from passive inhalation of someone else's smoke. Also, if you are a pregnant woman, the adverse effects of smoking may be transmitted to the child and to future generations. (See Box 1.4.)

| 1.4 | *DEATH FROM PASSIVE SMOKE* |

The U.S. Environmental Protection Agency has confirmed that thousands of Americans die each year from passive smoke inhalation, or simply breathing in the smoke from smokers near you.

Dr. Stanton Glantz of the University of California at San Francisco is one of the leading epidemiologists, or statisticians of disease, in the world. He reported at a world conference on lung diseases in Boston in May 1990 on the risks of passive smoke. On the basis of his review of all available valid statistical studies in 1990, he estimated that *50,000 Americans die each year* from passive smoke inhalation.

Source: *New York Times*, May 29, 1990, p. B5.

Now consider this idea: Many individuals who smoke for a long time get some horrible and expensive disease such as lung cancer or emphysema. Later on they then "choose" or are simply ordered by doctors to be put on extremely expensive life-sustaining treatment, such as a $25,000-a-week heart-lung machine or respirator. To offset short-term heavy losses on costs like these, hospitals and insurance carriers charge higher fees for other medical services and raise insurance premiums. As you can see, individuals who think they are making individual choices to smoke but later receive expensive life-support are actually billing others for much of the cost through the magic of the market system. In the chapter on health care we will look at social accounting to see how some of the real intergenerational and consumer cost problems are passed on by so-called "individual" health practices.

A policy area with less obvious intergenerational consequences is the national budget deficit and the resulting national debt. By some estimates, the true national public and private debt in the early 1990s has soared close to $4 trillion (about $500 billion total debts of governments plus the much larger $3-plus trillion corporate and consumer debt). In the past the effects of this kind of debt were thought to be exclusively technical, limited to such things as inflation and higher interest rates. In recent years, however, prominent economists have analyzed the likely current and intergenerational effects of the ballooning national total debt as a strong drag on economic growth and a force that erodes our standard of living in ways not seen since the Great Depression of the 1930s (see Calleo 1992). They also note that accounting procedures need to be adjusted to show the present value in dollars of what the present and future generations can be expected to pay over their lifetime as a measure of the true burden to taxpayers. The purpose of this procedure would be to tell us how generations in the future will share in the burden of paying for today's excessive consumption and debt (see Kotlikoff 1987, p. 6).

The issue that emerges from this line of thinking is this: The present generation (consumers, corporations, and government) consumes too much and invests too little in the productive sectors of the economy. We pass on the effects of the huge current debt and a weakened economy to our grandchildren because of our unwillingness to save, or to invest out of current earnings, or to pay taxes. Thus the total national private and public debt no longer is merely a question of technical economics but instead has intergenerational costs and consequences. As the popular bumper sticker says, perhaps we *are* spending our grandchildren's inheritance.

THE REAL VALUE OF COMPARISONS WITH OTHER COUNTRIES AND LOCALITIES

Beyond the policy basics are more subtle but important issues. We have seen how policies can have unexpected consequences and can sometimes exhibit the puzzling traits of a paradox. We also have to be aware of how our own biases or interpretations of the world make these issues even trickier to understand. These problems suggest one of the most basic issues to consider as you read this book: How can we Americans get outside our own biases and understand the potential for solutions to public problems, solutions that come from the examples of successful policies in other settings? One way is to understand the typical American styles of thinking about policy and how they limit us (Chapter 3). Another is to look for successful policies somewhere else in the federal system. Yet another is to learn from solutions that are practiced overseas. These approaches comprise what we call the comparative policy advantage. By being aware of how we limit ourselves, and by comparing policies from elsewhere, we may be able to think ourselves into solutions at home.

The comparative policy advantage can also help settle two more questions that have plagued American policy analysts: (1) Can we get democratically chosen policies that do not sacrifice effective solutions? (2) Can we know what is policy success versus failure? The comparative policy advantage allows one to see how others have arrived at effective and democratic policies, and to see examples of success that have occurred outside of our biases and our usual line of sight. Furthermore, it becomes easier to determine the success of policies when you can see clear success elsewhere, not only in other states in the federal system but also overseas. We will cover comparative policy solutions in each of the policy problem chapters and in the last chapter.

POLICY CHANGE AND STALEMATE IN THE FEDERAL SYSTEM

In regard to policy, we need also to recognize some general reasons why it is difficult to reach solutions and stick with them in the American system. One of the major reasons why problem solving is slow in America lies in the *intergovernmental* system. The American federal system was not designed for quick policy action. It was designed rather to be a decentralized system of representation and decision making, partly to guard against political power takeovers. Therefore it allows different levels of government to do different things at different times on the same policy problem. It further allows various levels to alter policy considerably as it moves down from the national level to local systems and vice versa. Recognizing how the eight patterns of federalism work and affect policy (see Chapter 5) is an important step toward helping us solve public policy problems in a complex and slow-moving political system.

A second reason why problem solving is slow—as has been suggested by several studies—is that we have a sort of "policy stalemate" at the national level (Dolbeare 1986; Lowi 1969). This stalemate is traceable to several factors, including polarized opinions and declining consensus on national goals, increasingly opposed party goals in the long stretches of divided party control of national and state offices since World War II, the complexity of federalism and "hyperpluralism," a situation in which so many powerful interest groups compete for power that they tend to cancel each other out (Lowi 1969). Because policy consensus can be reached only through complex power balancing between interest groups, a kind of policy paralysis develops. Unable to reach consensus, and with no dominant interest group, government retreats, makes small incremental and contradictory policy steps, or makes no response at all. An example of policy stalemate today is abortion policy. With new Supreme Court decisions increasing state powers to regulate the intensely divisive act of abortion, no clear, single national policy direction is now detectable.

Not all is bleak in the federal system, however. The policy stalemate at the national level does not necessarily extend down to states and localities. There is a compensating "subnational policy momentum" (Hamilton and Wells 1990, pp. 314–316). Thus many have noticed a growing degree of substantial policy change at the state and local levels (Harrigan 1988, Chapters 16, 17). But policy innovation at one lower level does not necessarily spread to become a trend throughout the federal system; the spread of innovation is both slow and irregular in most instances. Also, state and local action cannot substitute for strong national policies to deal with tough international problems that can affect us all (ozone depletion, AIDS, international economic competition, etc.).

WHY DO WE HAVE POLICY CYCLES?

In many intergovernmental programs a stalemate occurs from one decade to the next because of policy cycles. Policy cycles occur when, as soon as a program is in place and gains some ground, an opposing interest group or coalition mounts an attack on it (Jones 1968; Lowi 1969). The result is that current policies are replaced with previously attempted programs while conditions return roughly to what they were before. Even the partial return of power to the states to regulate abortions in the 1990s (reminiscent of the 1960s) illustrates this cycle. One of the more common policy cycle stalemates occurs when periods of government activism are followed by periods of "market solutions" to public problems (see Hamilton and Wells 1990, Chapter 12).

One reason for policy cycles involves the American election cycle. As we change executive branch administrations we seem to swing back and forth in our policy direction. For example, the Carter administration emphasized national energy policy, yet only a few years later the Reagan administration made severe cutbacks in those same policies. By the early 1990s there was substantial talk again about the need for a national energy policy in the wake of environmental threats such as global warming and the energy independence and alternatives issues raised by the 1990–1991 United Nations/Iraq War—some even claimed that Reagan's action in suspending the Carter initiatives was a "national tragedy"—only to have the issue die out by the 1992 presidential election. Thus we seem to have a tendency to reach a solution but not to stick with it because of divergent administrations.

Another reason for policy cycles is periodic switches in our preferences among various policy styles and cultures (see Chapters 3 and 4 for a full description). Public issues often arise or are understood through the rhetoric of these different styles and cultures. From one generation to the next, Americans conduct debates over policy issues in terms that are hauntingly similar to debates in years past, cycling back and forth among a limited set of ideas. To see this process, imagine any proposal for change in which you have an interest—for example, in regard to medical care, taxes, or welfare. Think of the ways that proponents for different policies use images to characterize the policies as they try to influence others. Some argue "return power to the states," for example—a theme as old as the Constitution itself. Others argue for a strong, active response by the national government. If advocates of change can get policy to go their way for a while at least, then resistance will inevitably rise somewhere in the underlying intergovernmental system, with rhetoric associated with a competing policy style or culture. For example, the idea that "we need national action on this" is traceable to James Madison's convention speeches as easily as it is to Lyndon Johnson on civil rights.

Another reason for policy cycles is that Americans simply like to reuse ideas from among our competing policy styles and cultures and thereby imagine they are introducing "something new." Americans seem to have only so much patience with a particular policy solution. After a few years, policy actors find some justification to modify the policy. Thus the issues and problems raised by policy cycles are never really resolved.

The shift of ideas on what is "best" for housing policy is an excellent example. In the early 1980s the Reagan administration advocated a policy of returning the housing function to the private sector. Reagan's position was that the tradition of highly centralized, direct national action to supply public housing had been a failure. By the spring of 1988, however, Congress and the media were debating the need for strong national action and the resurrection of government spending for housing the poor and the homeless; yet by May of 1992 the proposed House and Senate budgets called for the virtual elimination of new public housing construction and deep cuts in public housing maintenance. Such unresolved bouts about problems are common.

On a broader level, yet another reason for cycles is that Americans have been debating for 200 years where in the three competing federalist traditions policy responsibility ought to be concentrated. For example, in the 1950s in the Eisenhower administration there was much talk from the President and from study commissions he appointed about the need to return more power to the states and divide and separate responsibilities of the national level from the states (the tradition of dualism). By the 1960s, however, most academic specialists on federalism were arguing that this kind of dualism was both unrealistic and improbable. They often pointed to the inability of the Eisenhower commissions to persuade Congress and state and local governments that such a radical shift in responsibility could be made or was even desired. The Eisenhower proposals died quickly in Congress because of state and local resistance.

And so the 1960s analysts proclaimed that dualism was virtually dead, replaced by "new" forms of cooperative or centralist federalism (Elazar 1964; Grodzins 1966). Far from it: In the 1980s President Reagan dramatically raised again the issue of the need for "returning power to the states," and a major effort at a "new federalism" initiative was put forth by his administration. The Reagan proposal went even further than Eisenhower's in calling for a swapping of federal and state health and welfare responsibilities. Again, most of the proposal died in congressional committees, primarily because of state and city resistance. Thus complaints about too strong a national action in the 1950s had resurfaced in the 1980s. The policy cycle had made its rounds again.

THE ENDURING POLICY ISSUES

In addition to the various policy solutions that seem to cycle back into vogue periodically, there are enduring *political* issues that concern the ultimate goals and processes of the policy system. These questions give rise to many of the continuing debates about policy. Seven of the more important underlying enduring policy issues are summarized as follows.

1. *Democracy*. Abraham Lincoln's formulation of "government of the people by the people and for the people" has become a central feature of policy debates in this country. Most people believe that democracy literally *is* the expression of majority public opinion. However, considerable research and expert opinion cast doubts about whether "majority opinion" exists on most issues, and whether public opinion is an effective guide for directing government to "do what's best." Furthermore, democracy *is* more than just majority rule, and majority rule may not even be the best principle of democracy by which to guide public policy. The United States has not given serious consideration to European ideas of proportional representation or economic, social, and work group consultation in the policy process, for example.

2. *The public interest*. The "public interest" is a very elusive concept indeed, but hard as it may be to find and achieve, it is a powerful concept in public policy. Much of the conflict in public policy is rooted in people's effort to define and control what is thought to be in the public interest. We like the way Stone (1988, p. 14) expresses the idea: "Because politics and policy can happen only in communities, community must be the starting point of our policy. Public policy is about communities trying to achieve something as communities." This effort to achieve something as a political community could involve policy on which nearly everyone is in agreement, such as clean air or good education. It could mean something as specific as an individual's idea of what the community should do. It could be understood simply as "what is good for the community as a whole." One can clarify the phrase somewhat by examining options and consequences; by using standards of democratic human rights, efficiency, or ecological values; and by careful use of statistics—but in the end the "public interest" is in the eye of the beholder, and thus the debate about it drives the debates about policies.

3. *Equity or fairness*. If public policy and politics are about who gets what, when, and how, as the noted political scientist Harold Lasswell claimed, then the question of how the benefits and costs go to individuals becomes a crucial issue. A concern for distributive justice has become central to thinking about outcomes of government decisions. Are the outcomes of government *fair*? And what is meant by fairness? We suggest that you think about the concepts of fairness as the starting point in answering this question. First, Plato defined fairness as giv-

ing everyone his or her due. By this he meant that all are to get what is coming to them in both the positive service sense and the negative law enforcement sense. Bentham argued that fairness is giving the greatest good to the greatest number. Pareto (1971) developed his well-known theorem that action is to be taken in such a way that each individual is as "well off" as every other individual. Optimality is achieved when the benefits of individual A are the same as those of individual B. However defined, the concept of fairness is always a top burner issue in public policy debates.

4. *Efficiency*. Efficiency traditionally has been about minimizing waste. It has been defined as an input-output ratio. If an outcome is produced with the minimum of effort, expense, and waste, the activity is generally accepted as "efficient." Efficiency is thus a guide as to *how* to do things, not *what* to do. As the periodic outcries over "waste in government" indicate, efficiency is a powerful issue in public policy. But it is not a simple one. The public may demand a government program that is inherently inefficient. Police protection, for example, may be deemed necessary by the public, but because it is inherently inefficient the private sector will not provide it. Also, redundancy—the need to do the same thing at least twice—often conflicts with the goal of efficiency. One example is the American insistence on having three levels of government (national, state, local). Also the public insists on fail-safe systems. Will the public allow astronauts to go into space with only one life support system? Are nuclear power plants to have only one layer of safety systems with no backups? Will a city allow a police officer to patrol a high-crime area alone? Efficiency may not be as simple a guide to "good" policy as the economists or the input-output ratio definition might suggest.

5. *Equality*. The Declaration of Independence declares flatly that "all men are created equal." Of course, at that time women could not vote, nor could black slaves, nor, in certain states, could men who did not own enough property. Some people have always been "more equal" than others. Since that time, a central struggle in public policy has been to identify what equality means and to make it a feature of all policy. This struggle, best reflected in the civil rights movement, has been intense and protracted. What does equality mean? We like Deborah Stone's explanation (Stone 1988). She asks students to engage in a thought experiment involving how a cake can be divided equally among all claimants. Stone says that there are eight ways this question can be answered. (1) There can be equal slices but unequal invitations to the cake cutting; (2) There can be unequal slices for unequal ranks (e.g., freshman, sophomore, etc.) but equal slices for equal ranks; (3) There can be unequal slices but equal blocs of the cake assured for groups and individuals; (4) There can be unequal slices of the cake but equal overall meals; (5) There can be unequal slices that carry equal value; (6) There can be unequal slices but equal starting resources; (7) There can be unequal slices but equal statistical chances of getting a large slice; (8) There can be unequal slices but equal votes in the decision as to who will get what slice. The debate about how important equality really is, and even what it means, lies behind many policy conflicts.

6. *Effectiveness.* Here the issue is whether policy has accomplished the purpose it was *intended* to accomplish. Do schools actually educate students? Do welfare programs actually raise people out of poverty? Such questions are continually asked of all policy areas and are the basis for much of the accountability movement today. Accountability is usually defined as the duty to accomplish something and to make that accomplishment known to review officers (superiors) in the policy system. Thus program directors are called upon to develop "output measures" of performance, in contrast to input measures that identify the resources committed to the activity. The key issue of policy debate in this regard is always: What is success and how do you know it when you've got it?

7. *Representation.* Issues of representation carry great emotional and symbolic value in relation to political power. The central question of who has power in the policy system is critical to determining who gets what out of the system. The debate here is between those who think power is in the hands of elites and those who think it is held by interest groups in competition with each other (pluralists). Representation is an important issue because it has to do with giving people either the appearance of or the actual power to affect the direction of policies. Because the issue is so emotionally laden, it is the basis for much acrimony.

These seven policy issues are stable and enduring components in the debate over public policy and federalism in the United States. The public square, that arena where ideas and issues are debated, seems always to ring with discussions of these issues.

CRITICAL POLICY CHOICES IN AMERICA TODAY

While there is not universal agreement on what critical policy choices America faces today, all can agree that certain policy problems are critical. Our presentation of problems here in no way suggests that we rank them in order of importance. Each is critical and each is international, intergenerational, and intergovernmental in nature and scope.

The *health care crisis*, symbolized by Baby Catherine, is one problem. A related concern has to do with various issues of *medical ethics*, most of them involving the extreme ages of life: abortion, the use of fetal tissue in research, contract babies, test tube babies, euthanasia (or mercy killing), and the living will. Second the decade of the 1990s was ushered in with substantial attention to the *environment*. Earth Day was celebrated, President Bush declared himself the environmental president, and politicians and corporations generally postured themselves as environmentalists. Whether all this hoopla (Environmental Protection Agency Chief William Reilly labeled it the national morality play) means anything in real policy change is debatable. But few debate the fact that the trends, dilemmas, and issues of environmental quality are among the critical choices America faces into the twenty-first century. Third, we believe that the *education crisis* is a critical problem. Finally, one of the front-burner issues of the contemporary period is the economy, and more specifically, government's role in the economy. Thus *economic policy* is a critical choice. What is strange is that other countries have often reacted successfully to these problems, yet our awareness of how they do it is low. We will explore these issues and possible policy solutions in the middle and later chapters of the book.

Our approach will be to describe the various issues that guide the specific debates and to rethink possible options for resolving them. We will draw on our description of the American policy styles in Chapters 3 and 4 to help define what solutions are culturally tolerable within the American policy styles. In considering the practices of other countries, or even innovative practices in the states, we will keep a clear and cold eye on what can be adapted to the American policy limitations. In Chapters 6 through 11 we will try to find solutions that come into view as we consider what is feasible here and what has worked in other places. In particular we will look at health care policy solutions as they might be adapted from the American states and Canada; we will look at environmental solutions as they might be adapted from the European Economic Community; we will look at abortion and euthanasia solutions as they might be adapted from the various states and the Netherlands; and we will look at education solutions as they might be adapted from Japan, Europe, and various American states. The search for feasible solutions, in our opinion, should be one of the major objectives in the study of public policy.

As we indicated earlier, in addition to finding *effective* solutions, it is necessary at the same time to maintain democratic control over public policy. This task is a very tricky one; it involves determining who has clout in America, determining how to increase democracy without sacrificing effective policy solutions, and determining whether the intergovernmental policy system has built-in obstacles to the implementation of solutions, and, if so, how that problem might be eased. We will examine these issues regarding democratic control in Chapter 11. First we will consider the difficult issues of public policy and political power.

WHO HAS CLOUT: POLICY AND POLITICAL POWER

The question of how to increase democratic control is tied to the issue of who has power in America. Political power has been examined through a long series of investigations of power structures at all levels. It has captured the attention of both sociologists and political scientists (Dye 1986). The sociologists usually conclude that power is in the hands of the elites. This *elite theory* claims that a ruling class controls most of the important policy decisions most of the time. Political scientists seem divided in their findings: Some have found support for the elite theory, but since the 1960s their dominant approach has been pluralism. Pluralist theories, while conceding that elites are more powerful than other interests, do not find evidence for a ruling class. Rather, they see power as fragmented and dispersed among competing groups. A considerable amount of public policy is a result of the competition between these groups. Can these two great theories be combined and would this synthesis be a more accurate view of power in America? We think so.

Grover Starling suggested the concept of *pluralistic elitism* as the best approach to linking power with the study of policy (1979, p. 126ff). This view holds that vast power in America is exercised by diverse, occasionally competing, but limited-access elites. One example is the elite-dominated, exceedingly powerful Federal Reserve Board. But this view rejects the existence of a *single* dominant elite. On occasion these separate elites agree with one another, and on other occasions they are in substantial competition. Pluralistic elitism *also* recognizes the ability of ordinary pluralistic groups occasionally to override elite interests for more populist purposes.

INTERGOVERNMENTAL POLICY CLOUT

If we are to link power with policy, we must see more than just *who* is powerful. We must also see *how* power works in the intergovernmental process and what *results* are produced. The effective exercise of power over policy requires *maintaining* influence over time through the stages of formulating, enacting, implementing, and getting policy benefits. The time span often is very substantial. For those who would exercise policy power, there is a dual problem. First, policy actors must have enough resources to maintain influence over time. Second, they must project their influence across intergovernmental jurisdictions through effective intergovernmental strategies. In effect, it is not easy to exercise intergovernmental power over policy in the United States. (For a study of how this happens, and with what results, see Hamilton and Wells 1990, Part 2).

DEMOCRATIC CONTROL OVER POLICY

Because large resources and sophisticated strategies are necessary for exercising policy power, it might seem that the ordinary citizen and the great bulk of organizations have little hope of significantly doing so. But getting ordinary people to have influence is desirable, given the earlier stated importance of democratic problem solving. The key issues (see Chapter 11) are these: Can ways be found to increase democratic control over policy and maintain effective solutions? Is it possible to "empower the people"?

The conditions for an increase in democratic control, we believe, can be identified if we agree on what is needed for a democracy and what policy solutions can be both effective and arrived at democratically. But before we explore such ideas we need to look at the American policy system and the major policy dilemmas.

 CHAPTER **2**

POLICY CHANGE
IN THE TWENTIETH CENTURY

A LOOK AT THE EARLY TWENTIETH CENTURY

Time travel is a favorite topic of science fiction, yet most Americans are unaware of real history and what it can teach us. Most of us would be bewildered, even shocked, by the conditions and social attitudes we would see if we were put into the immediate past, say about 1900. Only a few things about life and policies are the same today as in 1900. Many of us may not be aware that in 1900 children could be forced into factory labor, organizing labor unions was illegal, and our public health system as we know it today was nonexistent. People knew little of inoculation, especially outside of cities. Hygiene was the only major approach to preventing diseases.

At that time, too, thousands of Native-American children were ripped away from their families by the federal government and put into "boarding schools," run as virtual concentration camps, where a child who even spoke his or her native language was put into solitary confinement and denied food. This system of "instruction" was intended to destroy all knowledge of their culture and family roots. In southern and other states blacks were subjected to periodic waves of attacks in the despicable "coon hunts" or lynchings without trial. A few decades before that, by an order of a Missouri governor, hunting and killing Mormons became legal in the state. Although Mormons had not been killed for over a hundred years, the order was not technically overturned until the 1970s by order of a Republican governor, Christopher Bond. And this was not yet "the land of the free" for women: Not only could women not vote, but they also had virtually no property or employment rights, nor even custody rights to children in many states. This is not an America most of us would recognize as being in

21

the twentieth century, yet it is the America of 1900. Truly this century has witnessed incredible reforms, and a large part of them are due to the role government plays in society.

This chapter will provide a detailed picture of policy history—how life has changed in part through political movements and the policy reforms of governments. We will see how the nature of problems in the United States, and the distribution of government responsibilities to deal with them, have evolved. The American policy system most certainly has not been static; it has experienced often dramatic changes decade by decade.

But why study policy history? A basic reason is that if we live only in the immediate moment we do not learn from our policy past. We all want relief from certain problems we share. If years of opinion polls are to be believed, Americans want better economic job security, pollution control, education for our children, cheaper health care, and control of crime, to mention a few concerns. And despite recent pessimism about governments, Americans expect governments to "do something that works" about these problems. But it is next to impossible to make good public choices if we know little of what has or has not worked in the past. There are many lessons to be drawn from knowing at least our immediate past, and particularly that of American policy history.

This chapter uses policy history as a preparation for making better choices and seeing possibilities. First, it explains the evolution of major problems and policy solutions in the mid-twentieth century. Second, it traces the evolution of the responsibilities of different governments in the federal system. Third, it describes the current distribution of policy burdens and problems inside the federal system. Who does what to solve what? And what are the trends of change over the last decade or so? Finally, the chapter considers some of the major issues faced by state and local governments.

Let's return first to our time travel. By the 1930s very few things had changed except in the realm of technology, transportation, and production. Women achieved the right to vote by 1919, yet they still had very few property or employment rights. Blacks were still lynched; they were still largely banned from and discriminated against in higher education and faced insurmountable obstacles in exercising their right to vote (despite the Fifteenth Amendment of sixty years before). Until 1936 labor unions were still illegal, and until 1937 child labor was still practiced. The Supreme Court simply refused to hear such cases.

As for the the 1930s, most Americans are aware—either dimly or through some highly colored ideological point of view—of the changes produced by the New Deal. It introduced many changes in economics and public policy systems, mostly to cope with the problems of the most severe depression the nation had suffered. At the beginning of the Great Depression 25 percent or more of the adult population were jobless, bankruptcies were common in the stock market crash, the bank system was unstable, and soon all the banks in America closed their doors, causing millions to lose their life savings. We were still largely an agricultural nation, although we had thoroughly transformed ourselves through the industrial and urban revolutions. By the end of the decade, partly because of the New Deal policies and partly because of a natural economic recovery, the percentage of unemployed was reduced to about 15 percent. Today such a rate would be considered a major economic crisis, but at that time it was a partial recovery. Despite all the New Deal changes, the America of that time would still be scarcely recognizable to many of us.

Historians of the era tend to place great emphasis on the economic changes that resulted from the New Deal. For the most part, the national government in the 1930s and 1940s had only two new major roles: serving as a national stabilizer of economic recovery in the 1930s, and planning the war production effort in the 1940s. Even so, those two decades formed the basic skeleton of modern policy responsibilities in the American federal system. These responsibilities included defense, macro economic management, labor management disputes, and general stabilization of the economy. The national government had not been involved in these activities in a major way before that time.

Also it was clear by the late 1930s that the national and state governments would share many responsibilities for welfare, retirement benefits, and scenic and recreational facilities. It was clear then, as it is today, that the states tend to monopolize the definition and control of crime, the regulation of justice, marriage, property rights, the powers of municipalities, the control of insurance, and the provision and control of most professions. In other words, the basic shape of American life and the basic distribution of policy responsibilities had been solidified by the late 1930s. By the late 1940s, mostly in response to World War II, the basic outlines of modern life in America were in place and the public problems that we know today were taking root.

THE RISE OF MODERN PROBLEMS, AND HOW GOVERNMENT GOT INVOLVED

There are many explanations for the increased role of government in American society in the twentieth century. One of the best explanations is that in the latter part of the nineteenth and beginning of the twentieth centuries our society began to undergo urbanization and industrialization. These tremendous processes of change affected our country dramatically, leading us from an agricultural society based partly on slavery before the Civil War to an industrial, urbanized society with fundamentally different problems, lifestyles, and hazards.

According to the social sciences, urbanization and industrialization produced modern social problems. Larry Gersten (1983) has summarized a number of more specific explanations of how the problems arose and how government got involved in them. He points to four triggering factors: natural catastrophes, technological breakthroughs, changes in the ecology and natural environment, and social evolution that leads to changes in values.

Natural catastrophes, something as simple as a hurricane or as complex as a new disease like AIDS, produce multiple problems and questions about what government should do in response. *Technological breakthroughs*, such as computerization and robotics technology, replace many forms of labor, leading to questions about government's role in the job retraining of workers whose jobs become obsolete. As for *ecological changes,* for over 200 years it was acceptable to dump poisonous toxic wastes and other forms of solid waste in streams or elsewhere, with little concern about adverse effects on health. Today accelerating changes in the ecology have produced pressing problems and a demand for government action; the declining availability of land for solid waste disposal and the accumulation of hundreds of millions of tons of dangerous chemicals in water and landfills have proven to be health hazards. The fourth factor is the *evolution of social values.* Problems arise because of the way groups have responded to modern issues. People react to issues according to their core values: Some groups hold "modernistic" values, while others have traditional cultural and religious values. Thus policy issues—such as the morning-after pill for birth control, or the use of fetal tissue in medical testing—are complicated because they are also moral issues. Thus the four factors identified by Gersten are important influences on our perceptions of problems.

There are several other factors that help explain how problems get to be problems. Certainly, the *cultural make-up of society* is one of the biggest factors. While the cultural and ethnic makeup of the United States is very diverse, it can be organized into two very broad camps (Hunter 1991). One consists of progressive groups who tend to question traditional values and advocate an expanding agenda of social rights. They tend to be opposed by the second camp, a loose collection of traditionalists who hold conventional religious and social values or emphasize the primacy of property in the marketplace. Some scholars (Jones 1968; Hamilton and Wells 1990; Palumbo and Calista 1990) argue that these deeply rooted differences produce an action-reaction cycle of struggle between these and other groups, which tends to play out over several decades. This struggle yields *policy cycles,* whereby ideals and government activities that are favored in one era come to be disfavored in another. Thus we have sexual liberation in the late 1960s and through the 1970s, and a return in the 1980s to traditional family values promoted in reaction to these liberalizing trends. (See Chapter 11 for a more detailed picture on the latest features of cultural and ethnic conflict in America and how it is affecting our politics, policy demands and cycles.)

Other factors can also give rise to conflicts over government roles in society and public policies. Charismatic leaders emerge periodically to form *organizations* that press their ideas on society. Famous examples are the brilliant W. E. B. Du Bois, who helped found the NAACP in 1909, and the fiery John L. Lewis, the great labor union leader of the 1930s. Also *the media* has come to play a different role in American society. Until the 1960s the media held a rather traditional stance of supporting public institutions with little criticism of public figures, but since the late 1960s it has defined for itself an expanded role as "watchdog," primarily over government abuses and shortcomings and secondarily over big business abuses. The issues highlighted by the media tend eventually to be adopted by the general population. And in a self-fulfilling way, as the media has helped prompt the anti-government sentiment prevalent today, general confidence in governmental institutions (including the media) have declined fairly steadily over the last thirty years.

All of these explanations of how modern problems arose have a certain validity. The strength of a particular factor varies with the problem, but there are broad patterns. We offer the idea that the majority of public policy problems get to be perceived as problems, and government gets involved in trying to deal with them, because of three general patterns of development.

Pattern one is the *Cultural Reaction Syndrome* (Figure 2.1). The general explanation here is that as urbanization and industrialization increased in the United States through the late nineteenth and early twentieth centuries problems actually got worse (unemployment, child labor, the destitute homeless, pollution, etc). As the years went by, these problems tended to come into conflict with aspects of cherished federalist, cultural, or religious values which had justified inaction or only limited actions by government to solve such problems. Reformers, motivated by competing values, formed interest groups, which put continual pressure on legislatures, executives, or courts to take action. Policy actors and institutions tend to react slowly to adopt the reform proposals of new, crusading interest groups. Eventually pressure on officials rises enough that the proposals begin to be taken seriously in the halls of government, and ultimately laws are passed and programs partially implemented that pursue the reformist laws. As effects settle in, however, opposing interest groups become "outraged" by the effects of these policies, and counterresistance is mobilized both inside and outside the arenas of official decision. At some point pressures may build up strongly enough that laws, regulations, and court decisions are rendered

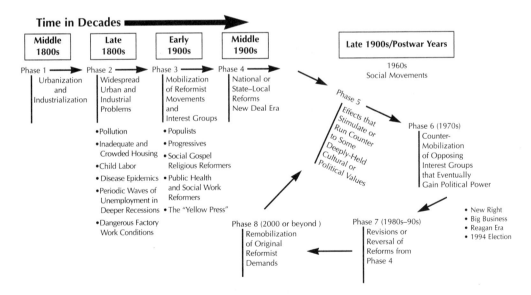

FIGURE 2.1   THE CULTURAL REACTION SYNDROME CAUSES POLICY CHANGE, REVISIONS, AND CYCLES OVER TIME

"reformed" or reversed. Thus there are several years or perhaps decades of continual "action and reaction" during which attempts to implement policies produce oscillating cultural counterreactions and political resistance.

This explanation of American policy as swinging back and forth due to a political-cultural action-reaction cycle is a valid explanation for the rise and fall of several reform efforts in the twentieth century, including the progressive movement in the late 1800s, environmental and women's groups in the mid-twentieth century, the pro-abortion versus anti-abortion battle through the 1990s, and possibly the civil rights/affirmative action debate as well as the electoral swings from left to right in the 1980s–1990s (see Chapter 11 for more on this syndrome in American politics).

Pattern two is less rational, and it short circuits the process of the cultural reaction syndrome. The *Modernization/Disaster Syndrome* (see Figure 2.2) goes basically like this: The same process of urbanization and industrialization that builds up and accumulates problems over time may not necessarily lead to the formation of interest groups that pressure officials to act. Instead, it may lead to *policy neglect*, that is, inaction, until a series of major disasters occur. Eventually one truly big disaster (or sequence of difficult years) gets attention somewhere in the intergovernmental system. At least one level of government debates proposals until it achieves some kind of policy consensus, and more laws, regula-

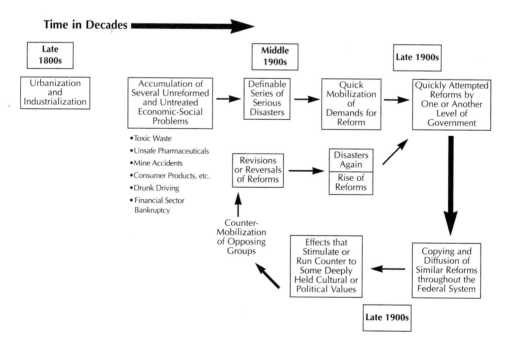

FIGURE 2.2   THE MODERNIZATION/DISASTER SYNDROME AND CYCLE CAUSES POLICY CHANGE, REVISIONS, AND CYCLES OVER TIME

tions, or court decisions are issued. At that point, other governments begin to copy the idea, and "solutions" begin to spread through the intergovernmental system. The pattern continues as in the Cultural Reaction Pattern: Laws and policies are partly implemented, producing action and reaction either in specific locations or in the general population. Two examples that fit this scenario are the series of disastrous mine cave-ins in the mid- and late 1960s, which led to the first strong national law in the United States to regulate coal mining safety in 1969, and the spread of drunk driving laws among the states in the 1980s.

A third pattern is the *Innovative Leadership Pattern.* Here an effective visionary leader at the local, state, or national level perceives a problem usually before the rest of the population and calls for action to deal with it. This leader is often either a rising new political figure or a policy entrepreneur who works inside the bureaucracy. Such a figure essentially defines problems her or his way and pursues solutions to them. If this leader is not able to capture power in government, she or he may organize an interest group to press government over time for major changes. Examples of innovative leadership would include Martin Luther King, Jr., in the late 1950s and early 1960s, consumer activist Ralph Nader in the late 1960s and 1970s, and perhaps Newt Gingrich of Georgia, the new Republican House Speaker in the mid-1990s.

These three intertwined patterns of policy change have produced most of the changes since World War II. They have informed the reactions we have had to each other, and the choices we have come to believe we must make. *They have produced a new distribution of policy responsibilities in the federal system.*

THE EVOLUTION OF GOVERNMENTAL RESPONSIBILITIES IN THE MID-TWENTIETH CENTURY

We shall use these ideas now to show our recent evolution of problems and responsibilities in the federalist or intergovernmental system. We will start by looking at the reforms attempted in the 1930s by the New Deal to resolve the tremendous problems created by the Great Depression, and more important, we will see what was *not* done by the New Deal. We will then move past the war years into the 1950s and 1960s, when most people followed the Cultural Reaction Syndrome to modern problems that arose from industrialization and the postwar era. We will then show the fairly quick explosion in the 1950s and 1960s of modern interest groups and, by the 1970s, a major readjustment of the distribution of federal, state, and local responsibilities for policies. Next we will briefly describe how, from the late 1960s through the 1970s, a virtual "culture war" led to increased national government responsibility in three categories: social policy, regulation of industry, and new cooperative and regulatory relations with state and local governments. And then we will describe how, by the late 1970s, a complex cultural reaction syndrome set in that sought to slow or replace these new policy thrusts, resulting in a limited redistribution of problems and policy responsibilities in the federal system. In the 1970s and after, entirely new kinds of problems began impacting all levels of government and the general population, coming from sources not seen before: the new international economy, growing global policy problems, and the inability of national governments to cope with these problems. In the 1980s American state governments rose to the occasion to cope with many of these problems. At the same time, however, the national government was attempting to follow the lead of the Reagan Administration to reduce government involvement in the economy and in society while these new external forces were changing the terms of life, business, and government in America.

We begin with the 1930s, to trace how the conditions of the Depression and the response of the New Deal under Franklin Roosevelt led to the first skeleton of modern policy functions in the American federal system.

The "natural catastrophe" of the first major global depression in the Industrial Era produced panic and disaster. No modern leader in an industrial, democratic system had ever had to cope with the problems that Roosevelt encountered upon taking office. The general system of investments and securities had collapsed starting in 1929, leading to the bankruptcy of hundreds of thousands of wealthier investors and nearly as many millions of middle-class investors. This was followed in short order by the collapse of banks and culminated in the laying off of large segments of the population by the mid-1930s. It was clear that the American economic system was not "self-regulating." And the headlines from overseas indicated that conditions were even worse in a number of other countries, particularly Germany.

It is sufficient to recall some of the major changes the New Deal wrought in the 1930s. By the end of the decade child labor had been banned by the Supreme Court, labor unions had been given the legal right to strike, and enormous public work projects had been established by the national government to bolster employment. The securities and investment sector had undergone a detailed regime of regulation, the banking system had been stabilized and regulated and uprooted from the insurance industry, which was (and substantially still is) regulated by the states alone. The first major forms of national government to local government grants had been established in the United States, largely for construction of infrastructure. Programs for rural and southern electrification and economic development were started, and the federal courts gave a green light to increased Congressional regulation of interstate trade and commerce. Despite the fact that unemployment still stood at 15 percent in 1937, the New Deal had seemed to reach its end. However, these changes in the basic political and economic structure and in the role of government in society had been clearly laid out. The distribution of policy functions had been significantly reordered, and even through the war years, when the economy was put on a semi-planned footing, the new formula was unaltered. The basic skeleton of the modern American federal system had been established. Table 2.1 shows the distribution of policy functions as of the 1940s.

**TABLE 2.1   THE DISTRIBUTION OF POLICY FUNCTIONS IN AMERICAN FEDERALISM IN THE 1940S
FOLLOWING THE CHANGES PRODUCED BY THE NEW DEAL**

Monopolized by the National Government	Macroeconomics, defense, immigration, social security, labor-management disputes, workplace safety, regulation of monopolies and banking, land conservation, airlines, railroads, broadcast licensing, international trade, foreign aid, foreign relations, postal services, counterintelligence, regulation of banking and securities, regional economic development, war-related economic controls and planned production, urban grants
Shared Rather Evenly by the National Government and the States	Welfare Benefits, social order, scenic recreation facilities, farm subsidies, taxing, highways, wilderness areas
Monopolized by the States	Control of Insurance, regulation of utilities, definition of crime, justice administration, marriage, property rights, powers of municipalities, civil rights, divorce, women's rights, status of children
Monopolized by Local Municipalities and Jurisdictions	Most of the important aspects of primary and secondary education (personnel, curriculum, programs, facilities, etc.), city growth and zoning, land use, public sanitation, fire and water services, parks, recreation, libraries, maintenance and provision of streets and roads, crime control, cultural life, political party organization and participation, property taxes, medical care for the elderly, segregation and discrimination, role of religious life in society

The New Deal, however, did not change everything about America, nor did it establish the entire pattern for postwar life. For example, blacks were still required to use segregated facilities and faced severe impediments to working and voting. Women still had few property rights and, perhaps more important, had little opportunity in higher education or in the workplace. The national government was little involved (except for labor affairs) in the regulation of what we would call the modern social issues such as women's rights. The courts were virtually silent about civil rights and liberties except for expanding limited access to higher education for minorities.

Furthermore, this was still an age of rampant pollution and almost no control of poisonous toxic waste. The industrial system was still based on a "do as you wish" ethic of pollution, and people were free to dispose of all forms of chemicals and wastes without government regulation. There were virtually no labor, health, or safety regulations in the United States, except those operating under state laws. Medicine was still in a fairly primitive state; antibiotics had not yet been developed and mass-produced. In fact, the manufacture and distribution of medicinal drugs was still an industry largely in the formative stage. Pharmaceuticals testing and safety were nonexistent. In addition, at the end of the New Deal the United States did not have a national economic accounting system, medical care programs for the elderly, or consumer product safety protection, and it had only a few farm assistance programs. Even the basic liberties were in a state that would be considered backward or unrecognizable by most of us today. For example, the right merely to protest peacefully against government policies or harsh conditions was virtually nonexistent. Even peaceful demonstrations usually landed the demonstrators in jail. In short, this was an era when medical drugs were not tested for safety or effectiveness, environmental pollution was rampant, and civil rights and liberties were rarely protected or advanced.

CHANGES DURING AND IMMEDIATELY AFTER WORLD WAR II

The changes wrought by World War II led to new demands in society in the late 1940s and early 1950s and eventually altered the mix of responsibilities in the federal system. The postwar demands were induced largely by the war itself or by Cold War problems. For example, black veterans organized to obtain the same services as white veterans for public housing, education, and other veterans benefits. As Professor William H. Chafey argues (1991), the war brought massive changes to American blacks. In 1940, 75 percent of blacks were still living in the rural South, but during the decade after the war more than 2 million moved to northern industrial areas or to the West. During the 1930s lynching had still been common in the South, and federal officials rarely condemned it; even in the 1940s anti-black terrorism still was common, but by then the White House under both Roosevelt and Truman started to respond. The war had produced some recognition of black rights to equality, and President Truman ordered the integration of the armed services in the latter part of the war. Similarly, throughout the Depression virtually no one had challenged the separate but equal education system that spent three times as many dollars on white people as on black people. By the end of the 1940s, however, the Jim Crow schools plus the "freeze out" from higher education increasingly came under legal and political attack from black activists. The black determination to challenge white racism first became obvious with a big march on Washington, D.C. in 1941, when A. Philip Randolph organized black protests demanding an end to blatant discrimination in the work force, particularly in defense industries. Franklin Roosevelt responded with Executive Order 8802 in June 1941, calling for the banning of discrimination based on color or creed in defense industries and government, and creating a fair employment committee to investigate claims of discrimination. This committee did little, however, and had little enforcement power.

The problem increasingly became the obvious and shameful mismatch between the sacrifices black Americans had made for the war effort, allegedly to protect democracy, and the fact that they were denied equality at home both before and after the war. For example, after the war, veteran and FHA housing loans were initially made available only to whites. Professor Chafey concludes:

> ... Government propaganda that emphasized America's fight against racism abroad helped to highlight the hypocrisy of racism at home, and the need to struggle against it.... The interaction of some improvements and differences during the war together with daily reminders of an on-going repression [after the war produced] ... a chemistry that was crucial. Simultaneous with new exposure to travel, the prospect of better jobs, and higher expectations came the reality of day-to-day contact with Jim Crow [discrimination] in the Armed Forces, housing, and on the job. (1991, p. 21)

A huge tide of black anger and frustration eventually led to black migration to the North and West, and to political protests.

In many other areas as well, the new demands created by the war and by its aftermath led to changes in American policy. Returning veterans demanded and eventually got more funds for housing and schools, college loans, health care, and veterans' hospitals. Since the late 1940s the national government literally opened its wallet to spend billions for all veterans.

CHANGES IN THE POSTWAR YEARS

Many changes in the society and the economy resulting from the war carried over to change America permanently. Initially the American military spending dropped as the armed forces were reduced to less than 500,000 from a wartime total of more than 2 million, but the Cold War quickly brought a military buildup in the late 1940s, which lasted nearly fifty years until the 1990s. Military spending rose during the Korean War and remained high thereafter. In the wake of this buildup, the military-industrial complex (namely, the new military contracting lobbies) emerged to become a most powerful element in Washington. Likewise, the pharmaceutical industry had exploded onto the scene because of the need to develop drugs and inoculate overseas armed forces during the war. After the war pharmaceutical lobbyists were very effective in delaying and preventing government regulation of their many new products until the late 1950s, when the Thalidomide disaster occurred. Despite a 1938 drug safety law, prescription drugs had until then been mass marketed without rigorous safety testing. It was then discovered that Thalidomide, a drug taken during pregnancy, produced deformations in fetuses. From 1959 to 1962, thousands of infants in different nations were born with severely deformed arms and legs. This disaster finally put an end to untested, mass marketed drugs. In 1962 Congress passed a tough drug safety act.

When America came home from the war it was basically a rail transport nation, with a weak system of national highways. This condition was not to last for long, largely because of the American love affair with the automobile, and partly because of the marketing and developing strategies of the big three automakers. These companies had spent billions of dollars during the war to convert their production line facilities to make tanks and airplanes. Now they faced the high costs of reconverting to civilian production of automobiles. They needed to recapture the civilian market, and to aid themselves during the costly era of reconversion. In the late 1940s and 1950s Detroit automakers pursued a dual strategy. They mass marketed the automobile to the American public, and they attempted to abolish competition by purchasing many mass transit operations in major American cities and dismantling them by selling off the properties. This dual strategy artificially increased the demand for automobiles. And of course more government spending on roads and highways throughout the 1950s also helped increase sales for Detroit autos.

Another factor in the new demands was that the postwar population boom was in full swing in the 1950s. There were increased demands for government to spend, especially on schools, housing, and hospital construction, and a large number of national programs were created for these purposes. Among these many acts were the Hill Burton Hospital Construction Act of 1946, which created a vast new network of hospitals across the nation. A number of national defense acts, passed in both the Truman and Eisenhower administrations, created hundreds of vocational-technical schools, public schools around military bases, and schools in rural areas.

Also the wartime use of nuclear technology had created motives (perhaps based on profit and guilt) to invest in developing ways to convert nuclear fission into electrical power. Thus President Eisenhower established his famous Atoms for Peace program in the early 1950s. The major feature of this program was to have the national government assume all of the expensive front-end costs of developing nuclear power in the navy's nuclear submarine program. This program literally developed nuclear power technology at public expense, to be adopted later by private utility companies for generating nuclear power.

The "biggest fish of all," and truly the largest capital investment program in American history, was Eisenhower's creation of the interstate highway system in the mid-1950s. The establishment of the Interstate Highway Trust fund was the linchpin in this program. The interstate highways were seen as a cure-all for the economy as well as for defense. Hundreds of billions of dollars would be spent on road construction throughout the United States over several decades. This would strongly stimulate the growth of giant shopping malls, retail and urban development, and the building of even more roads. Of course this also meant even more demand for automobiles. It was no secret that the big three automakers were strong supporters of the interstate highway system. In the wake of superhighways paid for by the national government, Americans went ever-more nuts for the automobile, car sales soared, and rail travel went out the window, all with massive government assistance. (This was not exactly the free market at work.) The benefit for defense would be the provision of an "American Autobahn" with highways thick enough to carry military transports. In short, the system would provide a quick moving national road system to transport civilian products in peacetime and military equipment and troops in case of a Soviet threat.

All of these war-generated and postwar demands led to the first wave of powerful interest groups and lobbies that gained strength in the 1950s. These groups, including the American Medical Association, the American Hospital Association, the pharmaceutical and the military contractors, the big three automakers, and state and local government lobbies, are still among the most powerful national lobbying organizations.

All these events could be said to follow the Modernization/Disaster Model, whereby the demands and forces associated with a war (World War II, then the Cold War), plus the problems of an increasingly urban and industrial society, spur on social changes, disasters, and demands for policy changes. In the mid-twentieth century these forces and problems stimulated the formation of enduring interest groups. As was mentioned earlier, the New Deal and the postwar policy systems through the mid-1950s neglected certain problems in the American society, especially civil rights, environmental degradation, pollution, hazards in the workplace, and unsafe consumer products. All these problems became more conspicuous in the increasingly urbanized and industrial society. Governmental neglect could not last forever.

Many of these problems also had a tendency to lead to disasters. Thus in the 1950s and 1960s certain developments followed the modernization/disaster model, which explains most policy changes through the early 1960s. Major disasters through the 1960s, such as Thalidomide, the overuse of the deadly pesticide DDT, mine disasters, and extreme pollution led to increased public attention and subsequent laws to reduce these hazards.

CHANGES FROM THE LATE 1950s TO THE 1990s

However, social controversies and policies followed a path of change that was considerably different in postwar America. Through the 1950s and 1960s social conflicts and changes mostly followed the Cultural Reaction Model, leading to the explosive growth of public interest and social lobbies. The civil rights movement had set the main example of protest and successful change through the new strategy of nonviolent protest. Several other groups followed more or less the same path to demand solutions to neglected social problems. These included the environmental and consumer movements of the mid-1960s and the feminist and anti-war protest movements of the late 1960s and 1970s. Thus by the late 1960s the cultural action-reaction path of change had led many have-not social groups to demand increased national responsibility for social issues.

By the late 1960s the cultural reaction model was beginning to dominate policy change. The new policies of the national government to resolve social problems and discrimination had set up counterreactions from the 1970s to the 1990s by those trying to reverse those trends. Figure 2.3 is an action-versus-reaction time chart that lists new laws and policies won by some groups and subsequent counterreaction by "anti" groups demanding a reversal.

Certainly by the time of the Nixon presidency the two main paths of policy change had led to a near monopolization by the national government of policy in three main areas: social policy, regulation of industry, and the cooperative and regulatory relations with the states and local governments. Thus by the late 1960s in the United States the distribution of problems and policy responsibilities had changed significantly from that in the New Deal and postwar eras. These changes are summarized in Table 2.2. This arrangement was rather stable at least through the early years of the Reagan administration, and began to change only in the late 1980s, with the setting in of a complex conservative cultural reaction.

A conservative counterreaction and mobilization of interest groups against the policies of the 1960s and 1970s started in the 1960s and crystallized in the early to mid-1970s. These groups included the anti-ERA movement, the Business Roundtable, the politicized southern and evangelical churches most prominently known as the Moral Majority established by the Reverend Jerry Falwell (and the Christian Coalition in the 1990s), and the anti-abortion movement. These groups sought to replace the policy changes of the earlier decades with new conservative policies and leaders in Washington.

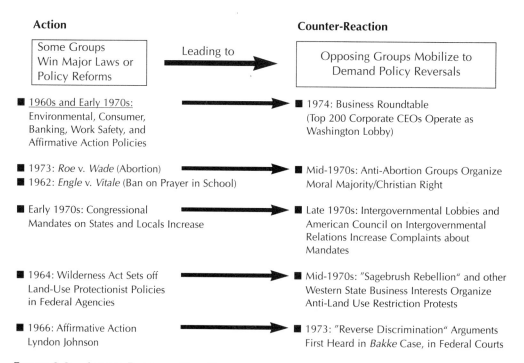

Action

| Some Groups Win Major Laws or Policy Reforms | Leading to → | Opposing Groups Mobilize to Demand Policy Reversals |

Counter-Reaction

- **1960s and Early 1970s:** Environmental, Consumer, Banking, Work Safety, and Affirmative Action Policies → ■ 1974: Business Roundtable (Top 200 Corporate CEOs Operate as Washington Lobby)

- 1973: *Roe* v. *Wade* (Abortion)
- 1962: *Engle* v. *Vitale* (Ban on Prayer in School) → ■ Mid-1970s: Anti-Abortion Groups Organize Moral Majority/Christian Right

- Early 1970s: Congressional Mandates on States and Locals Increase → ■ Late 1970s: Intergovernmental Lobbies and American Council on Intergovernmental Relations Increase Complaints about Mandates

- 1964: Wilderness Act Sets off Land-Use Protectionist Policies in Federal Agencies → ■ Mid-1970s: "Sagebrush Rebellion" and other Western State Business Interests Organize Anti-Land Use Restriction Protests

- 1966: Affirmative Action Lyndon Johnson → ■ 1973: "Reverse Discrimination" Arguments First Heard in *Bakke* Case, in Federal Courts

FIGURE 2.3   ACTION-REACTION TIME CHART

TABLE 2.2   THE DISTRIBUTION OF POLICY RESPONSIBILITIES IN AMERICAN FEDERALISM, APPROX. 1970

Monopolized by the National Government	Macroeconomics, defense, immigration, social security, labor-management disputes, workplace safety, regulation of monopolies and banking, wilderness areas and land conservation, atomic power and waste, airlines, railroads, broadcast licensing, outer-space exploration, international trade, foreign aid, foreign relations, postal services, counterintelligence, civil liberties and civil rights interpretation, intergovernmental mandates, urban and development grants
Shared Rather Evenly by the National Government and the States	Medical care for the elderly and disadvantaged, welfare benefits, environmental protection, social order, scenic recreation facilities, farm subsidies, industrial incentives, taxing, highways
Monopolized by the States	Welfare rules, control of insurance, regulation of professions, higher education, regulation of utilities, definition of crime, justice administration, marriage, property rights, powers of municipalities, divorce, women's rights, status of children
Monopolized by Local Municipalities and Jurisdictions	Most of the important aspects of primary and secondary education (personnel, curriculum, programs, facilities, etc.), city growth and zoning, land use, public sanitation, fire and water services, parks, recreation, libraries, maintenance and provision of streets and roads, crime control, cultural life, political party organization and participation, property taxes
Shared Rather Evenly by All Governmental Jurisdictions	Taxes, housing, urban growth and services, highways

As the conservative counterreaction gained power, it resulted in an ever-widening split within the political parties and in most religious denominations. J. D. Hunter later referred to this split as a growing "culture war" in the United States (1991). The counterattack had mobilized a broad coalition of business and traditionalistic groups seeking to form the basis of a conservative and neo-conservative revival. This coalition built up its steam out of a broad cultural and religious opposition—led by the more traditionalistic groups based in southern religions—mainly to the women's movement and abortion. By the late 1970s an easy alliance eventually grew between this wing and a coalition of business interests that sought to repeal what they saw as an anti-business and excessively regulatory environment. A key event in the growth of this coalition was the establishment of the Business Roundtable in 1974, comprising the chief executive officers of the top 200 corporations who would operate as lobbyists on Capitol Hill. The BRT was an extension of the Conference Board, a long standing big business interest group. The conservative cultural counterreaction achieved its full strength in the election of 1980 and the growth of the Republican party in the South in subsequent years. However, the revitalization of anti-regulation business lobbies in the 1970s is best understood in the context of the longer history of the national regulation of industry in the postwar years.

The New Deal had advanced the national regulation of industry in several vital ways (discussed earlier). These included tighter controls over banks and securities, experimentation with welfare and public works grants, and the establishment in 1936 of the right to strike and later the arbitration of strikes by government. But we must recall that even by the 1950s there was virtually no regulation of labor hazards, pollution, toxic chemicals, or hazardous products or drugs. The key event that marked the serious acceleration of industrial regulation was the Thalidomide drug scandal, which led to the strengthening of the Food and Drug Administration. This was followed by the Wilderness Act of 1964, the Mine Safety Act of 1969, the environmental protection laws of 1969 and 1970, and the large system of consumer and work safety laws enacted in the late 1960s and early 1970s. Figure 2.4 compares some regulations in the mid-1970s with the 1950s. It is a rather startling list to examine!

Thus by the late 1970s the national government had come to assume generally the regulation of social equality and opportunities and increased regulation of business as well as state and local governments. Policy change in the most recent period has involved working out what level of government in the federal system will assume these significant new responsibilities.

THE NEW MAP OF RESPONSIBILITIES IN THE 1990s

By the late 1980s the state and local governments had become the major agents of change in the federal system. While policy paralysis and gridlock were at work in the national government, there was substantial policy momentum among subnational governments (Hamilton and Wells 1990; see also Chapter 11), resulting in a redirection of responsibilities within the federal system. By the mid-1990s the states had come to share power in policy areas previously monopolized by the national government, particularly social policy and business regulation.

Scholars are still sorting out the reasons for the shifting of responsibilities

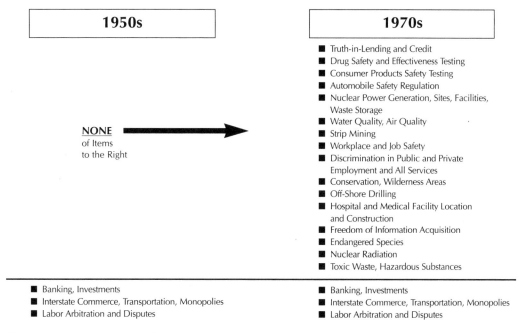

1950s	1970s
	■ Truth-in-Lending and Credit
	■ Drug Safety and Effectiveness Testing
	■ Consumer Products Safety Testing
	■ Automobile Safety Regulation
	■ Nuclear Power Generation, Sites, Facilities, Waste Storage
NONE ──────▶	■ Water Quality, Air Quality
of Items	■ Strip Mining
to the Right	■ Workplace and Job Safety
	■ Discrimination in Public and Private Employment and All Services
	■ Conservation, Wilderness Areas
	■ Off-Shore Drilling
	■ Hospital and Medical Facility Location and Construction
	■ Freedom of Information Acquisition
	■ Endangered Species
	■ Nuclear Radiation
	■ Toxic Waste, Hazardous Substances

1950s	1970s
■ Banking, Investments	■ Banking, Investments
■ Interstate Commerce, Transportation, Monopolies	■ Interstate Commerce, Transportation, Monopolies
■ Labor Arbitration and Disputes	■ Labor Arbitration and Disputes

FIGURE 2.4   BIG BUSINESS REGULATION, 1950s VERSUS 1970s

toward the states. Several important factors were at work. First, there were the continuing problems associated with industrialization and urbanization. Some of these problems, such as solid waste and the pollution of ground water supplies, most directly affected states and local governments. Also these policy areas had traditionally been dominated by subnational governments but had taken on a crisis dimension in some states.

Second, states and cities began to feel the effect of the new international economy and the growth of imports. This new economy reduced American market shares in formerly strong areas such as textiles, steel, and machine parts. The same effects have also begun to be felt in high-tech computer and electronics industries. The pressures of plant closings and unemployment are felt most directly at the local level. Thus state and local governments have jumped into the fray to try to retain industries and jobs.

Third, significant increases in certain public health problems placed more demands on state and local governments. The AIDS epidemic certainly led the list, but the growth of new antibiotic-resistant strains of bacteria, notably tuberculosis and pneumonia, joined the AIDS epidemic as serious problems facing public health officials.

Fourth, the fiscal and program cutbacks in the Reagan and Bush eras plus the growing power of the conservative counterreaction all helped promote the idea of the "turnback" of policy responsibilities to the states. There was a reduction in national spending on some social programs and a cutback in the flow of federal grant money to the states. This federal retreat from the policy priorities of the 1970s put pressures on state and local governments to find answers for such issues as urban services, environmental degradation, and economic development. Each of these four factors contributed to the growth of policy pressures on the states.

These developments resulted in a somewhat modified map of policy responsibilities in the federal system. By the mid-1990s the states had assumed from the national government a new wave of problems and responsibilities in the federal system. In general, states came to share more responsibility for macroeconomic development and attraction of foreign capital. States are now more active in economic development policies, foreign trade, bank regulation, savings and loan regulation, and insurance regulation. Thus they have somewhat replaced the national government as the leaders in economic policies (see Chapter 7). They have also become the leaders in areas where the feds had not taken the lead or had virtually neglected action, such as dealing with child abuse, child support enforcement, welfare reform, euthanasia regulation, criminal justice, and natural resource conservation, including wildlife, and rivers. States are also the leaders of reform efforts in what may be the leading needs in society today: health care reform, education reform, and economic development. (See later chapters and Table 2.3). Many of these areas had been nearly monopolized by the national government in the 1970s. In short, there has been a rather strong shift to equal sharing by the states and national government of responsibility for major national needs and policy demands.

Local governments, particularly cities, have also experienced substantial policy momentum. Cities are much more prone today to be involved in environmental and economic policies. Cities have also moved into areas that were previously neglected, such as responsibility for sports, for the privatization of services, for environmental recycling programs, and for certain disease prevention programs. Also, cities are more active in areas that were previously monopolized by the national government or the states through the system of cooperative block grants in the 1970s. These include local economic development, provision of mental health services, legal services for the poor, and certain social services such as family planning, spouse and child abuse and drug abuse prevention, environmental recycling, and values and character training (see especially Chapter 11 for the new social activism at the state and local levels).

Subnational policy momentum, then, resulted in a significant shift of policy responsibilities in the federal system. Such changes are due more to the changing problems of an industrial nation, forces from the international economy, or pressures from groups within the population than they are to deliberate seeking of policy changes by political executives. Such unanticipated changes are as much a feature of political life as of personal life. A study of policy history and the policy system's response to change can spotlight some possible options and the trends of change.

**Table 2.3   Changes in Major Policy Responsibilities in the Federal system
by the 1990s—Contrast to the 1970s**

Formerly Significant National Responsibilities for Which States Have Assumed the Major Responsibility	Criminal justice and crime prevention, foreign investment attraction, social welfare reform, healthcare reform and regulation, solid waste and ground water pollution, abortion regulation, economic development policies, education reform
New Areas States Have Assumed Due to National Inaction	Child support, child abuse regulation, spouse abuse regulation, AIDS and drug abuse regulation
New Areas of Mainly National Responsibility	Toxic waste cleanup, workplace and mine safety, consumer product safety testing, interstate drug trafficking, terrorism control, interstate missing children
New Areas of Mainly Local Responsibility	Environmental recycling and solid waste management, values and character education, third sector volunteerism (see Chapter 11), anti-drug abuse education, public health disease prevention, privatization of government services, sports and recreation programs, cultural arts, multiculturalism

 **CHAPTER 3**

THE LIMITS OF IMAGINATION

HOW POLICY MYTHS AND CULTURES AFFECT WHAT AMERICANS THINK AND DO ABOUT PUBLIC PROBLEMS

This chapter starts our picture of what Americans typically think and do about public policies. Here we look at our major beliefs about policies and see how these determine what we believe about government action. Policy myths can be defined as the beliefs about policy, which may or may not resemble what in fact is real or possible, but which always preset the American imagination and style of action on public problems. Perhaps we will discover much of ourselves in this and the following chapter, which describe our regional differences and thus completes the picture of how Americans "think and do" policies.

POLICY MYTHS AND CULTURES AND THEIR EFFECTS

A *political culture* is a widely shared set of political beliefs a people have about themselves and their political way of life. *Policy cultures* are those aspects of political culture that help define people's preferences about government's decisions and actions. The policy culture of a nation is a very powerful force and can be quite complex. It strongly conditions and somewhat predetermines the content of public policies. It strongly affects the policy style of leaders and interest groups— how they think about, choose, and implement policies, for example. In brief, policy cultures set the boundaries of what is acceptable for government activities.

For example, a society may accept the proposition (as most European societies do) that government has a responsibility to guarantee and promote the health of its citizens as a basic political right. American beliefs have not favored this idea; for instance, we are deeply divided about health care (see Chapter 9).

Thus cultural beliefs tend to provide "ready answers" to such issues. In fact, they tend to limit our picture of tolerable problems and solutions. Actions that are appropriate in one society or even within one region of a country may be illegal in others. Thus licensed prostitution is legal in parts of Nevada but certainly not elsewhere in the United States. Wife beating or child beating may be acceptable in some societies (and some parts of the United States) while it is illegal in all circumstances in some other societies.

Furthermore, in any given society, which actions are "acceptable" and "preferred" varies over time. For example, our attitudes and thus our laws regarding child abuse are starting to change in favor of protecting children and away from the historic practice of assuming that any parental "discipline" of children is largely off limits to public concern. Our ideas about protest and property have altered over time also. In the early history of the nation "demonstrations" often included the destruction of property. Americans are proud today of the famous Boston Tea Party, where British tea was thrown overboard to protest British taxes, but most Americans forget that in those day tea was a commodity that ranked with gold in value. Today our attitudes have "evolved." Demonstrators are expected to protest "peaceably," that is, they are expected to refrain from destroying or even trespassing on property. Our cultural values have shifted also in regard to what is property and who gets what rights to it. Thus humans can no longer be slave property, but children may still in some places be subjected to severe abuse with limited constitutional rights, treated like property.

Today's complex American policy culture is derived from many sources in our pluralistic society. A variety of religions, ethnic groups, and social and interest groups influence what people prefer about policies and governments. In fact, we are a more diverse society than ever before (see Figure 3.1a–c).

Most Americans do not consciously adopt a particular way of thinking about public policy. Studies of political socialization (what people believe about politics and policy) suggest that Americans form their general beliefs "bit by bit" as a result of random forces in the environment. This concept is referred to as the *accumulation theory*. Very few people, according to this view, form rational political beliefs, nor do they develop coherent political theories or world views. Instead, they pick up their political attitudes from their most important environmental influences. The result is our complex political and policy culture. And even though each individual is in a sense unique, we also have broad categories of shared policy beliefs. This chapter will describe these basic policy beliefs or cultures and will consider what difference they make.

Although there is a lot of talk in America about people as either liberal or conservative, most Americans tend not to be poles apart on policy issues, if only because most of our political beliefs are formed in a common environment, albeit a pluralistic one. Few persons, officials, or groups exhibit a consistently pure type of belief system. Rather, they mix one or more elements of the entire policy culture into their own thoughts and behaviors. Therefore it is possible to speak of a southern conservative who is a centralist on moral issues, who is decentral-

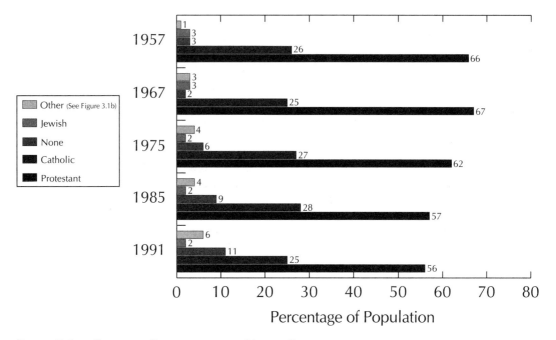

FIGURE 3.1a   RELIGIOUS PREFERENCE IN THE UNITED STATES
Source: *Statistical Abstract of the United States*, 1994, Table 203, p. 138.

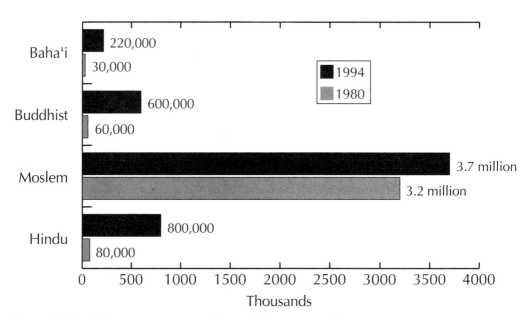

FIGURE 3.1b   A BREAKDOWN OF THE "OTHER" CATEGORY OF RELIGION
Sources: *The World Almanac* 1994, pp. 731–732; *The World Almanac* 1985; pp. 356–357;
The Handbook of Denominations, 1980, pp. 19–258; David B. Barrett, *1994 Encyclopedia Britannica Yearbook*,
p. 271; *Information Please Almanac 1980*, p. 435; U.S. Bahai National Center, Wilmette, Illinois.

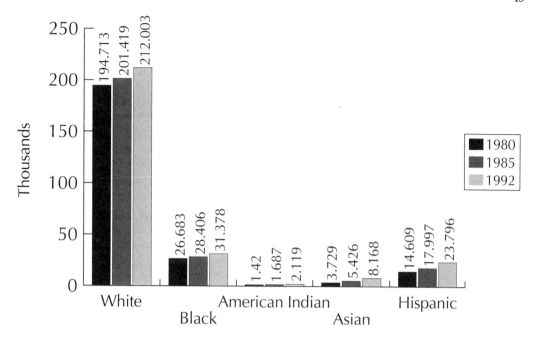

FIGURE 3.1c   ETHNIC DIVERSITY IN THE UNITED STATES
Source: *Statistical Abstract of the United States*, 1994, Table 19, p. 19.

ist on powers of government, but who also is internationalist in foreign policy. It is common to find one individual holding conservative beliefs on family policy, liberal beliefs on health policy, reactionary beliefs on moral legislation, and radical beliefs on environmental policy. Because of this trait of mixing and matching beliefs, most scholars maintain that there are very few pure *ideologues* in American politics. It would be misleading to accuse Americans of being "wishy-washy" or "irrational" in their beliefs. In fact, in their policy habits, Americans more likely reflect the complexity of our culture rather than inconsistency of political beliefs.

INFORMATION POLLUTION: THE GROWTH OF DISINFORMATION

One of the most interesting popular beliefs about our times is that we live in an "information age." Certainly it is undeniable that more knowledge exists of history, social systems, science, and so on than in times past. It is also undeniable that with modern communications media—satellite television, computers, information databases, and the internet, not to mention traditional print publishing— we have more ways of spreading more information more quickly. But part of the so-called information age are the modern systems of *packaged disinformation*: the mass marketing sciences and advertising in the business world, and the ever-more sophisticated political advertising, polling, speech writers, and the like in the political world.

The age of advertising is largely a twentieth-century development, as mass marketing developed out of mail order catalogues in the late 1800s. Advertising has now culminated in such things as half-hour "broadcasts" which are disguised as consumer shows or news reports but which are paid advertisements for items like Super Mops and Super Cleaners.

The legendary American skill of manipulating information in the business world has spread quickly into the political arena in this century, mostly since the days of President Kennedy, although it could likely be traced further back, particularly to the era of FDR. The manipulating of "the line of the day" reached its peak in the Nixon White House press team and has been masterfully described by those who turned the operation into an institutional part of American politics (see Kelly, *New York Times Magazine*, October 1993). The methods of political marketing have become even more sophisticated in modern-day campaigns, in political polling and ads for candidates, and in the Reagan and Clinton White houses.

The phenomenon of political public relations and manipulation of information has broadened and deepened in the latter part of this century into a social phenomenon that amounts to a disinformation system of propaganda, used in political advertising and in interest group lobbying, talk show hosting, and all forms of political advocacy. There is too little research on this darker side of the "information age"—the manipulative techniques and abuse of statistics, combined with powerful appeals to emotional and cultural symbols, especially as they bear on politics and public policy. There is research on the disinformation molding of the media and its focus on mythologies and hot issues of the time. There is some treatment of the institutionalization of propaganda in the presidency and in its supporting cast agencies, such as the Press Office, the politicization of analysis in the Office of Management and Budget, and a few other limited topics. Research methods textbooks have only just begun to include sections on countering disinformational techniques, especially the abuse of statistics. The Disinformation Society is still relatively unexplored territory.

We advance the tentative view that American public life is marked deeply but subtly by many widespread forms of policy and political "information pollution." Such disinformation occurs most significantly around controversial issues (e.g., gun control, abortion, the right to health care, etc.). Such pollution is created largely by intensely emotional, ideologically rigid, and mobilized groups that are motivated by deeply held beliefs and values. They seek to raise powerful arguments and they color or "massage" facts in such a way as to advocate a predecided point of view. Such groups, and their opponents, mobilize large amounts of money, memberships, lobbyists, and the like to "hit the streets" or "go lobby Congress," as they did in earlier decades. In addition, they now also use highly sophisticated marketing and demographic and political consultants to devise powerful marketing techniques to influence the public and leadership, especially by manipulating language and cultural symbols. Two of the most prominent groups that have developed such intensive propaganda campaigns are the National Rifle Association (NRA) and the American Medical Association (AMA). (See Chapter 9.)

American society has become increasingly polarized and ideological since the 1970s, dividing into large liberal, conservative, and populist camps (Maddox and Lilie 1984). Disinformation has no doubt played a role in this polarization. One of the most important methods of disinformation, which has increased social tensions, is to deliberately package issues by interpreting information according to beliefs out of certain American mythologies and stereotypes. (For a strongly partisan but revealing view of this method, one that documents the methods and challenges, see Parenti 1994).

In public conflicts, the politically organized segments of opposing camps tend to revert to two defensive or offensive strategies of information distortion. One is repetitious appeals to unprovable dogmatic assertions, and the second is emotionally charged manipulation of information through big cultural rallying symbols, statistical and scapegoat misrepresentation, and omission of facts. The historical record and expert information get swamped out. All claims start from rather dogmatically unquestioned preconceptions and assumptions put forth as universal truths.

In general, the most serious distortions of information are due to the manipulating of facts with powerful and appealing political ideologies or cultural symbols and myths. For instance, ideological liberals and radicals dogmatically insist that national problems require national solutions and deny that states or voluntaristic methods can solve anything. Ideological conservatives dogmatically insist that government always fails and taxes never serve any purpose, intone that markets always work on public problems, and omit any record of state, national, or foreign success in solving the problems. Finally, populists dogmatically assert that nothing big or centralized works, insist that both business and government are mutually corrupting and conspire with foreign interests to erode the lifestyle of average workers so that bureaucratic or business-oriented solutions rarely work, and insist that only "direct democracy" or limited voluntaristic or state or local solutions are possible (examples of populist ideas can be found in the "For the People" radio network broadcasts by Chuck Harder, highly popular now throughout the South and Midwest). These and other ideas that guide and distort American thinking about policies are described in greater detail later in this chapter.

HOW TO RECOGNIZE AND REVERSE DISINFORMATION

The disinformation problem, which has spread like a fog throughout public discourse, has made reasoned dialogue and uncolored, systematic policy analysis increasingly difficult. One way to clear the fog is to become aware of the possible manipulation of myths. (Study the myths described later in this chapter).

Another way to avoid disinformation is to learn valid uses of statistics and proper analysis of cause-and-effect relations. Table 3.1 presents the "Dirty

Dozen"—twelve common forms of statistical abuses and faulty arguments, versus twelve valid understandings and methods of presentation that serve to counter them. Correctives to disinformation appear in bold type in column 3 of Table 3.1. (This was developed in teaching advanced methods courses over a period of fifteen years).

TABLE 3.1   THE MOST COMMON FORMS OF INFORMATION POLLUTION IN THE UNITED STATES
THE DIRTY DOZEN: TWELVE MOST COMMON ERRORS, OR LIES, IN USING OR ABUSING STATISTICS AND INFORMATION

INCORRECT EXAMPLE	INCORRECT USE OF INFORMATION	CORRECT USE OF INFORMATION	CORRECT EXAMPLES
More people are at work now than ever.	1. Cite plain, raw numbers.	**Use percents through time.**	Annual unemployment percentage
The net family income rose for the last two years (1987–1988).	2. Cite only one to two years time.	**Use ten-to-twenty-year timelines.**	Use the last twenty years. Only 1987–1988 had increases.
Black family income rose since 1983.	3. Start a timeline at a favorable point for the argument.	**Start timelines ten to twenty years ago, or at a major change in time.**	1983 was the end of the worst postwar recession. Over twenty years the black income rose, fell deeply in 1982, and recovered slowly, only to fall to lower levels again in 1992.
Local governments *always* work better. National government almost *always* fails.	4. Confuse a popular myth with reality.	**Study the "General American Policy Myths" section in this chapter.**	See the "General American Policy Myths" section in this chapter. Also, see the record of national policy successes in Chapter 2.
A rooster crows first, then the sun rises. Other false associations are: Jimmy Carter is elected and inflation goes up. Ronald Reagan is elected and the nation falls into the worst recession since the 1930s.	5. Confuse statistical association of two things with cause and effect. This is a major problem.	**Know basic statistics. Examine several control variables; there may be other explanations.**	But the rooster didn't cause the sun to rise. Association proves nothing; appearances can deceive; things can work in reverse.

TABLE 3.1, CONT.

INCORRECT EXAMPLE	INCORRECT USE OF INFORMATION	CORRECT USE OF INFORMATION	CORRECT EXAMPLES
"The nation is ruined by" welfare queens, Christian fanatics selfish bankers, liberal democrats, fascist republicans, capitalist shysters, etc.	Exaggerate blame or credit by using a popular scapegoat.	**Recognize Scapegoating.**	See the "General American Policy Myths" section in this chapter.
Heart Disease is "caused" only by fat intake (or genetic inheritance or cholesterol or lack of exercise, etc.).	7. Cite studies with one supposed cause or no control groups.	**Most problems have four or five contributing causes.**	In fact, all of these factors combine to raise the risk of heart disease.
I was married to one man who was an abusive jerk; therefore, all men are abusive jerks.	8. One experience tells all.	**Many experiences and many samples are necessary to be able to make generalizations about behaviors.**	Just because I knew one man who was an abusive jerk does not mean all men are abusive jerks; each man has his own personality traits, values, etc.
We've passed a law to prohibit liquor sales; Now alcoholism will end.	9. Expect easy solutions.	**Again, most problems have four or five contributing causes. One solution does not cure all, and by itself may make the problem worse (witness Prohibition).**	Many factors contribute to alcoholism; it can be due to or exacerbated by genetics, dysfunctional family patterns, etc. A solution must focus on all factors.
Create socialized medicine or abolish Medicaid and Medicare.	10. Two extreme opposites are the only possibilities.	**There are many choices between the extremes.**	There are many ways to control health care costs and increase coverage. See Chapter 9.
Immediate results were expected from the 1980s space shuttle improvements.	11. Expect to get or measure real improvements within a short time period.	**Most new programs or reforms require a five-year "learning period" (or longer).**	It took many years to improve the space shuttle to reduce risk of accidents.
Cite the number of police patrols, drug arrests, etc.	12. Cite or use poor indicators of success, which actually show activities, not results.	**Develop measures of results, not just measures of activities.**	Measures of results: acreage of cultivated marijuana reduced, percent of teens admitting drug abuse, etc.

THE FOUR MAJOR AMERICAN POLICY CULTURES

There are four major types of American policy cultures—general political myths, ideologies, federalist cultures, and regional cultures—that mold our thinking about what are desirable and effective policies.

As in all nations, people in the United States hold dear some very important general political myths. Originally, the word *myth* meant a story that was used to explain something mysterious. Now the word is used most often in the social sciences for beliefs that explain something in a way favored by the believer. Thus a myth may be true, false, or partly true and partly false. The important point is that since the myth is accepted as *entirely true*, it becomes a basis for policy decisions and behaviors. Therefore the most important *general myths* have results in society that are somewhat self-fulfilling. For example, the major myth about poverty is that if people are poor they are probably personally to blame. After all, if America is the "land of opportunity" there must be no reason for poverty except laziness. Let's examine this myth.

Consider these facts: Most poor work full-time yet stay poor. Welfare scholars regard national and state anti-poverty programs to be modest at best, minimal in comparison to those of other industrial nations. American anti-poverty programs have been able to lift people out of poverty only to a certain extent, and mainly in the 1960s and 1970s (Schwarz 1988; Chelf 1992).

Yet our assumptions make us see facts in a predetermined way. Here is how most people misread the facts: Because most people believe that poor people are poor because of their own fault (an assumption), support and spending for government anti-poverty programs forever remain minimal (a fact that results from the assumption). Minimal government programs thus do not actually lift many out of poverty (a fact), and so the taxpayer always sees a lot of poor people out there (a fact—we have about 40 million poor people) despite or maybe because of the minimal government programs. Thus taxpayers and politicians easily conclude that since there are still so many poor people, despite poverty programs, they are "proof" that government programs don't work. The assumptions that government wastes money on poor people, that they stay poor only out of laziness and lack of initiative, becomes a self-fulfilling prophecy! Whatever the causes of poverty are, they *cannot* be reduced merely to one factor such as laziness.

A bit later in the chapter we will describe the other important general political myths, and the power they have to make us see and do things about policy in certain predictable ways.

Political ideologies are another, more complicated form of myth. They are generally understood as fully constructed political belief systems that guide policies and behaviors. Ideologies are distinct from other forms of myths in that they are usually based in a set of coherent political writings. Thus they provide a more general explanation of the way things ought to be, and they tend to capture the mind inside these beliefs in ways that may be more difficult to break out of than simple myths. Typically, we hear of liberal, conservative, or radical ideologies; later in the chapter we discuss how these are not the only important ideologies in America.

The third type of American policy culture are *federalist policy cultures* that are widely held over time. These belief systems are based in the American experience with federalism. They were present at the founding of the system and are still powerful forces today. An example is *dualism*, which argues that state powers should be generally increased and separated clearly from national government responsibilities, which should generally be reduced.

The fourth category consists of various *regional policy cultures*. Considerable differences exist between regions of the United States in ways of life, in attitudes, and in expectations about government and public policy. One reason that public policy in the United States is intergovernmental is the powerful influence of our regional policy cultures.

Now we will look in more detail at the powerful political and policy myths that emerge from these four American policy cultures, and estimate the degree to which these myths are true or false.

GENERAL AMERICAN POLICY MYTHS

The power of the myth lies in its ability to influence people to believe the myth is true and act in accordance with the myth. There are a number of such myths in America. The following list is selective, concentrating on those myths that have endured and seem to have the most influence.

GENERAL MYTH 1: AMERICA HAS THE WORLD'S HIGHEST LIVING STANDARD

Among the most commonly held myths is the belief that we have the highest standard of living in the world. This myth is a bit more fiction than fact. It is easy to believe because of false starting premises. For example, any American who has lived in or traveled to one of the formerly communist countries or a Third World country can easily see that we have a great deal of wealth in this society. But the issue is not whether we have wealth, but rather how much there is and how it gets sliced up and distributed. What we read into this myth is that most Americans can "naturally" get a big slice. But the distortions and inaccuracies in this myth are readily provable, and the reality is more complex.

First, if "the highest standard of living" means merely gross national or domestic product (the common measure of total national economic activity), then without doubt the United States ranks first as the largest world economy. But if "standard of living" means GDP per capita (or annual domestic production and consumption hypothetically divided evenly among all citizens), then the United States has fallen in rank from first in 1960 to ninth by 1988 among the modern industrialized countries (Dolbeare 1986, p. 62; and Table 3.2).

TABLE 3.2   GROSS NATIONAL PRODUCT PER CAPITA: TOP TEN NATIONS
             IN CONSTANT 1988 DOLLARS

1980			1988		
Rank			*Rank*		
1	Switzerland	26,266	1	Switzerland	29,539
2	Iceland	20,000	2	Japan	23,255
3	Sweden	18,291	3	Iceland	22,800
4	Japan	17,758	4	Norway	21,214
5	Norway	17,506	5	Sweden	20,853
6	Denmark	17,383	6	Finland	20,303
7	West Germany	17,283	7	Denmark	20,195
8	United States	16,945	8	West Germany	19,907
9	Finland	16,423	9	United States	19,813
10	Canada	15,067	10	Canada	18,015

Source: *Statistical Abstract of the United States*, 1990, Table 1447, p. 841.

Furthermore, we might want to consider whether some people dispropor-tionately enjoy a "higher living standard" over others. One way economists and sociologists frequently do this is to track and compare over time who has wealth and how concentrated it is. Wealth is extremely concentrated in the United States and is not widely dispersed to the middle class or the poor. The concentra-tion of wealth among the wealthiest 5 percent of the U.S. population in the 1980s has increased rather than decreased over the years since the mid-1970s.

At the same time, salaries and incomes for average Americans have not increased for decades, but have slightly declined. The best measure of this is median spendable net family income, which for over twenty years has been less every year than in the peak year of 1973 (except for 1987 and 1988) and has declined more steeply for the lower economic groups (see Figure 3.2). Finally, our poor are worse off than the poor of other industrial nations. An international study found that in 1995 the United States had the biggest annual income gap (of $54,613) between average rich families (at $65, 536) and poor families (at $10,923) among eighteen industrial nations. U.S. poor families of four were the poorest, except for in Ireland and Israel (AP news story, August 15, 1995). Our economic standard by these measures has clearly not been the highest and actually has fallen a bit for most Americans since the 1970s while it has risen for a much smaller and wealthier percentage. (Who does not know that it takes two paychecks in a family in the 1990s to equal the one-earner husband's paycheck of the 1960s?)

Another way to evaluate the American standard of living is to look at qual-ity-of-life measures. One good measure of the quality of life is health statistics. Infant mortality is one of several universal indicators. It is usually expressed as the number of deaths per 1,000 live births in a population. The U.S. infant mor-

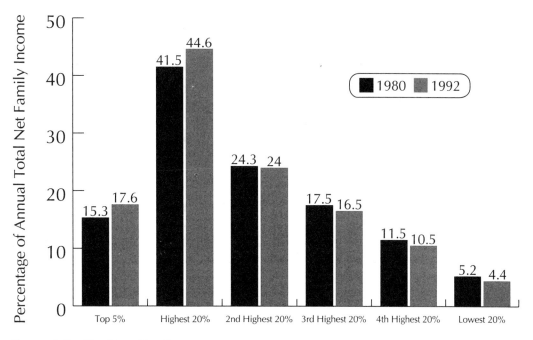

FIGURE 3.2   THE RICH GOT RICHER

Source: *Statistical Abstract of the United States,* 1994, Table 716, p. 470.

tality rate has improved slightly since the 1970s but has lowered in rank compared with other nations, dropping from about eighth among industrialized
nations in the late l970s to eighteenth or nineteenth by the early 1990s. The relative health situation for black babies has not improved at all, and compared with
whites has actually worsened from 1978 to 1986. In 1978 black infant mortality
was 1.89 times that of white newborns (38.6 deaths per 1,000 births for blacks,
20.4 per 1,000 for whites). By 1986 black infant mortality remained nearly the
same, but when compared with the white population it worsened to 2.11 times
that of white babies (35.5 deaths to 14.1 deaths per 1,000. (See Figure 3.3 and *U.S.
Statistical Abstract,* 1990, Table 110, p. 77.) Yet the myth continues that America
has the best health system in the world as part of the idea that we have the highest living standard in the world.

The real meaning of the myth is not to be found in statistics. One purpose
of this widely shared idea must be simply to express national pride. Second, this
belief allows people to downplay or gloss over problems in the economy, perhaps to help people believe that the economic standing of the country is not
actually worsening, when at times it is. Third, it also tends to gloss over problems that are due to our historic, highly uneven distribution of wealth. Crucial
issues of distributive justice—who gets how much of what—generally get less
attention in part because of the myth. Finally, this belief can help justify conservative philosophy that insists we need to keep the involvement of governments in

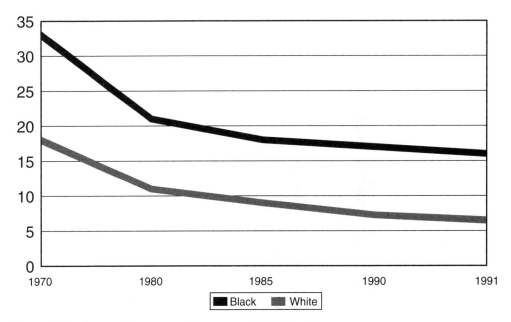

FIGURE 3.3   INFANT MORTALITY, DEATHS PER 1,000 LIVE BIRTHS
Source: *Statistical Abstract of the United States,* 1994, Table 120, p. 91.

the economy at a minimum. After all, why "fix" the economy with government tinkering if it is believed that not much is wrong with the economy that cannot be better handled by laissez-faire private sector freedom?

GENERAL MYTH 2: THE MIDDLE CLASS IS GETTING HIT THE HARDEST

Over the past two decades another widely shared myth has enjoyed great influence. This one does have somewhat more of a basis in fact. This myth is an example of one that is partly true and partly false, or is at least misconstrued in several ways. What is interesting is how this idea is seen differently by radicals, conservatives, and populists.

Conservatives use the belief that the middle class is being squeezed to point blame at high taxation, regulations on business, and "expensive" welfare programs whose burdens conservatives claim tend to fall disproportionately on the middle class. Radicals and civil rights advocates have responded by maintaining that a racist and anti-poor agenda is behind this currently popularized conservative view.

Populists also see the middle class as being squeezed, but in different terms. They generally believe that the middle class is being squeezed by big business, through such scams as the disastrous savings and loan debt crisis. They believe all Americans share their view that the middle and working classes increasingly bear the costs for such boondoggles, and for taxes. How that idea is interpreted, however, varies among Americans.

How much of the myth is true? Many studies of income and wages, including census data, do indicate that middle- and working-class Americans have seen their net incomes drop since 1973. It is apparently true that they are being squeezed, if the squeeze is being measured by the drop in net family incomes.

Another argument that is often made is that the general tax burden for working- and middle-class people rose in recent decades. This claim is not strongly supported by the facts, except perhaps in the 1980s. If all taxes (local, state, and national) are considered, as David Calleo (1992) has shown, from 1980 to 1988 the real tax burden as a percentage of net national product fell for the bottom 30 percent of the population and for the top 10 percent, but rose only very slightly for the rest of the middle income earners. To be precise, those who ranged from the fortieth to the ninetieth percentiles of net income (the middle income earners) were taxed about 1 percent higher on their net incomes in 1988 than in 1980. However, the tax bite of the net earnings for the same middle-income groups was the same in 1970 as it was in 1988. This means that average earners saw their tax rates remain about the same over the period, except for a slight rise mainly in the 1980s, not the 1970s!

The American tax rate is actually one of the lowest in the industrial world, with all taxes as a percent of the domestic economy (Gross Domestic Product) at 31.5 percent in the United States, 40.7 percent in Great Britain, 43.7 percent in Germany, and 47.1 percent in France in 1988 (Calleo 1992, p. 20). Middle-class Americans—defined as the middle 40 percent of incomes—have 23.7 percent of income going to all forms of taxes. This is actually *less* than the top 30 percent of wealth earners, who pay 26.7 percent and the top 10 percent, who pay 26.8 percent. The poorest 30 percent pay the least, 16.7 percent of their income (Pechman 1990, p. 4, cited in Calleo 1992, p. 98). As you can see, a stronger argument can be made that it is not taxes, but the drop in real income earnings that has squeezed the middle class over the last two decades or so.

It must be remembered that these incomes have dropped since the early 1970s in spite of the fact that the average family received a second paycheck as more women entered the work force in the 1970s than ever before. It simply takes two paychecks now to equal the real earnings of one paycheck in the 1960s. From this point of view, middle-income families *are* being squeezed, particularly when studies show that working mothers (and single parents) who work full-time still perform more than 75 percent of the household chores. Perhaps much closer to the truth is that middle class *women* are being squeezed.

This myth is thus mostly true. But it is particularly true for women, mainly those who are working-class or middle-income parents and working full-time.

This belief tends to heighten political conflicts in the society, as the facts are used differently by rigid partisans to bolster their own beliefs. They then tend to heighten the rhetoric, for example, complaining about either "tax-and-spend Democrats" or "fat-cat, cut-and-slash Republicans." As fingers are pointed at favorite scapegoats, the deep divisions between social groups are worsened. As whites blame blacks and vice versa, racism rises. As management blames labor and vice versa, and as environmentalists on one side and conservatives, economists, and businessmen on the other blame each other for loss of jobs and income, the divisions worsen.

Studies show that all voters are becoming more alienated, angry, and hostile. They are unhappy with the system and their perceived "opponents," and distrustful of political leaders. The political exploitation of the problems of middle income-earners, and their legitimate complaints about this problem, have no doubt heightened these tensions in America.

GENERAL MYTH 3: WE ARE BETTER OFF ISOLATED

Another durable policy myth concerns the alleged benefits of isolationism. One of the ideas inherent in isolationism is the populist idea that we should stop spending so much money on foreign aid and spend the money back home. The facts of foreign policy spending basically undermine this common belief that we spend lavishly on foreign aid. The United States has normally spent much more on arms sales and military aid than on nonmilitary economic assistance. Nonmilitary foreign aid is under $4 billion per year (arms sales to the Third World rose during the 1980s; see Table 3.3).

TABLE 3.3   THE FALL AND RISE IN MILITARY AID 1970–1988: TOTAL U.S. FOREIGN ECONOMIC VERSUS MILITARY AID, IN MILLIONS OF DOLLARS

	TOTAL ECONOMIC FOREIGN AID	MILITARY AID ONLY	MILITARY AID AS A PERCENTAGE OF TOTAL AID
1970	$3,676	$2,892	78.6% (Vietnam War)
1975	4,908	2,009	40.9% (post-vietnam)
1980	7,571	2,122	28.0%
1983	8,603	5,599	65.1%
1984	9,038	6,486	71.7%
1988	8,749	4,831	55.2%

Source: *Statistical Abstract of the United States*, 1990, Table 1400, p. 802.

Isolationism is based on strong American patriotism. One of its results is a general lack of information about foreign countries and their public policies. This lack of information extends to the mass media and the educational system. Even in higher education we rarely find courses in comparative public policies, economic systems, or education, for example.

The isolationist sentiment that we are better off alone expresses itself in different ways. The sentiment that we need to take care of only our own, that we need to pull out of the United Nations, that we need to reduce foreign aid drastically are examples. The basic lack of information about the geographies, societies, government, or policies of other countries also reflects this sentiment.

Isolationism might have some grains of truth in that it may stimulate us to pay more attention to our domestic problems, and it may stimulate us to search for what to do in foreign policy now that the Cold War has probably ended for good. But in the end, isolationism is counterproductive, even self-defeating.

Because the isolationist sentiment keeps us culturally ignorant of other peoples, we are easy victims to stereotypes at best and easy prey to xenophobia and exaggerated militarism at worst. As a result isolationism hinders foreign policy by making it difficult for us to understand issues in "hot spots," such as the Middle East. It reduces our awareness of our international economic position. Our lack of knowledge and languages reduces our ability to develop markets elsewhere or compete in foreign markets with leading competitors such as Japan and Germany. Finally, it makes it extremely difficult for us to learn practical improvements developed in other societies, both in government policies and business innovations.

Isolationism is not only self-defeating, it is increasingly infeasible. It is infeasible, for instance, to gain much money by squeezing it out of foreign aid, since the amounts are too small to make much difference for domestic problems. Much more important, it is unrealistic to cut ties to parts of the world with which we have close and long-running cultural and economic ties, such as Israel, Canada, Mexico, Europe, and Japan.

Most important, we simply *cannot* become more isolated in an increasingly interdependent world, that is, a world in which there is increasing dependence on foreign supplies and resources, and in which national economies and societies are increasingly tied into regional and global systems, both economically and culturally. Interdependence also refers to the rise of certain global problems that cannot be solved by one or a few countries' actions. Examples include AIDS, the depletion of ozone, the spread of nuclear weapons, and the destruction of rain forests along with many thousands of species. We would not escape these problems even if we put tanks at the borders and kept out contact with the world. In this physical sense, isolationism is impossible. All peoples are increasingly dependent upon one another for livelihoods, economic trade, food, disease control, science, languages, information, and the effects and solutions of common problems. The rise of the interdependent world—and the decline of the sovereign power of nations over domestic economies, international economics, policy problems, environment threats, and the problems of natural conservation—makes it more and more unrealistic to return to some dream world of isolationism.

A sign of the interdependent world can be seen even in local government activities these days. Economic interdependency has forced state and local governments to take on foreign policy type activities, such as attracting the investments of foreign firms or seeking out overseas markets for local businesses. The challenges to isolationism are stronger and more irresistible than ever before.

GENERAL MYTH 4: THE GOVERNMENT ALWAYS FAILS AND THE FREE
MARKET ALWAYS WORKS

Another national policy myth concerns beliefs about what is the "best way" to
organize and deliver goods and services to people. Many Americans advocate
the free-market myth. They assume the alleged inherent superiority of business and market institutions and values over all other kinds of institutions and
values. A strong form of this belief, common among partisan conservatives
and zealous free-market economists or businessmen (the prominent conservative economist Milton Friedman, for example), is the insistence that government programs are *always* failures. In its weaker forms (common among moderate economists and corporate circles) the assertion is that government
programs are *always* less efficient and *always* inferior in quality to the private
sector. In addition, the myth pictures government as less efficient or productive now than in the past. The crass denouncing of government is the most
extreme version of these beliefs and is somewhat the fad of the times. All are
descendants of the venerable traditional American beliefs that favor limited
government.

These views, especially the more extreme ones, are not strongly supported
by any convincing body of scholarly or systematic evidence. The evidence is
much more complicated than is characterized by these views. Any knowledge of
policy history (see Chapter 2) will show not only that the issue is not that simple,
but also that even the national government has sometimes "worked."

There are also considerable survey and scientific data that show that governments sometimes work well, satisfy consumers and citizens, and can work
better than no action, or private sector alternatives.

One group of prominent scholars summarized the contradictions to this
point of view from numerous studies (Wamsley et al. 1992):

1. Most clients of public bureaucracy are not dissatisfied; in fact the vast majority
   of them are very pleased with services and treatments received.
2. The rate of productivity increase in the public sector is not clearly lower than in
   the private sector; it is probably higher overall.
3. The federal government has not grown in number of employees since the early
   1950s.
4. The bureaucracy is not a "giant monster" or monolith; it is composed of many
   small and diverse bureaus and offices.
5. Public agencies stimulate and implement change; resistance to change is no
   more common in organizations of the public sector than in the private sector.
6. Studies have shown that the private sector is in fact more top-heavy with administrative personnel than the public sector.
7. Waste and inefficiency are no more prevalent in the public sector than in the private. It is simply that in the public sector they are seen as a waste of the taxpayer's money, while in the private sector we often fail to see that waste and
   inefficiency are more invisibly passed on to us in the prices that we pay as consumers. (Read the Chapter 9 description of medical cost-shifting for a very
   important example.)

Probably the best evidence that government programs *can* sometimes work lies in the record of the actions of state and local governments, especially in the 1980s and 1990s as responsibilities and the reform momentum has shifted downward in the federal system. In Chapters 5 to 11 you will see detailed evidence of the increasing success of state and local policies in intergovernmental affairs, environmental regulation, economic development, education reform, and health care reform, among others.

Many comparative policy studies of other nations also bear out the view that there is simply no clear pattern of evidence that public forms of organizations deliver services or products in ways inferior to private firms (Heclo 1983).

If this myth is basically exaggerated, what are its effects? It is possible to imagine several positive benefits from the assumption that governments never work and that the private sector is always superior. For one, it is important to expose whatever failures and inefficiencies of government programs exist. Extremely costly and corrupt programs, such as the $1.4 trillion savings and loan bankruptcies, as well as cost-overruns and disservice also deserve attention. For many years Senator William Proxmire issued his famous "Golden Fleece Award" exposing some of the sillier sides of government waste and inefficiency. Certainly avoiding the waste of taxpayer money is a laudable goal.

But there are also strong negative effects of the exaggeration of government failures. For one, it unfairly reduces confidence in, and the capacities and morale and productivity of, government workers. For another, it can unfairly twist people's assessments of government in general, even when surveys show that the people support many of the programs, especially the ones that benefit them. Perhaps one of the strongest negative effects is that it fosters an unrealistically pessimistic picture of state governments. There are many successful programs in the states, and they tend to be overlooked as potential real solutions. Untold lost opportunities to solve problems may well be the price paid as solutions to public problems go unnoticed.

In the l980s President Reagan was an outspoken promoter of anti-government ideas. He often invoked in his speeches the image of a massive federal bureaucracy larger than it ever had been, that intruded more than ever with long regulatory fingers into the lives of all Americans. The conservative picture that government is always a failure is stressed possibly even more in the 1990s (see Schwarz 1988; and Republican analyst Kevin Phillips 1994). This view is promoted in its most exaggerated versions by the many conservative radio talk show hosts (the prominent Rush Limbaugh is only one of numerous examples). Polling data, however, do not show such a clear antagonism for government actions. The majority of scientific polling shows that consistent public majorities *desire* government actions on problems, sometimes even if it means raising taxes (health care reform, crime, drug control and prevention, and environmental regulation are long-standing examples in survey research).

This myth of government failure is mostly false, although there are enough facts to help sustain the idea. For instance, there *are* more regulations and governmental programs now than in the 1950s. And they *do* cost business money, which either is absorbed by firms (in highly competitive situations) or is passed on as higher prices (in more monopolistic situations). But so much of the myth is not only false but is also historically naive and distorting. Historical evidence and research clearly show that workers and other citizens are much better off today as a result of increased government regulation. We will list briefly the undeniable improvements enjoyed by Americans over the last forty years due to public policies.

Since the 1950s new laws and enforcement have meant that air and water are cleaner, drugs are tested for safety before release to the public, auto safety and flame retardants on infant nightgowns prevent deadly fires and accidents, and dangerous chemicals and hazardous work are now far less dangerous to workers in industry. These benefits are attributable mostly to government laws and regulations, of which none existed before the 1950s (see Chapter 2).

Despite this evidence of government program success (for example, see Schwartz 1988), the stubborn myth still persists that almost all government bureaucracies and programs are inefficient failures.

The more extreme conservative spokespersons (for instance, Pat Buchanan) who cling doggedly to this assumption also voice some strangely contradictory sentiments. For example, they want to replace the policy activities of governments with private for-profit services, yet they express strong pride in the very same American government and institutions they scathingly criticize for threats to liberties. At these extremes such ideas can have the effect of eroding confidence in government even while being motivated by patriotism. The denouncing of democratic government can thus become a self-fulfilling prophecy that erodes democracy even more.

The final problem that could come from exaggerating the myth of government failure is that it could contribute to the decline of democratic participation and some of the basis of democracy in America. (Chapter 11 develops this argument and traces the connection between the rise of group conflict and gridlock and the decline of trust in governments and politics.)

GENERAL MYTH 5: GOVERNMENT EXECUTIVES WIELD GREAT POWER

A prime example of myth is the myth of executive power, the belief that government executives—presidents, governors, mayors—have great leadership power and should be held personally responsible for public problems. Presidential specialists have written for years about the exaggerated powers of the presidency in the American mind, yet the myth persists. Thus the public tends to hold executives accountable for events that occur during their tenure. For example, it is part of the myth of executive power to blame presidents for trouble in the economy even though the economic powers of presidents are severely limited by law, the independence of business practices, and conditions and forces from the international economy. For instance, laws give the Federal Reserve virtual control over interest rates and money supply. Corporations and banks have virtual freedom to conduct business, move capital, close plants, and shift manufacturing over-seas—with little executive branch power to influence these decisions.

GENERAL MYTH 6: CONGRESS IS A SNAKEPIT

Another myth about government institutions is that of the corrupt Congress. This view paints Congress as ineffective at best, corrupt at worst. Probably the dominant myth about Congress is that it is "rotten to the core." The picture changes a little over the years. In the 1970s Congress was pictured as consisting of entrenched seniority politicians who made budgets and laws without accountability or concern for popular needs, deep within a system of committees ruled by iron-fisted, white-haired chairmen. The members of the "power structure" were often depicted as corrupt politicians accepting big campaign donations or involved in sleaze, money, or sex scandals. This myth has changed somewhat. In the 1990s it says that Congress is made up mainly of rich, pork-barrel oriented incumbents who are not interested in meeting the needs of average citizens but are interested in pandering to special interests, lobby groups, and political action committees who fund their campaigns. The populist image of Congress today is that the rich, disconnected incumbents vote themselves pay increases while cutting budgets and raising taxes. These beliefs, probably the strongest images the public holds today of politics, combine to form a strong picture of a nonworking and nonrepresentative, even venal and corrupt, legislature. The major effect of this institution myth, which has heightened since the mid-1970s, is to exaggerate negative images and reduce the abilities of legislatures.

It is the American policy style to complain about legislatures and to take frequent and often extreme measures to reform them. The persistent efforts at reform, aimed at disempowering the supposedly universal "good old boy network," included the 1970s reduction of the congressional seniority system, the introduction of professional legislative and committee staffs, and the 1990s proposals for term limitations.

One of the problems with these reform movements is the unexpected and sometimes adverse results. For example, as a result of campaign finance reform laws in the 1970s, candidates running against incumbents could not compete with them for big PAC money, and so by the 1990s incumbents were outspending competitors by seven to one and were even more routinely returned to office—at least until the 1994 congressional elections.

GENERAL MYTH 7: LOCALS ALWAYS KNOW BEST AND ALWAYS WORK BETTER FOR COMMON FOLK

The final governmental myth that we will discuss is the idea that local governments are not only more effective and democratic than other levels of government but also closer, more accountable, more effective, wiser in decisions, and more responsive than other levels of government. The belief is partly traceable to dualism, a federalist culture we will discuss in the next chapter. It is also traceable to the strong influence of Thomas Jefferson, who promoted this idea along with his views that America should remain largely agricultural and nonurban so as to enhance democracy.

At this point, it should be emphasized that the federal tradition of dualism never gave powers to local government. The dualism found in the American Constitution gave power to the *states* and to the *national* government (mainly the Congress), but it said nothing about local governments. Given this constitutional silence, the federal courts in the nineteenth century declared local governments to be the creatures of state governments. As a result, the power of local governments has been limited substantially by state laws and state constitutions. Local governments must perform what is expected of them (and a lot is expected, given the myth) encumbered by these legal straightjackets.

There is evidence to suggest that local governments are improving their effectiveness significantly in the 1980s and 1990s (see later chapters). Historically, however, they have not been so effective, for a variety of reasons. For instance, they have low taxing abilities. They are subject to regulation by state laws in severe ways. Local elected officials are often amateurs who serve on a very limited part-time basis, with little advisory staff and little expertise or experience in government or public problems. Local offices are often filled by influential businesspeople who may favor the interests of developers or cronies rather than the interests of the disabled, the elderly, average citizens, or the poor or minorities. Local governments and voters often turn down such reforms as tax increases for school districts, proposals for city government restructure, or city-county mergers. In spite of evidence such as this (see Schultze 1985, Chapter 4, pp. 92–95), the myth persists that local government is always more effective at meeting local needs than are other levels of government.

AMERICAN POLITICAL IDEOLOGIES

A part of the American political culture is *political ideology*. Political ideologies are fully constructed political belief systems that guide policies and actions in politics and economics. Sometimes these belief systems are based in a set of political writings, some coherent and some polemical. At the personal level, ideologies are highly individual, as was explained earlier, and are the result of the political socialization process a given individual has experienced.

Political ideologies are not as strong in America as in some European countries. Public opinion polls have indicated for several decades that Americans, when asked whether they regard themselves as conservative or liberal, consistently answer "I don't know" (mid-thirty percentile) or "I am moderate" (mid-twenty percentile) (see review by Mayer 1992). Most people, approximately 40 to 60 percent, depending on the survey, cannot identify themselves as belonging to the liberal-conservative categories of ideologies commonly used in political analysis.

There is an additional complicating factor. As with the policy styles, Americans generally mix ideologies in their belief system according to the issue. The political socialization process in the United States does not create many pure ideologues, that is, people who are consistently liberal or conservative on all issues. As has been mentioned, it is not uncommon to find individuals who are conservative on some issues, liberal on others, radical on some, and populist on others. As a result, political ideology tends to have a complicating and confusing impact as a factor in the policy system.

However, this is not how the mass media tries to depict American politics and policy. Generally the mass media approaches policies in a point-counterpoint, liberal versus conservative fashion. The assumption is that if "both sides" of an issue are presented—that is, the conservative and the liberal point of view—more light than heat will result and the public will be able to decide what they believe. Even highly regarded news programs such as the MacNeil-Lehrer Hour operate on the method of contrasting controversies. Yet this perspective is intellectually understandable to less than a third of the American population. To what extent this approach distorts information for most people is unclear, but probably the information distortion is rather high.

There are several ways to categorize the ideological strains in American politics. The student is presented with a confusing array of terms, often accompanied by the prefix *neo* as in neo-conservative or neo-liberal. For public policy purposes, we will follow a four-category system that we think best captures the division of American ideology and clarifies much of the confusion about the 60 percent who are not liberals or conservatives. In analyzing the data from the University of Michigan Survey Research Center for political studies, Maddox and Lilie found that with four categories they could classify the 84 percent of the American population who even vaguely associate themselves with an ideology (Maddox and Lilie 1984, p. xxii). The categories are *conservative, liberal, populist,* and *libertarian*. A summary of the beliefs of these groups is shown in Table 3.4.

TABLE 3.4   WHAT DO AMERICANS BELIEVE?

LIBERALS	LIBERTARIANS	POPULISTS	CONSERVATIVES
24 percent 1980	*18 percent 1980*	*26 percent 1980*	*16.5 percent 1980*
nonmilitary internationalism	nongovernmental internationalism	strongly isolationist	military internationalism
48 percent anti-communist	50 percent anti-communist	61 percent strongly anti-communist	72 percent strongly anti-communist
support government economic intervention to promote individual welfare and regulate the economy	maximum personal freedom, reject government censorship, regulation of morality, etc.	anti-big government and big business	strident nationalists

TABLE 3.4, CONT.

LIBERALS	LIBERTARIANS	POPULISTS	CONSERVATIVES
high personal liberties	minimum social and economic role of government	suspicious of business and government (cooperation to exploit the poor)	favor government regulation of morality and some liberties to return to "traditional values" of religion
	property central— unregulated free market	regulation of business, redistribution of unfair profits	minimal government regulation of economy (except for pro-business subsidy)
	private voluntarism, not government programs	favor rural life	
	neglects equality	retain personal property rights	
		use government to enforce "traditional sectarian" values	

Source: Maddox and Lilie, *Beyond Liberal and Conservative*, 1985.

Conservatives (about 17 percent of the population in the 1980s) prefer the activities of the unregulated private market to government involvement in the economy. On the other hand, conservatives generally support government control of social behavior, particularly in the area of moral behavior. So, for example, conservatives are usually willing to support controls over marijuana, rock music, pornography, abortion, drug use, and alcohol abuse. What is the reason that conservatives oppose regulation of the economy but support regulation of moral behavior? The most likely explanation is that they tend to want to "control society" in order to return to an America that is rooted in the family, church, and traditional values. But, because they are skeptical of government's ability to meet social and economic needs better than the market can, they prefer minimum government involvement in the market.

Liberals (about 24 percent of the population in the 1980s) are more willing to accept increased government action in the economy in order to guarantee conditions of equality. Liberals are stronger believers in personal liberty and social equality than are conservatives. This is so because they are more likely to distrust traditional social institutions, which they do not view in such glowing terms as do conservatives. For the liberal, the "good old days" and the traditional social institutions are darkened by the inequality for women, slavery for blacks, inequality for minorities, and economic disasters resulting from periodic business cycles such as the Great Depression of the 1930s. For the liberal, unregulated traditional social institutions have produced much prejudice, racism, sexism, unemployment, and poverty. Liberals see traditional social institutions, then, as obstacles to individual progress, and they accept government as a means for removing these obstacles.

The primary concern of the populist (about 26 percent of the population) is for the interest of the "common man." Populists are deeply suspicious of *both* big government and big business. This attitude does not make them anti-capitalist. They accept the notions of private property and the market economy, but they see in centralization an increasing tendency of big government and big business to serve the interests of the privileged few. The basic populist policy style is toward the type of reform that would produce a wider distribution of wealth and opportunity for common folk. Maddox and Lilie describe the populist's reform ideas this way: "Populists support government regulation of the economy to prevent concentrations of wealth and to ensure a more equal distribution of private property—but not to destroy private property or capitalism" (Maddox and Lilie 1984, p. 20).

The 18 percent of the population who are libertarians are rigidly individualistic. They believe that few social institutions should exist at all, whether government, business or other. In the ideal libertarian world there are only individuals, and individuals have rights, the most important of which is to be free. Equality is a concept that does not play very strongly in libertarian thinking. To libertarians, most human needs can be met by individuals acting on their own for their welfare or for the welfare of their neighbors. Libertarians emphasize the autonomy of the individual and thus reject government control of individual behavior, especially moral behavior. Even more than populists, libertarians are suspicious of any social institution as a capricious controller of individual fate and freedoms.

One way to get an objective perspective on the four strains of American political ideologies is to compare them to European ideologies. For example, a comparison of American liberal beliefs and British conservative beliefs produces some striking findings. The most important conclusion to be drawn from such a comparison is that the modern American political spectrum is somewhat more to the right than the British political spectrum. In other words, a liberal in the United States is much closer to a conservative in England, at least on social welfare ideals, while a laborite in England would be labeled as a politically unacceptable left-wing radical in America. This point has some very important policy implications. To illustrate, the Thatcher government was understood as a strongly conservative government, but even Margaret Thatcher, the staunchest of British conservatives, did not openly advocate the abolishment of the national health insurance system in England, much less try to dismantle it. On the other hand, in the United States one would have to be an extreme liberal even to propose a nationalized health service. Most liberals would not (President Clinton certainly did not).

A comparison of American beliefs with those on the European continent produces even more striking contrasts. Consider, for example, the fact that few Americans, perhaps less than 2 percent, identify themselves as left-wing radicals. Yet if American radicals were transported to Europe, they would generally be regarded as mainstream social democrats, who constitute the majority of most governments and most ruling voting coalitions in Europe.

The four American ideologies seem to reflect a cycle of high tides versus low ebbs of influence in the policy system. The dominant policy style of the 1980s was conservative; that of the 1960s and 1970s was liberal. It is possible that the dominant style of the 1990s will be populist. The libertarian policy style has not had a broad-based organized appeal in the United States—the 1980s was the period in which it had the most impact on public policy. Key policy ideas of mainstream liberals such as social security for the old, civil rights for minorities, equal rights for women, and government safety regulation of the economy have been significant features of public policy for the most recent four decades. While the appeal of these ideas eroded somewhat among segments of the population, there is no convincing evidence that opinion swung strongly to the right in the 1980s (see Schwarz 1988). Instead, there was polarization of public opinion on several significant issues such as abortion and taxes.

SUMMARY

Americans think about themselves, government, policies, and solutions in ways culturally typical only to us. The policy myths—whether true, partly true, or mainly false—tend to determine our ideas and limit our imaginations about ourselves, our problems, and possible solutions. Examining how these myths limit our imaginations allows us to free our minds to find feasible solutions that may in the end be culturally acceptable. This chapter begins to set the stage for comparing and searching for solutions, which we will pursue in later chapters.

The story is not yet complete on how Americans typically "think and do" policies; we also have to appreciate the vast regional and federal differences in the way people think about public policies. Chapter 4 will complete this picture.

 CHAPTER **4**

THE AMERICAN TAPESTRY

THE DIVERSITY OF FEDERALIST
AND REGIONAL POLICY CULTURES

This chapter depicts how diversity in the American federal system and the remarkable regional differences in the United States make for rather striking varieties in the policies and lifestyles of Americans. It rounds out our picture of what Americans typically "think and do" about public policies. It not only sets the stage for the bigger picture of how federalism determines policies (Chapter 5), but also will enable us to develop a perspective for feasible alternatives to public problems in later chapters. Besides, it is fascinating to look at ourselves and appreciate the diversity with which the various regions of our country respond to public problems. We will start with the national federalist traditions that shape policies and then turn to our regional differences.

FEDERALIST POLICY CULTURES

The *federalist policy cultures* are the shared ways of thinking about and acting on public policy that can be traced to the American experience with federalism. These beliefs and practices have evolved out of the colonial period and were given forceful articulation in the Constitutional Convention. They are durable and powerful forces in the American policy system. The three federalist policy cultures are *compound federalism, dual federalism,* and *centralist federalism* (Hamilton and Wells 1990).

COMPOUND FEDERALISM

The compound federal culture is the belief that evolved from James Madison's influence over the original constitution design and early practice. Madison referred to compound federalism as a blend of national-level and state-level economics and politics (*Federalist Papers*, no. 39). A key element in Madison's compound federalism is the separation-of-powers principle.

In Madison's system, the division of powers was to have two effects. The first was to limit the power of social groups to influence the higher levels of government. This might be called the *horizontal function* of Madison's system. The basis of this idea was Madison's suspicion of human nature and of majorities. His reasoning went like this: Human nature leads people to form essentially self-interested factions which seek to win out over others and even misguide public opinion. This is especially true if the factions are composed of misguided passionate elites or uneducated and volatile social groups. Majorities are essential to democracy, Madison admitted, yet they constitute its greatest threat since they are often unstable, uninformed, and easily misled by political factions to repress human rights or minorities (see *Federalist Papers*, no. 10; *Federalist Papers*, no. 51, last paragraph).

To guard against these dangers, certain features of government design were built into the constitution. Government power was fractured among three branches of government. Strong limits were imposed on the amount of direct public representation: Thus the indirect election of the President by state legislature elites through the Electoral College. The election to the U.S. Senate was by the vote of the same state legislatures and not by popular vote. Different terms were set for House and Senate members, with the wealthier senators serving longer terms. Finally, an obstacle to change in any of these elements was the requirement that constitutional amendments be ratified by three-fourths of the states. All of these measures were meant to place strong limits on public opinion, to divide power among groups, to control horizontal social alliances or power concentrations, and to fragment government power and its ability to respond to these social pressures.

The second function of the separation of powers is its *vertical function*. The branches of government were constructed to represent different social groups in the population and to place these groups in competition with each other in government institutions at the top. Madison argued that the protection of minority rights and democratic stability required a balance among interests inside three branches. Thus there are those who represent the wise (the hierarchy in the federal courts), those who represent the powerful (the wealthy landowners from states in the Senate), and those who represent more of the common interest (the average man in the House) (see *Federalist Papers*, nos. 51, 53, and 57).

This design was to ensure competition both between social groups and between governmental branches and institutions. Its purpose was to slow down decision making and prevent political takeovers.

What made this system *compound* was that it had areas of overlapping responsibility for policy. Although economic subsidies, stabilization, interstate economics and growth were lodged primarily at the national level, states had a partial responsibility for these policies. Other areas where the states and the national government shared responsibilities were taxes, building of economic infrastructure, and defense (in the original system the states had state militia). The compound design allowed the states primary control over social life regulation, intrastate business, law, and crime. Today these policy responsibilities are much the same as when they were incorporated into the Constitution of 1787.

DUAL FEDERALISM

The second federalist policy style which has widespread appeal in the United States is the *dualist culture*. Dualism, more than the other traditions, favors separate and equal levels of government and decentralized government power. Its deepest roots are found in preconstitutional practice, in the anti-federalists, in the southern states, and in the profound influence of Thomas Jefferson. Dualists generally argue that having separate and equally powerful levels of government is the best kind of macropolitical arrangement. In fact, most dualists believe that the more the separation, the better the government.

Dualism has meant that economics, social life, and political liberties in the first century and a half of the republic were in practice largely controlled at local and state levels. Consequently the development and effects of these policies were uneven across the nation. The dual culture meant that the national government infrequently interfered in the business or social life of states. The major exceptions were the Civil War and Reconstruction, and the occasional "maintenance of order," such as the use of national power to suppress native Americans, restive farmers, or labor unions.

The dual tradition made a strong comeback during the 1950s and again in the 1980s, surprising some analysts who had declared its death in the 1960s (Elazar 1964, Chapter 3). From the beginning, the ideas of dualism have been favored by a significant minority and from time to time they are very popular. Both Eisenhower and Reagan, for example, called for a dramatic reordering of powers "back to the states," and for limiting national powers in the economy and in business regulation. More important, the demographic, economic, and electoral swing toward the South and West in recent decades made it almost inevitable that the strong dualist ideas in these regions would filter back into national politics.

CENTRALIST FEDERALISM

The last federal policy culture is *centralism*, which is the belief, partly traceable to Alexander Hamilton, that relatively strong national control of economics and politics by national elites is necessary for the most efficient and effective socioeconomic system. In the centralist culture, "business elites know best." Furthermore, centralists believe that elite control ought to be built into law and into the decision institutions of government.

Centralism asserts that elite policy and political control should be especially strong in order to achieve the following goals:

1. Maintain social and political order
2. Manage public involvement in politics
3. Maintain capitalism and national economic development
4. Secure economic stabilization and subsidy
5. Limit but not eliminate representation
6. Subordinate state and local goals to national elite and business goals

An excellent illustration of these goals is found in many policies of the Reagan administration. In the 1980s centralists' views came to dominate the administration's approach to intergovernmental economic affairs. A centralist slant was especially strong in Reagan policies of business deregulation, reduction of environmental protection, increase in defense spending, and policy relative to morality, such as abortion and prayer in the public schools. The administration's position was a potent marriage of the rhetoric of "free marketeering" and centralist federalism, designed, as David Stockman argued, primarily by and for big business. The administration's economic approach to federalism was to restore business-class centralism to dominance—a goal that was in conflict with the President's stated official goals of dualism. The Reagan federal style drew from both centralism and dualism, illustrating our point that there are few pure policy styles in American public policy.

REGIONAL POLICY CULTURES

Possibly the most fascinating force guiding the preferences for public policy in the United States is regionalism. One common way of discussing regionalism is to divide the country into sun belt and frost belt regions. The *sun belt* region consists of the southeastern and southwestern regions, including southern California (Dye 1986). These are the new-wealth growth regions where in-migration and new industry expanded after World War II. The *frost belt* consists of those states north of a line drawn from Richmond, Virginia, to San Francisco, California. These states are sometimes called the *rust belt* because they were the center of older "smokestack" industries and they have not had as rapid economic growth as in the sun belt. Analysts in the 1960s and 1970s were describing the "second civil war" between the sun belt and the frost belt because of the competition between the two regions for federal grants to encourage economic development and for the location of industries in their regions.

This traditional way of looking at the U.S. regions as two broad areas has both advantages and disadvantages. It does focus on the differences of population migration since the end of the Second World War. It also highlights some of the issues of competition between the states and the uneven economic growth. However, there are certain features of the American policy system that this simple North–South division masks. It tends to ignore the obvious social demographic differences between regions and the attendant differences in lifestyles and communities. The North–South idea also tends to nationalize the discussion of economics and to deemphasize the idea that there are actually many regional economies that operate in the American federal system. Most important for our purposes, it tends to overlook some of the very important public policy differences between the different regions of the United States.

Joel Garreau (1980), the cultural geographers (Zelinsky 1980), and a few political scientists have produced an important body of research that richly describes the important cultural and political distinctions between different regions of North America. We draw on this work and the very extensive material on state and regional policies for our discussions of regional policy cultures. We will describe the policy styles that are typical to each of seven regions (see Figure 4.1) and will note the differences they make.

THE NEW ENGLAND POLICY STYLE

The New England region is one of the least homogeneous of the American regions. It is traditionally broken into two distinct parts, the traditional rural Yankee New England of Maine, Vermont, and New Hampshire, and the rather different states of Massachusetts, Connecticut, and Rhode Island. The upstate, or traditional, area exhibits what we call the traditional Yankee policy culture.

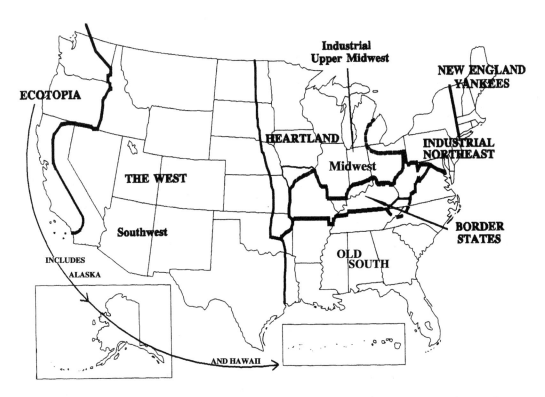

FIGURE 4.1   POLITICAL-CULTURAL REGIONS OF THE UNITED STATES THAT DETERMINE POLICY STYLES

Vermont has somewhat different traditions, associated with historic grass roots town meetings. Vermont is also a relatively strong spender in welfare and environmental policies. This relatively anti-urban, proenvironmental slant is rooted in Vermont's current demographics. Thus the state today is a mixture of traditional old-line Protestant Vermonters, and new immigrants associated with high-tech industries, universities, and the service-tourism industry.

The New Hampshire Yankee culture is noticeably different from that of Vermont. It is more like the "rock-ribbed conservative old Yankee" image, even though the two societies have shared rural beginnings and historical immigrant groups. New Hampshire has a tradition of very low state taxes and is virtually unique among the American states in not having a state income tax. This low-tax profile results partly from the combination of the conservative rural areas of upper New Hampshire and the white-collar labor and mostly white middle-class conservative suburban commuters of southern New Hampshire. The conservatism of New Hampshire, then, has been strengthened by white-collar suburbanization of towns and cities in the southern part of the state. As a result of its low-tax sentiments, New Hampshire has poorer school districts, has lower expenditures per student, and is less generous in programs for the elderly and for welfare services than other New England states.

As a result of these modern developments, Yankee New England today has three *traditional Yankee styles*: (1) The *new Yankees*, who are new immigrants, baby-boomers, city dwelling, service oriented, and slightly more liberal and environmentally inclined; they reside mainly in Vermont and the bigger cities of New Hampshire and Maine; (2) the socially and fiscally conservative *traditional Yankees*, particularly of rural New England and upstate New Hampshire; and (3) the *lower Yankee progressives* in Massachusetts, Connecticut, and Rhode Island (including far south New Hampshire), who are considerably more urbanized, more socially complex, more Catholic, more ethnic, and more industrial than the northern-tier states of Vermont, upstate New Hampshire, and Maine.

The lower Yankee states exhibit what could be called *urban Yankee progressivism*. These states have generally higher levels of taxation and greater expenditure on elementary, secondary, and higher education than the rest of the northern-tier states, and they are generally very active and innovative in elderly and welfare programs. They have strong government regulations and environmental programs. These programs are traceable to the demands of their urbanized societies and to the cosmopolitan mix of ethnic groups.

THE INDUSTRIAL NORTHEAST POLICY STYLE

The urban industrial states consist of the northeastern states of New York, Pennsylvania, Delaware, New Jersey, and Maryland, and the Great Lakes industrial midwestern states of Illinois, Michigan, Ohio, the northern part of Indiana, and the eastern part of Wisconsin. While these two groups are quite different in their social makeup and political traditions, they are similar in their policy cultures, probably because they share a similar social demography and economic base. Both regions are the heartland of American ethnic groups. Many immigrant groups, particularly northern and eastern Europeans, Italians, Poles, and central Europeans, came to both the upper Midwest and the industrial Northeast from the Civil War years to the 1930s. These immigrant groups went to work in America's factories around the turn of the century, contributing to the development of the industrial base in the United States and to the rise of labor unions, the Democratic party, and the urban middle classes.

Today this region shares certain problems associated with the 1980s decline of smokestack industries and the postwar rise of service industries. These problems give rise to voters' demands for public policies that are different from those desired in the Yankee New England or the Southern regions. Common throughout the region are the problems of the rust belt and the efforts of the "renaissance cities" to cope with those problems.

The "renaissance cities" must deal with the decline of smokestack industries with efforts to restore and revitalize urban areas, attract foreign capital or new service industries, and maintain the viability of the industry core and the status of the city in nationwide trade and politics. Perhaps the best examples of these efforts are Pittsburgh and Detroit. Both cities have worked to attract new service or high-tech industries, rebuild their downtown areas, and retain their population base. They typically have had aggressive, high-profile mayors or progressive city council members who try to recruit capital and investment. These self-starting renewal efforts took place in the midst of the great experiment to reduce government aid to cities in the early 1980s under President Reagan. Political leaders of the region led the fight against federal cutbacks and generally reflected a willingness to raise taxes to plug the gap created by declining federal aid.

This area of the country has historically been favorable toward labor unions, including the formation of unions in the public sector (even in universities and in services such as fire and police)—a policy style that is not found in other parts of the country. It is typically these states that have state job training or retraining programs for sectors that are experiencing loss of jobs.

Another aspect of the industrial urban policy culture focuses on the service-oriented economies of states such as Wisconsin and its heartland neighbor Minnesota. The policy cultures of these urban areas are even more strongly oriented than in other parts of the nation toward spending for education, social welfare services, and urban planning. The emphasis on economic development has resulted in active economic development offices at the state level. Cabinet-level agencies function to attract foreign investment as well as service industries from other regions of the country. Governors from these parts of the country are high-profile actors who pursue new capital investment.

THE HEARTLAND POLICY STYLE

The heartland of the central plains and upper midwestern states consists of the midwestern states of Iowa, Minnesota, most of Wisconsin, the northwestern part of Missouri, and the eastern parts of the generally more western states of Kansas,

Nebraska, Oklahoma, North Dakota, and South Dakota. Aside from sharing a common farm economy and having similar farm- and service-oriented cities, these states had similar waves of immigrants, mostly from northern and central Europe, in the last half of the nineteenth century.

The progressive heartland policy culture has always been associated with state and local reforms that reach back to the Progressive and the Populist parties of the 1880s and 1890s. At the state level, these reforms include legislation for financial audit and program review functions, and the reorganization of the executive agencies of government. More recently, progressive government reforms have included a broad mix of trends such as computerized welfare procedures, a strong effort to prevent child abuse, rehabilitative prison reform and alternative sentencing programs, deeply penetrating reforms of public education, and stress on environmental protection. These reforms continue the tradition of progressivism which stretches back to the last century.

Grass roots volunteerism is a very strong element in the central plains and upper Midwest states. It involves public participation in associations devoted to civic improvements. Thus in this region business and civil associations, church-based associations, and traditional volunteer service associations are active. Other forms of grass roots volunteerism include church-based associations against social problems such as Mothers Against Drunk Driving or Parents Anonymous against child abuse. The volunteer service associations include the Shriners, who operate the hospitals, the grass roots rural-based insurance associations such as Modern Woodmen of America, the social lodges such as the Elks, the Odd Fellows, the Moose, the Knights of Columbus, the Masonic Lodges, and also the Boy and Girl Scouts. In the heartland policy style, volunteerism is not a substitute for progressive government, but rather an important addition, a thrust in the same direction of civic betterment, understood as "neighbors working for neighbors."

Moralism takes several forms in the heartland style of public policy. Moralism results in active scrutiny and regulation of social behavior through statewide legislation. Among these regulations are limitations on liquor, detailed coverage of personal corruption of public officials, the control of pornography (even restrictions on public display of art regarded as pornographic), and restrictions on massage parlors. In the heartland style, prostitution is barely tolerated, drinking and driving are severely regulated, marijuana growers are hunted down, and driver substance abuse education in schools is highly stressed. Moralism in this sense is an expression of religious or civic values as expectations for the conduct of public officials, and as social goals in society.

However, moralism in the heartland policy style is not so strongly associated with religious fundamentalism or parochialism as in some other regions. There is a greater tendency than in Southern or border states to enforce Supreme Court rulings regarding the separation of church and state and the banning of prayer in schools. In the heartland such national regulatory policies are viewed less as "dictates by outsiders," than they might be in the southern or border states, or perhaps the western states. Indeed, regulations of social behavior imposed by the federal courts carry a certain moral legitimacy. Moralism, therefore, involves the enforcement of centralist decisions of *legitimate* government.

Social liberalism in public policies in the heartland policy style does not reflect liberal or radical values, that is, social legislation or program liberalism is not acceptable if its goals are to redistribute income. However, if the goals are to regulate the hazards of business operation, to promote individual initiative or betterment, or to express the "social Christian gospel concern" for the elderly and the disadvantaged, then those kinds of public policies are acceptable, and indeed strongly promoted. Thus attempts have been made to minimize the drastic national budget cuts and eligibility restrictions in health care support, welfare, and aid to families with dependent children. The emphasis in this region is on providing adequate support for the disadvantaged, the out-of-work, the minorities, and families with dependent children. The main emphasis is on high or maintenance levels of expenditure and innovation for education, economic development, and capital attraction for the state.

THE WESTERN POLICY STYLE

The Rocky Mountain western states combine with the central and western parts of Oklahoma, Kansas, Nebraska, and the Dakotas, and with the Southwestern states to form the Western policy culture. The Rocky Mountain states are Colorado, Idaho, northeast Washington, Montana, Utah, Wyoming, Nevada, and central and northern Alaska; the Southwestern states are Arizona, the far south of California, New Mexico, and Texas. Of course there are great differences between these vast areas. For example, the geography of Arizona and New Mexico is not at all similar to that of Alaska, nor is the social makeup very similar. For example, the Southwestern states have a much higher percentage of Hispanic peoples. Even so, the policy styles of all these states have a certain commonality.

The most important elements of the Western policy style include conservationism, a cowboy capitalist style of economic development and attitude toward government regulation, and a sharing of mountain state economic problems, including the issue of private exploitation of resources such as oil, timber, and coal. In this sense the conservationist policy is usually in conflict with both the "high-roller developer style" and the interests of big energy and timber corporations that wish to exploit natural resources.

The Western policy style is also characterized by an enduring anti-Eastern sentiment, which pits Westerners against "eastern" or "outsider" corporations or development interests and/or "Washington." This attitude, common among ranchers, farmers, and industrial workers, grows out of the Western tradition of high-spirited rugged individualism as well as frontier history. It gives rise to the demand of Western states for sovereignty in social regulation. For example, a fairly serious effort by about one-fourth of the western counties of Kansas to secede from the rest of the state over tax and state program inequities made for headlines and nervous state officials in Topeka in the early 1990s. A secession sentiment has also been strong in northern California. These social sentiments are also very strong in the more western plains states from Oklahoma to North Dakota. These states attempt to handle disputes between themselves with inter-state agreements over such issues as water rights, air pollution, and public transit. Consistent with their independence-from-Washington sentiments, they generally resist all forms of federal mandates on these issues.

An element in the Western style that appears only on the surface to run counter to anti-Eastern sentiments is the desire in recent decades to promote tourism. However, Westerners typically want only the "tourist dollars" to come and stay, not the tourists. This ambivalence about tourism and in-migration from other regions is rooted in the conflict Westerners feel between their desire for economic development and their wish to be independent of the East, live a free, uncrowded lifestyle, and the like. Much of Western public policy will show this deep ambivalence by promoting tourism or economic development while at the same time flirting with limits to growth policies. These limits include attempts to restrict building development, housing permits, and the shipping of tax resources (such as oil or coal) out of state, as well as to tax earnings from exports headed for the East. Some states have even put a ceiling on enrollment in their public universities in order to control the immigration from other parts of the country.

The venture capitalist attitude in this region combines with the sentiment of rugged individualism to yield a general preference for low property taxes and high sales taxes (especially since it places a tax burden on outsiders). It also results in the frontier style existence of certain "sin industries" which are allowed to prosper as sources of revenue—such as legalized prostitution in Nevada, gambling, horse racing, big lotteries, and the like. In the Western policy culture, vices are culturally tolerable, having been a tradition of the West dating back to the exuberant lifestyles of the early settlers. Moral legislation to control public behavior, except for the Mormon areas, is not an important requirement for civic life.

A major policy characteristic of this region is the severe conflict between conservationists and high-roller developers. In this sense the Western policy style has a split personality. On the one hand, ranchers and environmentalists have long been strongly devoted to preservation of the land and water and protection of the West's incomparable natural resources and scenic wonders. More recently they have been devoted to the reduction of pollution and hazardous wastes. On the other hand, mining interests, oil and energy companies, real estate developers, and new-wealth postwar entrepreneurs favor unregulated business and natural resource exploitation. Probably the most famous exponent of this view has been the beer mogul Adolph Coors, who played a strong part in the Reagan administration in getting prodevelopment and anti-conservation persons appointed to top government posts, including James Watt as interior secretary and Ann Gorsuch as President Reagan's EPA administrator.

The arguments between these antagonists are, of course, framed in the rhetoric of the greater public interest. In this battle Western environmentalists and conservationists are often pitted against government agencies that want to develop resources of natural areas. Conservationists have fought influence battles against the Army Corps of Engineers (which favor converting wild scenic rivers and canyons into hydroelectric plants or motor boat paradises), and against the Reagan Department of Interior, which had sought to unfreeze public lands held by the federal government for off-shore oil leasing or other forms of business exploitation. Particularly critical now is the current dispute in Alaska regarding whether to open up to oil developers wilderness range areas currently protected by law. This argument was intensified by the nation's need for oil and energy independence (fueled by the 1990 Gulf Crisis oil shortage) versus the spectre of "environmental rape" of virgin wilderness (as seen in the catastrophic off-shore oil spill from the Exxon *Valdez* oil tanker in 1989). One could justifiably describe the conflicts between environmentalists and developers as a new "range war" in the West (Lash et.al. 1986).

State spending on social welfare services in the Western policy culture is relatively low. The reasons are the tradition of rugged individualism and the relative lack of minority population in inland urban areas (except for black, Latin, and Asian concentrations in some cities of the Southwest). The Rocky Mountain West states and the Southwest states rank sixth and seventh respectively among the U.S. regions in the average AFDC grants to families (See Table 4.1). At the same time, the effect of moralism is low in the Western states and consequently tends to reduce the level of expenditure on public education.

TABLE 4.1   RANK OF THE REGIONS OF THE UNITED STATES IN 1985
IN AID TO FAMILIES WITH DEPENDENT CHILDREN (AFDC)

RANK	REGION	AVERAGE MONTHLY PAYMENT
1	*Ecotopia: Far West* California $617, Washington $492, Oregon $397, Alaska $749, Hawaii $468	545 dollars
2	*Yankee New England* Connecticut $590, Massachusetts $491, Vermont $572, Maine $405, Rhode Island $503, New Hampshire $397	493 dollars
3	*Heartland: Industrial Upper Midwest* Illinois $342, Michigan $488, Ohio $302, Iowa $381, Minnesota $532, Wisconsin $544	431 dollars
4	*Industrial Northeast* New York $550, New Jersey $404, Delaware $310, Pennsylvania $382, Maryland $345, Washington, DC $364	392 dollars
5	*Western Plains* Kansas $403, Nebraska $350, Oklahoma $310, North Dakota $371, South Dakota $366	360 dollars
6	*Rocky Mountain West* Colorado $346, Utah $376, Nevada $258, Idaho $304, Wyoming $360, Montana $354	337 dollars

TABLE 4.1, CONT.

RANK	REGION	AVERAGE MONTHLY PAYMENT
7	*Desert Southwest* Arizona $293, New Mexico $258, Texas $184	245 dollars
8	*The Border States (tied for 7th)* Kentucky $197, Indiana $256, Missouri $279, West Virginia $249	245 dollars
9	*Dixie: The Old South* Alabama $118, Arkansas $192, South Carolina $199, Virginia $354, Georgia $256, Louisiana $190, North Carolina $259, Tennessee $155, Florida $264, Mississippi $120	211 dollars

Source: Calculated from Dresang and Gosling, *Political Economy and Policy Performance in the American States,* 1985, pp. 225–226.

An interesting variation in the Western policy style is the political effect of the Mormon religion. The Mormon effect on the church member as a citizen and on government officials stresses quite different elements in public policy.

The church has a strong effect in Western states where church members constitute a significant minority and especially a majority of the population (Utah, Arizona). Mormon ethics place a strong emphasis on the sanctity of marriage and the importance of families as the basic social unit. Families are viewed as important transmitters of moral and civic attitudes to children. There is also an interesting emphasis on community values. Community values find their expression in the intense social life and ethics surrounding the Mormon church. Thus the community scrutinizes individual morality, encourages civic-mindedness among young people, and even promotes welfare-type arrangements whereby the church as a community bands together to aid other church members in need.

There is a strong stress also in the Mormon ethics on self-sufficiency tempered by a spirit of civil volunteerism, individual hard work, participation in community work, and the creation of wealth for one's self and one's family. Wealth is generally to be pursued through entrepreneurial endeavors, which are thought to advance self-sufficiency, and an entrepreneurial lifestyle is informally favored over other choices, such as social-service or public-service careers. Yet a cooperative style of business along with volunteerism are all consistent with and promoted by Mormon ethics, rather than "robber barren" capitalist attitudes.

As a result, Mormonism tends to produce a tradition that favors policies of individual civic activism, volunteerism, and a limited government that mainly promotes "progressive individualism." This philosophy does not stress the social democratic obligations of the state to provide programs for citizens. Mormonism promotes its own brand of Western style policy and communitarian ethics in the regions where the Mormon church is strong.

4.1 UNDERSTANDING THE STYLES OF POLICY ACTORS

An understanding of policy styles is useful in explaining why policy actors behave as they do. A good illustration of this fact is Senator Orin Hatch of Utah. Senator Hatch is a Mormon representing Utah, a primarily Mormon state. His policy views are generally in line with the dominant Mormon culture. On the one hand, Senator Hatch has been a strong proponent of certain conservative causes in alliance with conservatives from Southern states. Examples include his opposition to abortion, his strong support of the defense industry, and his active support of the Reagan administration's efforts at deregulation—all fitting the stereotype of the typical conservative. On the other hand, he has been one of the strongest supporters of family legislation, day care services, and parental leave, including significantly increased spending in these areas. This position has produced a strange alliance on these issues between Senator Hatch, the "conservative," and Pat Schroeder, the "social liberal" from neighboring Colorado.

Your thought experiment is to identify the elements in the policy style of Orin Hatch. What importance do elements of the Western political style take? What is the significance of traditional conservatism? Of the Mormon religion?

Extend your thinking to other policy actors with whom you are familiar. What elements in the various policy styles help explain what those actors do or do not do?

And we would emphasize the importance again of examining your own policy style. Why do you believe the way you do about policy? What factors influenced your approach to the policy system?

ECOTOPIA: THE PACIFIC COAST PROGRESSIVE POLICY STYLE

The Ecotopia policy region (Joel Garreau 1980) consists of the far west coastal states—California, Oregon, Washington, Hawaii, and also south-coastal Alaska. The cultural mecca, or informal capital of Ecotopia, is probably San Francisco, with its mystique of progressive social groups, environmentalists, and free thinkers.

These states strongly promote or attempt to strike a balance between environmental regulation and pressures by developers to use or develop natural resources. Ecotopia states are far more likely to have strong state and local environmental regulations than most other states. These states also have most commonly used referenda and recall procedures in their state constitutions. The Ecotopia style, then, makes considerable use of direct democracy techniques on controversial public issues rather than relying solely on decision making by elected representatives.

In the states of the far western coastal areas, including southern coastal Alaska and Hawaii, the vast and inspiring natural areas are much more important in public thinking than in other regions. In the West and in Ecotopia the land is variously pictured as a wilderness trust to be guarded for its own sake and for future generations, as a capitalist traditional frontier "ripe for exploitation," as a haven for native and individualist ways of life, and as an attraction for tourism.

Intense competition results from these competing views of the land. Thus the desire of oil companies and developers to drill or develop land raises the divisive issues of pollution and industrial "rape of the land." Conflicts over the land are especially intense between oil and developer interests versus native Americans, environmentalists, fishing industries, small fishermen, and the tourism industry. These conflicts are particularly strong in northern California, Alaska, and Hawaii but also exist in Oregon and Washington.

Another element of the policy culture of Ecotopia is that its big cities are frequently policy innovators. Often cities in the Pacific coastal states undertake unusual programs of public assistance, welfare, daycare, waste recycling, toxic waste control, energy alternatives, or other such "ecotopian ideas." These cities are then perceived elsewhere as leaders in local or urban attempts to deal with social or environmental problems. To some extent, this image of Ectopia as the bellwether producer of law and policy applies to state legislatures in this region.

But this image often masks underlying conflicts. For example, there is often strong conflict between urban and rural areas. Sometimes it translates into upstate versus downstate conflicts, or coastal versus inland. Conflicts have been severe over referenda issues on the environment, taxation, the redistribution of water supply from rural to urban areas, pesticides that drain off into what come to be downstream water supplies, and the development of federal lands and wilderness areas.

Conflicts in this region also revolve around issues of services for new ethnic minorities and immigrant groups. In the extreme Southwest, particularly in southern California, growing ethnic and immigrant groups include Asians, Southeast Asians, and Hispanics. These groups and their needs often erupt into visible conflicts with whites over issues such as multiple language training in schools, redistribution of income from white middle-class suburbs to inner-city areas, and race-based conflicts over crime control. The 1990 governors' race in California captured national attention when it featured many aspects of these conflicts: upstate versus downstate California, rural versus urban California, and ethnic versus white middle-class California. Democrat candidate Diane Feinstein was said to represent the liberal, upstate, environmental, ecotopian, and ethnic-urban segments of California, while the Republican candidate (and winner) Pete Wilson stood for traditional conservative, white upper middle-class, downstate, suburban segments—and their fiscally conservative policies and anti-crime attitudes in regard to citizens' rights, incarceration, and swiftness of punishment. This issue polarized the Feinstein voters, particularly the ethnic supporters, as implying that "these minorities were the problem." The California race conflicts spread to the rest of the nation in the early 1990s after the brutal beating of Rodney King by Los Angeles police in March 1991 was captured on video, which led to the explosive L.A. Riots of 1992 following a white jury's acquittal of police charged with the brutality. The Ecotopian experience, therefore, is not all about referenda, big city innovation, or environmental paradise. The region is also plagued with issues of conflict between social groups and substate regions.

THE BORDER STATES POLICY STYLE

The border states are those states that were divided both in geography and in loyalty during the Civil War: Kentucky, Missouri, Indiana, and West Virginia. They are said to have a mixture of mountain folk, urban versus rural, and Yankee versus Southern attitudes. Traditionally, Indiana is not included in this group, although we include it here for our discussion because southern Indiana has more in common with Southern states than does northern Indiana.*

The strong split in border states focuses around the Northern versus Southern sympathetic regions (Lockard 1957). The city versus country distinctions and the wealthy areas versus the mountain folk Appalachian areas are strong contrasts indeed. Because of such divisions, the border states find themselves lying midway between the Midwest and the Southern states in their social policy styles, their lifestyles, and their spending patterns. They rank in the middle to slightly lower groups of states in support of education, higher education, and social services (Table 4.1).

The border states rather strongly restrict the taxing and regulation powers of cities (Book of the States, 1988). Officials of cities in this region, such as Louisville, often speak of constraints imposed upon them by state legislatures. In Bowling Green, Kentucky, as in most sizable midsized Kentucky cities, for example, state regulations prevent the city annexation of outlying areas, and county residents oppose merger with the city's school districts because it would raise county taxes and cross psychological lines of school rivalries. The central city schools tend to suffer loss of students and tax base as the city grows outward. All these forces combine to create a kind of "fiscal death trap" for city schools as the cities are unable to expand their school system or their tax base. These restrictions do not hamper schools in neighboring Midwestern states, where schools and cities themselves operate more as independent municipalities, school unification tends to be state initiated, and cultural attitudes are more accepting of school unification and other forms of city-county consolidations.

These restrictions likely reflect a rural suspicion of city government, trace-

*One might also argue that Illinois falls in this category, but probably the portions of Indiana that make up its rural, conservative, and southern-leaning zone are simply larger and denser in population than similar areas of southern Illinois. Sociologically, Illinois is more a Midwest state.

able probably to the dualistic traditions and beliefs of the Thomas Jefferson era in the early frontier that is now the border states.

The border states have traditionally been marked by a low value on education and thus low spending on education. This historic trait may be changing. In Kentucky in 1989 the entire school system below the university level was declared unconstitutional by the state Supreme Court, an unprecedented action in the history of states. The 1990 school reform laws that ensued, as mandated by the Court, boosted state revenues by close to a billion dollars and introduced rather startling innovations (such as abolishment of the old State Department of Education, radical funding redistributions from rich to poor schools, school funding based on student performance levels). This reform, by most outside accounts, has been the most radical state experiment in education reform. It may have the potential to boost the Kentucky school system practices and performance closer to those of the better public schools in other regions of the country. But there is no missing the fact that this law is highly controversial in Kentucky, and local communities resent many of its progressive features. For example, the law seeks to eliminate nepotism in schools, a practice long abolished in most states. So what is often seen as progressive or even "radical" in border states is fairly standard fare in other regions.

In the border states one finds the strongest battlegrounds in the country today over issues of social regulation, such as abortion and spousal and child abuse laws. The controversy is due to the split personality of the states, and the polarization by urban–rural, wealthy–poor, city–country, Northern–Southern policy conflicts and social preferences. For example, Louisville and Lexington in Kentucky, along with nearby Owensboro, Kentucky, are more like industrial Midwest cities by demography and politics. There are relatively high concentrations of liberal democrats, Catholics, and minorities, including European ethnic groups, in these cities. In the same way, Kansas City and St. Louis in the border state of Missouri contrast sharply with downstate, more "Southern grits style" Springfield, Missouri, or with Missouri's southeastern section "boot heel" and Cape Girardeau. The southern and rural zones of the border states are much more "Bible Belt" and socially conservative, and generally share more in the Southern cultural experience.

The border states are also uniformly marked by slightly schizophrenic border zone style conflicts. Labor union conflict with management is high and has been especially strong in West Virginia, Missouri, and Kentucky. These states have passed limited right-to-work laws that allow workers to opt out of unions, but at the same time unions traditionally are strong in the mining, manufacturing, and heavy industries. On the other hand, unions are either weak or banned by law in certain important public sector areas, such as universities.

But there are also strong trends of reform in the border states, illustrating their "split personality." Education reform, drunk driving laws, progressive reforms in marital and divorce, child support, and child abuse laws are all strong trends that are being promoted these days.

Another important trend in the border states is that some of their traditional industries are declining, and as a result the states and cities are giving increased attention to economic development. For example, tobacco and coal mining are on the decline as tobacco use drops in the United States and the demand for coal has softened as a result of coal pollution problems and generally lower oil prices. The economic development policy of the border states today is to compete strongly to attract new foreign investment to help replace the dying industries. Missouri has one of the most aggressive of the state departments of foreign trade and economic development.

The border states are thus a *faultline fracture zone* of conflicting patterns of policies, business, labor, and social attitudes.

THE OLD SOUTH POLICY STYLE

The Old South consists of the southern states of the Confederacy, excluding Texas, which is probably more a part of the Southwest. The Old South states are Alabama, Arkansas, Florida, Georgia, Louisiana, Mississippi, North Carolina, South Carolina, Tennessee, and Virginia. While arguments can be made that Florida and Virginia do not share strong similarities with the other Deep South states in such things as demography and social attitudes, they simply cannot be separated from the South. Florida was a key part of the Confederacy, and Virginia along with Georgia was the home, if not the social soul, of Confederate resistance.

The Old South is the region that has maintained the most powerful and distinctive culture. As a result, it may have been studied and written about more than any other region of the world. V. O. Key, Jr., in his monumental book *Southern Politics* (1949) observed dryly, "Of books about the South there is no end," and proceeded to add another one. A never-ending stream of books have attempted to explain "the mind of the South." The obvious differences among these books suggest that if anyone has adequately explained the uniqueness of the South, scholars have not been able to unite behind that theory. We certainly do not claim to be able to accomplish that task. Rather, we will limit our discussion to the major characteristics of the *Old South policy culture*.

The South is a distinctive region in part because the people *believe* they are distinctive (Reed 1972). Southerners believe that there is a "Southern-ness" about them that sets them apart from the rest of the nation, yet what this Southern-ness is remains in dispute. This feeling of distinctiveness has a profound impact on the policy system. For one thing, it helps explain the South's willingness to fly in the face of prevailing national trends and retain established patterns of doing things. Thus movements such as the modernization of state governments, urban government reform, and the professionalization of the public service were slow in coming to the South. Indeed, they have not penetrated vast areas of the rural south even on the threshold of the twenty-first century.

When such modernizing reforms do occur in the South, they tend to take on regional characteristics. Southern policymakers tend to recoil at being considered copy-cats. Beyond this tendency, the belief about Southern-ness explains the region's willingness to resist national authority even when used in pursuit of legitimate national objectives. The Supreme Court's mandate for school integration in the 1954 *Brown* v. *Board of Education* case was resisted, at least in part, because it was viewed as threatening the "Southern way of life," and the preservation of that way of life seemed a higher value to some Southerners than the granting of equal opportunity to all Americans. This sense of distinctiveness does not seem to have been weakened much by the cultural forces of mass society (Reed 1972, p. 90).

Probably the most important force in the Old South is religion. It is almost commonplace now to say that there was a religious solid South before there was a political solid South. The dominance of fundamentalist Protestant denominations has at least remained stable, if it has not strengthened in recent decades. The religious hegemony has many implications for the policy style of the Old South. First, it would be hard to find a region of the country in which public policy takes a harder line on issues of private morality. The "thou shalt nots" of moral legislation are more extensive, and the penalties for violating them are more severe, in the Deep South than in other regions. At the same time, fundamentalist Protestants emphasize the necessity of the separation of church and state—a view that on the surface seems inconsistent with the idea of using the power of the state to enforce Judeo-Christian morality. What the concept of the separation of church and state means to most Southerners is that the church is to be silent on progressive social issues. The liberal social gospel movement—strong in the Catholic Church and Methodism, for example—is viewed with almost uniform derision in the Old South. For this and other reasons, it is difficult to stimulate informed and serious discussion of social policy issues such as poverty, birth control, AIDS, teen pregnancy, drug addiction, and the like.

In some respects the legacy of the Civil War has been the creation of a "civil religion" in the South. After all, the Old South is the only *region* with its own flag, anthem, and holidays. For non-Southerners these symbols of the Southern civil religion stir up highly negative images, such as slavery or the Ku Klux Klan, but for most Southerners they stir up quite different emotions and pride in the region. In our judgment, the primary impact of this civil religion on the policy style of the region is to keep the heavy hand of tradition on the policy system. "But we have always done it this way," seems a more convincing argument to some Southerners than the argument "this is the most effective way." Tradition serves as a powerful force to prevent certain controversial issues from reaching the public policy agenda.

Tradition also helps explain the persistent localism that is characteristic of the Old South's policy style. Politics in the South may best be described by three words: local, local, and local. We have remarked elsewhere on the power of locals in the policy system, even arguing that a localization of national policy objectives has swept the nation since the 1980s (Hamilton and Wells 1990). Nowhere is this localism more starkly played out than in the Old South. Resistance to many public policies, especially if they involve "outsider regulation," is rooted predominantly in the desire to retain local control. National regulations on school prayer, labor unions, affirmative action, or business practices are seen as illegitimate intrusions from Washington.

A darker side to the Civil War legacy and the civil religion that it spawned is the subculture of violence that exists in the South. The region is the most violent in a violent nation. A part of its policy style is to respond to crime and violence with vigorous enforcement of highly punitive laws. Thus the South leads the nation in prison population, in severity of sentence, in criminals on death row, and in executions.

The policy style of the Old South is also strongly shaped by deep concern for kin. It has been said that Southerners challenge the Japanese in the worship of ancestors. This trait has far-reaching effects on family law; most Southern states make it hard to obtain a divorce, for example. On the other hand, issues such as child abuse, teen pregnancy, and abortion are viewed as family matters that should be settled within the family. Many Southern states were late in adopting laws regulating these matters.

Finally, a look at the Old South policy style must include a look at the effect of one-party politics. V. O. Key, Jr., found that the primary effects of such politics were the suppressing of issues and the skewing of public policy to favor the haves over the have-nots. There are several problems with this view, however. The first is that political parties are not effective raisers of issues even when there is two party competition. The second is that, as E. E. Schattschneider observed, political parties are extractive institutions even when there is two-party competition (1942). By this he means that political parties extract "plunder" from the political system in the form of patronage, at the expense of the have-nots.

What then *is* the effect of one-party politics in the Old South? The primary effect is the suppression of political participation. Again, it is not so much that two party politics fosters political participation by raising issues and getting the vote out. Rather, in the Old South one-party dominance came by way of the disenfranchisement movement in the late 1800s. Bourbon democrats stirred Civil War sympathies as the political base for the Jim Crow laws. These laws were designed to break the back of the Populist party by disenfranchising both poor whites and blacks (Woodward 1966), thereby establishing the tradition of non-participation, which persists as one of the South's most important policy characteristics.

Much has been written about the "New South." The assumption underlying much of this literature is that the forces of mass society and modernization are eroding the traditionalism and distinctiveness of the Old South and the region is becoming like the rest of America. Social theorists usually argue that traditionalism (clinging to preindustrial folkways) is eroded and eventually eradicated by industrialization and its secular society. We do not believe this to be the case in the Old South (a view shared by Reed 1972, p. 90). The traditional culture of the Old South is not incompatible with the requirements of an urban society with an expanding economy. Japan retained its traditional culture while experiencing rapid economic development. Similarly, there is in fact much in the

Old South culture that facilitates an expanding economy. Southerners' belief in the distinctiveness of their region can express itself in a boundless faith that they can make a future together. A European type of secular and progressive ethos that is fairly strong in some areas of the country is very weak in the chromium gleam of the South's great cities. Southern religion is what makes traditionalists able to accept and survive modernization because it instills a sense of responsibility and nurtures virtues of hard work, industry, and thrift.

The civil religion of the South is also the basis for an instrumental view of government in which political institutions are cooperative participants in the drive for the future. This helps explain what many have thought is a paradox about the Old South: a ready acceptance of active government in certain areas of policy, especially for economic growth or education improvements, existing alongside a deep conservative suspicion of government. This mystery is easily explained: The Southern concern for kin breeds a commitment to the future—to leaving the world a better place, and to ensuring that the next generation is better off than the present one. And while participation (a requirement of democratic life) should remain the goal, high levels of nonparticipation in the South have left the politics of economic development to the economic elites and allowed them to guide the process without the messy problems associated with mass politics. Thus in its traditional culture, the Old South may have one of the most powerful social forces to continue economic development into the twenty-first century—while it maintains its conservative society.

SUMMARY

Policy cultures are the distinctive ways people think about, choose, and act upon policies and government activities. In the last two chapters we have examined the four types of important American policy cultures—widely held general myths, ideologies, federalist cultures, and regional policy cultures.

Any effort to understand public policy without understanding these policy cultures seriously impedes our abilities to understand ourselves, our problems, and potential solutions. Distinctive differences in regions and other policy cultures help determine the variations in the policy system by influencing what a society typically thinks is appropriate for public action. Policy cultures help predetermine the content of policy, the likely government actions, the preferences and behavior styles of officials and interest groups, and the benefits and conditions of life in the society.

 **CHAPTER 5**

THE INTERGOVERNMENTAL PLAYING FIELDS OF POLICY

A much-quoted line by Alexander Pope reflects much of the past literature on public administration and public policy: "For forms of government let fools contest; whatever is best administered is best." According to this idea, government structures and institutions mean very little. They are merely conduits for the more critical actions of individuals and groups. But is this the case? Probably not. It is more realistic to say that government structures guide and affect what actually takes place.

Yet government to most people in the United States is very elusive. Thus we hear citizens asking: Who is responsible for X? Where is policy Y made? Where do I get something done? And there is in nearly all interactions between citizens and government the question: Who is in charge here? Without answers to these kinds of questions, citizens cannot fix responsibility and hold accountable those individuals who exercise governmental power.

Several large, interconnected issues are at work here. If government arrangements make a difference, how so? Can a government be held accountable, made "more democratic"? How? And can a government that is made more democratic also be more effective (when many say no)? How?

These are the main questions of *democratic* policymaking. The first step in getting answers—and one of the most important steps in understanding the policy system and improving its outcomes—is to map out where, how, and what does and does not happen with public policy. In doing so in this chapter, we will use a viewpoint known as *structural functional theory*. Before we draw our policy map, we look at what this theory can say about public policies and public policymaking.

WHAT IS THE ROLE OF POLICY STRUCTURES?

The critical question for policy theorists is this: What roles, if any, do government structures such as branches of governments or specific bureaucracies play in the policy system? The answer has divided contemporary policy scientists into several camps. A brief review of each style is helpful in understanding the policy system, since each style illuminates some features of the system.

The first theoretical position is *contextualism*. In this view, public policies are a response to forces within the general policy environment but outside policy structures. Analysts who subscribe to this view differ on what are the specific "big external" forces. Some argue that the policy system is "caused" by the social or class stratification of modern industrial societies. For example, among the things that separate Marxists and non-Marxists views is how much importance the theorists give to the differences in wealth of social groups in politics. Other contextualists find demographic factors to be the most important determinants of the nature and scope of public policy. In this perspective, differences in age, education, income, levels of urbanization and industrialization, and the like drive the policy system. Still other contextualists place heavy emphasis on culture—a people's basic set of enduring beliefs about government and politics. Whatever the specific forces, contextualists agree that the content, direction, and outcomes of the policy system are more the result of these forces within the policy environment than the result of policy structures.

A second theoretical style is *public choice*. This view assumes that public policy is little more than the aggregation of the individual preferences of policy actors, that the content of public policy is determined by the interaction of individuals, often through organized interest groups. Thus to the public choice theorists the basic unit of study is the voter and those organizations that represent the voter's preferences. This approach draws heavily on two assumptions. The first comes from marketing within the field of economics, which assumes that a "rational" consumer makes choices between products offered by competing firms. In terms of public policy, then, we are seen as mostly rational citizens making clear and informed choices among competing policy alternatives. This theory also assumes that we have a simpler, automatically opinion-driven democracy in which policy structures are the arenas of choice made by the people. But like the contextualists, public choice theorists view structures as essentially neutral toward participants.

The third view is called the new *institutionalism*. March and Olsen describe it as follows:

> Without denying the importance of both the social context of politics and the motives of individual actors, the new institutionalism insists on a more autonomous role for political institutions. The state is not only affected by society but also affects it. Political democracy depends not only on economic and social conditions but also on the design of political institutions. The bureaucratic agency, the legislative committee, and the appellate court are arenas for contending social

forces, but they are also collections of standard operating procedures and structures that define and defend interests. They are political actors in their own right. (March and Olsen 1984, p. 783)

In this view, then, political institutions are not "robots for the people," rather, they are powerful semi-free policy agents.

Following this perspective, we stress that policy structures are more than neutral or weak conduits through which social forces play themselves out. They do react to social forces, but more often than not this reaction is an attempt to direct social forces in ways favorable to the views of the policy structures. Philip Selznick's theory of cooptation was one of the first of many detailed studies that show how policy structures manipulate social forces to their advantage (Selznick 1949, p. 72). In a classic study of the Tennessee Valley Authority, Selznick found that organizations reduce opposition by seeming to give them a role in the decision process, such as through an "advisory committee." Policy structures do not simply "deliver a service" or "operate a facility" in response to external forces; they perform important general social functions, some with positive and others with negative impacts.

At this point we need to identify several of the important ways in which structures work as semi-free agents in the policy process. First, structures often work semi-autonomously to *distribute resources*. Many of these resources are intangible, such as prestige, status, and deference. These qualities are often attached to specific offices, regardless of who actually occupies them. A good example is the office of lieutenant governor in most states.

Other resources are more substantive. These include money, expertise, information, and human resources. For example, as the old adage declares, "knowledge is power." Structures convey access to information to some and deny it to others. To possess information is to have power; to be denied information or to fail to seek it is to extend power to another. The control of information is so important to policy structures that such things as freedom of information, open-meetings acts, and right-to-know provisions were very late in coming to the American policy system (the 1970s) and are still resisted and circumvented by many agencies. The important point is that policy structures act somewhat autonomously to distribute resources.

Second, policy structures are semi-free to *determine or modify individual preferences* because they can manipulate the symbols, myths, and rituals of society in many of the ways that private firms use sophisticated advertising based partly on behavioral sciences. (The presidency itself has been transformed recently through these techniques. The *New York Times Magazine* presented a startling history of this phenomenon centering on media sorcerer David Gergen [Kelly 1993].) Consider the public hearing. Policy scientists have known for years that program directors use public hearings to develop public support for programs (or to defuse opponents) by inducing a sense of participation in government. The theory is that if an individual believes she or he has participated in a decision by attending a public hearing, that individual is either more likely to support a particular position or less likely to have a claim to oppose it. But the citizen is told *not* that the purpose of the public hearing is to develop public support or to lessen opposition but that the purpose is to "get input" as a means of democratic decision making. This approach invokes but also manipulates the myth of the town meeting that is historically so important in America.

What should be emphasized is that there is an extremely wide range of such symbols, myths, and rituals that can be strategically manipulated by public officials. Modern political systems have just as many symbols, myths, and rituals as do "primitive" societies, and the artful manipulation of those symbols are at least as powerful in modern societies because of the pervasiveness of the mass media. Furthermore, some have argued that this power of politicians and institutions to create "virtual reality" is so strong now that it is image-making, not substance or truth, that is the main trait or "Holy Grail" of public and business life in contemporary America (Kelly 1993, p. 64; Parenti 1986, 1991). At least there are many more avenues for communicating myths and symbols and more sophisticated techniques for making them believable in modern societies.

Deborah Stone (1988) reminds us that some of the most powerful symbols in the policy process are numbers. They are powerful symbols because they are used universally to define and describe a policy problem. Ask yourself how something "becomes" a policy problem. The most frequent answer is that we have measured or counted that something and determined that it has the characteristics of a problem. Consider how Stone makes this point:

> To count is to *form a category* by emphasizing some feature instead of others and excluding things that might be similar in important ways but do not share that feature. To count as unemployed (as the government does) only people who have looked for work in the past month is to *see unemployment as active job hunting.* That vision excludes from the unemployed people who desperately want to work but are unable or too discouraged to pound the pavement. (Stone 1988, p. 129)

Understood that way, numbers are symbols that involve important values. For example, one important value in the definition of unemployment as active job hunting is the assumption that an individual who is not job hunting does not want to work. Thus the very manner of counting implies a value judgment that this individual is lazy and content to live off welfare. In addition to defining the problem, numbers imply the need for action and the direction that action should take. In other words, some level of measurement becomes the standard for the solution to the problem. That standard becomes a very powerful symbol indeed. Who can doubt the appeal of the slogan, "Eliminate hunger in our lifetime." But there is a hidden number in that slogan and the number is 100 percent of the hungry people. A policy is judged to be a success or a failure on the basis of how closely the final numbers approximate the initial goals. The point is that policy structures by and large control the numbers, especially those that define the problem, and also those that suggest how effectively the problem has been solved.

Third, policy structures often *determine the rules of the political game.* This function is so important that structures are sometimes defined as accepted rules of behavior, collective norms, and routinized roles. But something much more important than the definition of structures is at stake. Since one of the themes of this book is the value of democratic control of the policy process, we will illustrate this point by using the concept of action channels.

One of the most important controls over the "political game" is how structures create accepted *action channels,* that is, accepted routines through which decisions are reached and other crucial actions are taken. Graham Allison summarized in excellent fashion the kinds of action channels: (1) preselecting the major players; (2) determining the players' points of entrance into the game; (3) distributing the advantages and disadvantages for each game; and (4) determining who gets a piece of the action in the first place (Allison 1971).

You should think about these strategies carefully since they explain a great deal of what takes place in the policy system. As a starting point, consider the following examples.

Iron triangles are informal alliances between interest groups, lobbyists, congressional committees, and executive agencies, which commonly preselect the major players, screen information, and draw up bills and amendments in Congress so as to control the policy process. The classic examples have been big military contractors and the tobacco lobby. It certainly is difficult for Jane and Joe Citizen to break into that process and "get a piece of the action."

At the state level there are some examples at least as impressive as the national iron triangles. For good or not (certainly it's a value judgment) the big-time sports establishments at big universities—such as football at Notre Dame and Alabama, basketball at Indiana and Kentucky—are clear examples of powerful and influential bureaucracies. All operate their budgets, which reach into the tens of millions and more in relative secrecy compared to the universities to which they are attached. All have rich alumni, supportive media, and patrons in the legislature. All have special systems of tutors, plush dormitories, free textbooks and meals, and other fringe benefits mainly for male athletes that are not available to general students (and usually not to female athletes either). All give their coaches big-time salaries that far exceed even those of the universities' presidents. (At the University of Kentucky, basketball coach Rick Pitino's "compensation package" and perks are worth more than $7 million, which exceeds the total combined salaries of *all* the science and liberal arts faculties *plus* the presidents of the state's three largest universities!)

Such structures exemplify the freewheeling, powerful government entity that virtually establishes its own cultural empire—so much so that it can set itself apart from control by university presidents, or even state budgetary controls that apply to the rest of the university.

At the local level the public hearing referred to earlier is an example of an action channel that determines players' points of entrance into the game.

Citizens are permitted to appear before an agency and give their views, but often not until after the more important decisions have been made.

| 5.1 | **ACTION CHANNELS IN ROUTINE GOVERNMENT FUNCTIONS** |

Anyone who has tried to fight a zoning decision has seen how action channels distribute advantages and disadvantages. Assume that a piece of property has been rezoned "commercial." Residents in the area believe that the rezoning benefits a select few and violates general land use patterns established for the area. The action channels established for resolving such policy problems involve a court hearing at which citizens can be heard. But will they be on equal terms with those who benefit from the rezoning? In most instances the answer is no. The process works this way. The jurisdiction that rezoned the property will defend the rezoning in court. That means that the county or city will provide the attorneys, public agencies will collect data (symbols in the form of numbers), and the legitimacy of public authority will be behind the action. The protesting citizens will have to pay the attorney who represents them, will have to overcome the image of being "obstructionists and troublemakers" opposed to economic progress and, in the absence of open records laws (and often even with such laws), will not have access to numbers available to the other side. Thus considerable advantage and disadvantage have been determined by the action channels designed ostensibly to ensure fairness. Such distribution of advantage and disadvantage is routine to the action channels in all policy areas.

But the question is, how can the policy process be made fair? What can be done so that all parties have the same relative advantage? Is the public defender in criminal cases an example of an attempt to solve this problem?

The fourth way that policy structures function somewhat independently is to *impose order* on a chaotic world. Think about the power of the terms *law, policy, regulations, administrative order,* and even *Constitution.* These words carry with them the assumption that events and behaviors will take place in regular and prescribed ways. A good example of power through control of terminology and knowledge is the obscure regulations used by the IRS when it audits your tax return. Their knowledge is not *your* knowledge (you must hire a tax expert). And you are assumed guilty by their terminology unless you prove differently. Bureaucratic terminology implies that the resultant order is reasonable and good, at least to be preferred to chaos and anarchy.

But the policy system pays a price for order. Order inherently favors the status quo. The discouraging of change carries serious implications for questions of progress and improvement. Are order and progress incompatible objectives? Is there such a thing as orderly progress? If so, is orderly progress to be preferred over disorderly progress? An authentic innovation violates the established order. Given all this, just how receptive are policy structures to change? Also, much like action channels, order distributes advantages to the privileged and disadvantages to the nonprivileged. Even the idea of disrupting order is viewed by some in a very negative way. Clearly there are serious questions of fairness associated with order. How can equity be served if order stacks the deck against those who are disadvantaged? Whatever the answer to these important questions, it is apparent that policy structures function somewhat autonomously to impose order on the policy environment and that such order has important outcomes.

These four things—distribution of resources, shaping of individual preferences, setting of the rules of the political game, and imposition of order on structures and procedures—suggest how policy structures operate as semi-free agents in the policy process. There are many ways in which policy structures control policy, but our primary purpose is to map what happens with public policy, where, and how.

THE POLICY MAP: THE EIGHT PATTERNS IN THE AMERICAN FEDERAL SYSTEM

Federalism is one of the most important elements in the American constitutional system, with profound impact on political power and on the development and implementation of public policy. In the United States federalism creates a complex array of policy structures. Within this complexity it is possible to identify which structures have the most influence over issue formulation, policy enactment, and implementation.

There are eight policy structures in the American federal system. First are the national, state, and local agencies of the three levels of government. How one views the proper role of each level is influenced by the federalist culture to which one subscribes. For example, a centralist argues for a strengthening of national government power. Republicans, for instance, in the 1980s generally supported a stronger presidency in foreign policy (and a weaker Congress) as well as a line item veto.

The second set of policy structures is created by the wide range of interactions *between the levels of government*. Many analysts argue that policy in the United States is inherently intergovernmental—that is, that policy inherently involves action at two or more levels. The intergovernmental policy structures are the national–state structure, the state–state structures, the state–local structure, the local–local structure, and the national–local structure. Later we will provide a brief overview of each.

LEVELS AND BRANCHES OF GOVERNMENT

Federalism involves the division of power among levels of government. Thus, in the United States there are national policy structures, policy structures in each of the fifty states, and policy structures in the approximately 60,000 local governments. While the actors in each set of structures vary significantly and the dynamics at each level are different, the policy structures at the national and state levels have many similar features and elements. The most important such element is associated with the separation of powers.

Separation of powers is the division (and partial competition) of authority among institutions, and the method of representation to the institutions, at the same level of government. As a typical example, the Constitution is written in such a way that Congress tends to have the major role in lawmaking and economic regulation while the presidency has a lesser lawmaking role in the veto power and technically has no constitutional economic powers. The separation of powers not only fragments power among branches of governments, but also fragments the representation of different interests among three branches. This latter purpose will be discussed later. It thereby creates a system of multiple, self-sustaining centers of power, representation, and policy.

Why fragment power? Would not a unified center of power be much more efficient in accomplishing policy objectives? The answer goes to the basic nature of our constitutional system. The underlying purpose of the separation of powers is to help protect against "majoritarianism," or the emergence of a dominant *popular* political movement, while at the same time making the exercise of *elite* power more difficult. James Madison, in arguing that this principle could protect the system from excessive influence either from popular majorities (a situation he especially feared) or from elites, wrote the following passage, which almost rings with both despair and hope:

> Either the existence of the same passion or interest in a majority at the same time must be prevented, or the majority, having such coexistent passion of interest, must be rendered, by their number and local situation, unable to concert and carry into effect schemes of oppression. If the impulse and the opportunity coincide, we well know that neither moral nor religious motives can be relied on as an adequate control. (*Federalist Papers*, no.10, p. 81)

Madison is saying that popular majorities have neither the moral character nor the religious commitment sufficient to prevent them from doing serious harm to the society, and therefore structures must be designed that will prevent majorities from forming and carrying out the majority will. Among those structures were federalism and the separation of powers.

Under federalism, popular majorities, sometimes allied with powerful interests, have to succeed *across levels* of government (national, state, local). With separation of powers, popular majorities have to succeed *across branches* of government at the same level (executive, legislative, judicial). To override *both* federalism and the separation of powers requires a very large organization with significant resources. An excellent illustration of this point is found in civil rights policy.

Civil rights organizations may be able to "win" in the Congress by getting civil rights legislation passed, but they can then "lose" in the enforcement of such legislation because the Executive Branch, for whatever reasons, is opposed to vigorous enforcement. Or civil rights groups can win at the national level, as they have in those instances where Congress passes legislation that the president and national courts are willing to enforce, but these groups still must win in each of the fifty states. The degree of state compliance may range from nearly full compliance to passivity to actual resistance and obstructionism. As this and many other examples demonstrate, federalism and separation of powers are powerful obstacles to the exercise of power across policy structures in the United States.

An understanding of federalism and the separation of powers can answer many important questions asked about the policy system. Why is the system so slow in initiating solutions to clear and perceived problems? Why does it take so long to get things done once there is agreement on policy? Who should be held accountable for inaction? Who is responsible for action? The answer lies in the fragmented system of multiple centers of power and policy.

The traditional way of describing American policy structures is to provide a brief explanation of the organization and function of institutions as separate actors. Each "box" or level of government is described as having separate powers and functions, with the possibility of conflict between the "boxes" (checks and balances, political disputes between the three branches, the states versus the nation, etc.). Most such studies tend to ignore institutions at the state and local level, emphasizing rather national institutions' issue conflicts, enactments, and implementation. (Prominent examples are Meier 1993; Gerston 1983.)

There is certainly much to be learned from focusing on single institutions as separate actors in the policy process, but a broader view is found in asking whether there are larger and more general structures (similar to the neglected tradition established in the classic study of all legislatures, Wahlke et al. 1962). Is it possible to identify the role of legislatures generally in the policy process? Are there similarities or differences in legislative functions at various levels? Answers to these questions represent important steps in developing a general explanation of the role of policy structures.

LEGISLATURES: MIRRORS OF SUBJURISDICTIONAL INTERESTS

The representation system in the United States has a powerful effect on legislatures in the policy process. Representation is the legalistic ways in which groups are allowed choice or influence in electing or participating in bodies of authority. It is the formal means by which groups are either "cut into" or "cut out of" power and influence in government. Unlike some European systems that provide for the representation of identifiable groups or interests in the society, the American system of representation is based on geographic areas. A member of a legislature in the United States gains his or her seat through election from a specific territory. If the area is the jurisdiction itself, the election is referred to as an *at-large election*. At-large elections are becoming less common because of concern about diluting minority voting strength. If the area is a portion of the jurisdiction, the election is referred to as a *district election*. In a system of geography-based representation there is no provision for representing any particular interests (especially since the Supreme Court's decision that at-large elections cannot be utilized to dilute minority voting strength). It is into this electoral void that interest groups have stepped. Lacking functional representation, specific interests find that they must organize and mobilize if they are to have any influence on the policy process. Interest groups, then, become the subjurisdictional interests that legislative bodies tend to mirror.

The primary problem is that interest groups vary greatly in size and resources. The geographic basis of representation makes the playing field for interests in the policy process uneven. Some interest groups "are more equal than others." One of the most important questions in the policy process, then, is whose interests are being represented.

The use of geographic districts as the basis for election means also that the representative system is highly fragmented. In effect, the electoral system creates multiple, self-sustaining centers of power. Such a situation is ripe for the development of oligarchic tendencies, that is, control by small, likely self-interested groups. Certainly in the early history of the nation the fragmented electoral system allowed local elites to establish virtual monopolies on the policy process. This tendency was strengthened at that time by state laws that limited the right to vote to about 10 percent of the population: free male landowners. These oligarchic tendencies mean that the subjurisdictional interests mirrored by legislatures tend to be those of local elites.

Much comment is made today about the power of incumbency, that is, the disproportionally high number of congresspersons who are reelected. While Americans are more dissatisfied with the legislative branch than either of the other two branches, up to 94 percent of the incumbents who run for congressional office are reelected. An easy explanation is that Americans hate Congress but like their own representative. A more probable explanation is that members of congress serve the interests of local (district) elites very well, and so the money, organization, and other resources necessary for reelection are available to them. It is because of these political realities that legislatures tend to mirror the subjurisdictional interests favored by local elites. The basic question at all levels, then, is: who (or what kinds of people) represents the jurisdiction? Who determines policies for the nation in Congress, who does so for the states in state legislatures, and who represents the city (particularly in large cities), rather than ward or district interests?

There is evidence suggesting that representation in state legislatures may be different from the national Congress. On the matter of incumbency, for example, there is a much higher rate of turnover in the states than in Washington. In some states up to 50 percent of the legislators are first termers. Also there is evidence that policy actors at the two levels function differently. It is argued that lobbyists have different tactics and motives at the state level because of less professionalization, lower income and expense of legislators, and differences in the general nature of politics at the two levels (Zeigler and Baer 1960). Certainly the different political cultures of the various states result in substantially different perceptions of what are proper government activities and political behaviors. In short, legislators bring to their positions different perceptions of what they should do and how they should do it, depending on the policy culture to which they subscribe. These differences are important. However, the general localistic and oligarchic bias still reigns. For instance, studies of the role orientations of state legislators yield a composite who is a district (localistic) oriented individual with very weak institutional (political party, legislative) loyalties. Each legislator tends to be most strongly oriented to the geographical entity that she or he represents, with particular orientation toward the district elite (Hedlund and Friesma 1972; Kuklinski and Elling 1977).

It is also important to understand that legislatures are the somewhat more dependent branches of government. They depend on the executive, committee staffers, and interest groups for policy initiation (Ripley and Franklin 1991). The exact issues and the agenda are by and large given formal reality in the executive branch and bureaucracies (Kelly 1993). The President's legislative program is well known. Through this legislative program the President by and large sets the agenda of Congress. But more often than not the genesis of a specific bill lies deep in the executive branch in its field of interplay with interest groups.

The process works something like this. "Field-level bureaucrats" encounter a problem or need while working with clients, encountering interest groups, or performing program functions. The bureaucrats inform their superiors of that need and eventually the agency makes a recommendation to the department office on the appropriate approach to the problem. If department personnel agree that the problem needs addressing, departmental lawyers actually draft proposed legislation. Since Harry Truman's presidency, when legislative clearance was instituted by executive order, the draft legislation has been sent to the Office of Management and Budget. The OMB reviews the proposal to determine whether it is consistent with "presidential objectives." If it is found to be consistent, it is sent to legislative liaison officers in the Executive Office of the President. These individuals plot legislative strategy, that is, they choose those actions most likely to result in the passage of the proposal, including the choice of senators and representatives to be sponsors of the bill. Ironically, then, the role of the senators or representatives who introduce the bill may be simply to allow their names to be placed at the top of the bill and to carry the bill into the chamber and give it to a page, who drops it in the hopper on the presiding officer's desk.

The degree of co-dependency of the state legislature on the executive varies among the states, although the process just described is quite similar in the states (Hamilton 1976). Some states are described as "strong governor states" and others as "weak governor states." It is important to point out that governors even in weak governor states can assume a proactive role in defining issues and formulating agendas. Any governor's effectiveness depends a great deal on the leadership skills and personal interests of the individual as well as the cooperation of active bureaucracies. But given these assets, governors are in a unique position to exercise policy leadership. This is true in part because, as we shall see, public policy in the United States is still remarkably state centered and there is substantial momentum at the state and local levels (see Chapter 11).

At all levels there is substantial policy initiation (if the indicator of the extent of policy initiation is the number of bills introduced). At the national level the average is about 20,000 bills introduced each session. Inventories of states are usually based in a biennial period; in recent years the 50 state legislatures have considered an average total of 190,000 bills in each biennium. The number varies greatly between the states, however. Alaska reflects a low of about 1,000 bills and New York a high of about 30,000. Enactment, however, is a different matter. In Washington less than 5 percent of the bills introduced become law. At the state level 22.8 percent of bills introduced are passed. On the average, state legislatures pass about 43,000 of the 190,000 introduced each biennium. Thus something very important has happened in recent decades to block action between the policy initiation stage and the enactment stage, especially at the national level.

Analysts refer to the situation at the enactment stage as *policy paralysis*. Political activists refer to it as *gridlock*. One of the best explanations for the growing national policy paralysis is found in Lowi's idea of hyperpluralism (1969). Hyperpluralism refers to the situation—beginning perhaps in the early 1960s—in which many interest groups became angry over social issues and divided into moralistic versus progressive camps, with historic splits within religions (Hunter 1991); these groups grew increasingly to compete with one another to the point that by the late 1970s the system was rendered incapable of taking any major action. In effect, interest groups cancel one another out in their influence on decision makers. From the standpoint of legislators, when they find themselves unable to respond to very powerful but competing interests and fear losing the votes they need for reelection, they respond to none. It is important to underscore the fact that gridlock has occurred at the enactment stage. Because some interests are able to initiate proposals, there is no gridlock at the policy initiation stage. Gridlock also seems to be more characteristic of the national than the state government. Indeed, there is considerable evidence that there was substantial policy momentum in new enactments at the state and local levels in the 1980s (Henig 1985; Hamilton and Wells 1990).

In summary, legislatures, as mirrors of subjurisdictional lobbies and forces, have had an increasingly difficult time developing a coherent, unified, and long-range view of policy. For a number of reasons, legislatures are not effective at policy formulation. Instead they are heavily dependent on executives, even in some weak governor states. While a bewildering array of proposals are made to legislatures, the national Congress is often paralyzed by the wide range of powerful interests that seek to influence it. Also, a number of institutional reforms, such as committee system reforms, have made it easier to kill a bill than to pass it. Even states have somewhat slowed their pace of enactments since the late 1980s.

Legislatures are less effective enactors of public policy today than thirty years ago. Several factors—modern issues, interests groups, geographic representation, image making—function as powerful impediments to innovation and reform. The most important recent compensator in the policy process, if not the single one, has been the substantial legislative policy activity at the state and local levels.

EXECUTIVES: THE SYSTEM'S PERSONIFICATION AND PSEUDO-MANAGER

Much emphasis is placed on the fact that campaigns in the United States are notoriously ineffective at defining and articulating issues (Nelson 1985). Such a view may be accurate for many individual campaigns, but over time the elections tend to reflect current policy concerns. Many of these concerns are simply positions recycled from the past, often reflecting swings in the relative strength of competing cultures. At other times the policy concerns arise from modern issues such as abortion and homelessness, and the solutions may be those tried in other jurisdictions.

The spread of innovation from one jurisdiction to another is an important phenomenon in the American policy system (Foster 1978). On rather rare occasions a policy concern is a hot topic or authentic issue raised by a particular candidate. The view that states and localities are great laboratories of democracy, while offering a limited definition of how those jurisdictions function, nevertheless describes how much policy experimentation originates at the state level. Many new trends in law in the 1980s spread among the states because of the actions of state-based interest groups, such as Mothers Against Drunk Driving.

It is important to note that many policy innovations devised by a state are coopted by a presidential candidate and made a part of the national agenda. One example is Bill Clinton's calls for welfare and health care reforms. All of these sources of new policy issues are blended with the candidate's own preferences to become issues on the agenda in campaigns.

Executives, then, find themselves in a favorable position for influencing the policy agenda (Denhardt and Stewart 1992). Their election is the nearest substitute for a plebescite in the American policy system. The U.S. President can take a nationwide perspective on issues. Voters perceive themselves as voting directly for the presidential candidates, even though they are actually voting for electors who will cast their votes as state units. Thus while it is not technically accurate to say that the constituency of the President is the American people, the appearance is there, and so presidential candidates are expected to take a national perspective on policy issues. At the state and local levels, executives are nearly always directly elected by the people. A candidate for governor, who may be from a particular region and wedded to that region's policy interests, must nevertheless convince the voters that she or he has a statewide perspective.

At the national level and in some subnational jurisdictions the legislature is heavily dependent on executive leadership for policy proposals and intervention in enactment stage. The President's legislative program tends to take center stage. This is true in part because legislative liaison officers in the White House Office are able to give coherent, continuous leadership to the President's program. The President also possesses some powerful political tools for influencing the Congress. Access to the media enables the President to make direct appeals to the American public. Ronald Reagan demonstrated the effectiveness of such appeals in influencing the Congress to adopt some of the more controversial features of his legislative program. Executives at the state and local level do not command the same media visibility.

Despite the title "chief executive," the role of executives in implementation can vary substantially. For example, some presidents, notably Richard Nixon and Ronald Reagan, have been effective in ensuring uniform implementation of their policies, in the bureaucracies especially. The intractability of the bureaucracy requires the expense of great time and effort; nearly all presidents have complained about the obstacles to effective direction of the bureaucracy. Other presidents have been ineffective in controlling bureaucracies, notably Jimmy Carter and Gerald Ford. President Nixon's frustrations in directing the bureaucracy were the basis for his extensive efforts to increase control over them, particularly through the rather extreme measure of withholding vast expenditure of appropriated funds.

Similar variation in the control of implementation is found at the state and local levels. The most important factors associated with executive effectiveness in this area seem to be the amount of time spent on policy concerns, the executive's political leadership and management skills, and the nature and intensity of interest group activity at the implementation stage. The bureaucracy, however, is the most significant influence over policy implementation.

BUREAUCRACY: GATEKEEPER OF GOVERNMENT ACTION CHANNELS

We referred earlier to how organizations can advantageously structure action channels. In many ways the gatekeepers of those action channels are the bureaucracies at each level of government.

Bureaucracies play a crucial role in identifying and promoting issues.

One of the key reasons is that they monopolize critical information and "control the numbers" that shape perceptions about the need for a policy response. Also, field bureaucrats are in constant interaction with a wide range of clientele, both influencing and being influenced by that clientele in forming perceptions. Developing a supportive clientele is the main strategy used both to mobilize support for ongoing programs and to cultivate perceptions of the need for new policies.

It is more difficult to track and evaluate how formal bureaucratic planning works to identify and promote issues. Street wisdom would have us believe that the formal planning process means little, that plans are formulated only to be set on shelves and gather dust. This view is partly correct, primarily because planning can become a strategy to divert criticism and neutralize opposition to the agency. People who are impatient with what the bureaucracy is or is not doing can be appeased somewhat by the promise that "we are looking seriously at the problem and planning to respond to it." On the other hand, as anyone who has been in education for any time at all will attest, the formal planning process in the bureaucracy is the arena where many issues are identified. In any case, bureaucracies affect what issues become issues through such activities as cultivating relations with media and key legislators, controlling information, interacting with clientele at the field level, and formally planning policy.

The separation of powers principle has led many individuals to the view that formulating and adopting policy is almost exclusively a legislative function. Such a view is not only simplistic but also inaccurate. Policy formulation takes place in a significant way within the bureaucracy—even to the details of drafting or revising probably more than half of all proposed legislation—but more subtle forces are at work as well. Two of them are crucial for an understanding of the role of the bureaucracy.

The first force is administrative discretion, which Congress builds into most laws. That is, the bureaucracy "fills in the blanks" with regard to the nature of the policy. While there is no such thing as a typical statute, the Resource Conservation and Recovery Act will serve as an excellent illustration. The RCRA is the statutory basis for policy on the management of hazardous chemical wastes. The act vests in the administrator of the Environmental Protection Agency (and thus in the agency itself) considerable discretion. The administrator is required to promulgate (1) criteria to identify the characteristics of hazardous waste; (2) standards applicable to hazardous waste generators; (3) standards for hazardous waste transporters; (4) regulations establishing performance standards for owners and operators of hazardous waste treatment, storage, and disposal facilities; (5) regulations requiring owners and operators of such facilities to have an EPA permit; and (6) guidelines to help the states develop their hazardous waste programs. Those six items represent substantial grants of discretion. Certainly it is possible to understand what policy has been formulated and adopted only by knowing the detailed regulations of the EPA.

The second force the bureaucracy has to form and adopt policy is the marginal definition of the law. The word *marginal* is used here in the sense in which economists use it, namely as "added" or "extra." Thus the marginal definition of the law means an added definition that must be given to policy especially at the point of field enforcement. Assume that both the RCRA and EPA regulations are in effect. The EPA inspector at a waste generation site (say a chemical plant) still must give that policy an extra interpretation in order to implement it. This added definition has two dimensions. The first has to do with determining what the policy is. What does it mean that no single furnace can emit more that X levels of inorganic chemicals? What is a single furnace? Other questions abound. In another work we estimated that over fifty such decisions have to be made in order to implement a simple risk assessment (Wells 1996). The second aspect has to do with stringency of enforcement. Will the inspector decide on strict enforcement of regulations or will he or she "cut industry some slack"? Anyone who has received a warning ticket rather than an actual citation for speeding on a highway has experienced an example of the marginal definition of the law.

Bureaucracies are the real structures that see to it that policy is effectively executed. Teachers teach, and police officers apply the "real" law, not governors or legislators. Thus bureaucracies are *the* critical actors in policy implementation. On the basis of an important work on implementation at the city level (Pressman and Wildavsky 1973), policy scientists now emphasize the importance of the implementation stage in shaping policy. Pressman and Wildavsky found that policies are constantly being transformed by decisions within the bureaucracy regarding which objectives are to be implemented, in what order, and with what proportion of available resources. The bureaucracy can even decide simply to delay or defeat implementation altogether, as has been the case repeatedly with target dates for environmental objectives, such as the reduction of automobile emissions. James Q. Wilson (1989) has recently reminded us that such decisions about implementation are largely the result of the organizational culture existing within the bureaucracy. In his view, organizations have an internal life of their own, which is far more important in determining what a bureaucracy does than are finances, clientele, or legal definitions of policy (this point is emphasized by decades of research in public administration; see Barnard 1938; Simon 1947).

This internal life with its shared values, commitments, and professional expectations is the source of substantial cohesion in the bureaucracy across governmental levels (Peterson, Rabe, and Wong 1987, p. 160). For one thing, it means that the bureaucracy is able to override even the effect of federalism. For example, specialists in local bureaucracies often feel more akin to their specialist counterparts in the national bureaucracy than they do to political decision makers or generalist bureaucrats at the state and local levels. This same cohesion also means that bureaucrats can and do bypass political decision makers. This is particularly true between levels of government. Educators are more likely to take their cues on educational policy from peers at other levels of government than from political decision makers at their own level. No deliberate strategy need be involved; the outcome can be simply the result of normal professional loyalties and career identities.

COURTS: THE POLITICAL ARBITRATION COUNCILS

The popular perception of the courts is that they give finality to questions and disputes within the political and policy system. A review of the effects of courts across levels of government on policy, however, yields a substantially different picture. The most accurate picture of the courts is that they are the policy system's political arbitration councils. The courts continually reconcile disputes. Court decisions about public policies are seldom final. Subsequent cases can modify points of emphasis, can restrict or expand allowable action, and on occasion can outright overrule previous decisions. We have demonstrated elsewhere that these oscillations of courts, while they often appear to be without coherence, actually fall into patterns that reflect courts' preference for one federalist culture over another (Hamilton and Wells 1990). Also, many instances of dramatic resistance to court decisions have occurred. Note Andrew Jackson's well-known statement that the Court (U.S. Supreme Court) "has made its decision, now let it enforce it." It is important to lay aside notions of the finality of court decisions and to understand that courts are actors in an ongoing policy process.

Courts often appear to be acting inconsistently on policy issues; Cynthia Cates Colella reached such a conclusion about the Burger Supreme Court (1986, p. 71). But when their decision making is analyzed by policy categories (environmental policy, etc.), the decisions reflect a rather consistent pattern. In addition to institutionalizing the prevailing values of the time, courts accommodate their decisions to the other branches of government or adapt their decisions to powerful political interests (Hamilton and Wells 1990, p. 81). The U.S. Supreme Court, like courts generally, rationalizes and legitimizes its highly political decision making by frequent appeal to one of the enduring federalist cultures.

Courts may also periodically protect elite interests by defining the interplay between economic enterprise and government. Felix Frankfurter, as a member of the U.S. Supreme Court, expressed this point well in an unusually candid observation:

> ... the raw material of modern government is business ... all our major domestic issues ... are phases of a single central problem, namely, the interplay of economic enterprise and government. These are the issues which for more than a generation have dominated the calendar of the court. (1961, p. 41)

Sidney Fine has carefully chronicled how the courts in some eras have favored elite interests. The most important was "... that during the period 1865–1901 laissez-faire was read into state and federal constitutions and ... judicial formulas were devised to limit the scope of ... social and economic regulation" (Fine 1956, p. 140).

Periodically, the courts have virtually defined public policy in the areas of social and economic regulation. As a result of substantial political pressures, particularly during the presidency of Franklin Roosevelt, courts loosened the rather strict laissez-faire limitations on government action. Some, including Fine, interpret this loosening as the judicial imposition of the welfare state. Yet when placed in a comparative perspective, say with Sweden or some other European democracies, American social and economic legislation appears to be more a modest strategic retreat from laissez-faire. In any event, a periodic function of the American courts has been to protect elite property interests.

PATTERNS OF INTERACTION AMONG GOVERNMENTS

Governments in the United States seldom act separately in the policy system. Instead, they are in continuous and dynamic interrelationships with other levels of government. The following sections will describe what the main intergovernmental structures and relations mean for public policy in the United States.

THE NATION-STATE STRUCTURE: THE FUNCTIONING OF A COMPLEX POLITICAL ECONOMY

The relationships between the national government and the fifty states comprise a complex political economy, whose functioning depends heavily on which federalist culture is prevalent at the time, whether dualism or centralism or compound federalism. This shift over time in the relative strength of the various federalist cultures produces the extremely important phenomenon of policy cycles in the American policy system. Which issues are debated at any given time is more frequently a result of a shift in the relative appeal of the federalist cultures. Thus certain aspects of the great issues are seldom genuinely new, but rather recycled arguments about whether central, dual, or compound control is the best approach.

For example, the highly intense debate over President Clinton's health care reform proposal, and about abortion rights and court restrictions on them, are controversial not just because of the policy but because of arguments about federalism. On the health care debate, relevant questions include: Should there be *national* standards and policies that strictly define and provide health care (centralism)? Or should the states be the major players in the reforms and the Feds stay largely out of providing coverage or services (dualism)? Or should the plan be much like Clinton's, which calls for national standards of coverage and prices that are controlled mainly by *private*, state-based networks of providers, with the states as the main regulators (a compound approach if there ever was one).

By devising a compound approach, President Clinton may have given his proposal the best chance of passage simply by making it fit the style most acceptable to most Americans—the idea that the "Feds" provide impetus and standards, but the provision and regulation of health care is left essentially to the private market under the regulation of individual states, in ways they see fit. Any health plan that might eventually get approved will no doubt carry a compound style (or it won't be popular enough to pass). But you can be sure that complaints will carry the familiar refrains from the other federalist ideas. From centralist advocates you might hear "It's not working because it provides terrible, uneven results." And from dualist speeches you might hear, "Too much Washington bureaucracy has produced terrible standards and too much intrusion into the states." For that reason, debates about policy, politics, and power are never really resolved.

Also, a particular federalist culture can undergird and legitimize a policy position even when a second culture is the current trend. For example, the centralist federalist culture dominates economic and monetary policy in the United States. The Federal Reserve central banking system has influence beyond the fondest dreams of Alexander Hamilton. Most Americans seem to accept with little question the centralist prescription for money and banking. Yet President Reagan got attention on the issue of restricting the Fed's ability to control interest rates when they threatened his tax-cutting programs of the early 1980s.

Also, on abortion policy the Supreme Court seems to have moved abortion rights slightly away from its still dominant centralist position (*Roe* v. *Wade*, 1973), whereby a woman had unrestricted, "sole choice" regarding abortion in the first three months of pregnancy. Since the Webster 1992 case, abortion rights are subject to a more compound influence: While the Court retains the concept of abortion as a woman's "constitutional right of privacy," states may now attach some qualifications to "sole choice" even in the first three months. Thus the federalist cultures can be both creators of policy cycles and creators of stability in policy. In either case, it is important to see how policy is guided by the federalists cultures.

The influence of compound federalism on the nation–state structure explains several important features of the American policy system. First, it helps explain constitutionally rooted conflicts over power and policy. A long list of such conflicts exists between levels of government: States that disagreed with conservatives' proposed urban grant cuts, cities that opposed reduced national grants for mass transit, and school systems that are concerned over proposals for national accreditation of schools. States and cities had been used to these compound-style forms of aid or cooperation and saw few reasons to cut them out. The separation of powers is an important element in the compound design, and it helps to explain conflict between institutions at the same level. Any morning newspaper will report such conflicts: the goal of balancing the budget is seen differently in the White House than on Capitol Hill; the president's health care reform is greeted with immediate opposition and a flurry of legislative counterproposals; the president attacks the Supreme Court for ignoring the intention of the framers. Compound federalism created many centers of competing power, and so what one "sees and seeks" in the policy system depends a great deal on "where one sits."

Second, compound federalism affects policy implementation. A mountain of research shows how policy gets altered in the federalist meat grinder. This occurs partly because of the power of the bureaucracy, referred to earlier. An excellent example is the Housing and Community Development Act, which mandated the deconcentration of low-income housing to all areas of a city. The policy issue was that these housing projects concentrated poor families into virtual ghettos, and thus the culture of poverty fed on itself. As with many other policies, the HCDA provided for the participation of local government officials in the implementation. A subsequent study showed that the locals in fact further concentrated the low-income housing. They made decisions on site locations on a "where needed" basis, which to them eliminated the middle- and upper-income neighborhoods. Their style of implementation raised the important question of what policy was being implemented (Wrightson 1986, p. 272). Clearly, national objectives are transformed in the intergovernmental implementation process.

Third, compound federalism helps explain policy and power stalemate. America is unable to make quick, clear decisions on important issues primarily because of the complex, noncentralized design of the compound model. Madison believed it was crucial to slow down the policy process through various balances of power. Because of the fragmented nature of the system, interest groups that may be powerful enough to win in one institution or level are forced to play the power game across institutions and levels. In doing so they encounter countervailing power that stops or slows down the process. Stalemate results because no single group is able to win across the fragmented decision system. The classic modern example was the failure of the Equal Rights Amendment. Despite strong, clear majority support over a decade, the pro-amendment forces failed to develop a strategy that targeted passage in the states, whereas the "Stop ERA" forces did exactly that. An example in the mid-1990s is the proposed amendment to balance the national budget, which needs approval by three-quarters of the states.

The nation–state structure when guided by centralism explains other features of the American policy system. Perhaps most important, it helps explain the vastly increased policy role of governments at all levels. The expansion of their policy functions since the 1930s occurred in part because the nature of American society changed by mid-century, evolving from a nonurban agricultural society to an urban post-industrial society. The centralist culture provided legitimization for this expansion by appealing to an enduring element in Americans' views of government, one consistent with Alexander Hamilton's belief in the necessity of an "energetic republic."

Among the more important elements in this expanded policy role are economic policy and regulatory policy. Centralism has provided the basis for both a national banking system and centrally directed macroeconomic policy. In fact, the history of the national banking system is the story of a titanic struggle between the three great federalist cultures. In this instance centralism was the winner and Hamilton's vision of a central bank became a reality. Centralism also provided the basis for expanded national efforts at macromanaging the economy in the face of the Great Depression and during World War II. The twin pillars of economic policy in this country, monetary and fiscal policy, are centrally directed strategies that reflect the preferences of national elites. The final area of expanded national policy is the wide scope of activity captured by the phrase "regulatory federalism." This regulatory activity, which began increasing in the 1950s, was targeted not only to private sector individuals and firms, but also to states and their political subdivisions. Such extensive national regulation of the states could be justified only through appeal to the centralist culture.

The nation–state structure when guided by dualism is probably the root cause of fragmentation in public policy in the United States. This fragmentation starts even at the policy formation stage, as dualistic interests conflict. Thus policy that comes out of Congress is the result of compromises between national and subnational interests, and it often seems poorly drawn up when looked at through the criteria of scientists or economists. Members of Congress cannot ignore home state interests, despite presidential pressures or the outcries of number-crunching technical advisors. As a result, national objectives get reworked deep in congressional committees. Second, the complexity of dualism explains in large part the slow implementation and enforcement. The Advisory Commission on Intergovernmental Relations sponsored a very informative study of regulatory federalism, and it found:

> [a] ... rulemaking process extended over a period of nine years is by no means unusual.... Most federal regulatory proceedings are characterized by seemingly interminable delays ... the regulatory process takes far too long to accomplish too little." (ACIR 1984, p. 109)

Delay is the inevitable consequence of the fact that dualistic federalism creates many state and local government hurdles that policy must clear before implementation.

Given the differences in policy outcomes between the competing federalists cultures, we emphasize that the primary policy influence of the nation–state structure is in channeling a seeming policy "decision" into a thicket of institutions and social forces, both national and subnational, for alteration and evolution. What comes out of that thicket years or even decades later may or may not coincide with the original policy intention. Thus the nation–state structure channels, alters, and recycles conflicts about public policy.

THE INTERSTATE STRUCTURE: IN THE THICKET OF GOVERNMENTS

One of the problems in identifying what the interstate structures explain about public policy is that the interstate and the dualistic national structure are closely related. In fact, many of the aspects of contemporary interstate relations have evolved historically out of dualism. For example, states under the Articles of Confederation were in a posture of much competition and conflict with each other, and this conflict, particularly over economic issues, was one of the most powerful forces leading to the Constitutional Convention of 1787. Two hundred years later one of the most important characteristics of interstate relations is competition and conflict. While the specific areas of conflict vary from those in the 1780s, much of the conflict is still over economic issues. The most publicized is in industrial development.

The interstate structure best explains several important features of the contemporary policy system. First issues are raised and sometimes suppressed that can be explained only because the states interact in patterned relationships with one another. Daniel Elazar refers to race as the issue where this point is seen most clearly. However, economic issues have been front-burner concerns in recent years. The states are pressure points in stimulating economic activities. It is ironic that much writing places emphasis on the national government's policies designed to ensure a developing industrial economy—activities such as building roads and canals and subsidizing on a massive scale construction of railroads. In fact, unlike most other industrial nations, the United States has never had an industrial policy. But states have. Nearly all states have policies designed to stimulate industrial growth. Many of these policies are highly sophisticated and, because of the size of the economic activity within the state, rival some nations in scope of activity. As a result of the differences in success rates among the states, some states have extensive "deindustrial policies," designed to offset the effects of "runaway" plants. Even given different successes, states have been important in stimulating an ever-expanding industrial economy (see Chapter 7).

As with industrial policy, most writing describes the national government as the regulator of U.S. economic activity. Given the expansion of the meaning of the interstate commerce clause, the national government, following centralist prescriptions, is the source of significant economic regulations. However, America is still a weakly regulated economy when compared with other nations, and states have in place significant regulations designed to protect business interests. A cursory glance at any state constitution, for example, will identify a number of provisions giving special protection to property. States also give grants of incorporation to business firms. There is little doubt that the national legislature could grant both charters and licenses to businesses operating in interstate commerce, but for a number of reasons states assumed the power to grant incorporation charters. When substantial competition developed between the states around the 1850s over attracting corporations, states began granting corporations more and more privileges. States with extremely generous corporate privileges are still the headquarters of a disproportionate number of corporations (Delaware and Connecticut, for example). This form of economic regulation was designed to protect the interests of the corporation, usually by making it more difficult for competing firms to be active in a given market. These sorts of outcomes of the interstate structures raise issues concerning the very nature of the economic system itself.

A second feature of the interstate structure is that states are at the center of implementation in the United States. This fact is a more powerful explanation of policy variations among states than are the socioeconomic differences. Take, for example, most environmental issues. Under the partial preemption implementation strategy, all fifty states have in place plans for the implementation of clean air, clean water, and chemical hazardous waste policies. But this phenomenon extends even to policy that would appear on the surface to be simply an "accounting matter." In the 1980s there was substantial interstate conflict over the formulas used for distributing national grant-in-aid monies to the states. In short, the so-called frost belt states claimed that the formulas were giving too much aid to the sun belt states, and that the bias was particularly inequitable given the shift in economic activity from the frost belt to the sun belt. What appeared to be a simple numbers-cruncher dispute became a powerfully divisive issue as it played itself out.

Of course conflict relations are not the only form of interaction within the interstate structure. States can and do cooperate with one another. There are even formal devices for such cooperation, such as interstate compacts and uniform state laws. We are most impressed, however, with two informal devices for interstate cooperation. The first is the extensive network of public interest groups. There is a vast array of organizations representing governors, state legislatures, state bureaucrats, cities, counties, and officials at all those levels. Such organizations are powerful forces stimulating interaction among the states and, perhaps more important, pressing subnational interests in national decision-making structures. Second, there are informal political networks within the interstate pattern. The most important outcome of these networks is the rapid diffusion of policy. The rapidity with which such reforms as the regulation of drunk driving and the protection of battered wives, abused children, and exploited children spread among the states in the 1980s is impressive. Other issues, such as the nuclear-free zones, simply fizzle out within the region of their origin. We suggest again that the interstate structure is an important force for raising and suppressing issues in the American policy system.

THE LOCAL–LOCAL STRUCTURE: LEGALLY SUBSERVIENT BUT POLITICALLY ACTIVE

Most students know that local units of government are political subdivisions of the states. Even though Americans were more attached to their local communities than to other political entities at the time of the framing of the Constitution in 1787, the Constitution is silent on the status of local governments. This deliberate silence was designed to avoid some of the divisive problems associated with the federal system, problems that might have jeopardized the ratification of the Constitution. As we pointed out earlier, nondecisions (what governments decide *not* to do) have important political and policy outcomes.

One important outcome of this nondecision is that the legal status of local governments was determined by case law. In such cases as *Trenton* v. *New Jersey*, the court declared local governments to be "creatures of the state" and "convenient administrative agencies" of the state. All these things mean that local governments and locals' relations among themselves are under the influence of and legally subservient to the states.

Subserviency and passivity are two entirely different things, however. Local governments have been anything but politically passive. Consider the existence of the local–local structure itself. This policy structure exists because there are patterned relations between local governments. If the ruling in *Trenton* v. *New Jersey* were strictly followed, such relationships could exist only if explicitly permitted by the state. But most of the local–local relationships exist because locals act on their own prerogatives. Such actions are so extensive that we ask, in a larger analysis of this topic, if locals are anyone's creatures (Hamilton and Wells 1990, p. 316). In any event, the local–local structure is a powerful force in the American policy system.

One of the most important results of the local–local structure is the influence of local interest in national representative institutions. We have discussed how legislatures are partly the mirrors of subjurisdictional interests. What we have not emphasized is the importance of federalism as the arbiter of political power in the United States. In Madison's terms, federalism made possible sufficient protection against "popular majorities" to prevent the "excesses of democracy." So locals simply cannot have things all their way in our Federal system, even though local interests, particularly local elite interests, play an important role in national institutions.

The front-burner issue for locals has been distributive politics. In the classic ideas of Harold Lasswell, the local–local structure has been most concerned with who gets what, and when and how. This is true even of their own spending. Where are sidewalks to be built? Where are street lights to be installed? Where are curbs and gutters to be constructed? Whose property is to be zoned for what? A cursory observation of virtually every city in the United States, as well as the facts documenting such cases as *Hawkins* v. *Shaw*, will confirm that distributive issues, or who is favored to get what, are more important than concerns for serving residents equally. These issues are also important in the local spending of federal grants, and have been since the earliest years of expanded national assistance to local governments. Lyle Dorsett has demonstrated that the acceleration in national grants during the New Deal did not disturb the status quo at the local level. These grants were directed locally, and so the new monies could be directed toward those individuals whom local decision makers wished to benefit and withheld from those whom local elites did not want to benefit (Dorsett 1977, p. 113). More recently, no one can understand "urban renewal" without understanding how local governments have assisted elite developers in acquiring land that they could not have acquired through normal market channels. Sometimes this link of local governments to local elites expresses itself in stark terms, as in 1981, when the city of Detroit worked with General Motors to destroy "Poletown," an established working class neighborhood, to build a Cadillac plant (*Washington Post*, March 1, 1981). In summary, how policies are really implemented at the local level depends more on the interactions of local officials, local elites, and local interest groups than on statutory provisions, administrative decision making, or court rulings at higher levels. (See the next section on national–local relations.)

Third, the local–local structure is very important in explaining the role of law as an instrument to protect property. Hamilton and Madison argued that the primary function of locals was to maintain order by protecting both lives and private property, but they did not specify *whose* lives and *whose* property. We must understand the local–local structure before we can define what property is at stake. For example, if an individual "steals" a can of gasoline from a store, that can is included in the definition of property to be protected. But if the store owner "steals" an equal amount of money through excess profits on the sale of the same gasoline, that lost money is not (yet) defined as property to be protected. The unequal administration of the law—even to the point of the law's practical content and meaning—is a function performed largely, and perhaps most effectively, by locals.

Finally, the local–local structure helps explain the heavy hand of tradition on the American policy system. The "maintenance of order" that James Madison prized so highly is realized in the bedrock of stable traditions at the local level. Political scientists often refer to the "spread of innovation" between units of government, but the suppression of innovation is accomplished by locals in two important ways. The first is simply the imposition of elite policy preferences, and the second is the imposition of the lowest common denominator of policy response in a number of policy areas. The most visible of such response is found in the public schools. While substantial national rhetoric occurs about quality education, policy response where it counts—in local school districts—is minimal at best. As we shall see in a later chapter, educational reforms that would cost the same dollar amounts as existing practices are largely ignored in many school systems. Something more is at work than inadequate communication. The primary force at work is the effectiveness of the local–local structure in maintaining traditional ways of carrying out policy.

THE NATION-LOCAL STRUCTURE: DISTRIBUTIVE POLITICS RUN RIOT

Much of the federalism literature depicts national–local relationships, often called *direct federalism*, as a twentieth-century development. In effect, the argument goes, direct federalism was not supposed to happen, because local governments are the creatures of the states, and states would not allow locals direct relationships with the national government. But such a view simply ignores history. At least from the early 1800s, cities were practicing partners with the national government in a wide range of projects (Elazar 1962), most of them programs of internal improvement. The first known national–local project, for example, was a joint venture between the U.S. Army Corps of Engineers and the city of Norfolk, Virginia, in the construction of a canal. Other early ventures included cooperation in the provision of educational facilities, public assistance programs, and to a lesser extent, a sound fiscal system. Given this historic reality, it is important to emphasize that the national–local structure was given substantial impetus during the 1930s. The operational features of the national–local structure, such as the grant in aid programs, were developed and expanded greatly during and since the administration of Franklin Roosevelt.

One of the important things that the national–local structure reveals is the capacity of national elites to accomplish their objectives through "extra-system" or indirect means. Expansion in this area was largely a result of the desire by centralist decision makers in the 1930s to bypass the states (with their own elite classes) to accomplish economic stabilization objectives. Thus the expansion demonstrates the ability of centralists to move outside the system and invent the means to change the policy system. As we have seen, the structure works both ways. The national government uses it to bypass the states to accomplish national objectives, and local governments use it to bypass states to accomplish local goals. What is good for the goose, presumably, is good for the gander. But the good of the states is seldom an issue. Again, whose creatures are local governments?

As with the local–local structure, the most important issue in this structure from its inception (accelerated in the New Deal) is distribution. As during the New Deal, the federal largesse today is largely distributed *through* local units of government. This has many important ramifications. For example, it has been rather popular for a number of years to berate the various anti-poverty programs for their alleged ineffectiveness in reducing poverty (Murray 1984). The generally accepted explanation for this "failure" was based in an assumption about the inherent inefficiency of the national design of the programs. An alternate and more plausible explanation is that the national–local structure distributes benefits inefficiently. Locals direct resources in ways preferred by local elites. For example, certain Office of Economic Opportunity officials complained not long after the start of the Appalachian programs that the programs were "a boon for the rich and for the well-entrenched political interests," which left the bulk of the poor in the region "largely untouched" (*New York Times*, November 29, 1970). Certainly such an outcome was not in the policy objectives of the program. The point is that the program could be a boon to the rich because of the freedom of locals to distribute benefits. Thus it may not be accurate to refer to a *general* distributive inefficiency. The structure is inefficient when measured in terms of statutory objectives, but highly efficient when measured in terms of the objectives of local political forces.

POLICY STRUCTURES: MORE THAN BOXES ON ORGANIZATIONAL CHARTS

The discussion in this chapter represents a radical departure from the view that structures mean little in the policy process. Clearly, structures condition and impact what happens in the policy system. Furthermore, structures directly affect how individuals in the policy system do or do not participate in the process. In other words, policy structures go a long way toward determining whether or not there is democratic policymaking. They also go a long way toward determining the interests to be served by the policy system. Outcomes are affected, at least in part, by policy structures.

Policy structures in the United States form a complex, multi-layered, inter-related system. Further, the way it "works" depends a great deal on the policy culture to which one subscribes. For a strict dualist, for example, direct federalism, or grants in the nation-to-local structure, would not work at all since it would be prohibited from the constitutional system. Are the intergovernmental playing fields of public policy appropriate ones for innovation and solution to America's critical problems? Success in dealing with problems depends heavily on the answer.

 **CHAPTER 6**

ENVIRONMENTAL POLICY

NECESSITY VERSUS DENIAL

Environmental policy may be defined as those actions of governments that seek to preserve the ecological basis of life. It involves some of the most critical choices that societies make. Immanuel Kant made the argument that individuals relating to others must never act on the basis of the ends justifying the means. This ethical imperative has a counterpart in public policy: Protecting the ecological basis of life is the ultimate policy imperative. Certainly, deterioration in the ecological basis of life would have important implications for the other critical choices that societies must make—in health, medical ethics, education, and economic policies. While all the critical public policy choices are interrelated, protecting the ecological basis of life is the *sine qua non* of human existence.

A second characteristic of environmental policy is that the "facts" are subject to denial. In fact, most analysts disagree over some aspect of the "environmental problem." Some even deny the existence of a problem (see *Insight*, April 27, 1992). When the subject moves beyond description to prescription, or from objectives to means, even wider disagreement occurs.

The opposing realities of the need for a policy to preserve the ecological basis of life on the one hand, and the potential deniability of both the problem and its solution on the other, pose great difficulty for any understanding of environmental policy. At the outset, therefore, it is necessary to examine what is happening to the ecological basis of life. The fact that we do not have basic information on some of the most important requirements for sustaining the ecological basis of life hinders this examination. The supposed information explosion simply has not yet clearly defined the problems of the environment. We should not try to fill in the blanks of an inadequate environmental database with guesses or opinions. We will attempt to deal honestly with the absence of data, for there is no other basis on which critical policy choices can be made.

A CAULDRON OF CONTAMINANTS: THE CRITICAL ISSUES

To define environmental policy as those actions taken by governments to preserve the ecological basis of life assumes that there is a threat to the ecology. Without such a threat, there would be no need for environmental policy. The basic premise of our approach is that there are substances added to the environment that pose a risk to the ecological basis of life. The most positive or active goal of environmental policy, then, would be to take actions that maintain environmental quality by *preventing* the release of such substances into the environment. The more minimal or negative goal would be to take actions that ameliorate environmental degradation when polluting substances have already been released into the environment.

One of the most controversial questions of environmental policy is which substances pose risks. Simply stated, what is pollution? The answer involves a distinction between a hazard and a risk. A hazard is a condition or situation that has the potential for harm. A risk is the more certain probability that harm will actually accrue from the hazard. The most common way of explaining the distinction is the analogy of an individual's plan to cross the ocean. Whatever the mode of crossing, there is the same hazard—crossing the ocean has the potential for harm. However, the risk of harm actually occurring is quite different depending on the mode of crossing. Crossing the ocean in the *Queen Mary* involves very little risk; navigating the same hazard in a single person sail boat is a very high risk. We view the individual crossing in the sailboat as a very courageous risk taker or a foolhardy thrill seeker, depending on our perspective.

So the debate rages. What substances pose hazards to the ecology? How do we determine what constitutes a hazard and what does not? How is risk to be assigned? These are not easy questions. The reader who would like to examine all these questions in some of their most stark applications should review the history of DDT, a brief outline of which is provided in Box 6.1.

| 6.1 | *AN AGRICULTURAL MIRACLE TURNS NIGHTMARE* |

DDT is a chemical that had widespread use in agriculture. In the initial years after its development it was hailed as a miracle substance, the basis of an agricultural revolution that would free the world from hunger, rather than as a hazard. A reversal of this view came only after extensive testing that revealed the full toxicity of the substance. Intense controversy surrounded both the testing and the findings. A ban on the use of DDT was a difficult policy objective to accomplish and came only after widespread use of the substance. It is significant to note that DDT is still utilized in the agricultural systems of some countries, including on some vegetables that are exported to the United States. While the nature and intensity of conflict varies from issue to issue in the environmental policy area, all efforts at resolving the most basic questions are fraught with considerable conflict.

How could the policy system have related to DDT in the beginning in order to avoid risk to human health and the environment? What should the American policy system do now relative to the export of DDT to other countries and the importation of vegetables sprayed with DDT into this country? How can such mistakes be avoided in the future?

The problem of determining what constitutes hazards and how to assign risks to them are made more complex by the fact that the environment is a single, interrelated system that is not fully understood. Analysts have tended to divide natural systems into categories and to study each category in artificial isolation from the others. For example, they divided the ocean into the Atlantic, the Pacific, and so forth. Actually, these great bodies of water are connected and comprise one ocean. What happens in one area of the ocean has important consequences in other parts. This aspect of environmental policy is what some commentators refer to as the "globalization of the environment." It is no longer possible to speak of environmental contamination as a local phenomenon (it was in the past only because of limited knowledge). Environmental degradation, wherever it occurs, always has some degree of global effect. This means that it is no longer possible to speak of either local or national solutions. Solutions must have some global dimensions.

Given the controversy surrounding the determination of hazards and the assignment of risks, is it possible to identify the major critical choices that societies need to make about environmental policies? This chapter identifies several areas of critical choices: the depletion of the ozone layer, global warming, acid rain, chemical hazardous waste, nuclear waste, air quality, and water quality. Of course, there are many who would disagree with this list. A good case can be made, for example, that overpopulation is the basis for most environmental problems. Certainly we would not want to detract attention from the effect that population growth has on environmental problems. While our selections are dictated in part by space limitations, it is clear that these problems discussed in the following sections pose serious and immediate choices for public officials.

THE OZONE LAYER: PLANET EARTH'S SUNSCREEN

Ozone is the basis of one of the environment's starkest paradoxes. When found in heavy concentrations at the earth's surface, ozone is one of the most dangerous elements in air pollution. In fact, ozone concentration levels are taken as the best measure of air quality in urban areas. High levels of ozone will trigger such regulations as mandatory inspection of automobile exhaust systems, for example. On the other hand, the ozone layer that envelops the earth is vital to the health of the ecology. This layer, located in the stratosphere between twenty and thirty miles above the surface of the earth, varies in thickness both by the regions of the world and over time. The basic issue with regard to the ozone layer is whether or not human activities either cause depletion (thinning) of the layer or create holes in it.

Ozone is a triatomic form of oxygen, that is, it consists of three atoms of oxygen. Oxygen in all its forms is highly unstable, so ozone is susceptible to being "destroyed." In simplified form, here is how the process works. Various commercial activities result in the release of chlorofluorocarbon molecules (CFCs). Part of the complex chlorofluorocarbon molecule is a chlorine atom. Ultraviolet radiation from the sun breaks off the chlorine atom from the molecule. This free chlorine atom then attacks and breaks up ozone molecules. It has been estimated that one chlorine atom can destroy up to 100,000 ozone molecules (Mintzer and Miller 1992, p. 84). The result is a thinning of the ozone layer or the appearance of a hole in the it, such as the one detected over Antarctica.

Because all conclusions about the environment are subject to denial, it is tempting to engage in a defense of the conclusion that CFCs contribute to thinning of the ozone layer. We will refrain from this temptation because our purpose is to identify the critical choices for policy systems. However, we would encourage the reader to look at the evidence derived from study of the ozone layer. At the core of that evidence are data collected from four major research efforts: the National Aeronautics and Space Administration's Upper Atmosphere Research Satellite, two American National Ozone Expeditions (dubbed NOZE I and NOZE II), a multinational research effort known as the Airborne Antarctica Ozone Experiment, and the Ozone Trends Panel, an international group of scientists who gather and interpret data from a variety of sources. We draw the conclusion from these data that CFCs have been a significant factor in the depletion of the ozone layer.

What is the hazard associated with a depletion of the ozone layer? The ozone layer functions as the earth's sunscreen with regard to certain wavelengths of ultraviolet rays. To explain this function, it is helpful to divide ultraviolet rays into three categories based on the length of the ray. The first category consists of ultraviolet waves shorter than 185 nanometers (for those interested in precision of measurement, a nanometer is one billionth of a meter). This category is the most dangerous but is filtered from the earth's atmosphere by ordinary oxygen. The second category is ultraviolet radiation in wavelengths from 185 to 290 nanometers. It is rays of this midrange wavelength that are filtered by the ozone layer. The third category is ultraviolet radiation in the range of 290 to 400 nanometers. This radiation is not filtered and reaches the earth. Therefore, the specific hazard posed by a thinning of the ozone layer is the increase in ultraviolet radiation in the 185 to 290 range that reaches the earth.

The second question, then, is whether or not the hazard poses a risk to the environment and to human well-being. The answer to this question requires identifying the effects of increased exposure to ultraviolet radiation of wavelengths between 185 and 290 nanometers. The most widely publicized of these effects is an increase in non-melanoma skin cancers among light-skinned people. There are less publicized effects, however, that may be more significant for human welfare. First, high levels of exposure to ultraviolet radiation can weaken or perhaps destroy the immune system. This is a phenomenon already associated with some types of chemotherapy and some medical radiation treatments. A related effect has to do with crop loss and forest damage. Some ecologists fear severe ecological damage in the Antarctica region as a result of the hole in the ozone layer. Over the earth's middle latitudes, where ozone depletion has been greater than was predicted, ultraviolet radiation is particularly dangerous to cotton, peas, beans, melons, cabbage, and the loblolly pine.

Assigning a specific level of risks to any of these potential effects is the most difficult task. Again, most work has been done on the risks of skin cancer. The Environment Programme of the United Nations estimated that for every 1 percent decrease in the ozone level there would be a 3 percent increase in skin cancers among light-skinned people. Using that relationship as the basis for its calculations, the U.S. Environmental Protection Agency estimated that 12 million Americans will develop skin cancer and 200,000 will lose their lives as a result of ozone thinning. These risks are significant and point to the fact that depletion of the ozone layer poses critical choices for policy systems.

One of the most important critical choices to be made is the issue of Third World participation in international efforts to protect the ozone layer. Third World policymakers argue that it is unfair to expect their nations to forego the economic development associated with the use of CFCs. Their argument is twofold. First, these nations have been making substantial investment in modernization technology, especially refrigeration. CFCs are the "propellants" for refrigeration and air conditioning. A ban on the use of CFCs would mean that much of that investment would be lost before it is fully depreciated. Second, replacement chemicals, to the extent that they are available, are more expensive than CFCs—up to six times the present cost of the most widely used refrigerant, CFC 11. Both of these factors, then, would impose substantial costs on Third World nations. Virtually all analysts are in agreement that any CFC policy is doomed to failure without Third World participation, particularly that of India and China (Makhijani, Bickel, and Makhijani 1990, p. 183). Clearly one of the critical issues facing the multinational policy system is to find ways to deal equitably with Third World needs.

A second critical choice has to do with finding acceptable substitutes for CFCs. In the first place, companies that have invested substantial amounts of money in developing substitutes have a stakeholder interest in the results of their efforts. This leads them to pressure regulatory agencies to approve their product. CFCs themselves were extremely significant commercially. At the height of CFC use, the five U.S. companies that manufactured them had annual sales in excess of $28 billion and employed 715,000 people. These numbers suggest that the stakes are high in developing substitutes for CFCs. Second, the timetables for the mandatory phase-out of CFCs encourage if not dictate an accelerated effort to develop substitutes, but these short-term substitutes carry their own risks. For example, the accelerated effort resulted in the development of HCFC as the most widely used substitute. HCFC is a molecule containing hydrogen, chlorine, fluorine, and carbon; it contributes to chlorine buildup in the stratosphere and to global warming.

The third critical choice is associated with the buildup of CFCs in the stratosphere. Even if there were an immediate and complete phase-out of the use of CFCs, the current buildup of chlorine atoms in the stratosphere will last for at least fifty years. Critical choices, then, need to be made not only relative to future release of CFC molecules but also in dealing with those that are already there.

Fourth, a major critical choice has to be made about the enforcement of agreements on substances that deplete the ozone layer. International agreements on CFCs leave enforcement to national regulatory agencies. Some nations have made serious attempts to give international agreements the force of domestic law. Examples are the 1990 Amendments to the Clean Air Act in the United States and various implementing legislation by the European Community. However, such legislation simply has been nonexistent or very weak in some nations that are party to the agreements. One of the unaddressed problems on the global level is the fact that international agreements are not self-enforcing. Critical choices have to be made about either an international enforcing organization or some mechanisms to ensure enforcement.

GLOBAL WARMING: A GREENHOUSE FOR PLANET EARTH

Global warming is an excellent example of the saying that little things mean a lot. The cause of this problem is substances called *trace gases*, so named because they make up less than 1 percent of atmospheric gases. In technical terms, trace gases are relatively transparent to incoming short wavelength sunlight but are opaque to the longer wavelength energy radiated from the earth's surface. In other words, trace gases allow energy to come into the earth's atmosphere but not to escape from it. Thus trace gases are often referred to as *greenhouse gases*. They allow heat from the sun to enter the earth's atmosphere and then trap it, thereby causing an increase in the earth's temperature. Ironically, it is the trace gases that ensure that the average temperature of the earth's surface is suitable for plant and animal life. Average ocean and land surface temperatures are 63 and 57 degrees Fahrenheit, respectively. Without the trace gases, surface temperatures might be as low as -4 degrees Fahrenheit. like the ozone layer, the greenhouse gases are vital to the health of the earth's ecology.

So how is the hazard created by greenhouse gases? Human activities have caused a buildup of these trace gases, increasing particularly the levels of carbon dioxide, chlorofluorocarbons, methane, and nitrous oxide. A good example is carbon dioxide, historically the most important of the greenhouse gases. Carbon dioxide is produced "naturally," providing an enormous stock of about 700 billion tons a year for nature's use. The biosphere then recycles the carbon dioxide, using it to good advantage in many ways. The best known of these recycling processes occurs in plants. An interesting feature of the ecosystem, suggesting perhaps an ecological balance, is the fact that the capacity of the ecosystem to recycle carbon dioxide is about 700 billion tons a year. Ecosystems have a certain natural capacity to recycle such byproducts of natural events. However, human activities produce another 24 billion tons a year, only about half of which is being recycled by natural processes. As a result, carbon dioxide concentrations in the atmosphere have been steadily building and are now about 25 percent higher than they were 100 years ago. A similar buildup is taking place with the other greenhouse gases. They all mix well in the atmosphere and are relatively long lived. These increased concentrations of greenhouse gases increase the capacity of the atmosphere to capture heat radiated from the earth's surface, thus raising the average temperature of the earth's surface.

There is rather common agreement on what would be the effects of global warming (Rosenburg, Easterling, Crosson, and Darmstadter 1989). The most obvious result would be a rise in sea level, estimated to be between thirty-five and sixty-five centimeters. This would produce flooding of low-lying areas, including wetland habitats, the regression of coastal islands and beaches, and the movement of saline water upstream in rivers that empty into the ocean. The associated losses would be catastrophic. A second result of global climate change would be a change in agricultural production patterns. This problem is particularly complex in the United States, where a commodity price support program encourages specific crop production in fixed locations. A shift in where crops can be raised would raise interesting questions relative to who benefits and who does not from agricultural policy. A third impact, more difficult to assess, is the effect of global warming on forests. It is easy to assume that the various species of trees would simply migrate to other areas and flourish. However, temperature is only one factor determining where trees will grow; other important elements are soil composition, topography, and elevation. Thus there is a wide range of factors associated with the effect of climate change on forests. Finally, with global warming there would almost certainly be increased warm weather patterns, including more precipitation, hurricanes, tornadoes, and monsoons.

These do not necessarily translate into more water for all, however, because many factors are involved in the availability of water, including greater evaporation and higher water demand associated with warmer temperatures. Most studies predict that the arid areas of the world will become more arid as a result of global warming. Clearly, global warming, should it occur, would be an ecological hazard with significant environmental, social, and economic outcomes.

An intense debate rages over whether or not human-produced greenhouse gases are causing global warming (U.S. Senate 1991). Again, our purpose here is merely to raise the questions posed for policy systems, not to evaluate scientific evidence. However, we urge the reader to review the elements in the debate, including computer modeling, called *general circulation models*, and meteorological events such as the thickness of the ice cap in the Dry Valleys of Antarctica. As a review of the debate will reveal, while the evidence for global warming is strong, it is not as conclusive as the evidence on thinning of the ozone layer.

This means that one of the critical choices for policy systems relates to making policy on global warming in the face of uncertain knowledge. Put simply, what should policymakers do when faced with significant disagreement among scientists? In dealing with this question, one must first understand the distinction between the role of science and the role of scientists in policymaking. Science is neutral and can and should inform the policy process to the fullest extent possible. Scientists, however, pose special problems for policy, simply because they are not as neutral as popularly believed. Scientists affiliated with industry, for example, are more politically and socially conservative than those who work in universities, for government, and for environmental groups. A study of 136 scientists on risk assessments for carcinogens found that industry scientists favored premises and judgments that made regulation of the substance under study less likely (Lynn 1986). Another important study found that when scientists became involved in the policy process, say as advisors to policymakers, there was a considerable weakening of their scientific perspective and a strengthening of perspective based on ideology (Dietz and Rycroft 1987, p. 17). In other words, scientists stopped acting like scientists and began acting more like politicians or political activists. On what basis, then, is global warming policy to be made?

The Intergovernmental Panel on Climate Change, an international group that studies global warming and assesses its results, was organized in 1987 by the World Meteorological Organization and the U.N. Environment Programme. The report of the Panel, issued in May 1990, is a model of a balanced, reasoned approach to policymaking in the context of an uncertain science. The Panel's most important conclusion was that, notwithstanding scientific uncertainty, all nations should take immediate steps to reduce greenhouse gases. These steps included strategies to lower rates of emission of the gases, such as catalytic converters on automobiles, and strategies to absorb excess gases already in the atmosphere, such as planting more forests. Without such actions, the Panel predicted, global warming will increase between 2 and 5 degrees centigrade in the next century, an unprecedented rate of warming with significant adverse effects on the ecological basis of life.

Thus a second set of critical choices posed by global warming has to do with the implementation strategies to decrease levels of greenhouse gases (National Academy of Sciences 1991). Can policy systems make the appropriate choices to reduce the emissions of these gases? Here, the experience of the American policy system is not encouraging. A key element in American strategy is automobile emission controls, but target dates for such controls have been delayed or simply ignored. A similar situation exists with regard to reduction of gases already in the atmosphere. For example, there has been a significant increase in the total acreage of forests in Europe, but these forests tend to be commercial "rapid growth" forests that do not have the ecological advantages of established hardwood forests.

The greenhouse effect poses critical choices about multinational cooperation. Some nations have taken the recommendations of the IPCC seriously and adopted policies designed to reduce greenhouse gases. These countries include the members of the European Community along with Australia, Canada, Finland, Japan, New Zealand, Norway, Sweden, and Switzerland. Other countries—most notably the United States, the nations of the former Soviet Union, and most Third World countries—have taken minimal or no action to reduce greenhouse gases. It is significant also that there has been no successful effort at developing an international convention on global warming, in spite of substantial effort on the part of certain groups and nations. A global policy problem does not necessarily evoke a global policy response.

Finally, the greenhouse effect poses critical choices for one of the most important unexamined aspects of environmental policy: the potential risks for environmental degradation. There are two basic choices that can be made. The first is to allow the degradation to occur. Costs associated with this choice include the impact of the degradation on the ecology, on economic activity, and on social life plus the costs of mitigation. The second choice is to adopt strategies, regulations, and the like that would prevent environmental degradation. Associated costs are referred to as compliance costs. One of the great paradoxes of U.S. environmental policy is that some environmental legislation requires the consideration of compliance costs when regulations are adopted, while there is no requirement to calculate the degradation costs or mitigation costs of pollution when regulations are *not* adopted. The risks of global warming present stark and imposing critical choices along these lines: What is the marginal difference between compliance costs and the sum of degradation and mitigation costs? For example, a 1989 study by the Environmental Protection Agency fixed a cost between $50 and $75 billion to mitigate the effects of a 1 millimeter rise in sea level on houses and roadways alone (Smith and Tirpak 1989). Clearly the degradation and mitigation costs of unregulated climate change would be substantial. Which costs should a policy system be willing to assume? Who is to bear the costs? At this point in the development of environmental policy, policy systems at least need to address the most basic question concerning costs: What are the full costs and who should incur them?

ACID RAIN: SINGING IN THE RAIN IS NOT WHAT IT USED TO BE

Acid rain is a shorthand way of referring to a wide range of acid precipitation. Acid precipitation is formed when sulphur dioxide and nitrogen oxide react chemically with hydrogen to form sulfuric and nitric acids, which then fall to the earth in rain, snow, hail, fog, mist, and dew. On a global average, rainwater is normally acidic, with a pH of about 5.6 (a neutral substance has a pH of 7; vinegar a pH of about 3.0). The increasing acidity of precipitation in some regions of the world creates an environmental hazard with significant outcomes.

The most widely publicized outcome is the effect of acid rain on lakes. The U.S. Congress established the Interagency Task Force on Acid Precipitation to study the problem in the United States. The research sponsored by this group demonstrated that acid precipitation resulting from industrial emissions was the major factor in destroying fresh water lakes in the northeast (Irving 1991). Also widely publicized is the effect of acid rain on forests. Dramatic pictures of dead trees in several regions of the country have appeared in the media. Recent research has concentrated on the effects of acid precipitation on the soil; chemical reactions triggered by acid rain result in the loss of large amounts of calcium and magnesium, and aluminum is leached from the soil as well. These outcomes pose significant critical choices for the policy system.

Among the most critical policymaking choices posed by acid rain is the context of political gridlock. In spite of the strong evidence linking acid precipitation to industrial emissions, the American policy system through the 1980s was deadlocked on the issue. The Reagan administration consistently opposed action until further study of the problem had been conducted. Most analysts agree that this position was the result of powerful constituencies within the Reagan coalition. But what constitutes enough study? When does study cease to have the purpose of advancing knowledge and become a ruse for inaction? How can the policy system relate to the influence of powerful, well-placed constituencies?

A second critical choice posed by acid rain is in the relations between nations in dealing with global environmental problems. Acid rain has been a source of policy contention between the United States and Canada (Schmandt, Clarkson, and Roderick 1988). Several important studies, including one sponsored by the National Academy of Sciences in 1983, directly linked acid precipitation in Canada with industrial emissions from the north central region of the United States. A similar situation exists within Europe. The Black Forest in particular has been hard hit by acid precipitation (Brown 1990), and some of the sulphur dioxide and nitrogen oxide emissions that cause it are from sources outside of Germany. As the protracted conflict between Canada and the United States suggests, it is not easy even for nations on the friendliest of terms to find effective means of cooperating on environmental objectives. How can nations chose those strategies that result in effective multinational cooperation?

Finally, acid rain poses critical choices about strategies for implementing environmental policy. The most important attempt in the United States to deal with the problem of acid rain is the Clean Air Act Amendments of 1990. This act is also the most significant application of the *marketable emission credits* strategy. In short, this strategy allocates amounts of allowable sulfur dioxide emissions to firms and allows the firms either to sell unused allocations or to purchase "credits" and emit more than their allocation. The presumption is that the appropriate level of emissions will be maintained within the total air shed. But this practice raises problems for individuals who live in the vicinity of high-emission firms. They breathe the air of their immediate area, the air with the high concentrations of pollutants made possible by the marketable emissions credit policy. So this strategy raises the important question of what is being marketed—people's health or pollution rights? Even if health is not an issue, should a policy system allow an individual or firm to pollute? Is environmental quality a commodity to be bought and sold?

CHEMICAL WASTE: SOCIETIES USE A LOT AND WASTE A LOT

The United States, along with the other advanced nations, is characterized by chemical dependency. Over 4 million chemicals are registered in the United States. Of those, approximately 70,000 are in regular use, produced by over 120,000 firms whose output represents about 8 percent of the gross national product. This extraordinary production and use of chemicals results in substantial waste. Combining all sources of chemical waste, there is the equivalent of one ton of waste created for each American every year. On the average, the United States produces over 260 million metric tons of chemical waste annually. Unfortunately, comprehensive data do not exist on worldwide production, but the most reliable study estimated 500 million metric tons for only nineteen countries (Sadik 1988, p. 12). These numbers suggest that the use of chemicals and the accompanying waste is a pervasive part of the global environment.

Determining the hazard associated with the large volume of hazardous waste is difficult for the simple reason that the toxic effects of approximately 70 percent of chemicals in use are not known (National Research Council 1984). Only 2 percent of all chemicals have been rigorously tested for their toxicity, partly because the testing of many chemicals is complicated, is expensive, and, particularly relative to human exposure, requires extensive time. This last factor is magnified by the almost compulsive drive, for both economic and social reasons, to increase the number of chemicals in use. All these factors add up to a snowballing effect: As the number of chemicals in use increases, so does the uncertainty regarding their hazards. The same situation exists for chemical waste; the larger the volume, the greater the uncertainty of the hazards they present for the environment.

The hazard associated with chemicals can be categorized on the basis of their short-term and long-term effects. The short-term effects can be relatively straightforward. These include allergenic effects (such as the reaction of some individuals to penicillin), central nervous system effects (headaches, convulsions, and tremors), and gastrointestinal effects (diarrhea, constipation, or ulceration). Long-term effects of exposure are more serious. These include various blood conditions (including effects on electrolytes, pH, protein, red and white blood cells, and the blood's oxygen-carrying and -releasing capacity), carcinogenic effects (production of cancers), glandular system effects, musculoskeletal effects (osteoporosis, muscular degeneration), mutagenic effects (transmissible changes produced in the offspring), and teratogenic effects (nontransmissible effects produced in the offspring). The assignment of risks to these hazards has been an ongoing activity since the important work of Lowrance (1976) brought the issue of risk to the policy agenda. As we emphasized earlier, however, the determination of risks is a long and costly process and has been conducted on only about 2 percent of chemicals in regular use.

Chemical wastes, then, present policy systems with a situation of significant hazards but undetermined risks. The most critical choice they pose may very well be whether advanced societies are willing to make the commitment to determine the level of associated risks. In part, such a decision would involve curbing the appetite for new chemicals—both in producing them and in consuming them. To put the matter simply, there is a lot of catching up to do with regard to risk assessment in chemical waste policy. However, as the experience with DDT should remind us, risk assessment for a particular chemical does not in itself solve the problem. There still remains the complex and difficult task of determining criteria, of setting standards, and of enforcing those standards. Companies that bring new chemicals to the market develop considerable stakeholder interests in those chemicals. In the past, some companies have been very active politically against regulatory efforts even in the face of the most convincing risk assessment results. Therefore, the determination of risks is only the first step in a long political struggle to develop and implement policy. How can the relative values of environmental quality, economic progress, and the conveniences of modern living be evaluated? What are the trade-offs between them? How can those trade-offs be accomplished in the highly political arena of the American policy system?

A second critical choice posed by chemical wastes has to do with which policy strategy is to be pursued. A policy system basically is faced with two strategies: a waste-reduction strategy or a hazard-reduction strategy. The nations forming the European Community have adopted a waste-reduction strategy (ECE 1984). The terms most widely used to refer to this strategy are "low-waste technology" and "clean technology." Underlying the European approach is the assumption that waste is an indication of inefficiencies in the production process. Thus when the environment is protected by the reduction of waste, the economics of production are also improved. Proponents of waste reduction strategy argue, therefore, that clean technology has environmental, economic, and production advantages.

On the other hand, American policy is based in the hazard-reduction strategy. This strategy seeks a reduction not in the volume of waste generated but in the hazard associated with the waste. The objective is to ensure an environmentally benign production and utilization of chemicals and, at the end of the waste stream, a safe disposal or containment of wastes. The containment strategy is employed for both wastes presently being produced and wastes that were inadequately or irresponsibly handled in the past.

It is difficult to determine whether the American strategy of hazard reduction or the European strategy of waste reduction is more effective in reducing pollution from chemical waste (Piasecki and Davis 1990). Only a modest beginning has been made in cross-national studies of environmental policy. However, several conclusions appear to be warranted from the data that exist. First, it is hard to avoid the conclusion that the American approach is more of an "easy fix" strategy than a determined effort to develop the best technology. An "out of sight, out of mind" position seems to be at the heart of American policy. Second, the European experience suggests that clean technology can reduce the volume of waste to the point where land disposal is unnecessary. Finally, waste reduction appears to be an incentive for effective recycling programs. In Europe there is both in-plant and off-site recovery of materials. In-plant, the waste generator recovers the material and reuses it in the production process. Off-site, the material is processed at a commercial recovery facility and sold on the market. Certainly there is sufficient evidence to suggest that an important critical choice facing the American policy system is to reexamine its basic strategy on chemical waste.

A third critical choice for the American policy system has to do with chemicals in everyday life—in food, in the home, and in the workplace (Samet and Spengler 1991). Americans are exposed to pervasive and personal hazards with little guidance as to the risk associated with that exposure. Food is an excellent example. The eating of prepared and packaged food is universal in advanced nations and widespread in less developed nations. Chemicals enter the food chain in many ways. Over 2,000 chemicals are directly added in the preparation or packaging of foods. Some, such as vitamins, minerals, and trace elements, are added to enhance the nutrient value of food. Others, such as colorings and texturing agents, are added simply to make the food look better. In addition to these direct additives, indirect additives are introduced in the food chain in either the production or processing phases. Pesticides, fertilizers, and growth hormones are examples of indirect additives in the production phase. Chemical changes resulting from processing food or induced by packaging materials are examples of indirect additives in the processing phase.

The American policy system first responded to additives in food with the Federal Food and Drug Act of 1906. Since then, chemical additives have been more studied, regulated, and controlled than any other area of the environment. On the other hand, the great number and variety of additives are a basis of concern. As risk assessment studies have shown, the human organism does seem to be able to tolerate small amounts of many different toxic substances simultaneously. However, not much is known about the carrying capacity of the body. What is the effect of chemical buildup in the body? Is the cumulative effect of chemicals the same as the effect of the last incremental dose? Will chemicals have antagonistic interactions once they accumulate to certain levels in the body? An additional problem is the fact that legal loopholes in the United States allow manufacturers to sell pesticides overseas that would be banned in this country (General Accounting Office 1989). For example, DDT and benzene hexachloride are banned in the United States but account for 75 percent of the pesticides used in India. Furthermore, some of the vegetables and fruits sold in the United States are produced in countries where there are few, if any, restrictions on the use of pesticides and where the people who apply the chemicals are untrained in their use.

A technology that may reduce the need for additives in food is *irradiation*, whereby the product is exposed to low levels of radiation, usually gamma rays emitted from Cobalt-60. Proponents of this process argue that irradiation does not induce radiation in the product, so no adverse effect occurs. Irradiation merely kills the bacteria and fungi responsible for spoilage, they state, reducing the need for preservatives. Opponents have serious reservations about irradiation. The major concern is that gamma rays break down every chemical bond in the food, and the "free" molecules can then recombine into any number of chemical components. Recombined chemicals found in irradiated food include formaldehyde, benzene, peroxide, and formic acid, hardly benign chemicals. So what should be the policy response to irradiation? Present American policy requires labeling of irradiated whole foods, but there is no requirement for notice of irradiation in packaged foods, restaurant food, or food sold in schools.

The last set of critical choices we will consider here has to do with possible surprises in the nuclear policy box. Serious policy concern for nuclear waste management is in fact less than two decades old. In the early stages of nuclear development, scientists and policymakers alike assumed that radioactive waste could be easily managed through deep geological disposal (the preferred technology today in American policy). Additionally, most individuals involved in the American nuclear program were more interested in developing new technology than in the dull and seemingly unproductive (at least from a career standpoint) question of waste disposal (Walker, Gould, and Woodhouse 1983, p. 2). Clearly, both scientists and policymakers preferred the development of technology over environmental objectives. Unfortunately, this goal preference has led to some choices that will raise serious policy questions in the future.

In 1994 the Department of Energy began releasing previously classified information that contained disturbing revelations—ranging from secret nuclear tests that the United States conducted, to confirmation of what a number of critics had suspected for some time, namely that the American government had been very careless in handling nuclear waste. The most politically explosive revelation was the information that human beings had been used in experiments to test the effects of exposure to radiation, many of them unaware that they were being used as guinea pigs. Some of the activities that had been considered but not implemented for a number of reasons were even more unbelievable. For example, a part of the Atoms for Peace program was planning for a "Panatomic Canal," using thermonuclear devices to excavate a new canal across Panama.

The U. S. government spent approximately $17 million studying the feasibility of a new canal (Hays 1991), but it is not known whether those studies actually led to the use of nuclear devices to excavate earth. Apparently the Soviet Union used nuclear devices to excavate lakes for water supply purposes.

So the question is, What is in the nuclear box? Will there ever be a full revelation of past practices? Nuclear nations face critical choices with regard to the disposal of what is already a part of the nuclear waste management system. The possibility that the problem may be many times larger than is generally known does not bode well for solution to the known problems.

AMBIENT QUALITY: THE AIR WE BREATH AND THE WATER WE DRINK

The word *ambient* is not in most individuals' vocabularies. It may seem to some to be one of those gobbledygook words specialists invent to make themselves seem more informed than other people. But ambient means simply "a surrounding environment." Thus *ambient air quality* means the quality of the air in an individual's immediate surroundings, and *ambient water quality* refers to water that is in the immediate area under consideration. In this sense, then, ambient air and water quality affect us more directly, personally, and immediately than other areas of environmental concern. What, then, is the quality of the air we breath and the water we drink?

The answer to that question is closely related to other aspects of the environment already discussed. For example, chemical and radioactive wastes that are not properly managed are absorbed by the air and water. In effect, deterioration in ambient air and water quality is a result of releasing into the environment larger volumes of contaminants than the natural systems are able to cleanse. In this respect, both air and water accept pollution readily. Water is a good example. Most schoolchildren know that the molecular formula for water is H_2O. What is not widely known is that the molecular structure of water allows it to accept pollution easily. In more formal language, water has a very high absorption rate. Only a few substances, oil for example, are not easily absorbed by water. So both air and water easily accept the "cauldron of contaminants" referred to in the first section of the chapter. The student is encouraged to review the extensive literature documenting the nature and scope of air and water contaminants. Our interest here, as in previous sections, is the range of critical choices ambient air and water pollution present to the policy system.

While a simple description of the legislation gives the appearance that policy progress has been made, there are a number of critical choices still to be made about air and water quality. First, there are a number of gaps in the American approach. The major gap is groundwater. Even though Americans withdraw approximately 83 billion gallons a day from groundwater sources, the Council on Environmental Policy did not even mention groundwater in its reports until 1979. Groundwater policy in the United States has evolved to what can only be described as "multiple sources of authority and diffusion of responsibility" (Kenski 1990, p. 60). Groundwater policy is diffused among sixteen different statutes and dispersed among at least eleven agencies at the national level. Also, groundwater laws vary substantially among the states. At least forty-seven states have more than one major agency responsible for groundwater policy.

With regard to air quality, the major gap is indoor air pollution. The EPA ranks indoor air pollution at the top of the list of eighteen cancer sources that affect the American population. The United Nations Environment Programme estimates that the world's population spends an average of 80 to 90 percent of its time indoors (U.N. Environment Programme 1988, p. 81). For most Americans, then, the risks of air pollution may be greater indoors than outdoors. American policy response to the wide range of indoor air pollutants has been limited and ineffective. Radon gas, a colorless and odorless gas linked to lung cancer, is a good example. The Radon Program Development Act of 1988 did not authorize the EPA to establish safe levels of radon in homes or to prescribe radon abatement methods through regulations. The act simply empowered EPA to provide information on the hazards associated with radon. Thus EPA's activity under the act has been limited to issuing a pamphlet entitled "A Citizen's Guide to Radon."

A second critical choice has to do with monitoring the effectiveness of policy that is in place. A number of problems exist, many of them substantive in nature rather than simply matters of methodology. The effort to monitor water quality is a good example of these substantive problems. The National Academy of Sciences administers a number of water-quality-monitoring stations, known as NASQUAN stations, throughout the United States. The NASQUAN data suggest that the effort to reduce oxygen-demanding wastes through the construction of municipal and industrial waste facilities has been effective in improving the oxygen content of surface waters in the United States. But the data also suggest that the algae growth in American surface waters has not improved. The reason is that the pollutants that stimulate algae growth, primarily nitrogen and phosphorus, come largely from nonpoint sources, that is, sources that are hard to detect, nearly impossible to monitor, and thus difficult to control. In effect, nonpoint contaminants seem to come out of nowhere because they come from everywhere.

A third critical choice for the American policy system, as well as the international community, has to do with the quality of the ocean. In the ecosystem the ocean functions in two important but not well-understood ways. First, the ocean produces roughly the same plant life as does the land mass, and so it is an important part of the carbon, oxygen, hydrogen, and nitrogen cycles. Second, the ocean is in constant interaction with the atmosphere. In this interaction, the ocean captures carbon dioxide. This absorption is one of the more important elements in controlling earth's temperature, making the ocean the "global regulator of climate." The ocean, then, is a complex interrelated system that will be put at risk by overloading with contaminants.

In this regard, the outlook is not encouraging. The ocean has been referred to as the world's ultimate septic tank. Waste comes into it from two sources. One is various land-based sources, primarily sewage, industrial discharges, and runoff from agricultural applications. The second is discharge directly into the ocean, primarily from oil spills, ocean dumping, and offshore energy production. For example, there have been spectacular and catastrophic oil spills. The largest single oil spill involved the ship *Atlantic Express*, which released 276,000 tons of oil off the coast of Tobago. By comparison, the Exxon *Valdez* released 35,000 tons of oil off the coast of Alaska in 1989. The perception of most Americans that sewage discharges in the ocean have been eliminated is simply inaccurate. The National Oceanic and Atmosphere Administration reported that treatment plants discharged 3.3 trillion gallons of sewage into the ocean in 1980 and estimated that the volume would rise to 5.4 trillion gallons by the year 2000 (*Newsweek* 1988, p. 45). About 35 percent of all municipal sewage in the United States is discharged into ocean waters. Historically, one of the most controversial uses of the ocean is for the dumping of wastes in all forms, including radionuclides. The United States, Japan, and some Western European countries engaged in ocean dumping of radioactive waste from 1940 until a moratorium was declared in 1983. As an example of the volume of such dumping, approximately 90,000 tons of nuclear waste were deposited in the ocean in 1983 (OECD 1985, p. 79).

Evaluating whether or not these and other contaminants put the ocean at risk is a difficult task. The ocean is a complex biotic system with adaptation capacities that are little known by marine scientists. In fact, monitoring the health of the ocean is itself fraught with great difficulties. Among the more important of these is the fact that authority for monitoring the ocean is scattered among 25 legislative acts, producing a fragmented approach that is seriously deficient. The critical choices that must be made about the ocean, then, will have to be made in the context of substantial uncertainty.

The fourth critical choice about ambient air and water quality has to do with the issue of fairness. Air provides the clearest example of this problem. Economists have long portrayed air as a "pure public good," meaning that if pure air is provided to one person it is provided for all. This is so, economists argue, because air is "indivisible," that is, it cannot be divided, priced, and sold to some and withheld from others. While this theory is appealing on the surface, in practice it simply is inaccurate. Because of developments in air-cleaning technology, clean air can now be delivered to some and withheld from others. Mexico City is an excellent case in point. In the affluent neighborhoods of the city, homes and offices are equipped with air-cleaning technology, so the people who live and work in those neighborhoods breathe essentially clean air (as long, of course, as they remain indoors). The great masses of the city, unable to afford air cleaning technology, are left to breathe essentially nonbreathable air. As the Mexico City situation illustrates, wherever ambient air is unbreathable within acceptable risks, breathable air is divisible and can be delivered to some and withheld from others. But is such a situation fair? Are air and water part of the "common pool resources" which should be accessible to all on an equal basis? Such questions go to the heart of the problem of environmental justice and pose critical choices for policy systems.

WHERE ARE WE NOW? POLICY RESPONSE TO THE CRITICAL CHOICES

In spite of the infinite deniability of the "environmental problem," policy systems have responded to the critical choices posed by environmental quality in a wide variety of ways. Some of these responses are in the form of multinational agreements. Other responses consist of actions taken by governments toward policies within their own borders. Taken together, the scope of these policy responses is large indeed. Since the wide scope of policy response makes it impossible to consider all policy in a summary chapter such as this, we will present selected policies that will illustrate the range and significance of policy response.

AMERICAN RESPONSE IN A MULTINATIONAL CONTEXT

Most of the general instruments of multinational agreement are employed in the environmental policy area. The most basic of these instruments is the *treaty*. Treaties are agreements between two or more nations that have the binding force of international law (in fact, treaties are a major source of international law). *Conventions* have the same character as treaties but deal with more specific and technical subjects. Since most international agreements on the environment have a specific subject (such as ozone depletion) or are technical in nature, conventions are important environmental policy instruments. *Protocols* are also common instruments of international agreement on environmental issues. A protocol is simply the record of a diplomatic conference, which shows the official agreements reached at the conference and which is signed by the participants. When there is disagreement on specific interpretations of a convention or protocol, many nations utilize a *declaration*, a statement of the policy of a particular government. While there are other forms of agreements between nations, such as the executive agreement, the convention, protocol, and declaration are the most frequently used in environmental policy.

Several important agreements relate to the problem of ozone depletion. The most important is the Montreal Protocol on Substances that Deplete the Ozone Layer. This protocol required that the thirty-seven signing nations reduce by one half their use of five CFCs and stop the use of three halons by 1998. But the Protocol left unregulated two of the most potent and widely used ozone-depleting compounds, methyl chloroform and carbon tetrachloride. Third World countries, especially India and China, refused to become parties to the agreement for reasons discussed earlier.

An important effort to strengthen the Montreal Protocol occurred in the London Accord of 1990. The London Accord provided for the complete phase-out of carbon tetrachloride by the year 2000 and of methyl chloroform by 2005, and it also accelerated the phase-out of the regulated CFCs and halons. More important, perhaps, the Accord addressed the problem of Third World participation. Third World nations were given a grace period of ten years to complete the phase-out. The Accord also authorized the creation of an international fund of $160 million for the purpose of helping Third World nations gain access to new technologies that do not use CFCs and providing financial assistance in implementing these technologies. As a result, China and India have become parties to the agreement. Taken together, then, the Montreal Protocol and the London Accord stand as important indicators that international cooperation in environmental concerns is possible.

On the other hand, the unsuccessful attempts to reach international agreements on global warming and acid rain are important indicators that substantial impediments exist to international cooperation on environmental problems. In spite of the convincing nature of the report of the Intergovernmental Panel on Climate Change, no general international agreement has been reached on global warming. Also, some nations have taken steps unilaterally to reduce greenhouse gases while other nations have virtually ignored the Panel's report. The former group includes the members of the European Community, Australia, Austria, Canada, Finland, Iceland, Japan, New Zealand, Norway, Sweden, and Switzerland. Among the nations that have virtually ignored the Panel's recommendations, the most notable is the United States. While the United States supported the IPCC and participates in various international conferences on global climate change, its policy response is best characterized by the words *minimal* and *cautious.*

The situation is the same with acid rain. There have been no general international agreements on acid rain, although several regional agreements have been reached, such as that between the United States and Canada. As with global warming, national action has been extensive in some countries and nonexistent in others. In the United States acid rain was caught in a political deadlock until the 1990s. The Clean Air Act Amendments of 1990 broke the deadlock and, as we shall see, made important provisions for reducing sulphur dioxide and nitrogen oxide emissions.

Protection of the ocean has been an area of significant international agreement. The most effective convention on ocean quality is the International Convention for the Prevention of Pollution from Ships, commonly known as MARPOL, adopted in 1973. The convention sets minimum distances from land for the dumping of sewage, garbage, and toxic waste from commercial ships. It also establishes limits on the amount of oil that can be discharged from ships. An annex to the convention, adopted in 1989, prohibits the dumping of plastics in the ocean and sets limits on other types of wastes. The London Dumping Convention of 1973 attempted to fill in the gaps of important pollutants not covered by MARPOL. It banned the discharge of heavy metals, petroleum products, and carcinogens, including radionuclides.

The largest body of international agreement on the ocean consists of various conventions entered into by nations on a regional basis. The most important effort in this regard is the regional seas program begun in 1974 under the sponsorship of the U.N. Environment Programme. This program attempts to set only general principles of pollution control and leave the detailed regulations of specific sources of pollution to separate protocols. The first agreement under the program was the 1976 Convention for the Protection of the Mediterranean Sea against Pollution. With the Mediterranean Plan as a model, other regional programs were adopted, including the Persian Gulf and the Gulf of Oman Plan in 1978, the Gulf of Guinea in 1981, the Caribbean and Gulf of Mexico in 1981, the Red Sea and the Gulf of Aden in 1982, and the South Pacific in 1986. More than 120 nations are participants in regional seas agreements. In addition, some have entered into agreements on inland waters. The most significant of these is the Great Lakes Water Quality Agreement of 1972 between the United States and Canada. Under the agreement, significant action has been directed to two of the major sources of contamination of the Great Lakes—municipal sewage and industrial waste water. The two countries have spent nearly $9 billion building and upgrading municipal sewage treatment facilities.

A final area of international effort to mitigate environmental deterioration has to do with the protection of endangered species. As its name implies, the Convention on International Trade in Endangered Species of Wild Fauna and Flora (CITES), adopted in 1973, attempts to protect endangered species by making it illegal to trade in the species. Species in need of protection are listed in three appendices. Those listed in Appendix I are rare and endangered, and trade in these species is prohibited. The species listed in Appendix II are threatened with extinction if trade is not strictly regulated. Listing in Appendix III affords the species the lowest degree of protection and simply calls attention to the danger to the species if long term trading practices continue. However, any nation can take out a reservation to (e.g., claim to be exempted from) an appendix listing. For example, five African nations have taken such reservations on the ban in ivory trading. As a result of these and other factors, opinion varies substantially on whether the CITES has reduced the threat to the elephant and the illegal trade in ivory (Honsang 1992, p. 66).

AMERICAN UNILATERAL POLICY RESPONSE

A second primary thrust of environmental policy is the unilateral response of individual nations. Because of space limitations, we will concentrate here on the United States, but we emphasize that many other nations have responded to various critical choices in the environment, some on a much more active basis. Nevertheless, the American policy response has been a varied one and can serve as a base line in analyzing and comparing the policy response of other nations. In looking at the United States, then, we will consider only those choices we believe all policy systems have to make about environmental issues.

The first effort at air quality legislation in the United States was the Clean

Air Act of 1970, which mandated the regulation of seven pollutants: particulates, sulfur dioxide, carbon monoxide, nitrogen oxide, ozone, hydrocarbons, and lead. Primary standards were to be set in such a way that the health of the vulnerable, especially the elderly and children, would be protected with an adequate margin of safety. Secondary standards were to be set to protect buildings, visibility, crops, and water. Together the two types of standards are referred to as National Ambient Air Quality Standards (NAAQS). On the basis of the NAAQS, the EPA was required to set emission standards for new stationary and mobile sources. New stationary source standards, called New Source Performance Standards, were to be set on an industry-by-industry basis. The act required EPA to take into account compliance costs, energy requirements, and environmental effects of each standard. With regard to mobile sources, the act established a detailed but flexible timetable for control of automobile and truck emissions. The EPA was given authority to change the timetables for compliance and has done so on several occasions. While the act vested authority for standards in the EPA, it also provided for the creation of state implementation plans. All fifty states have developed implementation plans, so the states, not the EPA, are the most important agents in the enforcement of standards.

The Clean Air Act was passed with the presumption that it would be amended, and Congress has done so several times. The most important amendments were the Clean Air Act Amendments of 1990, which mandated a reduction by the year 2006 in sulphur dioxide to 10 million tons less than 1980 emissions, and a reduction in nitrogen oxide to 2 to 4 million tons less than 1980 levels. This provision constituted a major break in the gridlock that had surrounded the acid rain issue in the United States. Additionally, the amendments called for a reduction in hydrocarbon levels of 35 percent and in nitrogen oxide levels of 60 percent from 1990 emission levels by the year 1996. The most contentious air quality issue is that of toxic air pollutants. The 1970 act specified only seven substances for regulation. The amendments identify 189 chemicals as being hazardous air pollutants. The EPA is required to identify emission sources of the chemicals and issue standards for emission. These standards are to require the installation of maximum achievable control technology, taking into account the cost.

The most innovative feature of the Clean Air Act Amendments is the establishment of marketable emission credits. First, imaginary "air sheds" are constructed, and total levels of emission of regulated substances are established for each air shed. Each emitter within an air shed is given an allowance determined on the basis of its average 1985–1987 fuel consumption. Emitters who released less than their allowance are permitted to sell a limited amount of their excess at a rate of $1,500 a ton; more allowances may be auctioned under certain circumstances. Emitters may emit more than their allowance if they are able to purchase credits. Presumably the total level of emissions within the air shed will stay within the range established by the standards. These provisions constitute one of the most extensive applications of market-driven strategies to environmental objectives.

The legislation that established the basis for surface water policy in the United States is the Clean Water Act. Originally passed in 1948, the act has been amended nine times, most significantly in 1972 (the Federal Water Pollution Control Act) and 1987 (the Water Quality Act). The two basic goals of surface water policy are to improve the nation's municipal sewage treatment plants and to reduce industrial effluents to zero discharge. For example, the 1972 legislation provided that there should be zero discharge by 1985 and that all the nation's surface waters be both fishable and swimmable by 1983. Both dates have long since passed and the goals obviously have not been realized. The policy strategy used is technology-forcing standards. To force the improvement of municipal sewage treatment technology, the 1972 amendments provided for substantial federal funding for the construction of sewage treatment plants. The 1987 amendments provided for federal funding through 1994, with a transition to full state and local responsibility for funding after that date. Concerning industrial emissions, firms in 1972 were originally given until 1977 to install "best practicable control technology" to reduce discharge to zero. The 1987 amendments required industry to install the "best available technology" no later than March 31, 1989, and failure to comply exposed the firm to enforcement action. The chief enforcement tool of the Clean Water Act is the National Pollutant Discharge Elimination System (NPDES) permit, which all industrial and municipal dischargers must obtain from the EPA, or from the states whose programs have been certified, before discharging effluents into the nation's surface waters. The permit is issued for five years and must be renewed to allow continued discharge. The EPA may issue a compliance order or bring a civil suit against a violator. In addition, individuals are authorized to bring "citizens' suits" in the U.S. district courts against violators of effluent limits.

A second major piece of legislation attempting to ensure a safe water supply is the Safe Drinking Water Act. The primary objective of the act, along with its five amendments, is to prevent harmful contaminants above specified levels in the nation's drinking water. Regulated contaminants include inorganic chemicals, organic chemicals, radionuclides, microbes, and turbidity. The EPA was required to contract with the National Academy of Sciences to study acceptable risks associated with regulated contaminants. Taking that study as the frame of reference, the administrator of the EPA was to establish maximum contaminant levels (referred to as MCLs) for each contaminant. These standards are not enforceable at the national level but are dependent on state action. The act also contained provisions relative to underground water, since it is an important source of drinking water. The most important of those provisions was the requirement that the EPA promulgate regulations for underground injection wells. Injection wells are used in a wide range of applications, and among the most important is the disposal of hazardous wastes. The act established a permit system for injection wells to be implemented by the states.

Finally, the United States has one of the most extensive networks of domestic legislation affecting the ocean of any nation in the world. There are thirteen

major pieces of legislation that attempt to establish marine policy: the Coastal
Zone Management Act (1972), the Deepwater Ports Act (1972), the Marine
Mammal Protection Act (1972), the Marine Protection Research and Sanctuaries
Act (1972), the Federal Water Pollution Control Act Amendments (1972), the
Endangered Species Act (1973), the Deep Water Port Act (1974), the Fisheries,
Conservation, and Management Act (1976), the Outer Continental Shelf Lands
Act (1978), the National Ocean Pollution Research and Monitoring Act (1978),
the Deep Seabed Hard Mineral Resources Act (1980), the American Fisheries
Promotion Act (1980), and the Ocean Thermal Energy Conversion Act (1980).
Two common themes run through all these acts (King 1986, p. 308). The first is
that the laws were anticipatory in nature, that is, they tried to prescribe policy
for conditions determined by analysts to lead to depletion, destruction, or
scarcity of marine resources with a "clear bias toward the future" (King 1986, p.
308). The second common theme is a concern for the ocean as a resource. The
objective of the legislation was to ensure a supply of energy and raw materials
from the ocean. Thus the future orientation of policymakers was directed not so
much toward environmental quality or the ecosystem as it was toward economic
objectives.

Hazardous waste has been the subject of extensive legislation. The first
effort at controlling toxic chemical waste was the Federal Insecticide, Fungicide,
and Rodenticide Act of 1947, aimed at controlling the use of pesticides in agricultural applications by requiring the registration of labels. Before a pesticide
could be marketed, it had to be registered, that is, a decision had to be made as
to what uses were safe and at what levels of application. The standard to be used
in the registration decision was the finding of "no unreasonable adverse effects"
from the use of the pesticides. The act was completely rewritten in 1972, updat-
ing both standards and the implementation process.

Two important components of hazardous waste policy were passed in
1976. These are the Toxic Substances Control Act and the Resource Conservation
and Recovery Act. The Toxic Substances Control Act, as its name implies, has as
its primary purpose the identification and control of toxic chemicals. Since as
few as 2 percent of all chemicals have been tested rigorously for their toxicity,
the act established a process for testing chemicals. An Interagency Testing
Committee was established to assist the EPA in determining which chemicals
should be tested. Also, the EPA was given general regulatory authority over
chemical hazards, including the prohibition of the manufacture, limitation on
the volume of production, restrictions on the use, the requirement of proper
notification of consumers, and selective controls over the disposal methods of
chemicals. The Resource Conservation and Recovery Act extended the TSCA's
provisions for control of disposal methods to the regulation of the "entire waste
stream." Producers of chemical waste were required to comply with regulations
regarding recordkeeping, reporting, the labeling of wastes, the use of appropriate containers, the provision of information on the waste composition, and the
use of a manifest system. Facilities that treat, store, or dispose of chemical waste
were also subjected to EPA regulation. Such facilities had to comply with regula-

tions regarding operating facilities, accident response plans, and closure requirements.

The TSCA and RCRA were designed to prevent contamination of the environment from chemical wastes. However, substantial contamination had already occurred. The Comprehensive Environmental Response, Compensation, and Liability Act of 1980, commonly known as Superfund, attempted to address this problem by giving the EPA broad statutory authority to respond to hazardous substances in the environment that posed any threat to the health of "any organism." The National Contingency Plan, developed under that grant of authority, established a strategy that involves two types of action. The first is the short-term removal of hazardous substances in emergency situations that pose a health or safety risk. The second is the long-term clean-up effort targeted to the "Superfund sites." These sites are listed on the National Priority List, which the EPA constructed using such standards as the quantity and nature of the hazardous materials, the likelihood of contaminating a water source, and the proximity of the release to population centers or sensitive natural environments. The National Priority List presently contains about 1,200 sites, and approximately 30,000 sites have been identified as potential Superfund sites.

The most intractable and long-lived hazardous waste is radioactive waste. As we indicated earlier, policy response was late in developing in the United States and is still the victim of policy paralysis. Ineffective as it is, American policy is based in several important distinctions about the types of nuclear waste. The first distinction is between nuclear waste resulting from military and that from commercial operations. Waste from military applications is stored at several U.S. locations, principally at the Savannah River Plant in South Carolina and the Hanford Reservation in the state of Washington. Military waste is not subject to the same public scrutiny as is commercial waste, but there is substantial evidence that most military sites have experienced considerable problems with containment.

The second distinction is between high-level waste, low-level waste, and uranium mill tailings. This distinction forms the basis of policy for regulating commercially produced nuclear waste. High-level nuclear waste is characterized by high radiotoxicity and heat output over a long period of time. The largest quantity of high-level waste is generated by the nuclear fuel process and by the reprocessing of spent fuel rods. Nuclear fuel production, usually referred to as fuel fabrication, results in high-level waste in the form of hulls or containers for the fuel elements and storage pond residues. The waste from the reprocessing of spent fuel rods is in liquid form and results from the exposure of the fuel rod to a solvent, usually tribtyl phosphate. Some spent fuel rods are unprocessed; these are highly radioactive and generate high levels of heat.

Commercial high-level waste is subject to the Nuclear Waste Policy Act of 1982, passed only after considerable debate and gridlock in Congress. General authority for regulating this waste was vested in the Nuclear Regulatory Commission, and specific authority over implementation was vested in the

Department of Energy. Strategy for containment of the waste was the construction of a deep underground depository. An amendment to the act in 1987 specified characteristics of the first site in such a way as to make Yucca Mountain, Nevada, the site for the first depository, which was authorized to receive either unprocessed spent fuel or the waste from reprocessing. The act also provided for temporary storage of some waste. For example, spent fuel rods from nuclear power plants had been stored either on site or at the few commercial facilities available, but those sites were strained to capacity. The Department of Energy was authorized to construct monitored, above-ground, retrievable facilities to store spent fuel until the rods could be retrieved for either reprocessing or permanent storage at the Yucca Mountain site. Costs of the overall program were to be met by a tax on the nuclear power industry. Fees levied on electricity generated by nuclear energy would be paid into a Nuclear Waste Fund targeted primarily to the construction and operation of the permanent facility.

Low-level nuclear waste in the United States is defined by exclusion. It consists of all radioactive waste other than high-level waste and uranium mine tailings. The waste takes many forms, including some very ordinary products, such as contaminated paper, gloves, construction debris, and other trash. Discarded contaminated equipment takes the form of tools, sealed carriers, and pipes. Wet waste consists of clean-up solutions, filter aids, oils, greases, and resins. Finally, various radioactive gases, such as Kr-85, are classified as low-level waste.

American policy on low-level waste was defined in the Low Level Radioactive Waste Act (LLRWA) of 1980, which vested primary responsibility for establishing management standards and criteria in the Nuclear Regulatory Commission. Beyond this, the act established two important policy principles. The first was the determination that low-level waste management is a state responsibility. In spite of the financial incentives designed to induce state action, however, a number of states simply failed to assume responsibility. The second principle encouraged states to form regional compacts for low-level waste management. There were serious problems in their efforts to do so, particularly the issue of which state would host the first site. Only one compact region, the Southeast, functioned at any level of effectiveness. The success of the Southeast was probably attributable to the existence of a low-level commercial facility already operating in the region. The LLRWA prescribes the technology of shallow land burial—near-surface disposal of the waste in excavated trenches. There is considerable uncertainty surrounding trench technology. The most significant problem is the bathtub effect. When the trench is filled, it is covered with two to ten feet of fill dirt. This capping material can be compromised by several forces, allowing water to infiltrate the trench, much as water fills a bathtub. The water in the trench seeps out into the ground, carrying with it radionuclides. At the Oak Ridge National Laboratory, for example, radionuclides leached from trenches installed below groundwater tables have been detected as far south as the city of Knoxville.

The final category of nuclear waste is uranium mine tailings. Considerable low-level waste is produced in the mining of uranium-bearing ore. Mill tailings are various soils and rocks left over from the mining process. Most have been simply left on site. Abandoned mine buildings and equipment may also be contaminated. There are twenty-four sites that have problems associated with uranium mine tailings, all but one in the West.

The American policy response to uranium mine tailings is the Uranium Mine Tailings Radiation Control Act of 1978. The act places overall authority for nuclear mine tailings in the Nuclear Regulatory Commission. Specific authority to implement the act was vested in the Department of Energy, which is required to meet EPA standards and to obtain a license from the Nuclear Regulatory Commission for its program at each site. The EPA was to promulgate standards by March 1983 and the DOE was to complete the stabilization program by March 1990. These schedules, like most in the environmental policy area, simply were not met. In fact, the DOE has become more a monitor of tailings sites than the remediator of such sites.

This section has sketched in summary form only the most significant legislation establishing environmental policy. There are a number of other statutes as well as volumes of regulations in the Federal Registry that constitute the full body of environmental policy. We now turn to the issue of how we got to where we are and the prospects for getting where we ought to be in environmental policy.

UNSCRAMBLING THE PUZZLE: HOW WE GOT TO WHERE WE ARE

We conclude this discussion with an important question: What is feasible policy, given the impediments to innovation? Environmental policy poses a troublesome dilemma in this regard. On the one hand, public support for policy action is high, and in fact it has remained consistently high for over twenty years (Dunlap and Mertig 1992). On the other hand, U.S. governments at all levels have failed to respond proportionately to public support. Such a dilemma suggests that the obstacles to policy action are particularly strong. A quick review of the most important impediments will provide a basis for what we believe is feasible environmental policy.

Certainly, policy cultures and myths are important elements in explaining American policy on the environment. The dualist culture is the dominant federalist culture within which U.S. environmental policy is rooted. The belief is pervasive that the national government is best at setting base-line standards and the states are best at implementing those standards. Thus dualism, with its highly decentralized power centers, helps explain why initial environmental policy decisions (new laws and regulations) often seem compromised or poorly constructed. As a result of pressures from lower levels in the federal system, environmental laws are softened, regulations are compromised, target dates are pushed further into the future, and critical policy needs are pushed aside in favor of regional or local preferences.

In some respects, dualism's effect on implementation is even more important. Environmental policy is implemented at separate levels of government, and what comes out of the "federalist meat grinder" may or may not be what was intended at the formulation stage. At the most basic level, state and local decision makers can simply stonewall the national policy objective. Beyond this, they can and do alter national objectives to fit their policy preferences (Wrightson 1986). Among other things, this means that national base-line standards are not implemented uniformly across the nation. Implementation can be very vigorous in some areas and very lax in others (Lester, Franke, Bowman, and Kraemer 1983).

The policy myths in the United States are also powerful impediments to policy action. Several of them are the basis for the argument that environmental quality is accomplished only at the cost of jobs. This argument carries the implication that the pursuit of environmental quality will also lower the standard of living for all Americans. The myth that the middle class is hit hardest by government action fuels this paranoia. The myth of government failure leads some Americans to have little faith in the capability of the system to respond to environmental degradation. The belief that we are better off isolated from other nations spawns a "go it our own way" mentality that undercuts efforts to work with other nations to solve problems that have global dimensions. These myths, along with others, have resulted in a cautious, limited, and sometimes contradictory approach to environmental policy.

The regional policy styles also contain elements that are impediments to policy action (see Box 6.2). Federalism accommodates the regions easily, and dualism further legitimizes the decentralized policy patterns. There are some regions, Ecotopia for example, in which environmental quality is given a high priority. In other regions, the word "environmentalism" is negatively charged and there is minimal commitment to policy that would enhance environmental quality.

| 6.2 | | *REGIONAL PREFERENCES AND NATIONAL POLICY* |

Very seldom does a specific piece of legislation make the national news media, but during 1994 the Federal Mining Act of 1872 was front-page news. The law was originally designed to stimulate development in the West by offering virtually free access to that region's mineral resources. The idea was that by giving away rights to gold and other minerals, mining companies would establish operations in the West, workers would move there, and the region would develop.

A hundred and twenty years later the act has become a nightmarish giveaway of American resources, often to foreign-owned firms. The media reported the following consequences of modern use of the act. The average price per acre paid by mining companies for public lands that they purchased for mining operations was between $2.50 and $5.00. The National Wildlife Federation estimated that the value of minerals removed from such lands each year was $3.6 billion. The national government collected no royalties on those minerals. Two companies in particular seem to benefit greatly: American Barrick Resources paid the national government $9,765 for land that has an estimated $10 billion in minerals, and Homestake Mining Company paid $310 for land with an estimated $646 million in gold deposits.

Any attempt to change the 1872 law to stop this massive giveaway of public resources is met with fierce opposition from Western politicians. These politicians have been successful to date in stopping any change in the law.

How can Western politicians exercise such power? Why should they want to stop reform? What is there in the Western regional culture that helps explain this bizarre situation?

Within the limited space of a single chapter we cannot discuss the implications for environmental quality of the culture of each region. Students should consider the following questions: What are the implications of the policy culture of my region for environmental policy? How active or inactive is my region in efforts to ensure environmental quality? Why is environmental policy in my region the way it is?

Some of the most serious impediments to policy are found in the policy structures themselves. In one of the most critical areas of environmental policy, that of international cooperation on global issues, policy structures are simply inadequate for effective functioning (see Box 6.3). While the range of multinational organizations for environmental policy is impressive, the primary problem is that of enforcement (Wells 1996). Although there are some sanctions that can be imposed, they are seldom applied in the environmental policy area. When sanctions are applied, their effectiveness depends a great deal on specific circumstances. Structures in the American policy system are fragmented and decentralized. Anyone who has attempted to gain information from or affect the decision of an environmental agency has encountered the problems of this fragmentation. State agency personnel claim that it is the Feds' responsibility, national agency personnel claim that the state should act, and local agency personnel tend to disclaim any power to act. Given the important functions that structures perform in the policy system, the impediments that they pose are especially difficult ones.

| 6.3 | *Is Global Enforcement of Multinational Agreements Possible?* |

The most far-reaching proposal for resolving the problem of enforcement of international agreements is the suggestion for a world legislative body with the power to impose environmental policy on nations. New Zealand was a strong advocate for this action at a conference held at the Hague in 1989. New Zealand's plan called for the establishment of an Environmental Protection Council as a unit of the United Nations. The Council would be empowered to supersede national authority on matters of environmental policy. A precedent for this sort of institution is found in the European Community: While the twelve member-nations retain sovereignty, policy adopted by the EC can have the same force as national legislation.

What do you think would be the various responses to such a proposal in the United States? How would our various policy cultures affect that response? How would our policy structures react to such a proposal?

In spite of strong public support for environmental policy, then, there are powerful impediments to policy action. Given these impediments, what is feasible policy? We believe that there are several courses of action the American policy system can and should take.

Concerning the threat to the ozone layer, all nations should take immediate steps to reduce the use of CFCs and other ozone-depleting substances. The Montreal Protocol represents an attempt by the participating nations to implement that principle. Most of the nations have made serious, good-faith efforts to structure national policy in ways consistent with the Protocol. The major problem remaining was participation by Third World nations. This problem was addressed by the London Accord. The Accord gave Third World nations a grace period of ten years to complete the phase-out of regulated substances, and it also authorized the establishment of an international fund, with an initial subscription of $160 million, to assist these nations in gaining access to new technologies. This action may well be the most important effort to date to accomplish environmental objectives through technology transfer. The necessary institutional structure and financial resources are present, and the technology transfer strategies should encourage Third World efforts to reduce ozone-threatening chemicals.

Several years ago the Intergovernmental Panel on Climate Change, an international group of scientists established under the auspices of the U.N. Environment Programme, devised a set of guidelines for government action on global warming. The report of the Panel provides an approach for defining feasible policy in all areas of critical choices in the environment. The report begins with a realistic assessment of greenhouse gases in the atmosphere and the current level of emissions of new gases. It then assesses the effects of the buildup on global climate. The result is a balanced, careful, and defensible statement of what can be expected if current rates of emissions continue. From this analysis, the report proceeds to a statement of the policy objective to be pursued: All nations should take immediate steps to reduce greenhouse gases. Implementation is to be on the basis of technological feasibility and cost effectiveness. Given these two criteria, the report recommends three strategies for the reduction of greenhouse gases: the more efficient use of energy, the employment of alternative fuels, and the planting of more forests to absorb greenhouse gases.

   The approach taken by the IPCC is an effective approach for all areas of the environment. In all critical choices, the American policy system should carefully identify what is happening, assess the results of current action, define a feasible policy objective, and identify strategies to accomplish that objective. A number of nations have attempted to implement the Panel's recommendation, and their experiences have demonstrated that the approach leads to feasible policy that judiciously takes on the serious issue of global warming and can serve as a model for other areas of environmental policy.

   Given the recommendations of the Intergovernmental Panel on Climate Change, reduction of greenhouse gases represents something of a test case of national will. Some nations, listed earlier in the chapter, have taken the Panel's recommendations seriously and adopted policies that have been effective in reducing greenhouse gases. Other nations, most notably the United States, have taken minimal action to implement the recommendations. A feasible approach for the United States would be to emphasize degradation and mitigation costs of global warming. This country has emphasized compliance costs almost exclusively, even to the point of requiring consideration of compliance costs in the decision to adopt new regulations, as was mentioned earlier. A policy that estimates full costing—including compliance, degradation, and mitigation costs—would provide the basis for more effective policy in this country.

   Concerning acid rain, it is certainly technically and economically feasible to reduce the emission of the sulphur dioxide and nitrogen oxide that form the chemical basis for acid rain. The Clean Air Act Amendments of 1990 suggest clearly that it is feasible to break the political deadlock that has prevented serious efforts in the past. The progress made between the United States and Canada, as well as the substantial multinational efforts in the European Community, suggest that multinational cooperation is possible. These signs indicate that an international protocol similar to the Montreal Protocol is feasible to reduce acid rain. The use of marketable emission credits, authorized by the Clean Air Act Amendments of 1990 in the United States, establishes a technological and cost-effective means of controlling overall emissions. All of these things mean that, barring a major change in political climate in the United States, the policy system should be able to respond effectively to the critical choices associated with acid rain.

The critical choices associated with chemical residuals are probably the most difficult ones to make. The reason for the intractability of the chemical waste problem is clear. The sheer number of chemicals in production and use yields a volume of waste beyond the capacity of current U.S. technology. The United States has adopted a hazard-reduction strategy, attempting only to reduce the hazards associated with chemical waste but with little or no concern about the amount of waste. A more feasible approach is the waste-reduction strategy of the European Community. The European experience suggests two very important things. First, waste-reduction strategies can reduce the volume of chemical waste to the point where land disposal is unnecessary or minimal. The United States places primary reliance on land disposal, but the land is no longer able to accommodate the volume of waste this country produces. Second, a waste-reduction strategy is an incentive for recycling programs. Many feasible policies for recycling are found in Japan and Australia also (Wells 1996). Certainly, the United States should add chemical waste reduction strategies to its policy and accelerate its emphasis on recycling.

There is simply not enough information available to be able to identify feasible policy for nuclear waste. The strategy of deep geological disposal is the most attractive for high-level nuclear waste. The selection of the Yucca Flats, Nevada, site suggests also that it is feasible to construct and operate a facility. However, if there are surprises in the nuclear wastebasket, as some have speculated, the problems associated with "controlling" the sites and disposing of irradiated materials may very well be beyond the capacity of current policy strategies.

The outlook for feasible policy for environmental problems, then, is both discouraging and encouraging. The serious problems are many and varied. A part of the problem is technological. For example, there simply is no known technology for the safe disposal of radioactive waste. What is most discouraging in the United States, however, is the issue of institutional capacity. The fragmented policy structures of the American system do not bode well for making the critical choices necessary for the ecological basis of life. Also, the wide gap between high public support of environmental policy and weak government action suggests that the obstacles to effective policy action are strong indeed.

We would emphasize, however, that the outlook for environmental policy is also encouraging. A number of effective actions have been taken. Among the most encouraging of these are the various international agreements on ozone depleting substances. The Montreal Protocol and the London Accord demonstrate that it is possible for nations to cooperate in solving environmental problems. Since most problems have global dimensions, these indicators of cooperation are especially important. Some policy actions in the United States are also grounds for optimism. The Clean Air Act Amendments of 1990 demonstrate that it is possible to break what appeared to be an intractable political gridlock. Actions at the state and local levels suggest considerable vitality at the grass roots, and the efforts of Los Angeles and Denver demonstrate that this vitality can be converted into effective policy action. The protection of the ecological basis of life should be a top priority of governments at all levels.

 **CHAPTER 7**

ECONOMIC POLICY

POLICIES AND CHOICES FOR PROSPERITY

This chapter examines the major domestic economic development strategies used by the national, state, and local governments. It starts with a look at the roots of governmental economic policies in the preferences of the Founders of the Republic which have guided the general traditions of government intervention in the market. It then describes the major policies of the national, state, and local governments and the issues surrounding how effective those policies are. Finally, it examines unresolved issues and critical choices posed for economic policies, especially those of economic justice in a consumption-oriented society, and the controversial and dubious claim that environmental protection sacrifices economic growth.

Issues about how government should relate to the economy have been front-burner topics from the earliest days of the nation. Considerable debate has occurred over the economic interests and motives of those who drafted the Constitution of 1787 (Beard 1941). Whatever those interests and motives were, economic problems were the catalyst for the convening of the Convention that proposed the Constitution. For example, the Annapolis Convention was called to settle economic issues between Maryland and Virginia, issues that were so intractable that the only thing the delegates could accomplish was to call a general convention to meet in Philadelphia in 1787. That convention produced the American constitution and sparked a continuing debate about governmental intervention in the economy.

But what kind of economic policies did the Constitution envision? More basically, what kind of economy was promoted in the Constitution? As the title of an important book on the subject asks, "How Capitalistic Is the Constitution?" (Goldwin and Schambia 1982). What is the proper relationship between government and the economy? What economic policy should the American government pursue? These are not easy questions. In the search for answers and potential solutions, we begin again with the critical economic policy choices that face us.

The United States has been in the process of developing an economic policy for 200 years. Considerable progress has been made, as reflected in the relatively well-developed strategies of national monetary and fiscal policy. However, the American policy system still faces critical choices about the economy. Ironically, the first is a choice among various views about the proper relationship between government and the economy.

THE SCOPE OF GOVERNMENT ECONOMIC ACTIVITY: COMPETING VISIONS

Delegates to the Constitutional Convention of 1787 brought at least three quite different visions of the relationship between government and the economy. Each had powerful and effective advocates. The first vision was that of James Madison and is known as the theory of *compound federalism*. The second was advocated by Thomas Jefferson and is known as *dualist federalism*. The third vision was associated with Alexander Hamilton and is designated *centralist federalism*. Each of these grand conceptualizations has formed great political cultures that have guided the policy and belief systems of most Americans. Within each culture are multifaceted and complex theories about how government should function in a society, including rather specific prescriptions on the role of government in the economy (Hamilton and Wells 1990). This chapter will focus on the economic policy elements in the three great visions of constitutional design.

James Madison no doubt had the most influence on the design of the new national government at the 1787 Constitutional Convention (see Epstein 1984; Farrand 1966). A key to understanding Madison's compound federalism theory is the word *compound*. Madison favored a constitutional system that blended various elements, including different institutions at the national level (separation of powers) and the different jurisdictions represented by the nation and the states (federalism). He argued that the new blending would be truly compound in that it would incorporate the tensions, powers, and functions of the many elements, and the result would be a total greater than the sum of the separate parts. Power to develop and implement economic policy, in Madison's scheme, was dispersed among the various institutions at the national level and between the nation and the states. Perhaps the primary goal to be sought in this blending of economic powers was economic development. The federal system would safeguard a stable economic order by securing property against the threat of strong factions, mass movements, or public revolts or interests. Madison also joined with Hamilton in supporting the use of government powers to stimulate commercial activity.

Alexander Hamilton, an intense and brilliant student of economics, supported an even more active role for government in the economy. The centralist political culture, which he largely created, was rooted in the belief that relatively strong control by national elites was necessary for the most effective economic system. In this view, the prosperity of the nation was virtually equivalent to the prosperity of the business classes. Long before the theories of trickle-down economics, Hamilton argued that government should subsidize commercial expansion with taxes, land grants, public works projects, and government financing, and the resultant benefits to the economic elite would "percolate down" to other groups in society (Fine 1956, p. 15). Within the new government, Hamilton's influence as secretary of the treasury was even stronger. The Federalist party, which Hamilton virtually created, led the nation in adopting policies that created central bank controls, stabilized government finances, imposed largely regressive taxes, provided numerous government subsidies for business elites, and established centralized control over imports and currencies. In this regard Hamilton may be regarded as the American Adam Smith, but with very different and much more energetic effects on governmental use of economic powers than Smith had on England with his distinctly *laissez-faire* ideas (Hacker 1970).

Thomas Jefferson's ideas, which partly echoed those of more Southern, agricultural, and rural interests, posed the most contrast to those of Madison and Hamilton. If Madison and Hamilton proposed the "positive state," then Jefferson proposed the "negative state." As Fine expressed the matter, "That governments should minister directly to the needs of the people by positive action, that it should regulate to any extent the economic life of the nation, were ideas foreign to [Jefferson]" (Fine 1956, p. 12). The phrase "a government is best that governs least" summarizes many of Jefferson's overall views. When government action is necessary, Jefferson argued, it should be the government "closest to the people" that takes action. Thus Jefferson supported an extreme decentralization that would have made local governments the determinors of most policy. But however extreme were his views of decentralization, Jefferson as President developed more active commercial goals. As President, he used national power in dramatic ways to accelerate national economic growth and commercial expansion. The best-known policy Jefferson pursued was the Louisiana Purchase, which literally doubled the size of the colonies, stretching it to the Missouri River. A great irony was that the Louisiana Purchase lessened the dominance of state government over economic development, since it led to vigorous use of central banking, westward expansion, and huge subsidies and land grants for railroad and canal construction. However, the main thrust of the dualist political culture articulated by Jefferson continues as our strong belief in populist democracy, grass roots local government, and our opposition to government interference in the economy, particularly in local business.

These three great political cultures, with their prescriptions for government's role in the economy, have remained powerful in guiding American economic policy. Each has varied in strength at different periods over the course of American history. This explains in large part the cyclical nature of American economic policy (Hamilton and Wells 1990, pp. 34–35). During the 1890s, for example, dualism largely determined national economic policies, especially those affecting the Supreme Court, which virtually read the theories of laissez faire into the Constitution and prevented vigorous national regulation of monopolies or even of child labor. Compound federalism gave rise to the "cooperative" style of federal and matching categorical grants popular in the 1960s and 1970s. Hamilton's centralism—conditioned by an occasional nod to dualism, as in the Reagan and Clinton presidencies—is the main guide to national economic policy in contemporary America. The three cultures frame most of the debates about critical economic policy issues, debates that are never clearly resolved: Should government be a positive force to affect economic conditions or should it assume a laissez-faire position that leaves economic development to the dynamics of the economy? If the choice is for positive government, then which vision of positive government? Should we choose Madison's compound vision, which has national, state, and local governments interacting to regulate or provide services or subsidies? (Environmental regulation and farm subsidy and development policies illustrate such choices.) Or should the choice be that of Hamilton's vision with centrally directed policy by the nation's economic elites (as illustrated by the regulation of nuclear power generation or by the nearly all-powerful Federal Reserve System)? Or should we turn to the currently popular idea of turning power back to the states, with more block grants, fewer requirements, and less national monies (the ideas of dualism, most popular among Republicans)?

IS A NATIONAL AMERICAN INDUSTRIAL POLICY POSSIBLE?

Economic development questions are inextricably bound up with two issues. The first is the more obvious of the two: How much can and should we produce and consume? The second is the character dimension: What kind of people do we want to be? Contemporary Americans are more accustomed to thinking about the first dimension than about the second. However, the framers of the American system were very concerned about both.

Several features of early American attitudes toward economic development deserve mention. The first has to do with the attitudes toward the use of land. Among the Founders, at least, these attitudes were deeply affected by the lingering shadow of the English manor. Morton Horwitz described those attitudes: "… land was not essentially an instrumental good or a productive asset but rather a private estate to be enjoyed for its own sake" (1977, p. 36). Early American courts interpreted the law in a way consistent with this view. Court decisions, particularly in the state courts (those courts closest to the people), were directed to discourage the use of land for economic development. As

Horwitz suggests, it took a transformation of American law to create conditions under which land could be used for productive purposes.

A second aspect of the attitudes of the Founders was their prevailing political theory, which saw a stable economy as desirable but viewed intensive economic growth as incompatible with a republican form of government (McDonald 1982, p. 53). This legacy included Plato, who argued that rough economic equality was necessary for a republic, and Montesquieu, who believed that if economic equality ceased to exist the republic would collapse. At a policy level these attitudes translated, especially in Andrew Jackson's presidency, into a strong bias against "privileged wealth" (perhaps the earliest form of American populism). This bias had many ramifications, not the least of which was the difficulty in establishing a system of national banks. These two general attitudes, along with others, suggest clearly that the Founders, while deeply committed to an expanding economy (especially Hamilton), were also deeply concerned with the nature of that economic development and its effect upon individuals and society (especially Madison, Jefferson, and the anti-federalists).

As we shall see later in the chapter, the twin pillars of U.S. national domestic economic policy are monetary policy and fiscal policy. The U.S. government, unlike that of most other advanced nations, has not developed an industrial policy. A fully developed industrial policy would almost certainly run counter to many Americans' beliefs about the proper role of government in the economy and would require acceptance of a positive role of government, reflecting Alexander Hamilton's dream of an energetic republic. Chalmers Johnson expresses this cultural factor in this way: "It [industrial policy] is first of all an attitude, and only then a matter of technique. It involves the specific recognition that all government measures ... have a significant impact on the well-being or ill health of whole sectors, industries and enterprises in a market economy" (Johnson 1984, p. 7). Johnson is certainly correct in saying we would need new attitudes to accept a wide range of government activities targeted to developing and retrenching industries for the purpose of global competitiveness. Such a change may be beyond the cultural values of many Americans. Robert Reich, secretary of labor under Clinton and Harvard professor of public policy and economics, has written about how Americans are so strongly entranced by myths of enemies abroad, triumphant entrepreneurialism, corruption, and poverty and laziness that we have great difficulty constructing policies not guided by these ideas, when there are many innovations practiced around the world (1987). In Reich's view, these respective myths cause Americans to be suspicious about government economic planning as "too foreign and dangerous, against the entrepreneurial spirit, and too corrupt and incompetent." In chapters 3 and 11 we explain also how *government* economic action such as planned industrial policy is severely limited by federalist traditions and other myths.

While such attitudinal impediments to industrial planning are a reality, in practice the United States has made substantial progress toward a national industrial policy, although uncoordinated and thus haphazard. The historic national spending on roads, defense research, the space program, and other infrastructure all illustrate giant steps toward an industrial policy. Both Hamilton and Madison wanted government to spend monies energetically to develop supporting facilities and technologies necessary for an expanding economy. Many economists recognize that government spending is not just consumption but is also investment for research, technology, product or policy demonstration (naval nuclear power led to electric nuclear power), and job stimulation, as policy history shows (see Chapter 2). The U.S. government was from the beginning engaged in road, canal, and postal construction. Presently there is a high level of concern for a "deteriorating" infrastructure. Centralized planning to revitalize our infrastructure (roads, sewers, transportation, bridges) means that our policy system is on the edge of national industrial planning. In fact, some states have almost full-blown industrial policies (described in the last half of this chapter), and all are involved in at least some planning toward making enterprises in their states competitive nationally and globally.

American conservatives have generally been opposed to a planned national industrial policy on cultural or ideological grounds. Many of them raise the spectre of a mercantilist or "socialist" state, with government bureaucrats deciding what and where goods can be produced and for whose benefit. On the other hand, the political leader who has had the most significant influence on the movement toward a national industrial policy is Ronald Reagan. Reagan, and later Bush and Clinton, virtually defined the economic policy agenda in terms that are at the heart of an industrial policy—job development, modernization of industry, world competitiveness, development of high technology, and orderly investment, all stimulated, underwritten, or subsidized by the government. So the critical choice is whether the American national policy system can proceed on an agenda defined in industrial policy terms and along the paths developed by state governments. In national politics we talk the game but so far have largely refused to play it.

WHAT DOES THE NATIONAL DEBT REALLY MEAN?

If the question of the general role of government in the economy has been divisive, the issue of the national debt has been even more so. The issue is not simply whether the debt has been a positive or negative factor in the American economy. Both analysts and the general public tend to divide sharply on many specific questions about the debt, creating a complex grab-bag of issues such as the following: Will the debt bankrupt the nation? Whose interests does the debt serve? On whom does the burden of the debt fall? Is the debt manageable? Can the American system afford the debt anymore? What is the economic impact of the debt?

Many conflicting answers are given to these important questions. Perhaps the most critical choice facing the American policy system in regard to the national debt has to do with coming to an agreement on which issues the debt raises for society. In short, what does the debt mean and what are its effects in the American economy and policy systems?

Virtually all of the explosive growth of the national debt occurred in the 1980s. In fiscal year 1979, Carter's last year in office, the federal deficit stood at $66 billion, but by 1991 it had dramatically mushroomed to $300 billion per year. As a percentage of the total economy (percent of GNP), the annual national deficit doubled in the 1980s compared with twenty years earlier, rising from between zero and 4 percent in the 1960s and 1970s to between 3 and 6.3 percent in the 1980s. The Clinton deficit reduction plan, passed in 1993, was claiming reductions of $125 billion, estimates that generally were supported by Congressional Budget Office analyses of the package the year before. David Calleo, a noted scholar of both public and private debt and its influence on the economy, concluded that the huge deficits were the result of four main factors: President Reagan's tax cuts, which did not spark increased revenues (as alleged by supply-side economists); increases in spending for defense; human resources; and net interest on the debt (mainly payments by the Treasury to investors in government bonds and securities). (See Calleo 1992, pp. 99, 143.)

Economists disagree how serious a threat the debt is. History can provide some clues. In fact, the United States has never been out of debt. The government of the Continental Congresses incurred debt as a means of financing the Revolutionary War. This debt was assumed by the government under the Articles of Confederation and passed on to the government that was established by the Constitution. Thus the United States was born as a debtor nation and has never been out of debt. The closest to a debt-free status was in 1840, when the national debt was $3.5 million.

In historic perspective, one of the important features of the national debt is that it has been an essential part of the nation's financial market. The debt has functioned as both a long-term and short-term medium of investment of great significance. As a long-term medium, the debt has provided individual savers and investment institutions with a wide variety of securities that offer the attractive feature of "being safe." As a short term medium, it has provided individuals and corporations a wide range of flexible short term securities. In both instances, national securities such as savings bonds and treasury notes have been extremely well managed. This means simply that the national debt is an essential part of the nation's financial markets. As one analyst observed several decades ago, "... if the national debt were to disappear, something would have to be invented to replace it" (Dale 1970, p. 106). The issue of whether or not the debt is manageable is faced by the simple historic fact that the financial markets managed the growing national budget deficits with remarkable efficiency through a complex array of short-term, medium-term, and long-term securities.

So what are the critical choices to be made about today's debt? In our view, choices must be made in two areas. The first has to do with the potentially inflationary tendency of the debt. The second has to do with its "burden," that is, the different ways the debt affects different people. In short, can the debt be managed without inflation and in such a way that its income distribution effect is equitably distributed across the population?

There are several factors to be considered about the potentially inflationary effect of the debt. The first is obvious: The debt may become so politically unpopular that policymakers will be tempted increasingly to use sleight-of-hand tricks, such as using Social Security Trust Fund revenues to help balance it out, or passing budget plans that call for action in the future, or even printing money to relieve debt pressures. Such action has been taken in the past. The budgets proposed by the Reagan and Bush administrations and passed by Congress in the 1980s became rather infamous for sleight-of-hand accounting. The budget deficits resulting from World War II, thought to be unacceptably large at the time, were financed largely by printing new money (which helped increase inflation from 1945 to 1948).

The second factor has to do with the debt's effect on private savings. Rather than print new money or use sleight-of-hand budgeting to obscure deficits, policymakers since 1945 have generally relied upon private savings (e.g., investments in government bonds and securities). There are two potentially inflationary dangers in such action. The first danger, argued by the supply side economists, is that private savings that are diverted to finance budget deficits are not available for investment in an expanding economy. Inadequate investment in the productive capability of the economy can have an inflationary impact, since monies are diverted to consumption (inflationary demand). A second danger is in the types of securities issued to fund the deficit. To make a complex issue overly simple, too heavy reliance upon short-term debt securities can be inflationary. This is the case because short-term securities are readily available for use—in street language they are "near money," and in technical language they are very "liquid"—and therefore movement from long-term to short-term securities has some of the same effect as does an increase in the money supply. Finally, the size of the debt, particularly as it is linked to the size of annual deficits, limits the use of fiscal policy (i.e., limits legislative spending) to stabilize the economy. We will discuss fiscal policy in a later section. Here it is sufficient to say that interest payments on the national debt are "uncontrollables" in the national budget—they must be paid. When such mandatory items are high, as they are today, they tend to limit the freedom of policymakers to use revenues for other purposes, thus reducing monies available for national needs. This means that critical choices have to be made to ensure that the debt is not inflationary. Can policymakers withstand the temptation to use sleight-of-hand measures or even to print money to relieve political pressures about the debt? What is the impact of the debt on private savings? When does the debt, and interest paid on it, become so large that it erodes the national ability to use revenues to pay for programs?

The second critical choice about the debt is on the issue of fairness. What

are the distributional effects of the debt and are those effects equally distributed across all segments of society? Are some made better off by the debt
while others are left worse off? While the numbers are very complex and difficult to obtain, the answer is that the debt has different impacts on different
segments of society.

The dynamics of the process are easy enough to sketch. Interest payments
on the national debt constitute a massive transfer of wealth. The total dollars in
interest payments vary over the years, depending on a number of factors. In
recent years the amounts are roughly between $200 and $250 billion annually,
making interest on the national debt the third largest single item in the national
government budget. Even when interest payments are at their lowest, the payments represent a significant transfer of wealth. Thus the question: Who benefits
and who pays? Beneficiaries are obviously those institutions and individuals
who hold debt instruments. Ironically, various government agencies, especially
the Federal Reserve Bank, which we will discuss later, owns a lot of the debt.
Many publicly supported retirement systems invest heavily in debt instruments
also. However, a disproportionate benefit from government securities goes to
upper-middle and upper-income individuals. Middle-income individuals invest
modestly in debt instruments and the poor virtually not at all. Taxpayers are
also obviously those who provide the revenues needed to make the interest payments. Again paying taxes is widely distributed among the American people,
but approximately 40.4 percent of taxes are paid by poor, working-class, and
middle-income individuals. Thus the national debt disproportionately benefits
upper-income groups and disproportionately costs middle-income groups.

This inequitable effect can be described as a "Robin Hood effect in
reverse," with the national debt taking from middle-income individuals and
giving to the rich. So one critical policy choice involves the question of how
government can structure its debt and its tax system so that benefits and costs
fall more equally on all groups in society.

THE BALANCED BUDGET AMENDMENT RIDES AGAIN: UNCERTAIN CHANGE, UNCERTAIN EFFECTS

The proposal to pass an amendment to the Constitution to balance the budget
is gaining consideration. After the 1992 elections the amendment quickly
passed the House of Representatives, where Republicans gained clear control,
but failed to pass in in the U.S. Senate. The proposed amendment would have
to pass the Senate by a two-thirds vote and then face the obstacle of approval
by three-quarters of the state legislatures.

To understand this proposal, it is important to examine the history of
such proposals. The recent amendment is just the latest of many proposals to
reform the budgetary process.

Prior to World War I the budget process at the national level was an uncoordinated wonderland of piecemeal action. Each congressional committee had certain agencies and programs under its jurisdiction and would recommend appropriations for them. Congress would act on each recommendation as it came out of a committee, without coordinating it with other appropriations it had made. Two significant results came from this system. First, congressional committees became little fiefdoms with special relationships to the agencies they controlled. All sorts of "pork barrel" and privileged deals resulted from this cozy arrangement. "Pork," or favoritism toward one's district, is as old as the nation, and not the invention of today's politicians. The second result was little attention to the overall levels of spending. While there were periodic outcries over national spending, this was not a serious problem. This was the age of laissez-faire economics, and national spending was not a large share of total production. Also, the United States was in a period of an expanding economy. World War I changed that situation, however. National expenditures went from a low of just over $734 million before 1915 to a wartime peak of $18.5 billion. More important, the postwar low expenditure was just under $3 billion. So World War I resulted in a massive expenditure during the war, and an increase in "normal" peacetime expenditures of 300 percent. Both increases were funded in large part by debt, as was the case also during World War II.

These circumstances produced the nation's first major battle over the budget. Much that was heard then is heard today. Like today, the President (Taft) called for the implementation of simple, businesslike budget systems (no one at that time paid attention to bloated businesses and the need to downsize them). Like today, the Republican party platform (of 1916) blamed the Democrats for all problems, accusing them of shameless raids on the Treasury. And like today, while calling for a balanced budget, the Republicans hoped to throw in a tax cut for businesses. The result: the nation's first major budget reform, the Budget and Accounting Act of 1921.

One thing the act called for was an executive budget process. The President would submit a unified budget to Congress, and Congress retained full power to appropriate. To assist the President, the act established the Bureau of the Budget. Expectations ran high. The second director of the Bureau addressed the President in lofty but familiar tones:

> "We still follow you, Mr. President, singing the old and tried battle song, economy with efficiency…. May we continue to sing it until in a noble paean of praise it heralds the day when taxes cease to be burdensome, and serve what is a grateful expression … of the numberless privileges and boundless blessings we enjoy in the most favored Nation of the earth." (quoted in Kimmel 1959, p. 96)

The experience of this reform was to be duplicated many times over. There have been numerous attempts by Congress to reform the budget process: the Budget and Impoundment Control Act of 1974, and the Gramm-

Rudman-Hollings Emergency Deficit Reduction and Balanced Budget Act of 1985 were two among many. Each made significant changes in both process and institutions, but none brought the budget under control, reduced the deficit, or lowered the national historical debt. Both the deficit and the debt increased significantly.

There have also been numerous attempts by the executive branch to reform the budget process: planning, programming, and budgeting of the Kennedy and Johnson administrations, zero-based budgeting of Jimmy Carter, the cost-benefit justifications under Reagan, and the line item veto proposals of Reagan, Bush, and Clinton. None had appreciable effects.

Numerous Presidential commissions have also been touted as ferreting out waste in the national government. Recently the "reinventing government" commissions of Vice-President Gore have been active. Probably less useful was the high-flying Grace Commission, under corporate magnate J. Peter Grace in the Reagan years. That commission spent literally millions, with great hoopla, while identifying very little real waste and reducing even less.

Today's balanced budget amendment is the latest in this long line. Several problems are associated with the amendment. First, it will not add new powers to either the legislative or the executive branch. If the political will to submit balanced budgets is lacking, what will happen? Politicians are clever enough to use "creative accounting" many times over, in addition to other methods. The states have much experience with this device, even though laws require most states to balance budgets. For example, Georgia has a balanced budget provision in its constitution, but it still has significant state debt. So do California and many others. Also, both in states and in the nation the law establishes many items as "off budget," that is, not part of the executive budgets submitted to legislatures. The current proposed amendment puts several items off limits from cuts or budget calculations: Social Security, defense, and interest paid on the national debt (i.e., rich foreign and domestic investors in government stocks and bonds).

Finally, what would happen if everyone took such an amendment seriously? Balancing the budget would require facing the grave difficulties of greatly increased taxes, deeply cut entitlements, or both. Which taxes? Which entitlements?

Most important, a balanced budget would have to face the problems of spending increases and lower revenues during a recession. Most economists insist that "good" deficits are run when increased monies are spent on unemployment compensation, which stabilizes economic demand in a recession and keeps people fed and basic bills paid while they wait out the cycle and search for work. Without that kind of deficit spending, the economy can quickly get worse. As the recessions in 1929 especially, and 1948, 1982, and 1991 clearly show, without a lot of temporary budget-busting *anti-recessionary* spending (mostly on unemployment compensation) the economy can nosedive quickly from a bad recession to a worse one and can even spin into a Depression (1930), partly *because of* restrictions on spending, or efforts to keep a budget balanced. (In 1929 and 1930 we had balanced budgets, which did not stave off, and in fact probably made worse the Great Depression.) Any amendment that does not temporarily lift the requirement for a balanced budget for anti-recession spending and conditions (the current one does not) can risk plunging the nation into a Depression. Some things are worse than mismatched numbers on a page.

We believe the most likely results of a balanced budget amendment will take one of four forms in the next ten years. First, it may not be passed by the Senate or by three-quarters of the states. Second, if it does eventually pass, there will be a period of initial cuts in programs amid gargantuan political conflicts over taxes and cuts, and there will be superbattles of resistance by states that do not want to pick up the bills for national program cuts. Third, such an amendment, if followed to the letter during a recession, would likely worsen the situation and potentially lead to Depression conditions. Thus the fourth and most likely path may be that politicians will eventually not want to stare into the barrels of both of these guns for too long. Instead, they will find ways to outmaneuver the amendment, as they so often have in the past. The national political culture has not yet resolved which it truly favors: what deficit spending provides for both good and ill, or what a balanced budget might lead to.

THE DOMESTIC ECONOMIC POLICIES OF GOVERNMENTS

Governments use four general kinds of policies to stabilize, substitute for, stimulate, and regulate the private market. Most of these policies actually occur in an intergovernmental sense, with the actions of national, state, or local governments combining to produce policy.

1. *Monetary policy*, except for state regulation of banks, insurance, and savings and loans, is mainly the province of the national government. It involves principally the direct regulation of the money supply and interest rates through the Federal Reserve system of banks, and secondarily it involves the national regulation of stocks, securities, and savings and loans.

2. *Fiscal policies* are under shared control by the national, state, and local legislatures. Fiscal policy covers all annual spending, but of particular interest to economists is spending that is deliberately targeted for economic stimulation, services, or jobs.

3. *Regulatory policies* are shared by the nation and the states, although regulation is somewhat dominated by national policies. The history of the growth of regulation—of industry, trade, social behavior, and state and local governments—and the current nature of shared responsibility for regulation are briefly covered in Chapter 2.

4. *Development policies* have become more the province of state and local governments than of the national government in the 1980s (described later in this chapter). Development policies are actually part of fiscal policies and include all forms of public spending and organization that provide services, subsidies, aid to business, and even direct products or services from govern-

ments (education, electricity, sewers) that promote or augment the growth of the economy.

Following the unusual activities of the government in the economy in World War II and the New Deal before it, the stance of national economic policy since the late 1940s has been described as macroeconomic. In macroeconomic policies the national government (and in fact the states also) seeks to stimulate or restrict production, consumption, trade, and employment so as to minimize the shock effects of recessions and expansions, and particularly to avoid a repeat of the Great Depression of the 1930s. Generally the economy is subject to a five- to eight-year business cycle—an oscillation between periods of high and low production and employment. The goals of monetary and fiscal policies are to minimize the inflation, unemployment, and other effects of recessions and expansions. Regulatory policies are intended to control the hazardous effects of business operation (pollution, accidents, unsafe products, etc.) and development policies are aimed at enhancing growth in sectors of the economy.

The Employment Act of 1946 has been referred to as the statutory statement of the postwar mixed economy. It formally defined the policy objectives of the national government relative to the economy. These objectives are three. First, the national government is to adopt the policy that ensures full employment, to ensure that every American who wants a job can find one. Second, the national government is to take action to ensure full production, to ensure that the factories, farms, and other enterprises of the American economy are producing at their full potential. Third, the national government is to adopt policy that will ensure the full purchasing power of the American dollar, to ensure that the value of American currency is not eroded by inflation. These three responsibilities—full employment, full production, and full purchasing power—set the parameters of national economic policy today. Such a policy role for the national government is probably beyond the fondest dreams of Alexander Hamilton and his energetic republic.

Certainly the national government has energetically pursued these three policy objectives. The instruments by which it attempts to do so are the twin strategies of fiscal and monetary policies. These two strategies were once thought to be incompatible with each other (Friedman and Heller 1969). Thus there were some policymakers who urged the adoption of monetary policy while others argued for fiscal policy. In fact, the government has used both strategies simultaneously from the beginning of its activity under the Employment Act. Monetary policy and fiscal policy have been the two great pillars of American postwar national economic policy.

MONETARY POLICY

Ask the average American what money is and how much of it is in circulation and he or she is likely to think you are crazy. Of course, money consists of those coins and greenbacks with which we are all familiar even if they are in short supply for us as individuals. And, of course, the average American will say, the amount of money in circulation is the sum total of all coins and green-backs that are held by individuals and institutions.

Economists, on the other hand, have had a somewhat more difficult time pinning down the slippery concept of money. Money obviously is the medium of exchange in any economy. Generally, governments assume a monopoly over what constitutes money and, by implication, over the amount of those objects in circulation. But this formulation is made complex by the power of other institutions to "create" money. Thus economists are forced to invent several different categories of money supply. *M-1*, for example, consists of "money" that can be spent right away. In technical terms, M-1 is the most liquid form of money. Over time, about 75 percent of M-1 is in the form of checking account deposits and 25 percent in currency. *M-2* is the money in M-1 plus savings accounts and time deposits. Savings accounts and time deposits are less liquid, since the money from them has to be transferred into a checking account before it can be spent. Finally, *M-3* consists of M-2 plus large time certificates such as certificates of deposits. Most such certificates are in large denominations, in excess of $100,000, and have at least a three-month maturity period. As these definitions of money suggest, institutions other than government can create money, even though only the government can legally print currency.

One almost universally held assumption about the financial systems of modern nations is that nations need a central bank. The assumption is so widely held that nearly all nations now have a central bank. These banks perform extremely important functions, including issuing notes (in most countries the central bank has the sole right of note issue), serving the needs of commercial banks, functioning as the fiscal agent for the government, maintaining the gold and foreign exchange reserves of the nation, and controlling the volume and use of money to ensure economic stability and growth (Beckhart 1972, p. 1). A strong central banking system for the United States was one of the top priorities of Alexander Hamilton. As the first U.S. secretary of the treasury, he pressed for the formation of a bank of the United States. The first Bank of the United States was chartered in 1791 and was headquartered in Philadelphia. Even with such an early and strong start, the history of the Bank of the United States was a very checkered one. Andrew Jackson's opposition to the bank is well known. With Jackson's election to the presidency, the charter of the Second Bank was not renewed in 1836. With the lapse of its national charter, the bank was chartered by the state of Pennsylvania, but it ultimately failed in 1841 with great loss to its stockholders.

The absence of a central bank resulted in several problems for the banking system. One problem was *par banking*. At issue was the question of whether or not the bank that cashed a check would pay 100 percent of its value (par value). Banks in different towns and states had different policies on par banking, so individuals or firms that accepted a check never knew how much value they would actually receive from it. The second problem was *elastic currency*. At issue here was seasonal variations in the need for money. For example, today extra currency is needed during the Christmas season. It is not a well-known practice, but the Federal Reserve central bank today routinely infuses the economy with approximately $5 billion in extra cash to meet the needs of the holiday season (Melton 1985, p. 17). During the periods when we lacked a central bank (from the 1840s to World War I) the seasonal need for additional money most affected farmers at harvest. Farmers were infuriated that interest rates would go up at peak harvest time, when demands for a relatively fixed supply of money increased.

A widespread consensus developed on the need to find solutions to the problems of par banking and an elastic currency. Today the value of par banking and elastic currency is one of the unquestioned assumptions of the central banking system in the United States. As Melton expresses the situation, "To the extent that anyone thinks about the subject at all these days, most regard an elastic currency as a self-evident good thing, not worth serious dispute" (Melton 1985, p. 17). This is an important point: There are many unexamined assumptions about money, its supply, and the institutions through which it is controlled, and these assumptions permeate the mountains of literature on money and banking.

These problems, along with others, provided the impetus for passage of the Federal Reserve Act in 1913. The central banking system that was thereby created is a unique institution in the American governmental system. Melton (1985, p. 7) calls it a "bizarre form of organization." The easiest way to understand the organization of the Fed (a shortened reference to the central banking system) is to start with the regional banks. These banks are chartered as privately owned banks, but their owners are the commercial banks who are members of the Federal Reserve System. For example, the Atlanta regional bank is "owned" by the commercial banks who are system members in the Atlanta region. These commercial banks, or *member banks*, are privately owned (usually by stockholders) profit-making banks who for a variety of reasons have chosen to become members of the Federal Reserve System. Each regional bank has its own board of governors, which functions as the policymaking body for that bank.

In addition to these regional boards, overall direction of the system is vested in a central board of governors. The 1935 Banking Act amended the original Federal Reserve Act to give the Board of Governors authority over monetary policy. Thus, although the organizational structure of the Fed is still "messy" (Melton 1985), at a policymaking level the control is clearly vested in the central Board of Governors of the Federal Reserve System.

There is much controversy that surrounds the status of the Federal Reserve System. One controversy centers on the independence of the Board of Governors. One of the best analyses of the system describes the independence of the Board of Governors this way: "In essence, the Reserve System is independent within but not independent *of* government ... while the System must endeavor to attain the general economic goals of Congress, it is free to use its own means to achieve them, subject ... to various statutory limitations"

(Beckhart 1972, p. 31). The fact that the regional banks are owned by commercial banks within their districts has been another source of continuing controversy. William Greider describes a humorous, but very illuminating, crusade by Wright Patman, a congressman from Texas. Patman reasoned that since the regional banks were owned by commercial banks, then the buildings themselves were privately owned and should be subject to property taxation. The tax commissioner for the District of Columbia, following Patman's reasoning, sent a property tax bill to the Board of Governors. The problem was resolved by the issuance of a quitclaim deed, which surrendered the bank's claim to the building in favor of the U.S. government (Greider 1987, p. 49).

At issue is the matter of democratic control of policy, a point to which we will return in a later chapter. At this point two questions are pertinent. First, is independence desirable? One observer described the elements involved in this question: The Fed "is asked to be politically neutral while regulating an economic system that is not neutral in its results. It is expected to act on the basis of reflective scientific judgment in an environment that stresses political responsiveness. It is asked to make technically correct decisions ... despite a highly conflictual scientific debate as to what correct policy is" (Wooley 1984, p. 12). In short, the Fed makes choices that have different impacts on citizens. For example, a policy designed to combat inflation may help the general consumer but hurt a retiree heavily dependent on interest income. Democratic administration requires political accountability in such matters, so in this regard independence is not desirable.

Second, does independent status guarantee independent behavior? One of the historic assumptions about the politics of monetary policy is that the Hamiltonian dream of elite control of such policy has been realized in the politics of the Fed (see, for example, Greider 1987). This view is strengthened by the fact that the Fed is the "bankers' bank." Thus while the Fed may be somewhat insulated from general political pressures, what about the insider influence of the banking community? Is the Fed a captive agency? Certainly, if we have learned anything from the numerous studies of government programs, it is that politics cannot be taken out of an important governmental function. Any attempts to do so accomplish only a change in the nature of the politics. With regard to the Fed it appears that "independence" means that the nature of the politics directing monetary policy is a limited access, elite dominated politics. Alexander Hamilton would be pleased, but should contemporary Americans?

The Fed has at its disposal several important policy instruments. For monetary policy purposes, the most important of these policy instruments are open-market transactions, control of the discount rate, and the capacity to adjust bank reserve requirements. Lesser strategies, such as public pronouncements of the Fed's views and limited influence over credit availability for individuals, are important but not as significant as the big three.

Open market transactions are the most important policy instruments available to the Fed. They consist of the buying and selling of various government debt securities, typically treasury bills, in the open financial markets. Control over open market policy is vested in the Federal Open Market Committee (FOMC), composed of the members of the Board of Governors and five of the regional bank presidents. It meets regularly throughout the year (normally eight times a year). Annual monetary targets are adopted in January and revised in July; in the other meetings short-term targets for monetary supply are adopted. The Board's decisions about both annual and short-term targets rely heavily on economic forecasts done by the board's staff. One basis of the chairman's power, however, is the ability to direct the FOMC to a consensus position (for a good discussion of the practical running of the FOMC, see Melton 1985, pp. 14–16). When policy is adopted, the transactions themselves can take several forms. In most cases the Fed will engage in direct buying or selling of securities in the open market. Increasingly, orders from foreign customers may be the basis for the Fed's action. In any event, the transaction is targeted toward adjustment in the short-run growth or contraction objectives in the M-1 supply.

A second instrument of monetary policy, the discount rate, is a rather complex set of relationships. It is best to begin with the idea that a central bank in all countries functions as a banker's bank. It is frequently referred to as the lender of last resort. Central banks are in an advantageous position in this regard because they nearly always have money to lend, since they have power to issue legal tender in the form of bank notes. Thus when all other banks have exhausted their liquidity (that is, they are out of money to lend), central banks can be called upon as a source of capital.

There are a number of circumstances under which member banks borrow from the Fed's regional banks. One of the most important was referred to earlier, namely, the seasonal variation in the need for money. Others are very complicated. For example, a change in the American gold position may force member banks to borrow from the Fed. In fact, such a development may force the Fed or the U.S. Treasury to borrow from foreign central banks or from the International Monetary Fund (a major international lender of development loans to developing countries, funded by 148 member nations). Historically, the Fed has discouraged member banks from borrowing money to be reloaned at a profit. The practice, however, varies among member banks, depending on a number of factors not the least of which is a bank's willingness to borrow for such a purpose.

Discounts are the loans made by Federal Reserve banks to member banks. The *discount rate* is the interest the Fed charges the member bank for the loan. Thus the discount rate is a Fed-administered central interest rate that serves as the actual cost of money to member banks as well as a base line from which interest rates for other purposes, such as consumer borrowing, can be calculated. These two aspects mean that adjustment of the rate can serve monetary policy objectives. A high rate tends to result in a contraction of the M-1 supply while a lower rate has an expansionist influence on M-1. It should be noted, however, that before discounts are made the Fed normally requires collateral, usually in the form of *eligible paper*, which consists of promissory notes held by the borrowing banks. The amount of collateral required is a matter of some discretion with the regional bank. The law simply stipulates that the regional banks, under general guidelines of the central board, are to limit the amount of collateral it requires to the minimum consistent with safety.

The third important instrument of monetary expansion or contraction is the reserve requirement, the most complex of the policy instruments. To understand the function, it is important to emphasize again that central banks are bankers' banks. Historically, other banks have utilized central banks as a place in which to deposit their excess balances. This depositing function served many objectives, including facilitating the clearing of checks drawn on the deposition banks (an early effort to solve the "par banking" problem). The Federal Reserve Act mandated that a certain percentage of a member bank's total demand deposits be held on deposit in the regional bank. This number, called the *required reserve*, has fluctuated historically between 12 and 17 percent of a member bank's net demand deposits. *Total reserves* are the sum of a member bank's required reserves plus the cash the bank is holding internally. Here it is important to remember the practice of discounting. *Excess reserves*, that is, cash held above the reserve requirement, may be used as collateral for discounts. Thus excess reserves are also *credit balances* for a member bank at the regional bank. The Fed can use the reserve requirement, then, in two ways to accomplish monetary policy: It can raise or lower the required reserve percentage, and it can manage the credit balances of its member banks. The later practice is called the *federal funds market*.

Control of the required reserve percentage is vested in the Federal Reserve Board of Governors. If the reserve requirement is lowered, a not infrequent phenomenon, money flows from the regional banks to the member banks. Member banks then utilize the money for lending and other purposes, creating what is known as the multiple expansion of bank deposits. In other words, a $1 reduction in the reserve requirement will result in an approximately $3 increase in the money supply. If the reserve requirement is raised, on the other hand, member banks must transfer money or other assets to the regional banks, lowering the supply of money in circulation. A drastic increase in the reserve requirement is unlikely, except under extreme economic conditions. The reason for this lies in the fact that banks vary in their liquidity, that is, how much money they actually hold at any given point. If a bank's liquidity position is low, it may have to call in demand loans in order to satisfy the increased reserve requirement, creating hardship for its customers.

In summary, excess reserves create the federal funds market. These excess reserves are also credit balances of member banks in their regional banks. The federal funds market is simply a mechanism for allocating these credit balances among the banks in the Federal Reserve System. The allocation resembles a market in the fact that the regional banks lend those credit balances and the member banks borrow them. The interest rate is negotiable but usually follows the baseline established by the discount rate. For all practical purposes, then, the Fed sets the federal funds rate. The funds market is particularly useful to large banks; approximately seventy banks account for most transactions (Beckhart 1972, p. 72). However, the federal funds market is open to a wide range of users, including foreign banks, government securities dealers, and some corporations. The federal funds market results in fuller utilization of a member bank's reserves and increases the efficiency of the money market.

Current operations of the Federal Reserve System would surpass Alexander Hamilton's fondest dreams for a central bank. While it may be an exaggeration to refer to the Federal Reserve System as "running the country," its power to affect economic conditions is impressive. Certainly it has established monetary policy as one of the twin pillars of American economic policy. The other pillar is fiscal policy.

FISCAL POLICY

Fiscal policy involves the manipulation of national government revenues and expenditures for economic policy purposes. Thus fiscal policy is accomplished through the budget process. This means that the making of budgets involves both questions of resource allocation (the core budgeting questions) and questions of economic policy. Obviously, a core concern in budgeting is the important matter of obtaining the revenues to support government programs and then efficiently allocating those revenues among the competing demands of the various programs. In recent years, however, utilization of the budget as an instrument of economic policy has joined resource allocation as a core concern.

Budgets can serve as an instrument of economic policy for the simple reason that the size of the budget makes the national government the largest consumer of goods and services and the largest extractor of value from the economy (largely in the form of taxes). When the government increases taxes, it is converting private consumption to public consumption; if it lowers taxes, it converts public consumption to private consumption. If the government increases its consumption of goods and services, the action has a stimulative effect on the economy; if it reduces its expenditures, the action has a contraction (anti-inflationary) effect. Because it is both the largest extractor of resources and the largest consumer in the economy, government decisions about its revenue and expenditure policies have important economic policy results.

From the Employment Act of 1946 until the 1980s fiscal policy in the United States, as with the rest of the industrial world, was dominated by the thought of John Maynard Keynes. Both conservative and liberal politicians and academics voiced their commitment to Keynesianism. Richard Nixon, for example, announced in a television interview that "I am Keynesian." This statement was followed by Milton Friedman, the conservative monetarist we referred to earlier, who said, "We are all Keynesian now." A major countertheory of Keynesianism developed political strength in the 1980s. While supply-side economics had been around for some time, it was very much a minority view among economists. It was given political potency by the Reagan administration and is often known as Reaganomics. The two fiscal policy strategies, Keynesianism and supply side economics, have their ardent supporters and detractors.

Sorting out and comparing the elements in the two fiscal policy strategies is a complex issue. At the risk of oversimplification, Table 7.1 attempts to compare them. The two disruptions of concern to economic policymakers are recession and inflation. Technically, recession is a period of three consecutive quarters of declining GNP; practically, however, recession is a time of less than full employment of the nation's productive capacity. Plants are idle, workers are unemployed, and the economy is generally stagnant. Inflation, in contrast, is a period in which money is losing value. Practically, this means that prices that must be paid for goods and services are rising, usually faster than increases in wages. The more money loses value, the greater the stress on the price index. Monetary policy attempts to manipulate the revenue and expenditure policies of the national government to combat these economic disruptions.

TABLE 7.1   KEYNESIAN AND SUPPLY-SIDE FISCAL POLICIES

	KEYNESIANISM		SUPPLY SIDE	
	Recession[a]	Inflation[b]	Recession[c]	Inflation[c]
Expenditures (E)	E+	E-	E-	E-
Revenues (T)	T-	T+	T-	T-

[a]A rational policy for deficits.
[b]The "forgotten part" of Keynesianism.
[c]Is Reaganomics an excuse for reducing the size of government?

In order to understand Keynes, it is important to understand his emphasis on the concept of demand for goods and services. When Keynes speculated on the basis for recession, he concluded that recession is the result of inadequate demand; thus the appropriate policy for recession would be a policy that stimulated demand. When Keynes speculated on the basis of inflation, he concluded that inflation is the result of excessive demand, and thus the appropriate policy response would be policy that reduced demand. In Keynes' view, demand could be stimulated in times of recession by a combination of increases in government expenditures and decreases in taxes. An increase in government expenditures is important because what the largest consumer does is important. When the government reduces taxes, purchasing power is left in the hands of the consumer. As we have seen, the marginal propensity to spend among Americans is very high. In short, give an American an extra dollar and she or he will spend approximately 96 cents of it. Reducing taxes, then, means that individual consumers have more money that they are very willing to spend. Notice that the dual action of increasing government expenditures and decreasing taxes is likely to result in a budget deficit—that is, the governments are likely to spend more money than they take in. Keynes argued that in times of less than full employment, a budget deficit is a rational policy to adopt.

When Keynes looked at inflation, he saw excessive demand. He argued that if governments reduced demand, the economy would "cool off" by bringing supply and demand back into equilibrium. To accomplish this, Keynes argued that during inflation government should reduce its expenditures and increase its taxes on individuals. By reducing expenditures, government would decrease the demand of the economy's largest consumer thus lowering aggregate demand and cutting inflation. By increasing taxes, government would take money away from individual consumers, thus lowering consumer demand and further reducing inflation. Thus the economy would be able to produce those goods and services that were balanced with demand and prices and production would stabilize. Notice that the dual action of cutting expenditures and raising taxes would more than likely result in a budget surplus, that is, governments would take in more money than they spent. This result has often been called the "forgotten part" of Keynesianism.

Supply-side economists see something quite different. In both recession and inflation they see inadequate supply (thus the derivation of their name). Inflation to supply siders is not excessive demand but inadequate supply. To them, there is nothing essentially wrong in an expanding level of demand—human wants are legitimate and the role of the economy is to satisfy them. Thus the prescription for inflation is to increase the supply of goods and services to a level that is in equilibrium with demand. Likewise, supply siders see recession as inadequate supply. In this regard, the demand for goods and services seems almost a given—human beings will always want increased goods and services. In a recession, factories are shut down, workers are laid off, and the economy is not producing the goods and services consumers want. The prescription for recession, then, is to get the economy moving again, that is, to increase the production of goods and services to a point where supply is in equilibrium with demand.

Supply siders in the Reagan years had a deceptively simply strategy for increasing the supply of goods and services. That strategy was to cut taxes and reduce government expenditures during recessions, and even more so during inflationary "boom" times. In this way, supply siders argued, there would be created a pool of investment capital. With taxes cut, money would be left with individuals who would invest at least a part of it. With government expenditures reduced, especially any government borrowing that might soak up private loan capital, money would be left in the private sector, and at least a part of it would be invested. (This is possibly the weakest part of the theory. Because government can deficit spend without "going out of business," reduced expenditures don't return money to private hands, since that money would not otherwise have been in the private economy.) Both reducing taxes and reducing government expenditures, then, would create the pool of investment capital essential to increasing supply. Entrepreneurs would draw from this pool to build new plants, modernize old ones, and take other actions that would increase the supply of goods and services. Critics of the supply-side prescriptions, however, argued that the theory was simply a guise for the real purpose of reducing the size and importance of government, which was to lessen government interference with and regulation of business.

So how are the respective fiscal strategies of the Keynesians and the supply siders to be evaluated? One very important point is that both theories concern themselves only with inflation and recession as the dominant forms of economic disruptions. But the United States, like most other industrialized nations, has had to contend with other very intractable problems, such as increasing foreign industrial competition or *stagflation*. Stagflation is the simultaneous occurrence of inflation and recession, something many people had simply assumed could not happen. A recession would seem almost automatically to have a strong downward pressure on prices. But neither Keynesianism nor supply-side theories have much to say about foreign competition or stagflation, so those problems can almost render both theories useless.

A second point to consider is the respective emphasis of the two fiscal policy theories. As we noted, Keynesianism emphasizes the demand for goods and services. In fact, Keynes has often been described as a demand-side economist. Supply siders, as their name suggests, emphasize supply. The problem is that even the most rudimentary economics holds that economic activity is the result of a complex interaction between supply and demand. What is needed is a new revision of the Keynesian and supply-side positions. We believe economists have a new revision that can be added to the economic policy system— namely, a full-blown national industrial policy that is reconcilable with environmental needs (Daly 1991; Van Den Bergh 1994; Stokes 1992).

A final point to consider is that neither Keynesianism nor supply-side policy has been given a fair chance to prove its worth, because neither theory has been consistently applied. Several examples of this policy inconsistency will suffice. First, President Lyndon Johnson gained passage of a surtax as a means of combatting inflation. This surtax was literally a tax on the tax that an individual would normally pay. After computing his or her taxes, the individual would owe the government an additional 6 percent of the tax owed. The idea was pure Keynesian: Take money away from the individual consumer by raising taxes and thereby reduce demand. But Johnson then proceeded to spend the revenue on a combination of the Vietnam War and his domestic Great Society Programs. Not only did he spend the additional revenues generated by the surtax, but he also borrowed increasing amounts of money. The additional governmental expenditures were more than the aggregate reduction in individual demand resulting from the surtax. The effect was simply to spend with the right hand rather than the left. Inflation continued to rise. The other example comes from the Reagan presidency. President Reagan was such an ardent supporter of the supply-side theories that a second name for it is "Reaganomics." As a way of getting the economy moving again, Reagan argued forcefully for a reduction in taxes and in government expenditures. What actually happened was the opposite. Reagan first cut taxes in 1981 but later persuaded the Congress to pass the largest single tax increase in American history. It was called the Revenue Enhancement Act in an attempt to veil the fact that it was a tax increase. Even the Reagan income tax bill provided for selective tax reductions, leaving most Americans with a higher or equivalent income tax liability. Also, government expenditures were not reduced. A very few programs experienced an absolute reduction in their appropriations, some continued to receive what was appropriated in the pre-Reagan budget, and most had an increase in appropriations, especially the military budget, which nearly doubled to about $250 billion a year after 1981. The result was a significant increase in government expenditures. In fact, Reagan's overall fiscal policy looked so Keynesian that some analysts referred to Reagan as "the ultimate Keynesian" (Thurow 1984). Like Keynesianism, then, supply-side fiscal policy has not been consistently applied.

To say that neither fiscal policy has been consistently applied does not suggest that either would necessarily be successful if implemented consistently. The major flaws in both theories rest in their points of emphasis. Keynesian policy emphasizes the demand side, supply-side policy emphasizes the supply side. Both, then, are truncated and inadequate as an economic policy. What is needed is a policy triad consisting of monetary policy, fiscal policy, and industrial policy. We now turn to a significant aspect of the American economic policy system—namely, state and local economic development policy.

THE NEW FRONTIERS OF STATE AND LOCAL POLICIES

State and local governments have been involved in economic development in the 1980s and 1990s more than ever before. The reasons for this are many. Before the 1970s, state activities to promote the economy were not so necessary, since the American economy dominated the world with nearly 40 percent of world industrial production and 40 percent of exports. In those years, despite recessions, family income steadily climbed, the national government officials in the late 1940s spoke of achieving full employment, and in the 1960s they confidently spoke of having only 4 percent unemployment. There were few serious industrial or agricultural competitors for American exports on the world market. In short, there were few pressures on state and local governments to do more than they had traditionally done to subsidize local or state businesses: build roads, provide electricity, develop ports, and subsidize business or agriculture with taxes and technical assistance.

Beginning in the late 1960s the American economy steadily lost ground to international competitors in the world economy. Suddenly farmers found that their grain and beef had to compete with lower-priced products from Argentina and Brazil, and consumers were buying Japanese and Asian and European electronics, stereos, and automobiles. In the 1970s this international competition combined with other factors—a relative low level of American savings and business investments in new plants and technology, higher priced labor, higher energy costs, and inflationary pressures from excessive wartime and social spending—to reduce American economic strength. All these forces combined to erode net family income, employment, and the general industrial health and competitiveness of the American economy from the late 1960s to the late 1980s.

As a result of these developments, state and local governments were increasingly pressured to aid business and to alleviate unemployment. States came into a near-frenetic competition to attract big business or foreign investment. By the 1980s economic development policy had become a common term in state policy systems. Today it generally means the efforts by state and local governments to stimulate, attract, or retain business and to develop, train, or stabilize the supply and problems of the labor force in the state. By the late 1980s and into the 1990s it could be argued that state and local governments were doing more along these fronts than the national government.

State economic development policies have sparked considerable controversy, both academic and political. There are many issues to be considered carefully. We will look at the most important ones.

First, do the activities of state and local governments actually increase state and local jobs, or do they just relocate businesses that would be considering moving anyway? Some studies, such as that done by Susan Hansen (1986), concluded that there were few new economic activities achieved by the state industrial development policies. Other research (Fosler 1988; Hansen 1992, 1984) seems to indicate that certain targeted businesses, when attracted by government and matched well with the economic and labor characteristics of a state, can generate business activity and jobs. Such current research argues that a strategy designed to increase jobs in nonprofit services, white-collar services, and advanced corporate services such as legal accounting, computer insurance, and public relations is the best one to attract business and increase local employment.

Second, can the activities of state and local government be well-meaning but misled? That is, do such programs often benefit mainly rich investors or wealthier tourists rather than the majority of the middle and working classes of their state? For example, Virginia governor George Allen's proposal in 1993 to spend $163 million to bring a Disney theme park to Prince William County in Virginia cost more than $60,000 for each of the 2,700 full-time jobs created. This is one of the more lucrative incentives offered by a state in recent years. Many state officials have questioned the growing practice of spending such large sums of tax money to attract jobs, particularly when the money goes to help big corporations such as Mercedes or BMW.

The *Washington Post* (February 6, 1994, p. B-1) compared the cost per job among many of the high-profile incentive packages offered by states to attract major employers since 1985. South Carolina enticed BMW to set up manufacturing facilities, creating 1,900 direct jobs at a cost to the state of $71,000 per job. Kentucky made a gross offer of $140 million to attract Delfasco Steel, which would have produced only 400 jobs in the state at a cost of $350,000 per job. In 1984 Alabama promised $253 million to the Mercedes Benz Company to build a car plant there with 1,500 jobs. In 1992 Indiana beat out Virginia by promising $300 million to reel in a 6,000-worker United Airlines maintenance plant. In each of these cases the states offered from $50,000 per job (United) to $350,000 per job (Delfasco).

A third important issue is whether the business attracted to a locality will produce costly environmental problems that the state government will then have to alleviate. Most state and local governments likely pursue economic development without carefully assessing these issues. Such decisions usually feature a political battle between those who oppose spending money on environmentally damaging businesses versus those who want to attract business of any kind.

By the mid-1980s clear trends solidified among states relative to economic development policies. Two policies were most common. First, states were spending more on business and university research grants to promote their state economy. Second, states were increasingly issuing development bonds and were authorizing cities to do so also. In effect, the governments acted as an intermediary to help a company raise money at lower costs than if the company had to go on the market to sell its own securities. One major advantage of such bonds is that they are exempt from federal income tax. But states and cities bear part of the costs in the form of lower income tax revenues. In the 1970s and 1980s Industrial Development Revenue Bonds (IDRBs) became the most popular method of promoting urban economic development, until 1986, when Congress put a ceiling on the amount that states could issue.

State governments in the 1980s competed intensely to attract foreign investments or domestic companies to their state. This increasingly ferocious fight led to many other tactics—tax breaks, free land loans, small business loans, equity investments, and outright grants—as more and more states chased after fewer and fewer jobs. Kentucky, for instance, passed a law in 1992 giving companies tax credits so they could regain as much as 100 percent of the cost of the construction facilities plus moving expenses. Over a dozen states and cities opened offices in recession-ridden Southern California in the early 1990s to convince local businesses that greener pastures existed elsewhere. A half dozen states, including Texas and Pennsylvania, positioned themselves as major providers of venture capital, small business incubators, and even expensive research parks to develop high technology, electronics, and computers. States commonly opened foreign trade offices to promote export of their products. By 1988 eleven states had established major research parks, eighteen had established incubator programs, and ten were providing direct seed and venture capital to businesses. Thirty states had developed major technical and managerial assistance programs to small business and all states were big spenders on university research centers ($167 million in 1988). About a dozen states had passed labor retraining acts by the late 1980s to help alleviate unemployment caused by the severe recession of 1982–1983. More recent developments include loans and training targeted for specific firms. The areas of greatest interest for targeted technologies are computers and advanced manufacturing of biotechnology and medical technologies (Atkinson 1988, pp. 5–6).

Local governments had positioned themselves to provide slightly different economic development incentives by the 1980s. Those that had been the biggest issuers of industrial development revenue loans in the 1970s shifted efforts in the 1980s and 1990s to try to attract "designer targeted industries." Several cities, such as Memphis, Atlanta, and Los Angeles, were trying to develop rail services between metro areas. Others, like Nashville, St. Louis, and Chicago, have established themselves as airline hubs. High-tech industries were offered lucrative incentive packages by such "high-tech hot spots" as Central Florida, Philadelphia, Salt Lake City, Minneapolis, St. Paul, Austin (Texas), San Diego, and Tucson. These "new growth zones" have tended to form alliances with university, business, and government leaders to try to attract these businesses.

Many states vigorously pursue export policies and try to attract foreign investment. In a survey by the National Governors Association, states spent nearly $100 million on international operations in 1991. Forty-one states maintained 163 offices in 27 countries, and they extended their activities with emphasis on tax incentives, research and development, and credits to subsidize home-state firms. Twenty states, for example, have venture capital funds.

Thirty-six states have established urban enterprise zones that attempt to attract businesses back into declining urban areas (Clark 1986, p. 82). Many states are combining packages of incentives that include property tax abatement and federal seed money from sources such as block grants and municipal development funds. A good example is described in Box 7.1. Cities may create tax increment financing (TIF) districts. In TIF districts, a city declares a certain area or neighborhood to be a development area. It issues bonds to clear land and to attract developers. Because new commercial structures or businesses are more valuable than undeveloped land, property taxes increase. The additional revenues are then used to pay off bonds sold to attract the corporation. Beyond this, it is hoped that the development itself will create jobs for citizens.

| 7.1 | *COME SOUTH OF THE BORDER: HOW KENTUCKY ATTRACTED A CANADIAN COMPANY* |

State economic development officials in Kentucky offered a generous incentive package to Canadian steel companies to build a $400 million steel mill near the Gallatin-Carroll County line. The package included state income tax credits worth up to $140 million over 25 years, tax credits for the purchase and installation of pollution control equipment, a $4 million state loan for water and sewage facilities, and a state grant of $132,000 to train employees. Gallatin County kicked in industrial revenue bonds to pay for construction of the mill. In turn, the plant will pay about $500,000 a year to the Gallatin County school district in property taxes. These kinds of packages are similar to the *tax increment financing* districts developed by cities.

Are such efforts worth the costs? Will attracting one firm to an area stimulate the area's economy? Are there better ways to stimulate an area's economy?

There are five theories to explain the increased role of state and local governments. Probably all have a certain amount of validity, and in combination they help explain why state and locals are pressed to do more and are attempting to respond to those pressures.

The first explanation argues that state and locals are doing more because the international business economy has penetrated the American economy more. American industrial manufacturing has seen heightened foreign competition both for overseas markets and for the domestic consumer markets.

A second explanation, with several versions, involves the continuing urbanization and suburbanization of America. As the population increased after World War II, more businesses located themselves in the suburbs and retail trade drifted from the city center to the suburban malls. Meanwhile, FHA and VA government housing programs helped people in higher income brackets to flee to the outskirts of cities. The center of the city experienced a decline in population, businesses, land values, and tax revenues as America experienced the so-called "white flight" of the middle class out of the city. Over some twenty to thirty years, according to this explanation, the cities became divided into white middle-class suburbs and diverse nonwhite minority populations in the urban center areas. Therefore, cities eventually became pressed to regain the lost capital. First in the domestic context as a result of urban white flight, and then with the industrial core declining further because of foreign and international competition, cities found themselves "on their own" and "abandoned" by conservative administrations.

Another version of this explanation emphasizes that increased international competition since the 1970s hurt U.S. agriculture, forcing states to act more to aid farmers. In the postwar era American farmers had increasingly adopted large-scale farming, intensive use of fertilizers, use of larger equipment for higher crop yields per acre, and expensive loans for harvesting equipment. These developments led to declining farm family income in the early 1970s as overseas competitors began to flood the world market with products that could be raised more cheaply in foreign lands with cheaper labor. Thus farmers found themselves with high investment and capital costs, stable or declining world prices for export commodities, and high inflation in fuel, fertilizer, and equipment costs. To make matters worse, foreign competitors were raising grain and cattle in South America and other places that would compete with American markets overseas. As farming became a less viable economic career, the percentage of Americans choosing to remain in agriculture declined from approximately one-third of the work force in the 1920s to less than one percent of the workforce in 1990. The pressures on the American farmer forced states to adopt programs that would help farmers find new crops, utilize less cost-intensive methods of farming, and compete with international suppliers in export markets.

The third explanation may be termed the capital and business neglect explanation. Some economists (Reich 1987) offer the idea that regardless of partisan control, the national government has for the most part pursued a policy of free trade since the 1930s. State governments also generally do not interfere with the inflow or outflow of capital. The competitive international economy in the 1970s forced many U.S. corporations to opt for "capital flight." In other words, they simply closed down operations that were inefficient and moved them overseas to the cheaper labor markets. Most American electronics and many core industries, such as automobiles, followed this pattern. The result was a slow increase of unemployment levels.

By the mid-1980s protectionist pressures were starting to build up on all governments to alter such free-trade attitudes, to the point where they had some effect even on the free-trade advocates of the Reagan administration. For instance, quotas and tariffs on Japanese automobiles were imposed in the mid-1980s, a deviation from the administration's customary free-trade policies. But, the capital and business neglect theory argues, governments traditionally did nothing or little to impede free trade and capital flight or increase the rates of corporate or private investments or savings. Thus it was natural in the increasingly competitive international economy that U.S. unemployment would increase, periodic recessions would worsen, and the decline of the manufacturing base would deepen. And it would be natural, following this trend, that state and local governments would be pressured to respond more with economic development policies.

A fourth explanation has to do with national inaction. A number of analysts have argued that there existed a form of policy gridlock in the national government. As the national policy system was increasingly preoccupied with divided party government and interest group conflicts on many issues, economic development and urban conditions were neglected. In 1982 and 1983 the country went through the worst recession since the Great Depression. For the first time since the 1930s there were no countercyclical (anti-recession) grants from the national government to the states. Instead there was a deliberate effort to press state and local governments to pay their own way. Thus states and locals began to pick up the ball on urban issues, social problems, and taxation in the 1980s. State governments enacted plant-closing legislation that required notice if plants left a state or locality. They passed worker-retraining programs and experimented with workfare and welfare policy reforms. State and local governments had become the great engines of change and policy momentum in the American federal system.

A final explanation for increased state and local action on the economy has to do with the regionalized economy of the nation. Economists and political scientists more and more have taken note how the U.S. economy is, to a great extent, broken down into sub-economies or regionalized economies (Markusen 1987). This suggests that the "national economy" is also a sort of confederation of regional economies. And when a regional economy suffers and the national government is ignoring the problems, states and localities are forced to act.

The regional economies tend to operate largely independent of each other's fates and fortunes. Each tends also to experience its own booms and busts, which may or may not coincide with the national economy or with other regions. Box 7.2 summarizes the swings in the economic fortunes of the various regions in the United States. It is clear that the regional economies operate in separate cycles, with each region somewhat insulated from other regions and sometimes even experiencing opposite conditions for long periods.

| 7.2 | ***BOOM AND BUST IN REGIONAL ECONOMIES*** |

In the early Reagan years the Southeast, the New England states, California, and Texas were experiencing high growth rates based partly on new high-tech and computer industries, which were at that time leading the world in innovation. The industrial Northeast was faring fairly well, as were the farm states of the Midwest. The Pacific Northwest and the border states were experiencing relative declines in their economies. By 1982 to 1985 the terrific boom years for New England began to collapse. The New England states and the industrial states of the Northeast and upper Midwest experienced almost depression levels of unemployment and stagnation.

By the mid-1980s, following a worldwide oil glut, the oil-based Texas economy had also collapsed. The Southeast, the California coastal states, and the Midwest farm states still retained fairly good economic health. By the mid-1980s, however, the farm-economy states, the Midwest, and the central plains had entered into a severe recession as well, and the border states were soon to follow. By the late 1980s the Southeast had recovered, California, with its diversified economy, was still very healthy, and Texas and New England were making partial recoveries while the central and border states were still in relative stagnation. By the time the 1990 to 1993 recession set in, nearly opposite trends had occurred. California entered into near depression-level unemployment and stagnation. Significant population left the state and real estate prices finally began to level out and drop a little in certain areas. The farm states in the industrial Midwest had picked up as had the border states and the southeast, based largely on housing construction and lower real estate and housing prices and better farm crops and export markets. The New England states that had been with California in boom years in the early 1980s were suffering and the industrial Midwestern states had made some transition to a service economy and were moderately healthy.

This is another major reason why state and local governments had to take on the task of promoting their own economic situation. National economic policies were not targeted much toward subregions but were directed toward national goals, such as the defense buildup and the cutback of urban and social services grants. The implication of the regionalization of economic issues for national economic policy is that interest rate policy for the federal reserve and the spending policies of Congress and the executive branch should be redirected to regions, although they substantially still are targeted to the national economy.

What these five theories of economic development help explain about state and local activities is interesting. The theory of decline of the competitiveness of the national economy due to the penetration of the international economy helps explain why states felt so pressed to actively promote their own foreign trade. Also, the heightened competition of state bidding wars for new factories is best explained by that theory. Thus the states compete fiercely with each other to attract foreign and domestic investments.

The theory of the flight of capital and the lack of investment explains why states have worked so hard at such initiatives as state foreign trade and export offices, the targeting of specific industries to attract the promotion of research parks, the increased spending on research grants, plant-closing legislation, and spending on incubators—all policies aimed at retaining or attracting business *investment*. Also, as states undergo regionalized recessions or depressions, state governments work harder to attract big-ticket investments, and entering into bidding wars and other forms of competition with each other.

The theory of the postwar decline of urban America is a partial explanation of why states have resorted to certain tax and fiscal tools, including urban enterprise zones, city industrial development revenue bonds, and tax increment financing districts. All of these are designed to restore to the urban areas some form of the business presence that had fled to the suburbs or to other regions of the country.

The period of national gridlock and policy inaction in the 1980s helps explain why there was an increase in state and local innovation in job retraining programs, workfare proposals, and their like as welfare rolls increased while grants were cut back. National gridlock and cutbacks explain the rise in state-funded research and development as such funding declined at the national level. Perhaps more important, it helps explain why urban areas and states have had to begin targeting their own special industries to fit the demographic and economic profiles of their communities.

Finally, the existence of regionalized subeconomies helps explain why states have turned to competitive promotion of tourism and have conducted border wars to attract domestic businesses. Regional economic differences help explain why certain states and cities establish development offices to lure business from depression states such as California. Regionalism also explains the experimentations in intercity rail and transit and the attempt to attract airlines to hub cities. Regional differences also provide some explanation for the existence of high-tech and business service professions such as accounting in the areas with big universities, highly educated populations, and cultural amenities. Regionalism also helps to explain the efforts by such cities as Pittsburgh and Detroit to "re-create themselves" as renaissance cities after the decline of their industrial base. Also the rise of state foreign trade offices, plant-closing legislation, and worker retraining has taken place in regions that have suffered severe business cycles in the past two decades.

Whatever the explanation for the increase in state economic development activity, how well do these new plans and strategies actually work to produce job growth? Several studies seem to provide the answers. About 40 percent of job growth comes from new small businesses already in the state, and about 45 percent comes from large businesses already in the state. Thus the more effective job-growth policies probably are those that subsidize in-state business and that provide technology and research. Typically, only about 5 percent of job growth comes from the highly dramatic and competitive incentive packages that win foreign or major domestic businesses to a state (Hansen 1992, 1986). Strong arguments can be put forward that tourism developments may be among the better investments in this category.

Much argument occurs over the term *business climate*, or the policies of state and local governments in competing with one another to attract business. A number of ranking systems are available to evaluate a business climate. The Grant Thornton Index, announced each summer, uses such factors as labor costs, labor union strength, and unemployment compensation. This index is usually used by those businesses looking for low taxes. The Corporation for Enterprise Development, a private consulting group, uses a ranking system that equally mixes several factors such as distribution of income, public support for education, and low unemployment. In addition, each major business magazine seems to have its own rating methods and database. There is no common meaning of business climate, however; some ranking systems are concerned for small business, others for manufacturing firms, and so on, so the utility of such rankings is low. Also, one of the biggest ironies of efforts to rank business climate is that low-tax and cheap-labor states, such as Nebraska,

Kentucky, South Dakota, and Mississippi, are also states with declining business economies.

Studies seem to show that very few businesses base their location decision on taxes alone (Hansen 1986; Hansen 1984). Such research shows that the important factors vary with the nature of the business. Manufacturing markets are concerned about labor costs associated with workers' compensation, wages, and benefits. Firms that require a higher level of education for their labor force are often more concerned with public spending on schools, the quality of higher education, the quality of the arts in the community, the level of the well-trained work force in the state, and the proximity to cultural and geographic attractions. One of the best studies concluded that it was unclear that the amount of tax burden affected location choice (Eisinger 1988). Most studies seem to show other factors as being more important, particularly appropriately skilled labor, the quality of public education, the availability of energy, and the proximity to markets (Fosler 1988).

In summary, the most advantageous job growth policies can increase employment 5 to 10 percent at most. Many policies, especially the tax and urban redevelopment programs, seem to hold few benefits for the central city core. States are involved in very expensive bidding wars for domestic and foreign investment that might have already decided to come to the state. On the other hand, certain regions and cities have become fairly adept at building government–business partnerships that attract new industries. Also, industrial revenue bonds have been used successfully for pollution control, hospitals, housing, fast food malls, and real estate developments. But despite the mixed results of state and local economic development policies, the efforts to promote business and labor are likely to *increase* rather than *decrease* given the forces that have pressured states and locals to bolster their economic prospects.

DILEMMAS AND CRITICAL CHOICES IN ECONOMIC POLICY

How do the concerns for the nature and effects of economic development affect broader social concerns? We believe that there are at least two ways in which the Founders' concerns should be a part of the current economic policy agenda. The first involves the consumerist society and its effect upon present and future generations. The second is the issue of the relationship between economic growth and the environment. These two concerns present critical policy choices that have been too long neglected.

The first issue deals with the question of how an unfettered consumerist society can deal with the issues of inequality and equity. Are large inequalities in wealth detrimental to a democratic republic? Given the bias among early Americans against privileged wealth, should the American policy system underwrite and protect wealth in law? Does the accumulation of wealth with its attendant luxury result in a weakening of moral fiber? Recent years have seen a resurgence of interest in virtue (see William Bennett and the other "virtuecrats"). Is the weakening of virtue at least in part a result of an erosion in national character resulting from sustained prosperity? These are not easy questions to answer, but they are important because the accumulation of wealth is in part a privilege protected and encouraged by law.

In some ways, nearly all the questions concerning the effect of wealth on national character lead ultimately to the issue of fairness. The *sine qua non* of economic policy, in our view, is that economic policy should be informed by the theories of justice. John Rawls described truth and justice as the "first virtues of human activities" and, as such, beyond compromise (Rawls 1971, p. 4). Justice should be the starting point of economic policy.

Reaching agreement on a definition of justice that can inform policy has not been an easy task. The most commonly held definition was formulated by Aristotle. In his *Nichomachean Ethics* Aristotle argued that justice is refraining from gaining advantage for oneself by taking what belongs to another or by denying to another what is due him. Thus the statement "give every person his or her due" came to be the most widely accepted definition of justice. But what is due a person? Vilfredo Pareto sought to provide an answer to that question in such a way that policy decisions could be made on the basis of justice. Pareto held that policy action should be taken as long as some individuals' welfare would be made better while no individual's welfare would be made worse (Pareto 1971). In other words, government could act as long as someone was better off without anyone being worse off. But a number of people question whether such action is possible. A simple formulation of the problem would be this: If a factory is allowed to pollute, factory owners are made better off but those who have to breathe the polluted air are made worse off. If the factory is required to place scrubbers on its smokestacks and reduce pollution, those who breathe the air are made better off but factory owners have lost profits and are made worse off. So in the real world, is there such a thing as action that leaves some better off without leaving others worse off?

We think a better definition of justice for policy purposes is found in the work of John Rawls. Rawls began with the proposition that what is due a person is derived from social institutions. Thus "the justice of a social scheme depends essentially on how fundamental rights and duties are assigned and on the economic opportunities and social conditions in the various sectors of society" (Rawls 1971, p. 7). This is an extremely appealing notion: For justice to be accomplished, the basic structures of society must be just. Whether or not the basic structures are just can be determined by the application of two principles. The first principle is "equality in the assignment of basic rights and duties." The second principle holds that "social and economic inequalities ... are just only if they result in compensating benefits for everyone, and in particular for the least advantaged members of society" (Rawls 1971, pp. 14–15). Taken together, the two principles mean that at any given point in time it is unjust for some individuals to have less in order that a few others may prosper. The implications of such a theory for contemporary American economic policy are numerous indeed. However, the choices that the principles pose may be beyond the capacity of the American system to make, given the ideological and cultural views prevalent today.

As difficult as it is to accomplish justice in the present period, justice across generations is even more difficult. Indeed, Rawls concluded that intergenerational justice "subjects any ethical theory to severe if not impossible tests" (1971, p. 284). Adapting Rawls's basic definition of justice, we believe that intergenerational justice requires the recognition that each successive generation is entitled to equality in the enjoyment of a productive economy. Put negatively, no generation has the right to enjoy economic advantages at the expense of future generations. Enjoyment of wealth in the present at the expense of the well being of future generations is unjust. This means that one of the critical choices facing the American policy system is to stop overvaluing the present and undervaluing the future. The marginal propensity to save, that is, the extra savings an American will make out of an extra dollar of income, is among the lowest in the world. Thus, conversely, the marginal propensity to spend, that is, the extra spending an American will do out of an extra dollar of income, is among the highest in the world. Americans systematically undervalue the future and overvalue the present.

An important point to emphasize is that consumption patterns are based in choices. Those choices become widespread, largely as the result of mass advertisement, and become institutionalized in the social patterns of a society. Mass consumption in the present is an institutionalized feature of the United States. Thus the question that poses the critical choice is this: Is the present generation ethically bound by the requirement of justice to put aside a suitable amount of wealth to ensure the productive capacity of the economy in the future? What is a suitable amount? Rawls suggests a way to make the determination. He argues that we should imagine ourselves as parents and then ask ourselves how much of our wealth we should set aside to ensure the economic well-being of our children. Rawls argued that the answer to that question is the amount of wealth we believe that we are entitled to claim from our parents. In addition to that amount, some allowance should be made for improvement in the economic circumstances of future generations. Those two factors—what we would reasonably expect from our parents and what is necessary to accomplish due improvements for future generations—is what is just between generations. Making critical choices on that basis would significantly alter not only economic policy but much of the rest of the American policy system as well.

A second intergenerational concern is the relationship between economic growth and the ecology. One of the remarkable features of economic planning has been that it has taken the effect of economic activity on the ecology out of its frame of reference. This occurs at both the micro and macro levels of economic thinking. At the micro level, deterioration in the ecosystem or exhaustion of the resource base are seldom elements in the costing of a product. In fact, as the experience with oil demonstrates, government subsidies and supports keep the price of petroleum products artificially low, thus encouraging exhaustion of the resource base. If there was full costing of the price of gasoline at the pump, that is, if all government subsidies to the production, distribution, and use of oil were removed, it is almost certain that the price would rise sharply and the amount used would decline, slowing the rate of resource exhaustion. To put the situation differently, the ecosystem and the resource base are systematically undervalued by the market, and this undervaluing is aided and abetted by government policy. The twin forces of market and policy undervaluation encourage overconsumption and waste. Recall that both government action and inaction on industrial policy affect economic activity. One of the critical choices the American policy system must make is to stop systematically undervaluing the ecosystem and the resource base.

Economic thinking and planning have failed to take the ecosystem into account at the macro level as well. This failure is most clearly seen in one of the most frequently used economic concepts—the Gross National Product (GNP). The GNP is universally used as the measure of a nation's economic activity and well-being. The unstated assumption is that the higher a nation's GNP, the better off that nation and its people are. But the GNP and its sister measure of the domestic economy, the Gross Domestic Product (GDP), are calculated without any concern for the ecosystem. A society could overexploit its resource base and seriously erode its ecology and the GNP or GDP would show the society to be well off. Such a practice is at best a seriously deficient short-term view of economic well-being and at worst a tragic betrayal of a society's capacity to provide for economic well-being into the future. There have been various concepts proposed to replace the GNP—such measures as "real net national product," "sustainable social net national product," and "index of sustainable economic growth" (Ahmed, Serafy, and Lutz 1989). As these terms suggest, what is needed is a commitment to *sustainable* economic growth. While the concept of sustainable economic growth means different things to different people, common to all the concepts is the idea that the use of resources in the present should not diminish economic well-being in the future (Repetto 1986, p. 5). Such a concern would permeate the policy system and would be especially important for resource policy (oil, gas, etc.), agriculture policy, public lands policy (can anyone imagine the United States giving away billions of dollars worth of mineral resources to a foreign corporation for only a few hundred dollars in fees?), and trade policy. Clearly a critical choice the policy system must make concerns a means of expressing economic well-being that is more realistic over time than is the concept of the GNP.

Given the historic commitment to economic development, can the contemporary policy system rethink the issues of economic development in ways more friendly to future generations? What kind of development and under what circumstances should it occur? How are such values as a healthy environment and maintenance of the resource base to be factored into product pricing on the one hand and aggregate measures of the nation's economic well being on the other? What are the consequences of income and wealth inequalities on the nation as a political system? These are important questions, each posing a series of unresolved critical choices for the American policy system.

 CHAPTER **8**

EDUCATION POLICY

A NATION AT RISK

Few policy areas have evoked as much attention and provoked as much controversy in recent years as has education. Educational reform has been on the policy agenda for much of the twentieth century (Cuban 1990); and after nearly a century of front-burner status it is still a major issue in the American policy system. What are the issues that divide Americans over education questions? What are the forces that gave rise to and continue the vitality of these issues? What response has the policy system made, and how effective have those responses been? How did we get to where we are with current policy and how do we get to where we need to be? These are not easy questions. We begin with an identification of the issues that divide Americans over education policy.

FOUR RECURRING ISSUES

Education issues have been on the American policy agenda for a century, simply because the policy system recycles the questions, debating them over and over again without resolving them. We believe that four issues encapsulate most of the division among Americans on education. First, there is the basic question of who is to be educated and for what. In other words, is education for the masses or for a few? If education is for the masses, what kind of education should it be? What is the proper mix of liberal and vocational education? Second is the issue of institutional structure. A wide range of questions are involved here. What is the proper mix of private and public education? What is government's responsibility, if any, to assist private schools or to assist families whose children attend private schools? Third is the issue of administrative structure. Should administrative control of schools be contracted out to private providers or remain a government responsibility? If it remains a government responsibility, in what level of government should control of education be vested? Finally, there is the issue of accountability. The current policy debate includes much discussion over the word "empowerment," but who should be empowered—parents, teachers, or someone else? Accountability involves answerability. To whom should educators answer—to their professional consciences, to state legislatures, to national educational authorities? It is these four issues that pose the critical choices for education policy in the twenty-first century.

EDUCATION FOR WHOM?

One of the beliefs that dominates American thinking is that everyone needs an education. The roots of this idea are found in the thought of Thomas Jefferson, who believed and argued forcefully that a democratic republic required an educated citizenry. Following that belief, he committed much of his life to furthering the cause of education, including founding the University of Virginia. Today Jefferson's belief is one of the most widely held myths among Americans. But agreement on a policy objective, even when that agreement approximates consensus, does not necessarily resolve all issues.

The most serious issue posed by the objective of educating all Americans is the question of the kind of education that will be provided. Historically, America has emphasized a general education through the high school level and a liberal education (some call it general education also) at the college level. Thus all American youths were expected to be proficient in the language, including literature, in quantitative reasoning, in history, and in the natural and social sciences. If a student was lacking in any of those proficiencies, failure was assumed to have occurred either in the student or in the school. As a result of this assumption, there developed flippant policy rhetoric on the one hand and rather serious think-tank style analysis on the other. The flippant policy rhetoric is seen in bumper sticker slogans such as "Why can't Johnny read?" and "If you can read this, thank a teacher." The more serious analysis of the issue is well represented by a study sponsored by the National Commission on Excellence in Education and published under the title "A Nation at Risk." Both the rhetoric and the analysis simply fueled the persistent call for education reform.

One result of the reform movement has been the development of alternatives to general education high schools and colleges. The most important alternative is the vocational school, which has gained widespread support because of the belief that an education (in this regard, a "skills education,") is the basis for a more productive individual and thus a competitive economy. This belief is an extension of Jefferson's idea that an educated citizenry is necessary for a democracy. The belief in the necessity for an educated work force is particularly strong in the high-tech economy of the postindustrial age. Again, a near consensus does not resolve all the issues associated with vocational education.

One of the most intractable issues surrounding vocational education also involves the question of the kind of education that should be provided. Should vocational schools teach specific job-related skills? If this were the case, then vocational schools would survey the current inventory of jobs and structure their instruction to develop the skills needed for those jobs. Or should vocational schools develop cognitive skills that would enable the individual to learn specific skills through on-the-job training? If this were the case, then vocational schools would attempt to identify the requisite cognitive skills and then structure programs designed to impart those skills. In such an approach, if the recommendations of such advocates as the Department of Labor in its SCANS reports are taken as the model, vocational schools would offer general education programs similar to those of comprehensive high schools.

Vocational schools also have been subject to the charge of failure. Concern for the "work force crisis" has come to rival the concern for reading skills in policy rhetoric. The crisis, according to those who hold the view, has resulted in a deterioration of productivity and of wages. Comparison is also made with the skills of workers in other countries; measurement and comparability present many, if not more, problems than those associated with comparing reading and mathematics skills. And the process reaches its fruition in the call for reform (Magaziner 1990). The slogan of the vocational reform movement is "investing in people."

But what is the most effective way to invest in people? Is it through investing in comprehensive high schools and colleges or in vocational schools? If in vocational schools, what kind of training should be provided? What is the link between education and productivity? What is the link between education and the effective functioning of a democratic republic? Critical choices must still be made relative to the policy issues of education for whom and for what?

WHAT TYPE OF INSTITUTIONS SHOULD DELIVER EDUCATION?

A second critical choice relative to education has to do with the institutional structure through which education is delivered. The near consensus on the goal of educating all American youths makes this choice more difficult. The elements of this debate are the institutional preferences of each group in American society. The most basic question is: What is the proper mix of public and private schools? A host of questions follow. What is the responsibility of government to private schools? Should the same government aid be extended to private schools as to public schools? What about parents who do not want their children in educational institutions at all, public or private? Should they be allowed to educate their children at home? The American policy system has been divided over the these questions since the earliest days of the republic.

One specific form of government aid to religious schools has come to symbolize the issue. That form is the *voucher*, a government payment to a parent, who is to use it to buy a child's education from among any number of suppliers. There are several dimensions to the voucher issue. The first is the equity dimension. Is it fair to parents who send their children to private schools to have to pay taxes to support public schools? Is this double taxation? At the policy level it is argued that private schools relieve crowding in the public schools, thus reducing the tax burden on all citizens. Second, there is the competition argument. Here the concern is with the possible monopoly power of the public schools. If there are no other providers and there is mandatory attendance up to a certain age, what is the motivation of the public schools to provide quality education? Third is an ideological dimension. Those who support vouchers tend to have an anti-government orientation. They also tend to support "traditional" values and find fault with how the public schools are imparting those values. Fourth, there is the achievement argument. It is held that private schools deliver higher-quality education than public schools and thus student achievement is higher. Finally, there is the structural dimension of the issue. This relates to empowerment. The argument is made that the less hierarchical nature of private schools results in the greater empowerment of teachers and parents. Such empowerment is seen as furthering the cause of quality education. As the issue of vouchers indicates, a number of critical choices need to be made about the institutional structure for education.

WHO ADMINISTRATES THE SCHOOLS?

Alexander Pope, in a famous couplet, wrote, "For forms of government let fools contest; that which is best administered is best." While Pope's couplet may overstate the importance of administrative structure, the issue of administrative control of the educational system is a perennial one. The issue comes down to the question of who should manage the schools. Should education remain a government responsibility managed by publicly employed administrators, or should education be privatized? If schools are to remain under public management, at what level should that management be vested—local, state, or national? These questions constitute the third area of critical choices for the American policy system.

Of the many forms that privatization can take, "contracting out" has been the most frequently used in education. In the practice of contracting out, the public entity previously responsible for managing the schools contracts with a private management firm to run the schools. The belief is that the private firm will be more efficient in delivering educational services. But is this necessarily the case? Is the presumed greater efficiency of the private firm ascribed largely by privatization proponents? Is there evidence that the private firm will manage the public schools better? What will be the motive of the private firm, education of young people or profit maximization? Does privatization result in less public visibility of the program and thus invite corruption? How should the private management firm be monitored to ensure quality control and performance? What if the private firm goes bankrupt? These and other questions that surround the privatization question pose critical choices.

If management of the schools is retained by government, at what level of government should control be vested? Since colonial times, the belief has been very strong among Americans that control of the schools should be at the local level. A corollary belief is that education should be "taken out of politics." These two somewhat contradictory beliefs have led to the establishment of school districts, a practice common to all fifty states. School districts in most states are special district governments, that is, they are local units of government with most of the characteristics of cities and counties. But does vesting educational control in districts take education out of politics? Or does it merely change the nature of the politics from an accessible, higher visibility politics to a limited-access, lower visibility politics? What about quality control? How can the policy system be assured that all the districts are offering the same quality of education? What is the responsibility of state and national governments toward the special district? Should the state provide aid to its districts? Should the national government provide aid? And if aid is provided, do state and national governments have the right to insist on certain performance standards? Clearly, there are a number of critical choices the policy system must make in what might appear on the surface to be the mundane area of administrative control.

WHO IS ACCOUNTABLE?

The widespread belief that education has failed has spawned an extensive effort to identify the culprits and hold them accountable. No development has had more practical effect on educational institutions in recent years than has the accountability movement. In several ways the issue of accountability relates to the issue of administrative control. The most important of these ways is empowerment. In short, who should have the power to determine what the schools teach and how they teach it? To whom should such power be given—to teachers, parents, administrators? What role should students have in determining the nature of their education? These are difficult questions, and opinions differ sharply on them.

At the heart of the issue of accountability is the question of answerability. To whom should teachers and administrators answer? A number of possibilities exist. Should educators answer only to their conscience, particularly as that conscience is expressed through professional organizations? What role should accrediting agencies, largely in the form of professional associations, have in determining educational practice and in disciplining errant educators? Can the educational system be self-disciplining? Given that the special district is the structure for delivering education, what is the role of the state and nation in determining educational practice? Should there be uniform state standards, such as state-prescribed reading levels? Should national standards of performance be adopted? If standards external to the educational system are adopted, how are these standards to be enforced? For example, should prospective teachers have to pass a national examination before they are licensed to teach? Should teachers be regularly retested to ensure that they remain competent?

One of the great ironies of the American policy system is the fact that two centuries of emphasis on educational reform have left a host of critical choices still to be made. Before we turn to the question of viable choices that can be made, we ask, as we did with other policy areas, the question of where the American policy system is now. What are the major components of American education policy?

POLICY RESPONSES TO THE CRITICAL CHOICES IN EDUCATION

Education policy in the United States is developed at many points in the federal system. Thus, however primitive or well developed, there is a national education policy, an education policy in each of the 50 states, and an education policy in the 60,000 local school districts. The policy emphasis of each level is different. Presumably, national policy pursues national objectives, state policy pursues state objectives, and local policy pursues local objectives. At times, however, these objectives conflict with one another. As a result of the multiple points within the federal system at which education policy is developed, it is difficult to describe a comprehensive, coherent education policy in the United States. For our purposes, it is sufficient to describe where the policy system is now relative to the critical choices identified in the preceding sections.

EDUCATION TOWARD DISCIPLINED INTELLIGENCE VERSUS DISCIPLINED SKILLS

As we noted earlier, there is a near consensus on the proposition that all American youth are entitled to an education. Until the mid-twentieth century both public and private schools structured their curricula on the general education model, what a historian of the U.S. educational system referred to as the *disciplined intelligence* model. Bestor argued that "The founders of our public school system ... believed ... that ignorance is a handicap and disciplined intelligence a source of power" (1953, p. 3). A number of scholars, most notably Spring (1976), have shown that disciplined intelligence was not the only objective sought by the founders of the public school system. Various social objectives were also primary, for example. Horace Mann, sometimes referred to as the father of American public education, argued forcefully that one of the most important functions of a public system was the socialization of all American youth to appropriate social and political beliefs. To gain support, then, the public schools were promoted as agencies of socialization that would assimilate immigrants into American society, alleviate the problem of crime, reduce poverty, and solve labor problems by providing a trained, pliant labor force. These were high expectations indeed for any structure within a policy system. Some of these myriad expectations were simply incompatible with others. For example, is the objective of ensuring a trained labor force compatible with the objective of developing disciplined intelligence in all of America's youth?

During the first century of public education the preferred method for accomplishing educational objectives was the general curriculum. All students were expected to develop verbal and quantitative skills, know literature and history, understand the basics of natural science, and have familiarity with the social sciences. A number of forces combined to challenge this approach, however, and three developments were particularly important. The first was the great concern during the 1950s with the competitive standing of the United States relative to the Soviet Union. In some quarters a near hysteria developed over the presumed superiority of Russian students, particularly in the areas of science and mathematics. This concern led to the passage of the National Defense Education Act with its emphasis on science and mathematics education. This emphasis meant, among other things, identification of the "best and the brightest" American youth and concentrating educational resources on them. The second development was the civil rights movement in the 1960s. The civil rights movement broadened concern for excellence in education to all children, especially minority children and poor children. Equality of educational opportunity became an important objective. The third development, emerging with great strength in the 1970s, was concern for the competitive position of the United States in the emerging world economy. The belief was prevalent that the American work force was not as productive as the work force of other nations, particularly Germany and Japan. These three developments were the primary forces in a search for alternatives to the general education approach. As a result, the development of disciplined skills joined the development of disciplined intelligence as educational objectives. Career education and general education became the answers to the question: "Education for what?"

If it is appropriate to refer to Horace Mann as the father of public education, then Sidney P. Marland, Jr., should be designated the father of vocational education. Marland, commissioner of education during the Nixon administration, believed strongly that vocational education was the answer for a number of social ills, including juvenile delinquency, student rebellion in school, and unemployment among young adults. Conversely, he believed that general education did not provide young adults with job skills. He summarized his view in this way: "When we use the word 'meaningful,' we imply a strong obligation that our young people complete the first twelve grades in such a fashion that they are ready either to enter into some form of higher education or to proceed immediately into satisfying and appropriate employment" (1972, p. 4). Marland envisioned a two-track system in high school, one track consisting of the traditional general education curriculum for students who planned to attend college, the second track consisting of skills education for students who would enter the work force immediately upon graduation. Marland used his considerable influence as commissioner of education, including the disbursement of discretionary funds, to stimulate the vocational school movement.

Today vocational schools are a significant component of the public school system. In keeping with Marland's view, vocational education has always emphasized training in specific job-related skills. Appropriate administrators have surveyed the job market to determine what skills are needed, and then programs have been established to train students in those job-related skills. It is not uncommon for vocational schools to provide the equivalent of on-the-job training for specific industries. As an incentive to prospective industries some jurisdictions offer the services of the school in training workers in specific skills needed by that industry. Regular offerings have in the past included training in secretarial skills, automobile mechanics, and the like, but recently vocational schools have added more high-tech courses such as electronics and computer processing. This traditional emphasis on specific skills has come under serious attack in recent years. Within the vocational school movement, then, there still remains serious debate over the question: "Education for what?"

THE MIX OF PUBLIC AND PRIVATE INSTITUTIONS

The question of the proper mix of public and private education has been on the American policy agenda since the establishment of the public school system. More specifically, the issue is the role of government in assisting private schools operated by religious organizations. Aid to parochial schools has dominated the policy agenda on the mix of public and private education.

The outlines of modern policy on government aid to parochial schools began to take shape in the 1940s. By that time public policy, particularly in certain states, had been structured to support religious institutions in a variety of ways, most noticeably through direct provision of financial support. At the national level the Higher Education Facilities Act of 1963 authorized construction money for sectarian schools, a policy the Supreme Court sustained in *Tilton* v. *Richardson* (403 U.S. 672). The states gave parochial schools a wide range of direct financial support, including a bus fare reimbursement scheme in New Jersey, the provision of supplies and materials such as books and laboratory supplies, the exemption of church property from taxation—even in the case of commercial, profit-making property such as parking lots—and aid for religious instruction. Some states also supported specific religious practices, such as prayer in the public schools, the basis for *Engel* v. *Vitali* in 1962 (370 U.S. 421), and mandatory Bible reading, the issue in *Abbington School District* v. *Schempp* in 1963 (374 U.S. 203). While some of the practices were struck down by the Court, as were the prescribed prayer and mandatory Bible reading, a wide range of activities were upheld. The Court based its decisions on various grounds, including the "child benefit" doctrine, the "public purpose" doctrine, and the "purely secular purpose" theory. These practices and others meant that the states and religion had become very much entangled with one another.

The Supreme Court became the major policy actor in setting the boundaries of the entanglement. Several important cases provided the occasion for the Court to define the government's responsibility to provide financial aid to parochial schools. Three cases are especially important for an understanding of this complex issue. The first is *Everson* v. *Board of Education*, decided in 1947 (330 U.S. 1). In this case the Court ruled: "Neither a state nor the Federal Government can set up a church. Neither can pass laws which aid one religion, aid all religions, or prefer one religion over another.... No tax in any amount, large or small, can be levied to support any religious activities or institutions, whatever they may be called, or whatever form they may adopt to teach or practice religion" (pp. 15–16). This is strong language indeed and would seem to prohibit most forms of aid to religious schools as we know them today. In the second case, *McCullom* v. *Board of Education* (333 U.S. 203), the Court reiterated the Everson doctrine and struck down a policy in Illinois that allowed ministers and priests to come into the public schools and teach religion. The Court found that the state not only was allowing its tax supported public buildings to be used for religious instruction but was also putting the coercive power of the state behind attendance. The Court reasoned that the "State also affords sectarian groups an invaluable aid in that it helps to provide pupils for their religious classes through use of the State's compulsory public school machinery" (p. 5). In both the Everson and McCullom cases, lawyers for the religious groups had argued that the Court's position implied a hostility on the part of government toward religious groups and restricted the free exercise of religion as guaranteed by the First Amendment.

In the third case, *Zorach* v. *Clauson* (343 U.S. 306), the Court had to face the question of potential conflict between the establishment and free-exercise clauses of the First Amendment. The Zorach case in 1951 involved the issue of release time. Rather than using public school buildings for religious instruction, students were released from school to go to private facilities where religion was taught. Students who did not want to attend religion classes were allowed to go to study hall. The Court defined its problem in the case this way: "Our problem reduces itself to whether New York by this system has either prohibited the 'free exercise' of religion or has made a law 'respecting an establishment of religion' within the meaning of the First Amendment." The Court found that the release time plan violated neither of the clauses. In rather obtuse reasoning that it had earlier rejected, the Court held:

> ... so far as interference with the "free exercise" of religion and an "establishment" of religion are concerned, the separation must be complete and unequivocal. The First Amendment within the scope of its coverage permits no exception; the prohibition is absolute. The First Amendment, however, does not say that in every and all respects there shall be a separation of church and state. Rather, it studiously defines the manner, the specific ways, in which there shall be no concert or union or dependency one on the other.

Otherwise, the Court held, almost as if offended by the thought, "a fastidious atheist or agnostic could even object to the supplication with which the Court opens each session: 'God save the United States and this Honorable Court.'" The problem with the Court's reasoning is that the First Amendment does not studiously define the manner and the specific ways that the state may relate to religion.

Since the First Amendment does not specifically define the boundaries of the separation between church and state, the Court was faced with the necessity of finding some tests of the limits of entanglement. The 1971 case *Lemon* v. *Kurtzman* (403 U.S. 602) provided the opportunity. Pennsylvania had adopted a policy to reimburse sectarian schools for the cost of teachers' salaries, textbooks, and teaching materials in certain secular subjects. The Court disallowed the practice and announced the three-part Lemon test that required that any government activity involving religion reflect a purely secular purpose, that it neither advance nor inhibit religion, and that it avoid excessive governmental entanglement with religion. The Lemon test was then used to strike down a number of state practices supporting religion. Among other results of this curtailment of state involvement was an increased saliency of religious issues on the public policy agenda and an awakening of evangelical

Christians to political activism. The issue of the relationship between the state and religion is now as divisive as at any time since the colonial period.

THE LIMITS OF LOCAL ADMINISTRATIVE CONTROL

The federalist culture that guides American policy on control of public schools is dualism. The belief is very strong in America that schools should be controlled at the local level. As we saw earlier, this belief is joined by a belief, largely a result of the progressive reform movement in the early 1900s, that education should be taken "out of politics." These two myths have resulted in the vesting of control of public schools in special district governments.

The special district government is not well understood by most Americans. Several important characteristics need emphasis. The first should be the most obvious: Special district governments are local units of government, just as are cities and counties. Special districts have their own governing authority vested in them by the state through the charter that creates them, the authority to provide educational programs within the district. Special districts have their own governing structures, and for school districts these are school boards. In most states the members of the school board are elected by the voters living in the district. Special districts generally are given the power to tax, and in American tradition school districts have the power to levy taxes on property. The property tax, then, has been the primary means for financing public education throughout American history.

It is the reliance on the property tax to finance public education that placed the greatest strains on the tradition of local control. The problem arose because of the extreme differences among districts in the value of property. Some districts were "wealthy" in that they had high-value residential and commercial properties; others were "poor" in that their residential properties were of low value and they had few commercial properties. The wide variation in the value of property meant a wide variation in the resources available for financing education. Parents in the poor districts began to question whether the differences in resources resulted in a difference in the quality of education. Equalization of educational opportunity between districts became an important policy issue.

As with the aid to parochial schools issue, the courts became the most important policy actor. Two important cases set the direction of state decision making. The first case was *Serrano* v. *Priest*. Mr. Serrano lived in a poor school district in California, a state whose constitution guaranteed to every resident the "equal protection of the law." Attorneys for Mr. Serrano argued that state laws requiring his children to attend school in the poor district in which they lived denied them the equal protection of the law. In essence, children in the poor districts were forced by state law to attend schools that provided inferior education. The California Supreme Court agreed and ordered the state to adopt policy that provided equal educational opportunity to all children regardless of place of residence.

Following the Serrano decision, individuals and groups interested in the equalization of educational opportunity began to look to the national constitution. The Fourteenth Amendment also contains an equal protection clause, prohibiting states from denying "to any person within its jurisdiction the equal protection of the laws." The case of *Rodriquez* v. *The San Antonio Special District* challenged the unequal financial resources of districts as a violation of that clause. The national courts ruled differently than the California courts, however. Relying on the dualist federalist culture so heavily that it almost strained the concept to the breaking point, the Court found that unequal financing of public schools did not violate the Fourteenth Amendment. Public school financing, in essence, is a state question to be resolved at the state level.

With the failure to obtain a ruling that would require all fifty states to equalize educational expenditures of districts, proponents of equalization began to bring suit in various state courts. State legislatures, perhaps anticipating that the suits would be successful, began adopting policy designed to equalize educational opportunity across school districts. The primary features of state policy were *state funding* and *state mandates*. State funding of education increased dramatically in the 1960s to a point where education now receives the largest percentage of state aid to local governments. Its primary objective is the equalization of financing between school districts. Increased state funding has been accompanied by increased state mandates. Since school districts are local units of government, they are "creatures of the state" in the same way that cities and counties are. In short, they are subject to whatever controls the state places on them. States have increased dramatically the number of requirements they impose on school districts, covering the full range of school functioning, from recordkeeping to curriculum and learning materials. Since most of these mandates also involve the question of accountability, we will return to them later. At this point it is important to emphasize that the rapid increase in state mandates has reduced substantially local control of public education.

The privatization movement has not had much success in education. The most publicized privatization effort is probably that of Baltimore, but that issue was hardly one of comprehensive privatization. Only eight elementary schools and one middle school were privatized. Of the system's 113,000 students, 4,800 attended the privatized schools. As of the mid-1990s only Baltimore, Miami, and Minneapolis had privatized any part of their public school systems. Several high-visibility attempts at privatization were unsuccessful, including in Hartford, the District of Columbia, San Diego, and Nashville. Common to nearly all the unsuccessful attempts was strong opposition by teachers, particularly teachers' unions. A second factor, especially important in the large cities, was the racial factor. One observer described the racial factor this way: "To date, no major city has escaped a racially charged process. Part of the reason is that, in virtually all cases, the prospective management firms are headed by white entrepreneurs who are attempting to run urban schools with large minority enrollments" (Mahtesian 1994, p. 48). Because of the limited experience with privatization, we lack solid data with which to evaluate policy outcomes. Even with more extensive experience, data may be difficult to obtain. Private contractors are not as affected by state "sunshine laws" (requiring that meetings be public) and freedom of information acts as are public agencies. Additionally, the media are not as likely to provide the watchdog function for private firms that they do to public agencies. In any event, the many questions surrounding the privatization movement cannot be answered on the basis of policy history.

THE ACCOUNTABILITY MOVEMENT

The accountability movement has had more practical impact on education than any other single force in recent years. The movement gained strength because of the widely held myth of failure. Many Americans believe that the schools are not providing the education that they are capable of providing. Legislatures and state departments of education have turned to the various devices offered by the accountability movement as the strategy to reverse this perceived failure. These devices are targeted to teachers, to students and to curricula and teaching materials.

The most common devices to ensure teacher competency are certification requirements, teacher testing, and on-the-job evaluation of performance. Certification is the process by which a state vests in an individual the right to teach. Historically, requirements for certification varied widely among the states, but in recent years states have moved toward common requirements, thanks in large part to the work of the National Council for the Accreditation of Teacher Education (NCATE). NCATE has adopted a model program of study to be followed by students seeking certification. Schools of education can apply for NCATE accreditation. Since NCATE accreditation is a very important indicator of peer approval of a given program, college administrators are usually very anxious to obtain this accreditation. A private national professional association, then, has become an important policy actor in setting standards for certification of prospective teachers. A practical effect of NCATE influence is a more uniform set of requirements across the states.

Testing of teachers is often associated with initial certification. The most common form of testing is the National Teachers Examination (NTE), which attempts to test the general competency of an individual for the teaching profession. The test consists of two parts. The first part is a communication skills test and consists of writing, reading, and listening subtests. The second part is a general knowledge test, which include mathematics, science, social science, and literature/fine arts. The assumption underlying the test is that there is a minimal competency in each of these areas that is necessary to be an effective teacher. The primary policy choice to be made is in setting the *cut score*, or the minimal score required for certification. The problem is that the cut score will vary according to the method used to determine it. A study published by the American Psychological Association found that "there can be large discrepancies between the cut scores produced by the most common methods of setting cut scores" (American Education Research Association 1985, p. 50). These discrepancies raise a number of important issues, among them difficult legal issues of due process (Citron 1985).

One result of legal challenges to teacher testing has been the setting of cut scores in such a way as to minimize the possibility of penalizing an individual taking the test. A cut score can err in one of two directions. It can certify that an individual is competent when in fact he or she is not. This kind of error is called a *false positive error*. A cut score can also find that an individual is incompetent when in fact he or she is competent. This error is called a *false negative error*. In most states the risk of misclassifying a competent individual as incompetent is considered the more serious of the two (Busch and Jaeger 1989, p. 2). This is an interesting and significant choice—interesting because of the values that it reflects, and significant because as the probability of false negative errors decreases, the probability of false positive errors increases. In other words, the more you ensure that competent persons are not denied certification, the more you certify incompetent individuals. This is hardly an outcome that those supporting the accountability movement want.

As we noted, the NTE is a general test. It does not address an individual's competency in particular subjects. States have addressed this issue by adopting various subject matter tests, most frequently called *teaching field criterion referenced tests* in the jargon of educators. An individual seeking certification in mathematics, for example, would be required to take a mathematics competency test. The underlying assumption is that there are certain things an individual most know in order to teach a subject. However, similar problems exist with regard to setting the cut scores as are found in the NTE.

The third means by which teachers are held accountable is an on-the-job evaluation procedure. Annual evaluation of teacher performance is now an almost universal practice at all levels of education. In most instances there is a combination of a formal evaluation instrument and classroom observation. The formal assessment instrument is structured on the basis of the competencies teachers should exemplify. Presumably, the evaluator completing the instrument is competent and in a position to rate the teacher. Generally, the rater is the chairman of the department within which the individual teaches. Classroom observation is common mainly below the university level. The idea is to rate the actual performance of a teacher in the classroom setting. Many colleges and universities use student evaluation of professors in their assessment, but this practice is rare in elementary and high schools. Whatever the combination of rating methods, annual evaluations of teachers are used in a variety of ways. The most important objective is to improve teacher performance. Some institutions have formalized programs for the improvement of teaching that are linked to the annual evaluation procedure. Others leave improvement to the individual teacher and his or her response to the annual assessment. Additionally, it is common for the annual evaluations to be used for determining pay increases, promotion, and tenure. Thus the results of the annual evaluation process are important elements in the careers of teachers.

The accountability movement has also focused on the student. Much attention has been directed toward determining desired "learning outcomes" and the development of assessment instruments to monitor student progress. The determination of learning outcomes begins with the question of what the student should learn and culminates in an identification of various performance measures that assess whether students have actually learned what they should have. The development of learning outcomes can take place within a number of arenas. Obviously, each individual school is one such arena. The faculty develops the outcomes they believe appropriate for students graduating from their school. This is the process usually followed by colleges and universities. Learning outcomes are developed for each major area within the college. For example, if you are a Political Science major, it is likely that the faculty of your department have identified the competencies you will be expected to develop before you graduate. Also, this faculty will have specified an assessment process that enables them to determine whether or not you have developed those competencies. The assessment instrument may be a formal test, such as the field test of the Graduate Record Examination, or a portfolio containing examples of your work, such as class tests, term papers, and the like, or some other assessment device. At the high school and grammar school levels it is not uncommon for the learning objectives to be developed external to the school. Increasingly, professional associations are involved in the development of learning objectives. For example, the National Council of Teachers of Mathematics has developed competency levels for both elementary and high school mathematics. In other instances, learning objectives are developed at the state level, often through the state department of education, and are influenced by the contents and competitive aspects of standardized tests such as the ACT or SAT. In either case, students are expected to have developed the specified competencies before passing the course or graduating from the school.

| 8.1 | *WHAT SHOULD JOE AND JANE COLLEGE LEARN?* |

Chapter 1 should have made it clear that we have certain specific objectives in mind in this textbook. To put the matter in the jargon of educational accountability, we have specific learning objectives in mind. One of them will illustrate the problems associated with the accountability movement.

One of our learning objectives is that all students in public policy develop the ability to think about policy on a crossnational basis, since we believe it is imperative that nations learn from one another. To assess whether students are actually developing this capacity, two things are necessary: First we have to give operational meaning to "thinking on a crossnational basis"; second, we have to devise means to determine whether the student is developing those operational characteristics.

To get a flavor of how difficult these two things are, we suggest you try an experiment. First, give specific operational meaning to "thinking on a crossnational basis." What is a student able to do who can accomplish this objective? Second, devise methods to determine whether any given student has developed those abilities. How can you know that you or any other student in your class has developed that ability?

The third area of interest in the accountability movement is that of the curriculum and teaching materials. Relative to the curriculum, the primary focus has been on the development of learning outcomes and on building those outcomes into the curriculum. (Those outcomes would then be used in the student assessments discussed earlier). *Competency-based education,* as the concept is often called, attempts to ensure the development of those competencies deemed essential at a particular level of education or in a particular subject.

Most states also have adopted a wide range of mandates concerning teaching materials. Prominent among these mandates are those regarding textbooks. Nearly all states have a process by which textbooks are approved for use in the state, and only those texts on the approved textbook list may be adopted by a district. In some states the requirement extends to private schools that seek either certification or aid from the state. For example, if a private school receives aid for teaching the secular subject of natural science, then it would be required to adopt a text from the state-approved list. In addition to textbooks, there is a wide range of teaching materials that are prescribed by the states. These range all the way from the highly controversial sex education materials to laboratory equipment and supplies. The objective behind the mandates is to achieve a minimal level of adequacy in curriculum and materials.

What is the result of all these accountability devices? As surprising as it might be, very little effort has been expended to determine the results of accountability devices. Student assessment is a good example. The development of learning outcomes, the integration of those outcomes into the curriculum, and the assessment of how well students are accomplishing those outcomes is a difficult and time-consuming process, one that has certainly increased the paper work required of teachers. But has student assessment improved the quality of education? As one cynic on our faculty put it, "Who assesses assessment?" Have the time, effort, and resources expended on assessment resulted in higher-quality education? Unfortunately, at this point it is not possible to say. So we are left with only a question: Is the accountability movement a substantive process that improves the quality of education or is it an externally mandated process that simply increases paper work for already overloaded teachers?

STATE EDUCATION REFORMS

Along with the accountability movement, the issue of empowerment has been an important part of the debate on quality education (Blase and Blase 1994). In this regard, one trend is clear: State departments of education have become increasingly important in determining educational policy and practice. That is, there has been a centralization of power at the state level that has strained the concept of local control almost to the breaking point. A parallel development has been an increase in the power of administrators in the school districts and educational institutions. In the school districts the role and influence of principals and superintendents have increased significantly since the l960s. This double shift of power has led to calls for the empowerment of parents or teachers. Some districts have made good-faith efforts to increase parent participation in the affairs of the school. Techniques for doing so include stimulating organizations such as the parent–teacher association and relying on school district equivalents of state sunshine and open records laws. A much more ambitious plan, the charter school movement, has been proposed as a means of empowering teachers.

The *charter school* is an independent school run by teachers under a contract with the school district or state department of education. The idea is to free the school from the bureaucratic control now associated with the increased power of school administrators and state departments of education. A group of teachers may start a new school or convert an existing one to charter school status by entering into a contract with a school district. The contract will specify the program the school will offer and the student performance standards that it will guarantee. If students do not perform at the levels the contract specifies, the contract can be withdrawn. The charter school usually receives the same amount of financial assistance from the state that would have gone to the public school. An interesting feature of charter schools in the states where they have been approved is that the schools are "schools of choice," that is, students can choose to attend the charter school or the public school in their district. The charter school, however, may not screen students on the basis of their intellectual or athletic ability (there goes the football team). If there are more applications than the charter school has space for, students must be chosen by casting lots. A charter school is governed by a board of directors, which is elected by its teachers and by the parents. In this way, the school is granted considerable autonomy with regard to educational goals and methods. Certainly, teachers and parents experience considerable empowerment.

To date, only two states, Minnesota and California, have authorized charter schools. As a result of the limited application of the concept, it is difficult to evaluate the potential of charter schools. In theory, charter schools have the advantage of "combining aspects of schooling historically considered public, such as access and funding, with those considered private, such as responsiveness and freedom from bureaucratic entanglement" (Williams and Buechler 1993, p. 4). If these advantages work out in practice, they certainly would be compelling reasons for supporting charter schools. Minnesota's initial experience with charter schools, however, has not been altogether encouraging. Rather than having a number of applications from innovative schools and teachers, the first applications were from a private Montessori school and a small rural school scheduled for closing by the state. This led the president of the Minnesota Education Association to observe that charter schools in practice may be little more than elite academies created with public funds (Astrup 1992, p. 29). The direction that charter schools will take—whether they will become truly innovative schools combining the best of the public and private approach or elite academies funded by the state—is still to be determined.

FEASIBLE POLICIES FOR EDUCATION

One of the learning objectives we have emphasized strongly in this book is that of thinking about the policy experience of the United States compared to the policy experience of other countries. Much can be learned by focusing on the policy culture of and experience in other nations. The striking feature of educational policy in other nations is the almost universal occurrence of calls for educational reform. In a provocative essay entitled "Death, Taxes and School Reform," two observers of education policy across nations concluded: "There are few things in life that one can count on, but one is dissatisfaction with the schools. The United States is hardly unique in this respect: Campaigns to reform national education systems are launched regularly in countries around the world." In conclusion, the authors contend, "the belief that something is wrong with the schools and that 'reform' can fix it appears to be one of the few reliable features of modern life" (Plank and Adams 1989, p. 1). While specific education policy issues may vary across time periods and among nations, education reform is a perennial issue that dominates education policy in nearly all nations. Feasible education policy, in the United States and in other nations, must begin with a realistic approach to the phenomenon of school reform.

Two perceptions are central to the beliefs that underlie the continual call for school reform. The first is the myth of failure, the perception that something is wrong with the schools. The basis of this perception does vary between nations and over time. Currently, the basis for the myth of failure in the industrialized nations seems to be the notion that education has not responded adequately to the world economy and technological advances. In developing nations the basis for the myth of failure seems to be the perception that education is not adequately providing for development within the country. Thus across nations the perception of failure of the education system is commonly related to economic development and progress. The second common element in the constant call for school reform is the belief that reform will be successful, that it will fix whatever is wrong in the educational system. What are we to make of these two myths? Do they have substance in fact? Do they serve the interest of educational quality? Are the myths accelerators or impediments to educational progress?

A part of the perception that there is a critical failure in education may be a measurement problem. For example, if the question "Why can't Jane read better than she does?" is asked, then, "Read better in relation to what or to whom?" must also be asked. The most common answer the American public is given is that Jane does not read well in comparison with Japanese or German students. This answer points up one of the measurement problems. The United States is one of the few societies that is committed to education of all youths and virtually the only society that requires all students to submit to skills tests. However, not all Japanese students are given cognitive skills tests; generally only those who are progressing through the system to university-level education are tested. Therefore, only college-bound students in the United States should be in the pool for statistical comparison with other nations. An alternative way of evaluating contemporary education in all nations would be to compare present student scores on skills tests with those of students of previous generations. But insurmountable problems lie in the way of such an analysis. Among the more serious of them is the fact that the timeline is very short since skills testing is a relatively recent practice, the fact that the tests themselves have changed so that valid comparisons are difficult to make, and the fact that what is being tested today is considerably different from what was tested decades ago (few academic disciplines are the same today).

Should attempts to compare groups of students, then, be abandoned in favor of comparing students to some absolute standard? In other words, should a high school graduate be required to read X number of words per minute with Y comprehension level? The problem with utilizing such an approach on a cross-national basis is that such tests are subject to significant cultural bias. For example, the differences in the Japanese and American cultures account for most of the differences in the two educational systems

(Ohanian 1987, p. 14). For instance, the historic cultural isolationism in the United States (see Chapter 3) has led to Americans' lack of interest in world geography and the study of other cultures and societies—hence the omission of these subjects in U.S. elementary and high school curricula. The Japanese culture, however, has a broad interest in foreign societies, so Japanese students are required to take intensive courses in world geography and cultural studies. Therefore, when Japanese and U.S. students are tested in these areas, at least part of the result is a function of cultural factors and not of the school's success or failure in teaching the students.

It is important when thinking about American education to understand that some of the differences in education performance across the states is also attributable to a measurement problem. In this country the most frequently used measure of education achievement is the Scholastic Aptitude Test (SAT). There are significant problems in using the SAT score as the measure of educational quality across the states, however. Two analysts stated the problem succinctly: "... the major obstacle to state-by-state comparisons is the difference in the test-taking population in each state. Because the groups of students taking the SAT are qualitatively different from state to state, a large portion of the variation in state scores might have little to do with the quality of each state's system of education" (Steelman and Powell 1985, p. 604). The most obvious difference is found in the percentage of eligible seniors who take the test. In 1982 this percentage varied from a low of 2 percent in South Dakota to a high of 69 percent in Connecticut. Additionally, those who took the test were not random samples across the states; there were significant social and economic differences between the test-taking populations of the various states.

The beginning point in breaking the endless cycle of reform and instituting meaningful change is to deal honestly with the myth of failure. The absence of comparable statistics on school performance makes this task a very difficult one, although some meaningful work has been done on comparing educational performance across states. Steelman and Powell (1985) developed a method for "correcting" SAT scores across the states by controlling for the effect of different percentages of students taking the test and for the varied composition of the test-taking population. The rankings of states were significantly different from the ranking based on uncorrected scores. Additional work needs to be done in the United States on developing accurate measures of school performance. Equally important is the development of accurate measures of school performance across nations. Simply put, crossnational comparisons of educational performance presently represent only the beginning of what needs to be a long and careful effort.

If measures of educational performance are not as dependable as they should be, what then is to be made of the myth of educational failure? One thing can be said with confidence: The evidence does not support it. Unfortunately, the opposite is also true: The evidence is not sufficient to justify the claim of educational quality. Anecdotal and case study evidence can be amassed to support both the claim of failure and the claim of quality. A college graduate with a reading level of a fourth-grader would confirm the failure myth, and an individual with an extremely disadvantaged background who earned a Ph.D. at a prestigious university could support the quality myth. Case study evidence would consist of such things as analysis of the successful effort to reform Chicago's schools (Heck 1992) or studies of the charter school movement mentioned earlier.

It is difficult to evaluate such evidence. We suggest several conclusions. First, common sense indicates that the myth of failure is fraught with hyperbole. The fact is that the overwhelming number of Johnnys and Janes in the United States can read. Second, there is substantial evidence that the exaggerations found in the myth of failure are deliberate because they serve political purposes. Plank and Adams (1989, p. 2) found that the politics of school reform, in both rich and poor countries, centered around the issue of who would control the schools. In the United States, they found, the politics of reform typically is a struggle between those who work in the schools and those who pay for them, with elected politicians exploiting the conflict in any way they can. In poor countries the politics of reform tends to be a struggle between those who are well served by the system and those who are not. The result of the politics of reform is what several analysts call the "pendulum effect" (Tyack, Kirst, and Hansot 1980; Shimahara 1986). This effect occurs as one generation of actors in the politics of reform attempts to reverse the "successes" of its predecessors. Many of the policy cycles within education are attributable to this factor. Finally, all these things mean that there is a certain primacy of politics in educational policymaking. Herein is found one of the great ironies in the history of American education. The progressive movement of the early 1900s sought to take educational policymaking out of politics and place it in the hands of professionally competent individuals. What they did instead was to embroil educational policy in a political conflict between professional educators and various publics over the issue of who should control the schools.

Is meaningful change possible in a policy arena characterized by the primacy of politics? We believe that it is. The basic issue is that of the democratic control of policy. It is at this point that we can learn the most from a study of other countries. A number of other nations, especially Sweden, Japan, Germany, France, and England, have successfully reformed their educational systems, and all of those reform efforts occurred within a highly politicized context. The effort in Sweden, for example, involved some of the most basic tensions within that society, tensions between elite and mass control of the educational system. There are features of the reform effort that were common to each of these successful countries, and the most important of these features was the deliberate effort on the part of leadership to involve all affected parties in the change effort. Change was not an "insider's" process, but an open process involving a wide range of participants. "Reform" in the United States more often than not has been a process limited to the politicians or to the professionals. Educational change in this country needs to recapture the great potential found in civic involvement of all citizens. We return to this important point in Chapter 11.

 ## CHAPTER **9**

CODE BLUE FOR HEALTH CARE

AMERICA'S MEDICAL CRISIS

The hopes and fears of the nation were centered on Washington in 1993 and 1994 as one of the most titanic political battles since World War II played out. At issue was the proposal to reform the American health care system. Arrayed on one side were those who called for change: A newly elected president and the first lady, the automakers, most state governors, organizations representing the elderly and consumers, and the labor unions. On the other side were the opposition lobbies: the giant drug firms, many small businesses and organizations that represented them, the huge health insurance industry, and the American Hospital Association. Many groups were divided over the issue. The American Medical Association leadership, which favored universal insurance coverage paid for by required contributions from workers and employers, was at war with many of its convention delegates who opposed such ideas. A large alliance of nurses and the AMA's big rival, the American College of Surgeons, even supported a Canadian-style national health insurance plan. Never had the medical profession's house been so divided. But the major factor seemed to be public support for reform. During the summer of 1994 nearly 80 percent of voters supported the idea of universal insurance coverage (Newsweek polls, June, July, August). With such overwhelming public support and the support of powerful organizations, it seemed that the health care reform proposal was unstoppable.

THE DRUMBEAT OF DISINFORMATION: THE KILLING OF HEALTH CARE REFORM 1994

By midsummer of 1994 a strange turn of fate had infected the battle for health care reform. On the one hand, the opposition lobbies struck back with an intense and well-financed campaign. On the other hand, the general public was almost unaware of the megabuck anti-reform campaign. The unawareness of the public is explainable largely because the opposition flooded the Washington TV markets and created a near panic among members of Congress by instilling the belief that the public was turning against universal coverage (*New York Times*, July 17, 1994).

The anti-reform lobbying effort was the largest in recent American history. The opposition spent more than $300 million in less than a year. This giant sum was larger than all 1988 and 1992 presidential campaign expenses combined and dwarfed the second largest lobbying campaign, the $150 million effort by big business in 1978 to defeat the establishment of a cabinet level Department of Consumer Affairs. As the well-orchestrated campaign cranked up the heat on members of Congress, a logjam of contradictory proposals emerged. No coalition developed to protect the Clinton plan, and some observers argued that the White House had not been active enough in resisting opposition pressures. The Clinton plan suffered a major setback when several former supporters, including the AMA, the Business Roundtable, the Chamber of Commerce, and the Republican leadership in the Congress, announced their opposition. The results of the opposition effort were to kill the Clinton proposal in Congress and to leave the American policy system deeply divided over health care reform.

Several factors are important in explaining the failure of health care reform in 1994. The first is what we call the drumbeat of disinformation. In Chapter 3 we talked about the important concept of information pollution and stressed the fact that it tends to occur around controversial issues such as abortion and health care. Such pollution is created by intensely emotional, ideologically rigid, and highly mobilized groups that argue on the basis of deeply held beliefs and values. They color or massage facts in such a way as to advocate a predecided position and will use propagandistic and marketing techniques to influence public opinion and political leadership. These techniques rely on the repetitious appeal to unprovable dogmatic assertions and the manipulation of information through cultural rallying symbols, scapegoat misrepresentation, and omission of facts. The historic record gets shunted aside in the process.

The opposition lobby conducted a very effective disinformation campaign. It chose as its theme the claim that health care reform would create "a monster regulatory bureaucracy that would swoop down and impose regulations on small businesses to pay the total bill for health care." Employer mandates would supposedly finance a system in which the bureaucracy would make the determination of what health care each American would receive, ending forever patient choice of a doctor. The battle over health care reform, in this regard, was more than anything a war to manipulate cultural symbols.

A second factor in the defeat of the health care reform was the ambiguous attitudes about it among Americans. Public opinion polls consistently show that Americans are deeply worried about certain health care problems. Among the most important of these is the loss of health insurance and the inability to pay the high costs of nursing home care for elderly relatives. Such fears have led more than 70 percent of Americans to favor "fundamental reforms" in the health care system. But support drops by more than half when specific proposals are mentioned. Thus while pollsters found that up to 80 percent of Americans want universal health coverage, few people wanted anybody to pay for it. Less than half (45–49 percent) want employers to pay, while even fewer (40 percent) want to pay for the plans themselves without employer contributions. Further, about half want no tax increases to pay for reforms (*Newsweek*, June 27, 1994, p. 29; *New York Times*/CBS poll, July 14–17, 1994). It seems most Americans want reform but cannot agree on who should pay the costs.

Various academics have argued that the failure to get health care reform lay in the mixed feelings Americans have about the specifics (Fein 1994; Brown 1992). Brown argues that our split personality over the specifics of reform is due to a never-ending argument over the relative merits of the private versus the public sector, an argument that depends on values that cannot be proved or disproved. Fein agrees, arguing that health care reform failed in part because of the perception among political leaders that there is so much distrust of government that the American public favors the invisible hand of the market to the visible alternatives developed by government bureaucrats. Certainly, the disinformation effort appealed to such cultural factors in defeating the health care proposal.

The disinformation system means that the first victim in debates over health care is often the facts. As difficult as it is, we must get past the packaged onslaught of distortions to a body of verifiable, historical facts about health care issues. We must go below the ideological debate to explain how the health care system and its problems are typically depicted by various parties in the debate. This chapter will attempt to deprogram our politicized view of the facts. Ironically, our approach is best explained by a medical analogy: We first attempt to diagnose accurately what the system's problems are and then prescribe realistic solutions. But first a bit of perspective is in order on one of the most important features of the American health care system.

THE ECONOMIC GIANT: THE AMERICAN MEDICAL SYSTEM

An appreciation of the gigantic size of the American health care system is necessary to understand why it so important to different interests. The health care system is a $900 billion a year sector of the economy. By itself, as an economic sector, it is larger than the entire economy of any European country except Germany!

Few Americans truly understand how much is spent on the medical sector. Annual medical spending ($900 billion in 1994) is now roughly *three times larger* than the annual giant defense budgets in the peak years of the 1980s (roughly $300 billion a year). It far exceeds the annual spending on the entire American education system, public and private. It is almost equal to total corporate annual profits! And it is growing by about 10 percent a year, faster than most anything else in the economy.

As an economic giant, the American medical system truly has no peer in the world. No other medical system—in fact, no other single private industry or government expense on earth—generates and consumes so much money or such a high percentage of a large nation's wealth (15 percent of gross domestic product in 1994, and rising).

The point of these mind-boggling facts is this: To propose deep changes in *any* economic entity that is this wealthy, wealth generating, and politically powerful will be controversial to say the least. Mention of reform will inevitably stir up high levels of political conflict. To sort out the facts from the fog is a challenge.

THE CONTEXT OF MEDICAL SYSTEMS WORLDWIDE

It will be informative to see how medical systems around the world are different from ours. Experts differ on how to classify systems. One of the best ways to make sense of the different kinds of medical systems is to adapt several schemes from leading experts. Any national medical system has five parts (adapted from Anderson 1989b; Roemer, 1993; Graig 1993):

1. *Tangible medical methods and techniques*: prevailing medical arts, technologies, buildings and research centers, drugs, equipment

2. *Ownership*: professional guilds, private capitalists, churches, government services, co-ops

3. *Management*: professional licensing, facilities planning, organization public or private

4. *Economic support*: government taxes at different levels, social insurance, private insurance, charity, personal income

5. *Delivery style and modes*: preventive care, public disease control, curative care, long-term and old-age care, naturalistic medicine, Chinese, etc.

These separate parts can be organized in several ways. Health care organization is a nation's assumed principles of what are the best ways to own and deliver medicine to people. Four forms of medical organization are used around the world:

Private Organization ────────────────────────▶ Public Organization

United States before 1900	*United States Today*	*Canada Germany*	*Sweden England*
Guild and Competitive Market Model	Mixed Market Model	Comprehensive Service and Social Insurance Model	Public Service Model

In the *guild and competitive market* systems, professions are private, often organized into competitive medical guilds. Ownership of medical care is private property or at most a church or religious charity. This model was in Europe and the United States roughly before 1900 and is found in some developing countries today.

In the *mixed-market model* ownership and services are a mixture of private and public. However, the "market" or private sector part of the system is really not a true competitive market but rather a mixture of two things. The first is a combination of competitive and monopolistic features (small-town doctors, small insurers versus a few huge corporate insurance giants, corporate hospital chains and drug firms). The second is the fact that individuals receive medical care from professionals who are paid by a combination of third-party payers (insurance plans, government services) and individual fees. The mixed market model is what the United States has today.

The *comprehensive service and social insurance model* is what most European countries and Canada have. It provides universal, not-for-profit health insurance to all persons, through tax supports. The professions are both private (private fees for profit) and public (salaried government employees).

The *public service model* is often called "socialized medicine" and thus given a bad name in America. Actually this model resembles the public service tradition of certain widely admired professions in the United States—especially astronauts, military, police, firefighters, teachers, and Forest and Park Service rangers. In a public service medical system, all health services, professions, and insurance are publicly owned and operated by government-salaried employees, there are few market features, there is usually a lot of local or regional funding and control of medical care, and hospitals and medical professionals operate within defined and negotiated budgets. The U.S. Armed Forces, England, Sweden, and Norway have this system.

Given the varied ways of organizing a medical system, what *is* the American system? No other system has such unusual basic traits. Consider the following partial description of the American mixed market medical system:

1. Profit-oriented ownership (private hospitals)

2. Not-for-profit care (Catholic and Shriners hospitals)

3. Extremely high-paid and high-status careers marked by nearly total, almost authoritarian personal control of services provided (private surgeons, M.D.s, etc.)

4. Politically restricted practice of competing medical arts (Chinese medicine, naturopathy, homeopathy, chiropractic, and osteopathic medicines and nursing have all been severely restricted as a result of successful AMA lobbying over the years)

5. Low-status, fairly low-paid health technicians (nurse aids, social workers)

6. A "mixed market" marriage of private-owned systems (HMOs, PPOs, private hospitals, and clinics) tied to vast regimes of government subsidies and ser-

vices that provide income to select professions and needed services to special populations (tax code subsidies, Medicare and Medicaid, Armed Forces health care, veterans hospitals, etc.)

7. A group of truly huge, international, high profit-generating industries (drug companies, insurance companies, corporate hospital chains)

8. A crazy-quilt system of insurance coverage based on two layers: corporate employers providing employer/employee shared-cost medical plans for (increasingly less than) 50 percent of the population, plus public and government "contract for bid" and public-owned insurance funds that cover about 30 percent (Medicare for elderly, Veterans Administration and military, public employee insurance funds, etc.); the system thus misses about 17 percent of the population

Most analyses of the system consider only parts of it. This partial analysis leads to confusion and ambiguous attitudes about what the health care system is and what reform it needs.

Given this complex, unique system, what is the health care problem? The elusive answer to this deceptively simple question lies in what one is willing to see and in how one describes the health care system and its problem.

A simple analogy can offer a profound lesson about examining the health care crisis. Several blind men try to describe an elephant from touching specific parts of it. Some say it is long and skinny (the tail), some say it is like a tree (the leg), some say that it is hard and smooth (the tusks). So much of the beast, like the medical system, is left unknown as people consider only a small part and mistake it for the whole.

Like the parts of the elephant, each of the five expert pictures of health care, which we will present in the rest of this chapter, describes only part of the real facts, but when we add them together we will get closer to the more complicated truth. The five expert pictures are progressively revealing and each has a different assumption about the medical system and its problems. But even these five interpretations start from a deeper cultural ideal of medicine. The great debate about health care has focused largely inside certain cultural ideals and assumptions.

Therefore, to understand health care in America, it is not enough to understand a multitude of technical facts. We also have to grasp *how we think about medicine* in the shadow of our cultural beliefs. So we must first describe those cultural beliefs that shape the five definitions of the problems and that limit our understanding of what to do about them.

HOW THE GREAT AMERICAN CULTURAL TALE ABOUT MEDICINE LIMITS THE DEBATE

All Americans share an enduring picture of the "medical system" as a *small-town marketplace of scientific wonders*. Such an ideal is part of the powerful social mythology that Secretary of Labor and Harvard scholar Robert Reich says guides "who we are, and what we want for ourselves and one another" (1987, p. 5). In Chapter 2 we argued that social myths are not to be thought of as "falsehoods." They constitute a belief system so widely shared in a society that it can become a "self-fulfilling prophecy." Belief systems are appealing, enduring, and adaptable, and are powerful forces in a society. The American cultural ideal of medicine is one such belief system that guides social and governmental policies. Perhaps more important, the desire to keep that ideal limits our imagination about solutions and inspires intense conflict over any changes.

The cultural ideal is an early American storybook tale. It tells us that nearby we have our trusted small-town doctor and our hospital, complete with specialists, both operating like any Mom and Pop store. Except, of course, the good doctor is not just a store clerk, for the doctor is anointed with Science, and holds the purist of motives (self-sacrifice in public service). This vision is deeply rooted in our culture, embodying four specific cultural ideals that are among our most cherished beliefs: *small-town folks, secular worship of science, heroic self-sacrifice,* and the *heroic small businessman.*

Some health care experts and historians have rightfully argued that American political and social culture set the limits of American imagination about what's good and possible in the reform of health care (Fein 1994; Starr 1982; Freidson 1970). These four grand ideals are the forces that most shape the American medical imagination. They form four steps leading to a kind of medical sanctification, which has made reform of the system in the twentieth century so difficult to accomplish.

In the first step, some of our early medical beliefs were sanctified in the vision that doctors are neighborly, caring, independent agents, with a caring bedside manner (small-town folks). As a result, we historically granted "the doc" great trust and status. And because doctors were armed with Science (secular worship of science), we trusted them more, anointing them with almost unrivaled social status. With that status came tremendous independence and legal power over medical decisions in the doctor–patient relationship as advances in biology and bacteriology came to be associated with doctors in the early to mid-twentieth century. Medical sociologist Jewson (1976) described this phenomenon as a historical shift in medical social roles from bedside to hospital to laboratory medicine.

In the third and fourth steps we completed the medical sanctification process with beliefs that further strengthened our admiration: We all know that doctors worked so hard to get through medical school (heroic self-sacrifice); and they have come to our town to practice in our hospital, among our people (the heroic small businessman). These worshipful beliefs about doctors (charted best by Jewson) have also been carefully cultivated and politically nurtured in the twentieth century by the American Medical Association and "the profession" (Starr 1982).

The *economic* significance of these worshipful beliefs is that Americans apply little of their normal consumer attitudes to medicine. They absolve doctors and hospitals from the normal rules of the market. Reflect on how most of us act when negotiating with a car salesperson, or elbowing our way through a discount house to buy a stereo or even something highly technical like a computer. Now contrast that to how we act when we are with medical professionals—apologetic, unquestioning, almost fawning. In matters of medicine we behave most unlike the consumers we perceive ourselves to be.

From this small-town mythic tale, we retain the notion that we have a private health care system, providers who sell their services in an open market, just as in any other business—even though we see increasing amounts of government services and regulation. Similarly, we see ourselves as tough consumers, choosing medical care on the basis of good information provided by market feedback. (The facts are that most decisions to get medical help are made quickly, and most doctor choices are made entirely by chance or are based on hearsay). We also continue to assume, despite dwindling insurance coverage, that we have a lot of choice in selecting doctors, hospitals, and treatment options. We are, after all, a nation of choosers, aren't we?

In contrast to these assumptions, legal scholars, medical historians, economists, and academics for years have charted the slow establishment of near monopolism in medical practice as well as in other areas of the medical industry (Gelfand 1993; Fox 1993; Maggs 1993; Larkin 1993; Berlant 1975). Since we usually question and eventually limit overbearing monopolism elsewhere in our lives, why do we not do so with the medical system? Probably because of cultural-psychological rationalization. Rationalization is the process of coping with a loss or other difficulty or avoiding change by adjusting our understanding or perception of reality (Wheeler and Janis 1980, pp. 24–28). Thus we tell ourselves the following not exactly false but only partly correct story about the problems of the medical system:

> It's all about outrageous rising costs. The system is a bit out of whack, but it's not entirely broken—it just has out-of-control prices. Maybe some doctors or drug firms are a bit greedy. It is not something government needs to replace. Maybe at most we just need to regulate it a little bit, or provide coverage for most people.

This story about the "medical cost explosion," a descendant of the eroded mythic dream, is a comforting rationalization shared by both liberals and conservatives. And like all tempting rationalizations, *it is part of the truth*, but not all of it. Its place within the total picture can be seen from a careful look at the five main expert descriptions of the health care problem.

FIVE EXPERT PICTURES OF THE HEALTH CARE PROBLEM

The American debate on problems of the medical system has been guided by five different definitions of the problem. Three of these are simply descendants of the main cultural tale: Control the costs and you control the problem.

Problem Picture 1: "It's a Cost Explosion that Hurts Business" Here the picture is that rising health costs drain needed capital and profits from the economy and private businesses. Thus, this cost explosion is a threat primarily to business profits, to our international competitiveness, and secondarily to jobs and incomes. As such it drains off monies that could go into new product innovations, higher wages and benefits for workers, etc.

Solutions: Find mild ways to introduce competition (through managed care, HMOs, consumer information systems). Try to encourage negotiated or publicly bid contracts of fees and services for the private providers to compete against (Clinton-style plans).

Problem Picture 2: "It's a Cost Explosion that Is Threatening Government Budgets and Other Public Priorities" Here the picture is that rising health costs are a threat mainly because they are a severe drain on governments (see Figure 9.1). In this picture, budgets will hit panic levels by the beginning of the twenty-first century. Most worrisome, they are devouring revenues at a rate that now requires governments to make large reductions in vital areas such as defense (national) or education and universities (states), with no end in sight.

Solutions: Same as number 1, stressing state-led actions.

Problem Picture 3: "It's an Insurance Coverage Problem" This is the point of view advocated by insurance and small-business-oriented analysts. The main problems are said to be huge gaps, loopholes, and unnecessary costs and cancellations in the private insurance coverage most people have, and in the declining benefits (in Medicare and Medicaid) for the elderly for short- and long-term care.

Solutions: Fix the insurance problems—guarantee portability, pricing and policy truth statements, right to buy despite preexisting health problems, etc. (This is called "insurance reform" and "providing access.")

Problem Picture 4: "It's the Decline of Preventive Medicine and Public Health" This picture from public health experts stresses that we are backtracking to Third World levels in preventive medicine because of the decline of public health systems—low rates of immunization and preventive checkups, bad diet and care of young children, eroding public control of disease transmission, AIDs, etc.

Solutions: Return to our historic preventive medicine practices.

Problem Picture 5: "Our Health Costs Are Worse Because We Have a Giant, Nonmarket System of Medical Monopolism, with Politically Artificial Limits on Competing Medical Arts" This picture is a powerful historical point of view, the only view that is not a child of the great mythic tale of medi-

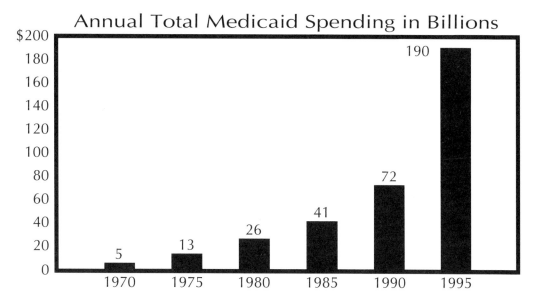

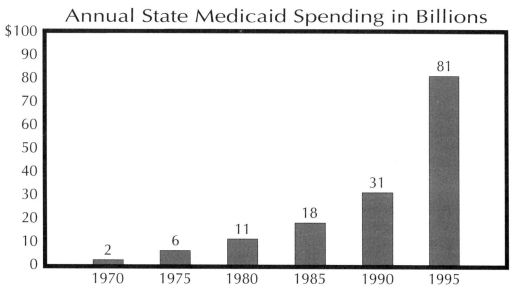

FIGURE 9.1   THE BIGGEST SUCKING SOUND: HOW THE MEDICAL COST EXPLOSION IS TAKING BILLIONS AND MORE EACH YEAR FROM GOVERNMENTS
Source: President Bush's 1992 and President Clinton's 1995 budget proposals to Congress.

cine. It is supported by historians of medicine, some health and labor economists, consumer groups, and competitive medical professions. It stresses that
we have less and less real choice (until recent years) and truly huge costs
because of three aspects of historic medical monopolism: (1) prices are tradi-

tionally unlimited and technology and drugs are super-pricey (costs aided by government subsidy); (2) doctors wooed states to slap severe artificial political restrictions on competing medical arts and self-care common elsewhere in the world; and (3) costs are exploding partly because of unrealistic treatment and deathbed "keep 'em alive" social expectations, made worse by a cult and culture of physician control of heroic intervention.

Solutions: Introduce true competition and true choice in medical arts, and competitively control pricing (see number 1 above).

We should now dig a little deeper into the facts that are used in each of these interpretations of the health care problem.

THE COMMON ELEMENT: COST, COST, COST

The main characteristic distinguishing the American medical system from those of other nations is that ours is marred by a combination of exploding costs *and* declining medical coverage and service to the population with some evidence of overall declining quality of health. Both of these trends have worsened over the last several decades. It is important at this point to explore the facts about these costs.

THE FACTS OF EXPLODING HEALTH COSTS

There are a number of key indicators of exploding health costs. The most important is that total medical costs in the mid-1990s are approaching $1 trillion a year. Worse, the costs have been accelerating for more than ten years at a rate of 10 percent a year, more than double the growth rate of the economy (which has been between 1 and 4 percent) and the general inflation rate (below 5 percent) At the start of the 1960s the United States was spending about the same as other industrial nations, such as Germany and Canada, or about 5.5 percent of GDP (the total annual value of domestic production and consumption). But while other industrial nations' share devoted to medical costs rose slightly over 35 years to the 6 to 8.5 percent rate, America's tripled to 15 percent of GDP, with the steepest rise in the 1980s (Graig 1993, p. 18).

These costs translate into higher costs for American businesses and families. Business, which covers not quite two-thirds of the population through employer/employee insurance plans, pays about $200 billion a year for health care costs. This is more than total annual corporate after-tax profits each year since 1990. Average costs per employee have tripled over the last decade to over $5,000 per worker. Individuals and families worry deeply about the problems associated with rising medical costs. They fear that losing their jobs will mean losing health insurance or that a preexisting health problem will prevent them from obtaining insurance. They worry about paying for nursing home care for parents and grandparents (averaging $37,000 per year, more than the median family income). And they worry that monthly costs of medical care are eating so severely into incomes that many families are now forced to delay or not seek routine medical care.

THE REASONS FOR EXPLODING COSTS: "LOOK, MA! NO REAL MARKET!"

Why does all this happen? In picture 1 of the medical system, which is the viewpoint of many health care policy experts and economists, the medical system is said to have inadequate price-controlling market mechanisms. In addition to dysfunctional markets at work, there is horrendous administrative overhead. While the out-of-control sectors are limited, they are powerful wasters of medical and financial resources. The argument made is that our dysfunctional medical system doesn't just let prices rise, it *forces* them to rise.

In this view, there are five main forces that have produced the health cost explosion. First is the *third-party payment system*, that is, somebody other than the patient-consumer pays the majority of relatively unrestricted bills. The main payers are insurance companies, and Medicare and Medicaid. Before the 1960s the majority of people had only private hospital coverage and little insurance of any kind for doctors' bills, so doctors kept their fees at competitive and affordable levels. When third-party payment took over by the late 1960s, however, prices shot through the roof as market supply and demand price restraints collapsed. Until 1984, for example, Medicare paid for virtually everything at virtually any price, and so did private insurers, encouraged by the big net of employer benefit plans covering two-thirds of the population. By 1990 health spending was transformed (Figure 9.2).

The second factor producing the health cost explosion is said to be *unrestrained entitlement attitudes*. Under the nonmarket third-party payment system, American consumer-patients came to believe that they had a right to all possible services with no sparing of the costs or effort. Patients tend to demand all-out efforts, especially in the case of traumatizing accidents, terrifying diseases, or family members near death. Some studies show that most Americans with deteriorative or old-age conditions will spend 90 percent of their lifetime medical expenses in the last several months of their lives (frequently hundreds of thousands of dollars) to stave off death for only days or weeks. This strange trend, which might be called the "Golden Coffin Syndrome," may account for as much as 15 percent of total medical spending. In most instances, patients are not told what any bill will be, and they don't directly pay for most of it later. Some studies show that doctors don't even know their own prices ("That's the billing department"). Neither the patient nor the doctor seems to care because a third party will pay. As one conservative expert writes:

> Real insurance does not "insure" routine, predictable events (and needs), but rather events that *might* happen in the future and would be calamitous if they did. If automobile insurance were written like health insurance, for example, it would pay for gas fillups, oil changes, lube jobs, wiper blades, etc. ... (with) no limit on

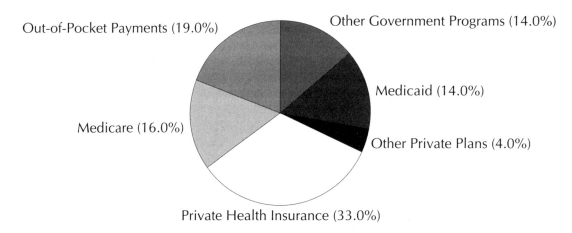

FIGURE 9.2   THE NATION'S HEALTH DOLLAR: 1991
Source: *Health Care Financing Review* 14, no. 2 (Winter 1992), p. 1.

the amount of goods and services.... To grasp the logic of it, imagine that you were to give a dozen people a duplicate of your credit card, tell them to head out to the malls, and have the bills sent back to you for payment.... Multiply this about 20 million times, and you have the shrewd financing method of our health care system. (Evans 1994, p. 11)

This is not a normal market. It has almost no competitive price restraints. More than $200 billion out of $900 billion is a conservative estimate of *expensive waste* in the dysfunctional market system (*Consumer Reports*, July 1992, p. 436).

Third, *unnecessary medical procedures* amount to about $130 billion, 14 percent of total health spending per year. A Rand Corporation study attributed this cost to a multitude of notoriously excessive, unnecessary procedures: heart bypass surgeries (44 percent unneeded), cesarean births (one in four births, twice the needed rate), back surgery, prostate surgery, and overuse of magnetic resonance imaging, to name a few. (See Table 9.1.)

TABLE 9.1   PERCENTAGE OF COMMON MEDICAL PROCEDURES THAT ARE UNNECESSARY AND OVERUSED

Hysterectomy	27%
Carpel tunnel syndrome surgery	17%
Tonsillectomy	16%
Laminectomy (most common type of back surgery)	14%
Pre-operative lab tests	60%

Cesarean section	50%
Upper gastrointestinal X-rays	30%
Removal of atherosclerotic plaque from carotid artery	32%
Heart bypass operations	14%
X-ray exam of blood flow to arteries	17%

Source: *Consumer Reports,* July 1992, pp. 439–440.

From the 1960s to the 1980s doctors had rather unlimited incentives to do and bill for more. Their code of ethics stressed "all available means," which also meant higher incomes. Thus in private practice more tests were ordered to "insure" for a diagnosis and to pay costly malpractice insurance in some specialties. Besides, third-parties would pay for the procedures.

The fourth factor said to contribute to the health cost explosion is an *incredibly expensive private bureaucracy*: $165 billion or 20 percent of medical costs are lost each year in insurance company excessive overhead costs, billing and delays, doctor billing, and office costs. In just insurance, for example, many studies show that about fourteen cents of every premium dollar is overhead expense in the private insurance industry, while the Medicare and Canadian public systems spend 2 percent (Health Care Financing Administration 1990).

Fifth is a *hospital medical arms race equal to the 1980s military arms race*. At 38 percent of national health care expenses, hospitals spend $340 billion per year (twice all doctor earnings; see Figure 9.3). Much of this spending started with a giant surge of hospital construction from the late 1940s through the 1960s aided by federal subsidies. This was followed by a Medicare policy that allowed hospitals to charge capital spending improvements to the system. This payment practice was cut off by Medicare regulations in the 1980s.

Today hospitals compensate by marketing themselves to richer patients, investing gargantuan sums in high-tech equipment to attract them. Experts point to profligate hospital spending on Hilton Hotel luxuries, urban hospital duplication and Madison-avenue marketing of state-of-the art technology. Today urban hospitals within a few blocks of each other all have their infant intensive care wards, heart transplant centers, sports complexes complete with big swimming pools, royal suite rooms, and MRI machines—while in contrast one can drive through hundreds of towns in some Western states in search of a single physician. This crazy medical arms race is financially equivalent to every city having its own aircraft carrier or B-52 bomber wing. In fact, some large U.S. cities have so much medical overbuilding that they have more MRI machines than all of Canada. Economists insist that such competition drives up prices, since the patients and doctors don't pay for the gold plating (insurance does). Economist James Robinson (1988) looked at 5,732 hospitals. Costs per admission for insured patients were 26 percent *higher* in hospitals that had more than nine major competitors in a fifteen-mile radius than in hospitals that had less competition.

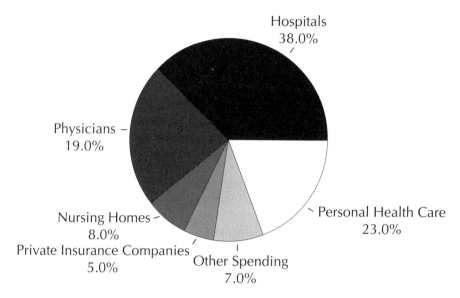

FIGURE 9.3   THE BREAKDOWN OF HEALTH CARE DOLLARS

Meanwhile, there's no convincing evidence of big increases in health care quality in proportion to all this spending, for two reasons. First, the 17 percent of the working population that has no insurance coverage, along with the larger 37 to 50 million who are uncovered at some time during a year, are almost always unable to obtain these high-tech services. Also, Medicare and Medicaid do not reimburse as lavishly for these services as in the past (for the elderly and really poor). Increasing numbers of hospitals and doctors deny expensive high-tech and emergency room care to uncovered patients unless state laws require immediate life-saving care. (Read typical family stories in Boxes 9.1a and 9.1b). Second, other industrial countries have most of the per capita use of technologies that we do (e.g., bone marrow transplants) without our arms race spending. Nor do they have the waiting alleged by distorted propaganda (see Box 9.1c).

| 9.1a | **AMERICAN FAMILY MEDICAL COSTS** |

Randy Sadler, his wife, Denise, and two sons live in Kernsville, North Carolina. Randy is self-employed and Denise works part-time for the Federal Government. The family earning combined is roughly the U.S. median income of $35,000 a year. Until recently, the Sadlers had no health insurance. Denise works too few hours to qualify for her employer's coverage and Randy, being self-employed, carries no insurance at all.

Realizing how risky it is to be without insurance, the family bought two policies from American Republic: one for Randy, with a $1,000 deductible, and one for Denise and the boys, who each must satisfy a $500 deductible every year. Monthly premiums total $227.

The insurance company promised a 5 percent premium reduction if, during any year, no covered members file a claim. If someone later submits a claim, the reduction is wiped out, and the premium reverts to what it would have been.

Ben, the youngest son, has severe allergies and is included in the policy; however, the insurance company refuses to cover this preexisting condition. The policy "waivers" his coverage for allergies, except for acute reactions that require hospitalization. This same waivering negates coverage for ear disorders and diseases of the tonsils and adenoids. Denise is covered for migraines and depression only because when she applied for the coverage she had not sought treatment for that ailment and the company was unaware she suffered from it. She put off seeing a doctor and even delayed a routine gynecological checkup because she knew insurance carriers disapproved of applicants who had recently seen a doctor. Recently, Ben has had two operations, which the family has paid for little by little out of their own pockets; other bills for Ben's bi-weekly allergy shots, medicines for recurring ear infections, and doctor visits are growing steadily, and the Sadlers' insurance policy is of little help. They feel they might as well not have insurance.

Their doctors, knowing the family's precarious financial situation, freely hand out samples of medications they need. However, in addition to this help and their health-insurance premiums, the family typically spends $100 to $200 a month on medical care and prescription drugs.

Source: "The Search for Solutions: Case Histories." Copyright 1992 by Consumers Union of U.S., Inc., Yonkers, NY 10703-1057. Condensed by permission from *Consumer Reports*, September 1992.

9.1b

HEALTH CARE PROBLEMS OF A TYPICAL SELF-EMPLOYED FAMILY

The Winslows of Lincolnville, Maine, are a young family with two children. Their oldest daughter was born with bipolar disorder, which causes manic depressive behavior—a rare condition in children; the youngest daughter has chronic ear infections, temporarily impairing her hearing and speech. Deb, the mother, suffers from asthma, skin rashes, and migraine headaches. Tom, the father, is a healthy, self-employed carpenter. His gross income in 1991 was about $21,000. The family's medical expenses eat up nearly 20 percent of that income.

Their Blue Cross policy, which costs $3,200 a year, pays the usual 80 percent for doctors' charges and prescription drugs, but only $84 a day for hospital care. The local hospital charges $500 a day. The policy also limits benefits for mental illness.

Deb quit her job as a bookkeeper to reduce the family's income so that they could qualify for Medicaid, and recently Blue Cross increased the Winslows' monthly premium by $60, so they have applied for a cheaper policy. The Winslows have to stay poor to provide care for their youngest daughter as well. She recently qualified for the Maine Health program, a plan that covers medical bills for approximately 5,400 of Maine's poorest children. The Winslows pay a monthly premium of $9.55.

Paperwork for the multiple plans has put Deb's bookkeeping skills to the test. The Blue Cross subsidiary, Blue Alliance (that provides the family's major medical coverage), must pay its share of the children's bills before Medicaid and the Maine Health Program kick in. The pharmacy that supplies the oldest daughter's $200 worth of prescriptions each month must first bill Medicaid. Medicaid then sends the Winslows a form to mail to Blue Alliance. Blue Alliance pays Medicaid 80 percent of the bill, and Medicaid then pays the pharmacy the amount it has received from Blue Alliance plus the portion it's obligated to cover. When Deb needs a prescription for herself, she pays the pharmacy, then must wait up to twelve weeks for reimbursement from the insurer, forcing the family to put off paying other bills.

Deb needs prescription-strength inhalers on a regular basis to prevent asthma attacks, but their $57 price tag forces her to use them only for emergencies; she then uses the money to buy the children clothes or shoes. But Deb also pays a price for delaying care when she has to go to the hospital emergency room for a Demerol shot for her migraines (she has made six such trips this year at a cost of $64 per visit). "You have to fight the bureaucracy, the insurance companies, and the legislators who don't want to listen. Nobody knows what a financial nightmare this is," observes Deb in frustration.

Source: "The Search for Solutions: Case Histories." Copyright 1992 by Consumers Union of U.S., Inc., Yonkers, NY 10703-1057. Condensed by permission from *Consumer Reports*, September 1992.

CANADA: NO WAITING FOR CARE

The Deveys of Burlington, Ontario, have lately been heavy users of medical services. Linda, forty-six, has had a number of gynecological procedures, and she also has severe allergies. Her sons, ages eighteen and twelve, have similar allergies. Their father, Robert, age fifty-one, suffers from recurring cysts on the cornea of the eye.

Robert is a teacher; Linda is a teacher's assistant. The family's gross income in 1991 was about $60,000 in U.S. dollars. Of that, they paid about $14,600 in federal and provincial taxes. Some of those taxes go to fund the Ontario Health Insurance Plan, which pays most of the family's medical bills.

The school district that employs Robert pays $600 a year for "extended health insurance" that pays for some of the medical treatment not covered by the province. The district also buys dental coverage for the family. That benefit costs the school district $700 a year. In Canada about 25 percent of all health expenditures are either paid out of pocket or covered by private insurance.

The Deveys' allergies are so severe that conventional treatment by an allergist is of no help. They look to a doctor of environmental medicine, who does more extensive testing to find the exact dosage that would neutralize the symptoms—a treatment which their health plan insists is experimental and so refuses to pay for testing. The Deveys look to their extended health coverage to pay the difference but still had to pay about $1,700 in 1991 for testing and allergy treatments.

Their out-of-pocket expenses used to be higher, but after the insurance underwriters refused to pay for the "experimental" treatment Linda appealed the decision to Ontario's Human Rights Commission and won. This reduced their injection expenses by half.

They have virtually no other medical expenses, since Ontario's plan takes care of just about everything else—fortunate for the Devey family, because in the past few years Linda has had two operations to remove benign cysts in her ovaries and breast, and because of her allergies she had to have a special hospital room during these times. She has also suffered whiplash from an automobile accident, and Robert needed treatment for his recurring problem in his eye. The boys also needed treatment for ear infections and often used an after-hours clinic. Such facilities are staffed by medical professionals and are popping up all over Canada, paid for by the provinces.

Doctors in Ontario are allowed to bill their patients small amounts—$5, $10, or $15—for such services as prescribing medication over the telephone, transferring medical records to another doctor, making appointments with specialists, filling out immunization reports or health forms for children's camps and schools. The Deveys' doctor gives his patients the choice of paying an annual fee of $54 that takes care of all those services, or paying as the need arises. The Deveys chose the latter.

Source: "The Search for Solutions: Case Histories." Copyright 1992 by Consumers Union of U.S., Inc., Yonkers, NY 10703-1057. Condensed by permission from *Consumer Reports*, September 1992.

What these five factors mean is that the United States, unlike other nations, has not been able to prevent escalating health care costs from robbing the rest of the economy, both business and government, of needed revenues. In fact, both business and government have been forced to "rob Peter to pay the health care Paul" in very clear ways. In private business and in the medical industry, this is known as cost shifting.

COST SHIFTING: METHODS OF DIVERTING HEALTH COSTS

Research shows businesses have identified exploding health costs as being perhaps the single greatest drag on corporate profits, capital investment in new technologies, and international competitiveness (Jasinowski and Canner 1989). They have compensated by shifting costs *internally* for these and other financial stresses, and by cutting benefits to workers. Cost shifting methods include reducing wages, making sweeping cuts in middle management (known as *downsizing* in the early 1990s), reducing health insurance benefits by increasing deductibles and requiring worker co-payments, and reducing employer contributions to pension funds.

Some businesses pass on health costs directly to consumers through higher product prices. This is especially true in the more oligopolistic sector, which does not experience much free-market price competition (e.g., oil companies, aerospace contractors) and for some firms that face fairly competitive domestic markets (e.g., tires, electronics). For instance, Robert Mercer, chairman of Goodyear Tire Company, reported that the company's annual health costs raised the price of each tire by $3.40 (Graig 1993, p. 23).

It is not only businesses that engage in cost shifting. The entire health care system is marked by a crazy-quilt of half visible cost shifting that can be likened to a large black-market or underground economy. Economists, health care specialists, and politicians are to differing degrees aware of these practices, but corporate health plan managers and hospital administrators are exposed to them on a daily basis.

Cost shifting works like this: (1) Doctors, hospitals, and some insurance companies shift higher premiums and less coverage to covered workers and patients to compensate for uncovered patients; (2) big businesses that are able to do so pass on health costs (see methods above) to workers and consumers; and; (3) middle-size businesses as well as consumers and workers pay this bill of cost-shifted health care through higher premiums, higher doctor and hospital charges, lower wages and benefits, and higher commodity prices in the general market.

There are three notable escapees who avoid these increased costs or income losses: (1) the doctors (who almost always get paid by someone); (2) the hospitals (who usually get paid, and who pass on unpaid costs in bills to covered patients); and (3) small businesses who generally can't and won't cover workers, and who provide benefits only voluntarily. (Small business lobbies ferociously fought off picking up some of these costs when they helped beat down the Clinton plan's employee–employer shared contributions plan in 1994.)

THE STRAIN OF THE COST EXPLOSION ON THE ECONOMY

Any economy is turned askew as a larger percentage of its total is devoted to any one sector. Wartime economies are the obvious example: Shortages occur in everything as the economy is rerouted to war production at levels of 20 percent of the total GDP or higher. Experience with industrial economies in the twentieth century shows that a danger point is reached when 20 percent or more of the GDP is diverted to one sector. Such a diversion produces severe economic hardships and distortions in the rest of the economy. The American medical system is not yet at 20 percent of the GDP, although if the current rate of costs continues to expand as it has over the past twenty years, it will likely reach 20 percent by the year 2004, according to the Congressional Budget Office, the Health Care Financing Administration, and most economists who study health costs. Already the private expenses on health care are reducing outlays for workers' benefits, wages, and business investment in product research and development.

A second effect of the health cost explosion is a severe drain on public budgets. Government outlays to defense, higher education, infrastructure, and urban problems are limited or reduced. In fact, increased expenses for health care is one of the factors restricting *national government* spending and contributing to the *national debt* (other factors are reduced revenues and increased outlays for interest on the debt; see Calleo 1992, pp. 98–99).

State governments, meanwhile, are seeing their public revenues being eaten up by health care costs. These costs now consume as much as or more tax revenues (17 percent and rising) than any of the historic "big items" of state expense: education, higher education, roads and highways, and state parks (see Figure 9.4). States—in their giant version of cost shifting—are now forced to spend less on these other items and on social services, since most state budgets are required to be balanced. The costs to the market and to government budgets are merely the two most visible pieces of the iceberg of economic distortion that results from exploding medical costs.

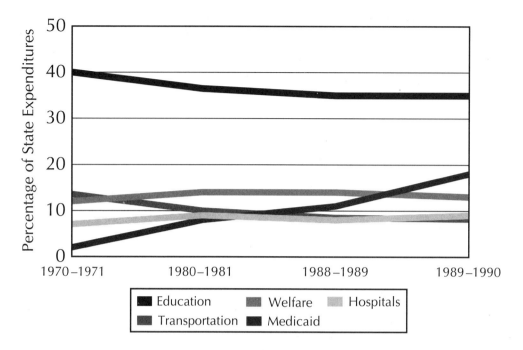

FIGURE 9.4   ROBBING PETER TO FEED PAUL: STATE GOVERNMENTS ARE TAKING MONEY
             AWAY FROM VITAL AREAS TO FUND MEDICAID

Source: 1992 Significant Features of Fiscal Federalism, Table 34:37.

As medical costs continue to approach 20 percent of GDP, a potentially
dangerous and ironic problem is worth considering. The leaders of old
Communist countries used to trivialize or deny the effects of their committing
20 percent of GDP to the military. American conservatives later boasted that
they buried the old Soviet Bloc under the Cold War arms race, which forced
the Soviets to devote so much to the military that it accelerated the collapse of
their other economic sectors. Today while the medical sector is approaching
the 20 percent of GDP mark, we should not engage in the same denial. Without
coping with our cost problem, we risk a collision with an iceberg (over 20 percent GDP) that many experts and big business leaders say could, as with the
Soviets, potentially sink the economy.

CODE BLUE RESPONSE: PROPOSED SOLUTIONS TO HEALTH CARE PROBLEMS

Many solutions to the health care crisis have been proposed: private insurance
reform, individual mandated purchase, managed care reforms, preventive
medicine proposals, proposals for "true competition" of medical arts, and sin-

gle-payer or national/state public insurance and service proposals. These are based on the various "problem pictures" described earlier, and each proposal has a number of effective advocates.

PRIVATE INSURANCE AND INDIVIDUAL MANDATED PURCHASE REFORMS

Private insurance and individual mandated purchase reforms are the minimum-action reforms. They target mainly the "insurance coverage" problem (problem picture 3) but not much else. This solution is to increase individuals' ability to obtain *private* insurance with government subsidies, and/or to require individuals to buy private insurance (with or without employer help), again with government subsidies for the poor. Both proposals are mild, voluntaristic stabs at controlling the cost explosion problems by increasing competition among private insurance companies (but not elsewhere in the corporate medical world), or by making medical cost information and insurance more available to patient-consumers. Once again, the particular diagnosis of the problem determines the prescription.

Private insurance reformers are still entranced by the mythic ideal of medicine and call only for incentives to expand private coverage and control costs (but not mandate coverage in any way). Several things are usually proposed to accomplish these objectives. Nearly all private insurance reformers want to eliminate the practice of refusing coverage for persons with preexisting medical problems. Most believe that private health plans should compete with a selection of health plans chosen through government "bids," the latter made available to state or federal employees and also sold to individuals and businesses. Finally, these reformers favor state laws preventing insurers from "cherry picking"—only insuring healthier groups of people. Government subsidies to the poor would be in the form of grant refundable tax credits or sliding scale discounts to cover most of the premiums, with no family facing an out-of-pocket cost of more than 10 percent of income (Graetz and Tobin 1994). The subsidies for low-income persons—often construed as twice the federal poverty level or below—would be paid for by eliminating tax shelters for employer-paid premiums or by replacing parts of Medicaid acute care for the elderly with the subsidies.

Individual mandate proposals put the duty to obtain coverage solely on individuals and families, thus lifting it from employers (the prevailing system in America) and avoiding placing it on government. To get coverage, persons would be required to buy insurance either through employers or in the private market. Government would significantly cover premium costs for lowest-income families. Employers could cover some of the premium costs—as is common practice now—but would not have to do so.

In most insurance reform proposals the assumption is that costs would be controlled primarily through greater competition among health plans. The underlying assumption is that increased insurance competition would result in increased insurance company pressure on doctor and hospital providers to rein in price increases. An additional factor would be limits on medical liability and malpractice suits. A secondary emphasis in some proposals is incentives to hold down costs by expanding HMOs and other managed care practices in the private sector, and establishing consumer medical information systems (now sorely lacking). Most of these ideas were in the proposal made by former Representative Jim Cooper (D. Tennessee) and supported by the insurance and small business communities.

The main problem with these proposals is the lack of research and resulting uncertainty about the effect on the population. A secondary problem is that most of these plans (at least the ones introduced in Congress) do not tackle the cost explosion head-on. They do not address price competition among doctors or hospitals, but place exclusive reliance on competition among insurance companies. But insurance costs, as we have seen, are only a part of the overall cost explosion monster.

More serious is the problem of leaving out the working poor. The Congressional Budget Office estimated that Cooper's bill would leave some 25 million people (of the 37 million or so uninsured) still without coverage. It would aid mainly those families near the official poverty level. If employers were not required to contribute, there is no reason to believe that trends would change much—some firms would contribute, some would not. So average premium costs would be unlikely to decline much *for the worker* from the current median of $5,550 per family of three now provided by employers. This cost, if borne by workers alone, would be about 15 percent of mean family income ($37,000 in 1994). Even worse, working-class families with two incomes that combine to put them slightly above minimum wage (totaling $24,000 or higher), would receive no public support under the Cooper plan. Instead, they could see employer support drop out, since the thrust of such bills is to get *individuals* to pay the cost of insurance. Already, three of four such uninsured adults are employed full-time but typically hold jobs that offer few or no benefits. They spend between 10 and 20 percent of net income on health care. The core problem, then, is the approximately 25 million uninsured working poor who earn joint incomes below $30,000 a year. The "voluntary buy private" plans offer them little ability to buy, give them little opportunity to overcome their health cost burdens, and perhaps risk encouraging businesses who presently share costs to drop support. For a story of a typical working poor family, see Box 9.1b.

Insurance access and individual mandate care acknowledge to differing degrees that costs are exploding and insurance coverage is decreasing. None of the solutions assumes or acknowledges, however, that the market is so dysfunctional that it might be a quasi-monopolistic, noncompetitive "engine out of control" that poses serious threats.

Thus there are several peculiar features (some would say gaps) in the assumptions that lie behind these kinds of limited reforms. First, by downplaying the cost problems and not acknowledging the monopolistic problems of the health care system, the private insurance access and individual mandate advocates can simply assume that neither moderate nor stringent government actions are needed. These solutions are based in incremental changes in the mythic ideal of medicine. Second, by minimizing the public health problems which generally require more government programs, the insurance proposals are limited to insurance reform and avoid the role of government in preventive medicine. Third, all of the proposals accept the dominant mode of medical science as curative (take chemicals or get surgery), and all assume that medical science is in the hands of the physicians, while ignoring alternative medicine forms.

MANAGED CARE SOLUTIONS

Managed care proposals are founded on the twin ideas of across-the-board competition and emphasis on preventive medicine. These solutions are based on extensive experience in big business health plans and on health reforms established by state governments. They make several assumptions about the medical system that the insurance reforms do not. The most important assumption is that medicine is a mixed market, with many serious nonmarket and near monopolistic traits. Some parts of the market are monopolistic (no pricing of services), some are competitive (medical equipment manufacture), some are subject to nonmarket pricing elements (third-party payments), some are provided by government (Medicare), and some are provided through government subsidy (tax code subsidies). Diagnosing medicine as a *dysfunctional market*, the managed care proposals prescribe solutions to fit the mixed-market disease.

Managed care began more than forty years ago when private businesses such as Kaiser and the Health Insurance Plan of Greater New York purchased their own hospitals and pharmacies, and/or employed their own doctors on contract, to provide health care for employees. They developed management strategies to keep costs down and to encourage workers to use preventive medicine. In the early 1970s the Nixon administration proposed Health Maintenance Organizations (HMOs), partly as a way to outflank proposals for national health insurance. The result was a 1973 federal law that allowed organizations to charter themselves in contract arrangements for the provision of health services. By 1991, 40 million Americans were enrolled in about 560 HMOs around the country, up from 10 million in 200 plans in 1980. By 1995 enrollment had risen to 50 million. In 1995, HMOs charge an average $1,740 for an individual policy and $4,704 for a family, $145 versus $392 a month respectively (Group Health Association of America 1995).

These prices are 10 to 50 percent lower than the national average, depending on the plan and the particular region (see later in the chapter). HMOs and their cousins use a range of practices to keep costs down. The HMO contracts with a number of physicians (doctors often join more than one HMO) who agree to provide care at the set prices. This arrangement guarantees doctors a steady supply of paying patients. HMOs generally emphasize primary-care physicians, rather than costlier specialists, for common problems. The HMO sets its own rates and benefits, and subscribers are limited to the hospitals, physicians, and other providers on the contract list. Other cost-cutting moves include pre-admission certification and price limits on specific services.

In contrast to traditional fee-for-service plans in which doctors may order many unnecessary procedures, managed-care systems have medical directors who oversee hundreds of physicians, and "utilization review" nurses who monitor individual cases. While patients are free to see physicians at any time, to order an expensive test the doctors must get prior approval by fax or telephone. This requirement reduces expensive "blank check" testing, or "defensive medicine." Patient education also is an important part of managed care. Patients are told about risks and procedures and allowed to influence medical decisions (not typical in past practices). Wellness programs are common, including weight management, anti-smoking programs, nutrition, cancer awareness, and stress management.

Monthly insurance premiums typically are only a little lower than in traditional plans, but overall annual costs are considerably lower, since the co-payments and deductibles are very low or nonexistent in managed care plans, as opposed to the expensive co-payments and high deductibles of traditional medical insurance plans. HMOs provided coverage for 40 million Americans in 1990 and 50 million in 1995 at an average out-of-pocket cost of $2,450 per person per year (averages of Group Health Association of America figures, 1990 and 1995). This is approximately 40 percent less than the $4,000 individual average cost of traditional plans with deductibles and co-payments averaged through the same five years (Congressional Budget Office 1994). These statistics alone explain why there is such a rapid movement to managed care.

Ownership managed care may be among the most efficient in cost control. Such organizations employ their own salaried services and work from an overall health budget. Managers and physicians have to be concerned with prices and volume of services within that budget. This is actually the logic of American business-owned HMOs, of hospital care in Australia, and of overall medical care in Canada, Germany, and France. In *third-party managed care* the payer (the HMO, the sponsoring hospital, the business, or an insurance company) pays fees for care but tries to manage volume through bureaucratic supervision of contracted and outside doctors and hospital. It is approximately one-quarter to one-third less cost efficient than the more tightly managed ownership HMOs.

HMOs provide care at least equal to and in many cases better than traditional practices. The best HMOs improve medicine and cut costs by screening doctors for skill, quality, and economy, by monitoring their performance, and by encouraging board certification (a series of postmedical school tests to certify that a doctor possesses advanced, "elite" knowledge). Industry experience and trends show that HMOs cut costs, provide high-quality care, and improve the overall health of subscribers, because of the wellness and prevention programs, compared with traditional medical and insurance practices.

Managed care became so popular among large businesses that an extremely influential confederation of insurance companies, health care providers, politicians, and leading health care academics formed a coalition lobby that promotes managed care known as the Jackson Hole Group. It publishes studies and lobbies Congress and the state legislatures. Actually such cost-conscious planning is rapidly replacing traditional health plans in the business world. In 1988, 89 percent of workers in company plans could choose traditional health plans with free choice of doctors, but by 1992 that number had declined to 65 percent (KPMG Peat Marwick survey 1992). More than 80 percent of insured workers were covered by HMOs in Washington, D.C., 33 percent in California, and 30 percent in Minnesota. It may well be that without health care reform, the ability to have unrestricted choice of doctors will vanish anyway.

Like the insurance proposals, managed care solutions assume minor problems in the medical market, do nothing to alleviate the problems of public health, and ignore the problems of medical monopolism. Managed care plans are beginning to emphasize preventive medicine aspects for the individual planholder, but they have not directly promoted public preventive medicine programs for larger segments of the population.

PUBLIC HEALTH SERVICES AND PREVENTIVE MEDICINE

Preventive medicine viewpoints argue that personal health is a strengthening of the body's natural mental and physical health defenses, better exercise, diet, and nutrition, and regular checkups before the onset of severe stages of illness or imparity. The traditional, minimum definition of *public health services* is government provision of essentially nonprofitable safeguards against disease for the entire population, through such measures as universal childhood immunization, public sanitation, water quality and food safety regulation, and health instruction in schools. Public health, like defense or natural wonders such as the Grand Canyon, is considered to be nearly a pure public good (rather than private property) in all industrial countries, and in all but the most extreme political ideologies.

Public health is more widely defined within the health care profession to include governmental promotion of health in the entire population and improvement of substandard health conditions among disadvantaged segments, including new immigrants, poor women and children, and the elderly. Few of these things can be made available to the general population through private, for-profit medical practice. At least since the Second World War the orthodox doctors, through the AMA, have supported public-funded health measures. The general view among public health and social workers is that as political trends tend to favor public health programs, public health indicators

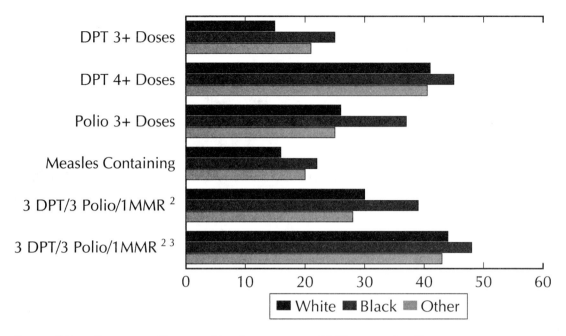

FIGURE 9.5A   PERCENT OF CHILDREN NOT IMMUNIZED IN 1992 BEFORE AGE THREE
Source: 1994 Statistical Abstract of the United States, Table 203, p. 138.

improve; if political trends do not favor such programs, as in recent years, public health indicators tend to decline (Ginzberg 1994).

In the mid-1980s the decline of many public health programs and public health indicators began to concern public health officials and medical academics. They pointed to the cuts in public health spending, the rise of "Third World diseases," the declining immunization rates in the United States, and other worsening health conditions, due to the neglect of public health programs (Figures 9.5a and 9.5b). By the late 1980s, for instance, the United States ranked third from last of all North and South American nations in the percentage of preschool children immunized against common deadly childhood diseases. Also, the number of children under age 6 living in poverty increased from 5 million to 6 million from 1987 to 1992, or 26 percent of all children of that age, the highest rate in 25 years (National Center for Children in Poverty 1995). These trends, according to the National Center report, have devastating consequences on youth from toddlers to teenagers. The highlighting of these problems, combined with the AIDS epidemic, the new wellness and nutrition movement, and a highly popular and pro-active surgeon general named C. Everett Koop, all helped to spark a growing interest in preventive medicine and public health measures in the late 1980s and 1990s.

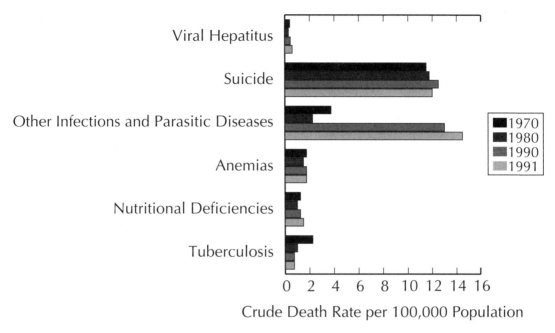

FIGURE 9.5B   DECLINING PUBLIC HEALTH INDICATORS
Source: 1994 Statistical Abstract of the United States, Table 125, p. 93.

COMBINING MANAGED CARE AND PUBLIC HEALTH: THE CLINTON PLAN

A NEUTRAL ASSESSMENT OF THE CLINTON PLAN

The Clinton plan for health reform was formed by a 500-member advisory committee made up of representatives from big businesses, state governors, insurance companies, and health care academic experts. The commission gathered input at meetings held around the country in 1992 and 1993. It did not build close connections with congressional leaders and health care experts, however, an oversight that came to haunt the proposal in 1994 when the White House needed help to stave off interest group pressures on key committees and legislators.

The Clinton plan tried to tackle some of the problems of the mixed market, particularly the noncompetitive features of pricing, the cost explosion, and several of the public health problems. In brief, the original Clinton plan was a complex, 1,300-page bill that called for universal coverage of citizens, basic coverage benefits for all, and a choice of insurance plans including state-sponsored "buyers' co-ops" of insurance (the so-called health alliances). The plan allowed a person to shop around in a reinvigorated competitive market and choose among three alternatives: (1) a traditional, private insurance plan (with total choice of physician, typical premiums, 15 to 20 percent uncovered copayments, 80 percent or so coverage after deductibles, etc.); (2) an HMO offered by private insurers or public pools (like teachers' insurance funds); or (3) a state-sponsored set of successful bidders who would pool providers and insurers and would meet a standard set of benefits at set prices. These state-sponsored alliances would provide a baseline of real competition and consumer information against which the private insurers and HMOs would compete.

With this plan, private insurers and HMOs would not be able to use cherry-picking or other selective practices to deny coverage. Every worker and family member would get coverage, and the working poor and poverty-level persons would receive subsidies to purchase coverage.

Proposed caps on annual premiums and expenses were the key to the universal insurance plan. Individuals would spend no more than $1,800 for premiums; families would spend no more than $4,200. Employees would also pay out-of-pocket expenses typical of but lower than usual private insurance: $10 per visit to an HMO, or 20 percent co-payments plus annual deductibles. These costs would be capped at $1,500 a year for individuals and $3,000 for a family. Employers would be required to offer plans and to pay 80 percent of the premium for whatever plan the worker picks, with the worker picking up the other 20 percent, subject to the spending limits. Otherwise the worker would choose the state alliance plan, and the employer would contribute 80 percent of the state-set premium cost.

The Clinton plan also called for providing at least partial coverage for many neglected public health and preventive services. These included routine checkups and tests; strongly expanded innoculations; neonatal, infant, and well-baby care; long-term health care and home care for the elderly and disabled; routine vision and hearing care; and mental health and substance abuse recovery programs.

The plan included several secondary features. The first was provision for "today's uninsured" such as retirees, part-time workers or workers moving from one job to others, disabled workers, and the "working poor" and those working for small businesses or self-employed. The plan would have established a "National Health Board" that would have set the benefits standards—with states having some ability to adjust these benefits—and determined levels of federal aid to the states.

A condensed summary of the plans was provided in an analysis by the New York Times (September 19, 1993). According to that summary the plan would have been funded by combined employer–employee contributions (80 percent for big employers only up to 7.9 percent of payroll; 20 percent for workers) rather than through a general income or national sales tax. Other monies would come from Medicare and Medicaid savings and a stiff tax on tobacco and alcohol.

To simplify the cost picture, if the major independent analyses (Wyatt 1994; Congressional Budget Office 1994; Lewin 1993) were roughly correct, probably the annual average of total medical costs to the individual or family would have been approximately $1,000 less than the current national average of $5,550, close to the caps proposed by the administration and a considerable reduction for most people. However, the actual public cost of universal coverage would have been perhaps $130 billion more than projected by the administration, spread out over the first seven years of the plan (see Box 9.2). The problems of the plan were insufficient financing, doubts about its ability to contain the cost explosion, and the long period (seven years) before the plan would reduce the national debt (compared with projected expenses for existing Medicare and Medicaid and other government subsidies). The plan was strong, however, in terms of benefits, lower consumer costs, coverage or quality.

9.2

THE CLINTON PLAN UNDERFINANCING PROBLEMS

1. The White House underestimated the costs of the new benefits, which would put inflationary pressures on all premiums because the plan's standard benefit package was "a tad more generous than that of the average working American's," Office of Management and Budget chief Reischauer told the House Ways and Means Committee on February 8, 1994.

2. Leak-through residual premium inflation was likely. As large groups of providers and purchasers of private policies remained outside the alliances and the HMOs, insurance premium costs would still go up in the private fee plus private insurance arena (although probably less slowly because of explicit price competition from alliances and HMOs).

3. Higher premiums (from 1 and 2) would lead to higher federal subsidy costs in covering the poor and the uninsured. The Congressional Budget Office estimated that the net increase of benefit costs plus subsidies would be $133 billion more than the first six years combined cost estimates, upping the deficit for those years to between $50 and $70 billion. After then the plan would reduce the deficit.

4. Some analysts believe that the cycle of cost shifting from cost-controlled Medicare and Medicaid programs and the new health alliances to the private sector might still take place, as private-fee doctors, private insurance companies, and the hospitals would seek more money among those who opt out of the alliances and HMOs. Doctors are able to hike prices slightly for only about 50 percent of private-pay patients (to compensate for Medicare limits on their pay), because insurance carriers are reluctant also to pay "any and all charges." Presumably the ability of doctors and hospitals to cost-shift losses in this way would lessen as competition increased with the presence of alliances and HMOs.

The administration claimed, and the CBO, Wyatt (1994), and Lewin (1993) analyses acknowledged, that there were significant potential savings that could offset the cost overruns, through malpractice liability limits, simplification of forms and billing practices (a major factor), preventive medicine, and consumer information. However, all the analyses refused to attach specific numbers to these savings because of quantification difficulties, so the overruns are probably less than cited above, possibly one-fourth to one-third lower.

Nevertheless, these inflationary loopholes in the cost-control abilities of the Clinton plan are due to the assumptions that we would get cost reduction mainly through heavily induced insurance competition plus premium caps in the alliance and HMO sectors. Other price increases would simply leak through the competitive and capping nets.

The alternative to these leak-through increases would be more direct regulation of costs, such as global budgets for each state or each hospital, or mandatory fee schedules negotiated on a state-by-state basis with doctors and hospitals (as is done in Canada).

As to benefits, Clinton's plan, particularly the much-attacked health care alliances and choice of traditional or HMO style plans, would have provided the typical consumer with far more real choices than are currently available (about 20 percent of the population and their families are *not covered at all* by the current schemes and many are restricted to what the employer offers). The plan would have granted a large-scale expansion of benefits to roughly 50 million persons (the uninsured populations) and a modest expansion of benefits over current coverages for the rest of us (see Box 9.3).

| 9.3 | ***SELECTED ADDITIONAL ADVANTAGES AND DISADVANTAGES OF THE CLINTON PLAN*** |

Advantages   The original proposal would increase preventive care in America but would delay some of it until after the year 2000 (mental health, substance abuse). It would increase funding for immunizations, prenatal and well-baby care, early cancer detection checkups, and routine eye and ear care, including glasses for children.

Early retirements might increase, a bonus to companies that are downsizing or that have large retiree health costs (e.g., unionized plants, automakers). This is so because the health alliances would pay 80 percent of the retiree costs; the company would pay 20 percent.

Health plan costs of unemployed or low-wage workers would be substantially covered by health regional alliances; disabled workers could no longer be excluded from coverage or forced to pay higher premiums.

Employed disabled who need assistance would receive aid in the form of a tax credit for 50 percent of their costs up to $15,000 a year to help cover daily home help and transportation.

Disadvantages   Small employers who would have to pay for health care would pay less on wages and other benefits and would lay more people off.

Companies that use a lot of uncovered part-timers or immigrant labor might decrease their use of full-timers, require more overtime for full-time workers, shift jobs offshore, or automate to replace workers.

Sources: CBO 1994; Wyatt 1994; Lewin 1993.

The plan was not—despite the shrill exaggeration of its opponents—anything like socialized medicine. That is, it was not a proposal for nationalizing health service workers as salaried employees of government. Nor was it a government takeover of more than one-tenth of the economy (as was alleged by Republican Senator Phil Gramm from Texas). Rather it was based on the freedom principles of retaining private-practice physicians, depending mainly on private insurance to provide coverage, and allowing states to devise their own plans to provide the standard benefits. In particular, it did not challenge either the market/profit basis of medicine or the dominant medicine referred to as "curative." In fact it took very few steps to break the monopolization of medical arts built up by the physicians, nor did it seek to outlaw private practice, hospitals, insurance, or drug firms and replace them with government corporations. Mainly it sought government-enforced means of public and market-based competition and choice of services, combined with increased public health measures and nationally guaranteed standards of largely private insurance for all.

INTERPRETATION OF THE CLINTON PLAN
THROUGH THE MEDICAL MONOPOLISM PICTURE

The medical monopolism interpretation of health care (theory 5) sees the resistance to the Clinton plan in a different light. (The historical evidence for this view will be given shortly. See for instance, Public Citizen, Fall 1994; Berlant 1975).

In this view, the high-spending resistance to the Clinton plan actually manufactured some startling forms of information pollution. In short, the opponents' propaganda about a "government takeover" was diversionary and often self-serving. Opponents refrained from mentioning how a "government takeover" at the behest of medical lobbies had established in this century a subsidized near-monopoly of medical arts enjoyed by M.D.s over their highly limited, state-regulated competitors (chiropractors, Chinese medical practition-ers, nutritionists, etc.; see Berlant 1975).

In this picture, the conservative-supported medical oligarchy had been built first on AMA lobbying of state legislatures to kill competition since at least 1910. Since then, medical monopolism grew along several paths: The M.D.s had quietly suppressed medical competition since the mid-1900s; the big drug firms grew after World War II to become one of the richest oligopolies in history; and now corporate hospital chains and insurance companies continue to merge and monopolize their markets year after year. In reality, the Clinton plan was far too timid to break up this medical-industrial monopolism. It would not even tackle the special interest takeover of medical arts by the M.D.s, much less create a truly competitive health service.

As a result, the opposition propagandists found it easy to form a remark-able alliance to defend medical monopolism, composed of the powerful com-bined lobbies of wealthy medical specialists, hospitals, the insurance industry, and pharmaceutical giants, in league with the small business lobbies. And the propaganda could deliver a double whammy—savage the plan as a "socialistic takeover" when it was not, and thereby divert attention from and protect *their own* monopolistic takeover that had served well-heeled interests for three gen-erations.

FINAL ASSESSMENT OF THE CLINTON PLAN

Regardless of these different views of the Clinton plan, several things are indisputable. Had the proposal passed, the U.S. health system would still have been the most privatized, most weakly regulated, least "nationalized" health service in the modern world. Yet in spite of the fact that it was rooted in forty years of primarily business managed care health plans, and it was designed and supported by major sectors of big business, the Clinton plan got sweep-ingly portrayed as a "radical departure" by its opponents and the historically naive mass media. The old scare word "socialized medicine" was exhumed again with the same killing effect. Even for many of its big business supporters the plan ironically came to be seen as a step beyond the normal incremental change in politics.

The Clintons' effort to take on the legalized, orthodox medical monopo-lism could be called the biggest effort by reformers to restore markets and break up and regulate the largest monopolistic segment of the economy since the busting up of the Standard Oil monopoly at the turn of the century. Reformers and journalists across the spectrum of national politics bewailed the "lost opportunity" to reform the system and contain costs by national action in 1994. Lost in the fog of the debate and the postmortems of the Clinton plan were the solutions from the perspective of one of the most powerful diagnoses of the medical crisis: the medical monopolism viewpoint.

THE MEDICAL MONOPOLISM PICTURE: RESTORING TRUE COMPETITION

This problem picture of medicine and its solution (theory 5) is the view that the "medical crisis" in America is rooted in long-developing aspects of monopolism in major segments of the health care system. The theory admits that the health care system in America has many interconnected parts, but it stresses that large parts evolved in staggered fashion in the twentieth century toward a medical-industrial complex. This complex exhibits markedly *nonmarket* behaviors at the least, and near-monopolistic tendencies in much of the system—traits that have been aided by clear historic government policies and subsidies. Reforms that ignore this monopolism and are limited to small segments of the health system, in this view, will fail to control costs. Weak, mistargeted, or partial measures lead inevitably to more distortions of service, cost shifting, or cost explosion.

The various manifestations of monopolism in the medical system provide answers to many serious, otherwise confusing, health care problems. Consider the following:

1. Why is there a cost explosion? *Answer*: Because of historically unrestrained drug, doctor, and hospital pricing and excessive services.

2. Why are there excessive defensive medicine with unnecessary procedures, too many specialists, not enough general practice doctors, and shortages of doctors in rural and Western regions? *Answer*: Doctors and hospitals still are essentially free to set up practice, charge fees, shift costs, and so on in spite of partial regulations or disincentives from Medicare, HCFA, other government regulations, and insurance pressures.

3. Why do we stress expensive curative medicine over preventive medicine when most medical ailments are self-induced, deteriorative, or environmental? *Answer*: Historically government subsidizes orthodox medicine and spends big bucks on curative hi-tech interventions.

4. Why do we lack clear knowledge and consumer information about medical arts performance? *Answer*: Because of historic monopolism of price, performance, and other information concealment by doctors and hospitals.

5. Why are there gaps in insurance coverage? *Answer*: There is no national plan, only weak state regulation of predatory insurance practices that avoid covering less profitable groups.

6. Why are alternative, sometimes cheaper medicine and medical arts legally restricted? *Answer*: Because of historical monopolization of practice by M.D.s, largely unrestrained by the courts.

7. Why are the better-heeled segments of the health professions especially opposed to cost reform, alternative medicine, and public insurance? *Answer*: Because of monopolistic profits, especially in drug companies and insurance, and to a lesser extent among high-income specialists and big hospitals.

To the degree that we understand historical medical monopolism, and how to reform and control it, we can figure out how to control and reduce these problems. Otherwise we misdiagnose the symptoms and will continue to experience the problems. The next section examines the historical details of monopolism in medicine.

THE HISTORICAL EVIDENCE OF MONOPOLISM

THE BEGINNING OF MONOPOLISM IN THE MEDICAL ARTS

Throughout the 1800s "medicine" was a fairly loose, unregulated conglomeration of medical sects. Physicians in the late 1800s were not "M.D.s" as we know them today: The most common type of physician was a tough competitor known as the *homeopath*. The M.D.s themselves were known as *allopaths*. Their approach to medicine, until the 1870s at least, relied on large doses of chemicals, purging of the body with water or other fluids, bloodletting, and semi-experimental forms of surgery. Allopaths were not particularly highly regarded (licensing was easy, schooling erratic or even nonexistent), especially among the educated urban dwellers, who tended to favor homeopaths until the turn of the century. Homeopaths, the largest of the various sects of scientific herbalists, mainly administered small doses of chemicals or herbs designed to produce reactions in the circulatory and immune systems (not quite understood that way then). This practice was based on a system of treatments developed by the German physician Samuel Hahnemann in the early 1800s. The small doses were designed to stimulate the body's natural defenses to slowly mobilize against the disease or condition. Allopaths/M.D.s came to adopt a number of the homeopathic practices in the early to mid-twentieth century, but only after largely eliminating this group from competition through the domination of state medical licensing among other tactics (Berlant 1975, Chapters 4 and 5).

After the 1880s allopaths were increasingly influenced by biological and bacteriological discoveries, mainly from Europe. American scientists and physicians trained mostly in Germany brought the message of laboratory science and bacteria to their brother allopaths in the United States. Allopaths became increasingly allied with biological science, changed their medical approach, and found themselves finally on strong ground against the herbalist competitors. A parallel trend around 1900 was the development of a political and business alliance of allopaths/M.D.s with their former enemies, the pharmaceutical companies, against homeopaths who offered serious professional competition against both drug companies and allopaths. As part of this strategy of eliminating what the M.D.s called outside quackery, the American Medical Association (worrying little about quackery in its own fold) borrowed a strategy of licensing from the English Royal Board physicians. It involved getting state legislatures to limit medical licensing to M.D.s and/or placing licensing under AMA-sanctioned medical boards from 1880 to 1900. By the second decade of the 1900s allopaths/M.D.s had "zoned out" their competition from license to practice "medicine," defined as surgery, prescriptions, and innoculations. The restriction was particularly on homeopaths but also included chiropractors, osteopaths, herbalists, and hydropaths (Berlant 1975, Chapters 5 and 6; Gelfand 1993).

The allopaths/M.D.s were also able to transform medical schools. They obtained lucrative financial support from the Carnegie Foundation to prepare its famous Flexner report, which the AMA presented in 1910 as a plan to obtain elite funding of AMA-sanctioned medical schools. "The transformation of American medical schools according to a scientific model (borrowed from German bacteriological science, applied first in the United States by John Hopkins University), presided over by university presidents and medical school deans, and generously funded by private foundations like Rockefeller, was firmly in place by the turn of the century" (Gelfand 1993, p. 141). Through Carnegie funding, the AMA expanded its membership, promoted its own curriculum in medical schools, lobbied to advance its own definitions of medical licensing requirements, and controlled state boards. The result was that competitor schools and practices were driven out of business, and the AMA's monopolization of medicine was established during an age of anti-trust (Berlant 1975, p. 247; Gelfand 1993, pp. 1140–1144).

The growing political clout of the AMA was exercised on numerous occasions after 1910. It helped oppose public health proposals in 1910, defeated compulsory health insurance proposals in states and in the Congress from 1913 to 1920, and allied with the Department of Agriculture's Bureau of Chemistry to fight homeopaths in rural areas after 1910. The AMA most notoriously opposed government subsidies for public health centers, group practice medicine, diagnostic clinics, and even innoculations by states or the national government during the 1920s and 1930s (actions the profession is not proud of today).

The AMA's drive to monopolize medical arts, fight off public health reforms, restrict competing arts, and maximize physician control culminated in almost complete success in the two decades after the Second World War. The AMA opposed President Truman's efforts to establish a national insurance program in the late 1940s. In addition, doctors began a strong wave of battles in state legislatures, lasting until about 1970, to limit the practice of the remaining competing medical arts. By the 1950s midwives had been ousted from hospitals and banned by state laws from assisting at births. At AMA behest, only doctors could now preside over births. Periodic assaults against the "quackery" of chiropractors have taken place since the turn of the century, but particularly since the 1940s. In contrast, the AMA has never mounted a serious assault on quackery in their own ranks; instead the M.D.s adhere to a code of silence about colleagues, and until the late 1960s they generally refused to testify against members in malpractice suits. During the same years the practices of nurses were proscribed by M.D.-dominated state lobbying, so that nurses cannot perform minor surgery (unless there are no physicians in the region), nor are nurses or pharmacists (who have much more intensive education about drugs than M.D.s) allowed to write prescription drug orders. Until the 1970s, M.D.s were successful in obtaining state laws freezing out chiropractors from insurance coverage, and commonly restricted most osteopaths and all chiropractors from hospital service. In response, osteopaths built their own hospitals. To a lesser extent the states also restricted other medical arts at the behest of the AMA in those years, including physical therapists (now more widely accepted by M.D.s), Chinese medicine, and herbalist doctors and pharmacies. The mid-1960s represented the peak years of the monopolization of medical arts via the M.D.s' strategy of controlling state regulation of medicine.

QUIET FORMS OF MARKET COLLUSION

Medical sociologists have had a difficult time penetrating the veil of secrecy about monopolistic medical practice and protocol among doctors themselves. The "inner workings of the guild" are part of the education and acculturation of young doctors. While the topic of "doctor society" is broad, it includes collusionary practices to ensure income stability or even high lifestyle. For instance, doctors typically agree among themselves informally on how many practicing new doctors or specialists will be allowed into the town, the clinical practice, or the hospital. The purpose is to guarantee limited competition and substantial incomes, especially for specialists. A young doctor fresh out of medical school has to have space in an expensive building and expensive equipment to practice, something typically impossible to finance when facing medical school loans, hungry and anxious families, and stingy bankers. Established doctors are already set up with the equipment and office space, and they exercise the power to admit or deny new doctors to their groups and to hospital practice. As a result, young doctors must shop around until they can "get admitted into the club," and they must also be socially acceptable—meaning race, religion, or nationality has sometimes excluded doctors. Faced with exclusion, a young doctor's other choices are unprofitable rural service or military service. From the turn of the last century until the 1960s, blacks, Jews, and other minorities, as well as women, were discriminated against. Quotas restricted their acceptance into medical schools, excluded them from medical societies, and denied them hospital privileges even if they did qualify (Beardsley 1987, Chapter 4; Rosen 1983, pp. 66–78, cited in Gelfand 1993, p. 1142).

There are other monopolistic collusionary behaviors among doctors. They include refusing to refer patients to chiropractors, setting fees to fit desired income levels, shifting higher fees from Medicare patients to private patients, refusing service to Medicare patients or the uninsured (common in obstetrics), refusing to give patients information about other doctors or about pricing, lucrative "self-referral"—that is, ordering expensive services and tests to partly self-owned labs for extra income—and Medicare fraud (estimated by the General Accounting Office to run at about $1 billion a year in fraudulent billings). Such monopolistic, unregulated practices are the little talked about, yet profitable, dirty laundry of the medical profession.

It is difficult to put price tags on the overall costs of the professional forms of monopolism. The Consumers Union, in a review of studies, estimated that unnecessary medical procedures, which would be one broad indicator of the larger costs, cost $130 billion in 1992, or as much as 20 percent of the $650 billion spent on patient care in that year (*Consumer Reports*, July 1992, p. 436). Malpractice suits and premiums, cited by doctors as a big villain in the cost explosion, amount to only 3.7 percent of physicians' income (double for high-risk specialties; *Medical Economics* 1990 annual survey) and less than 1 percent of total health outlays (U.S. Department of Health and Human Services, HFCA Fall Review, 1992, Table 9, p. 18).

COSTLY NONMARKET BEHAVIORS OF HOSPITALS

There are about 6,700 hospitals in the United States, 340 of which are federal hospitals open only to military personnel or native Americans. Of the nonfederal hospitals, approximately 60 percent are so-called nonprofit hospitals (a misleading label), 27 percent are local government-operated hospitals, and 14 percent are private for-profit hospitals. Most hospitals in the postwar years (not counting religious or philanthropic institutions) were constructed with the help of major federal and state laws, particularly the Hill-Burton Act of 1947, which covered about half of construction costs for over two decades (more evidence of nonmarket subsidy). Also, Medicare financed large parts of hospital capital improvements until the financing was ended in the mid-1980s.

Consumer groups and health economists have been active in revealing the nonmarket, cost-explosive practices of hospitals, including corporate hospital chains, in several major areas. These include overbuilding in urban areas, using political clout to avoid national health planning and siting restrictions intended to limit overbuilding, aiming for Cadillac services to insured patients to retain profitability, and, along with doctors, shifting costs to offset Medicare and insurance company limits intended to hold down costs.

Truly bizarre, opposing practices are a part of hospitals' market monopolism tactics. For example, marked-up prices are wildly enriching for plush suburban medical centers and hospital chains in growth regions of the United States, but the same gouging tactics are the desperate, last-ditch defense against hospital shutdown in inner-city areas. Hospital shutdown is a very serious trend in the inner cities (especially in regions of recession and high immigration), where even the arsenal of tactics to cost-shift and to mark up the price of services cannot counteract the heavy costs of providing emergency and other care to the masses of uninsured and poor. In Chicago, for example, the last downtown hospitals closed in the early 1990s, and hospital care for anyone in the populated urban center now requires a long ambulance trip to a suburban hospital, a pattern that is repeating itself in other big cities. Also, 92 of 549 hospital trauma centers closed their doors between 1985 and 1991, primarily because of costs of expensive care for the uninsured (Mabee, 1993 Annual National Trauma Symposium survey, in *Medical World News* 1994).

Monopolism partly contributes to such *rationing by geography* because of the largely unrestrained ability of corporate hospital chains and high-priced specialists to set up services where it is most profitable rather than where there is market need. Doctors tend to choose high-income specializations over lower-income family practice, and suburban settings where amenities are not lacking and third-party payment is common. Both doctors and hospitals are in fact fast disappearing from nonprofitable areas such as the sparsely populated rural settings, the Western and plains states, and the inner cities.

DRUG COMPANY PREDATORY PRICING

The final major form of monopolism is found in the super-markup prices of pharmaceutical companies.

The pharmaceuticals business was originally anti-doctor. Drug companies commonly advertised that doctors knew nothing and that consumers could fare better administering drugs to themselves, free of quackery. Regulation of drug safety and proof of effectiveness have been reform issues only in the twentieth century, after taking a long and rocky road. This section on the drug industry is based substantially on Julie Rovner's analysis (1992).

In 1906 the Pure Food and Drug Act was passed; it made possible government analysis of patent medicines, but it did not require disclosure of contents, it banned only false and fraudulent statements about ingredients, and it did not ban false claims about results. In 1938 the Congress passed the Food, Drug and Cosmetic Act, partly as a result of public reaction to the deaths of more than 100 persons who had taken a "miracle" drug that contained substances used in making anti-freeze. The new law mandated government approval of drugs for safety before marketing. Even then, safety testing was virtually nonexistent and there was no requirement relative to claims of effectiveness.

In 1962 the thalidomide drug scandal rocked the nation. Thalidomide was an essentially untested sedative marketed widely in England and Europe for use by pregnant women, one of thousands of untested drugs that were dumped on the market after World War II. It was linked to severe malformities in thousands of infants, who were born with arms or legs missing. The nerve-wracking controversy gripped the nation, and congressional hearings led to passage of amendments to the 1938 law which finally established stringent safety testing of the flood of new drugs. The amendments required drug firms to provide the FDA scientists with detailed safety testing information and pre-market evidence of effectiveness. In 1984 Congress passed the Drug Price Competition Act, making it easier for smaller drug firms to market generic copies of drugs whose patents had expired, with the idea that competition would bring down prices. Manufacturers were required to show only that their drug copies were bioequivalent to the original patented drug. Thus safety testing and false claims issues became settled areas of regulation.

However, despite the 1984 generics law, the price explosion has continued as the main issue of pharmaceutical monopolism in the last two decades. Analysts tend to agree that the drug business is a semicompetitive market. There is a high level of product competition, but it is between copycat drugs, which are marketed by the hundreds of thousands, often with little chemical differences. The basic problem is that there is no real price competition. Except for the generics, the industry has been marked by price inflation and high profits. In the fifteen years since 1980, prescription prices rose nearly three times faster than prices for other products, and 50 percent faster than even other health care costs. In 1995 drugs were nearly 200 percent higher than in 1980, an inflation rate of over 18 percent *per year* (Rovner, *Congressional Quarterly Researcher*, July 17, 1992, pp. 599–613).

Drug prices are a severe problem for most Americans for several reasons. First, many health plans do not cover prescription drugs. Second, the elderly commonly take daily doses of multiple prescriptions for such common conditions as diabetes, high blood pressure, and low potassium, which can cost hundreds of dollars per month. Third, Medicare, the federal program for the elderly and disabled, does not cover most outpatient prescriptions. This triple whammy, particularly on the elderly, pushed Senator David Pryor, chair of the Senate Special Committee on Aging, to say in February 1992, "Prescription drug price inflation now hits over 5 million people over 55 who are having to make daily choices between food and their prescription drugs, between fuel for their home for heat or paying for prescription drugs … what kind of a country have we become?"

Critics of the drug companies make a very good case against pharmaceuticals for monopolistic and collusionary pricing, in spite of product competition. Their arguments can be summarized as follows:

1. At the current pace, a prescription costing $20 in 1980 will cost $120 by the year 2000 (more than 500 percent inflation).

2. In the 1990s the annual inflation rate is about 3 to 3.5 percent, while prescription drug prices continue to increase more than 10 percent per year.

3. Drug companies have extremely high profit margins (as a percentage of sales), four times higher than the Fortune 500 average (12.8 percent per year versus 3.2 percent). Drug companies lead all U.S. industries in three common profit indicators: percentage of return on stockholders equity, percent return on sales, and percentage of return on assets.

4. Drug makers do spend a lot on research and development, but they spend even more on marketing and promotion—25 percent of sales for advertising, versus 22 percent for research.

5. Drug makers have no incentive to control prices because drugs aren't sold directly to consumers but mainly through doctors, who make the prescribing decisions knowing little or nothing about the prices. Also, the costs of the sales force of drug firms are exceedingly high (in contrast to department store or even insurance and car salespeople) since drug firms use virtual armies of very well-paid salespeople who visit doctors' offices and dispense large amounts of

sample drugs. (Conscionable doctors often give free samples to poorer patients, but the costs are still passed back to the point of pricing).

The drug makers counter with these arguments:

1. Drug firms do not overcharge since their drugs actually lower the total health bill by cutting down on hospital stays or averting surgery.

2. Drug costs are a pretty stable share of U.S. medical costs as a share of GDP. In 1960, drugs represented .53 of GNP, rising to only .58 by 1990. Also, drug-price inflation is somewhat slower in the 1990s, rising in the 8 percent a year range.

3. Costs rise because the costs of new drug development have increased even more. In 1976 a new drug on the market cost about $54 million, but by 1990 it was $231 million.

4. Pharmaceuticals are not rapacious profit-mongers, since they are among the biggest research and development spenders in the economy (three times the corporate average), plowing $12 billion a year from profits back into research. Pharmaceuticals lead the world in drug development, producing about 40 percent of all new drugs on the world market. Thus it is a major industry with a positive balance of foreign trade, with nearly $1 billion a year in overseas sales.

As Rovner (1992) argues, at best these are partial explanations for 200 percent price inflation since 1980. Drug companies apparently do maintain considerable profit margins, partly because of their excessive overhead, high salaries, and high rates of return to investors. At the heart of the drug companies' defense, however, is the argument that they save the system money. The drug firm Schering-Plough released a 1991 study that claimed that over the next 25 years drugs will save 5 million lives from and prevent 9 million cases of heart disease, reduce deaths from lung cancer by 662,000, and lower new arthritis cases by 2.1 million. These reductions in disease, the report maintained, will result in reduced spending of $211 billion for cardiovascular disease, $14 billion for lung, colon, and leukemia cancers, and $127 billion for arthritis. However, former Surgeon General C. Everett Koop has made an extremely powerful argument against this position. Koop maintains that preventive medicine earlier in the life cycle lowers costs and saves more lives more than expensive drugs and surgery near the end of life. Koop argues that about 60 percent of ailments among Americans are self-inflicted as a result of long years of neglect, bad diet, and hazardous health habits, or result from genetic susceptibility. The remaining 40 percent of ailments are mainly bacteriological. The self-inflicted and genetic ailments are more cheaply and effectively approached by preventive measures. Thus a more serious investment in public health and preventive medicine, and away from heroic or intrusive medical investments, could extend life expectancy by up to several decades for most people, with 20 percent lower annual costs (Koop 1995; Fries, Koop, et al. 1993). In other words, if the roughly $10 billion excessive profits earned by drug companies each year were diverted to preventive medicine, the investment would provide even better health and longer life at significantly lower costs.

We will next summarize some solutions to monopolism's problems, as incorporated in our proposal for an ideal and feasible national or state system of health care reform. Our solution draws from all five pictures of health problems. We will then describe the latest trends in state efforts to resolve the problems of health care, a trend that will probably accelerate in the absence of national health reforms.

AN OUTLINE FOR A POLITICALLY FEASIBLE HEALTH CARE REFORM

Items of reform in the following list are arranged from the weakest measures to the strongest:

1. Laws establishing "truth in pricing" and "truth in performance" information for consumers.
2. Broader use of managed care, or even state-sponsored negotiated fees.
3. Much stronger public and private investment in preventive and public health programs.
4. Establishment of true choice and a truly competitive medical arts market by liberalizing medical licensing and rights to practice of alternative medical arts.
5. Legal caps on malpractice; stronger enforcement against Medicare fraud.
6. State or national establishment of competitive "buyers' co-ops" for public employees, capable of marketing against private insurers, based on bids of prices and services, open to small business, uninsured, and open enrollment.
7. Legal restraints on profiteering and cherry-picking practices of insurance companies, and usury laws against overpricing of pharmaceuticals.
8. Single-payer/public financing of universal government health insurance, and the limitation or abolishment of private insurance.

These reform measures draw from all five pictures of health care problems, including the analysis of monopolism.

In our view, all items in the list should be present for an ideal nationally led reform. However, the defeat of the Clinton plan, and the political gridlock in Washington—exacerbated by divided party control of Congress and the Executive after the 1994 elections—probably preempts national action for the foreseeable future. Therefore, a politically feasible reform would ideally include all items but would involve either reforms led by state governments or a combination of state and national action. A "fair" reform pattern would be for the national government to pursue several of the weaker items (say from items one to three), while the states would be generally responsible for pursuit of *all* goals over the next half dozen years. It is our evaluation that the "fair" reform pattern is what is emerging in America, mainly by state-led reforms, and that it will be solidified as a new intergovernmental policy regime for the reform of medicine by the year 2000. If this intergovernmental regime does not take place—because of, for example, effective lobbying against further reforms in the states—then the crises in the health care system will escalate severely. However, as we shall show in the next section, state-led reforms are already far along and continuing, despite national inaction.

THE FINAL FRONTIER: HOW THE STATES ARE TAKING OVER

Over the last several years states have been passing comprehensive health care reforms which have followed one or more of the above directions. States have become the major source of health care reform, despite the media attention toward Washington. This is so because the states have been under tremendous pressures for reforms, mainly from rising health care budgets. In 1994 health care costs (mainly to the Medicaid program) ate up 18 percent of state budgets, and they will eat over 25 percent in the mid-1990s, according to current official estimates (see *Governing*, July 1993, figure on p. 28). From 1989 to 1993 state spending on Medicaid more than doubled to $55 billion. As a result of spending more on health care, states are being forced to spend less on higher education, roads, and other priorities (see Figure 9.4), a situation that simply cannot last. As a result, state efforts to reform health care accelerated in the early 1990s. "You can hardly keep up with what's going on," reported the head of the National Academy for State Health Policy in 1994.

It is clear that health care reform in the United States will not be led by the national government. State health reforms are the leading edge of change in the 1990s and are defining the outlines of the new health care system in the United States. State reforms are following several patterns, described in the following sections.

EXPANSION OR REPLACEMENT OF MEDICAID TO COVER MORE POOR

Since the late 1960s traditional Medicaid programs for the poor have covered mainly private doctor fees and hospital charges. States are now expanding or simply replacing Medicaid-style benefits to cover larger pools of the poor and uninsured with greater benefits. These are easy types of reform, since Medicaid benefits are well established and can easily be incrementally increased and targeted to larger pools of people. Such reform has accelerated since the Clinton administration eased the approval of state experiments in Medicaid reform and substitution (called *waivers*).

Several states have simply expanded Medicaid benefits to a wider circle of the uninsured and poor—often defined as those whose incomes are up to 200 or 300 percent higher than the official federal poverty rate—and they have increased covered services to include preventive care, prenatal and well-child care, and prescriptions. States that have led the reform wave in this direction include Rhode Island (November 1993) and Arizona, which has expanded coverages since 1982.

Several other states have experimented with wholesale replacement of Medicaid, with mixed state and federal funding of more lenient benefits and insurance coverage for nearly all of a state's poor, working poor, and uninsured. States that have produced this kind of reform are Arizona (since 1982), Minnesota (1992), and Florida (1993).

Minnesota has a well-developed program of this type. The Minnesota program covers a fairly broad category of the poor (defined as 275 percent of the federal poverty level definitions for families), plus those who have been uninsured for four months or without employer-supported insurance for eighteen months. Its benefit package is quite generous, especially preventive care measures. It is paid for by a 5 cent cigarette tax, a 2 percent tax on hospital, surgical, and other health care and drug providers, and premiums based on a sliding scale of family income.

The Arizona program is similar to that of Minnesota, except that it has been running much longer (since 1982), it does not cover those uninsured for short periods as does Minnesota, but it does include a children's care program which specifically aids low-income children, and it offers medical coverage to companies of forty or fewer employees that do not have group insurance. Studies by the Federal Health Care Financing Administration found that the Arizona program provided higher-quality care for children and had better access and less expensive care than traditional Medicaid systems. Arizona has been the basic model of state reforms along these lines. Furthermore, these states' experiences have inspired the adoption of managed care into Medicaid programs.

LIMITED INSURANCE GUARANTEES AND MANAGED CARE BUILT INTO MEDICAID-STYLE PROGRAMS

A variation on the trend of expanding or replacing Medicaid involves combining managed care networks, insurance guarantees to limited populations, and administrative changes in the Medicaid-style programs. Private-fee services are replaced with managed care systems that use networks of health providers to cut costs. Physicians are care managers, and normally the general practitioners must be visited before specialists, and approval of specialists' services is required. The leading state in these reforms, Tennessee, several years ago developed a managed care network for its state employees at a more cost-effective rate than traditional services. Tennessee's expanded 1994 Tenn Care program established a funding and benefit partnership with the federal government that essentially modifies Medicaid. It builds on its managed care state employee network to expand the Medicaid base by offering insurance benefits to an additional half million persons.

The trend of expanding managed care in states, mainly through bids to HMOS or preferred provider organizations, or creating managed care state insurance pools, as an alternative to private physicians in traditional Medicaid reimbursement, has expanded to about a half dozen states; in fact, forty-nine states are reported to be introducing at least limited elements of these ideas. Such limited population insurance guarantees provide coverage usually only to the poor, the uninsured, and/or the working poor without insurance. Maryland, New Jersey, Oregon, and Florida put such laws on the books in the early 1990s, with implementation deadlines established in the mid-1990s.

Such programs provide insurance through one of two ways: through bidding out to private providers who operate managed care networks, or through "pay or play" incentives for employers to provide (and usually partially pay for) employee insurance. *Pay or play* usually means that employers must work out the provision of split-cost insurance by a certain deadline (the "play" idea) or they will have to "pay" split costs of premiums or taxes into a state cooperative plan. There are usually pools of money that help small businesses cover such costs.

STATEWIDE SYSTEMS OF MANAGED CARE NETWORKS FOR WORKING POOR AND THE UNINSURED

About a dozen states have moved beyond the simple expansion of Medicaid to create *statewide systems of managed care* targeted at much larger segments of the population. This is now one of the biggest trends in the states. The Clinton plan substantially drew its ideas from the already established state programs. State-created comprehensive managed care systems for all or most citizens provide real competition to private insurance and fee-for-service doctors and hospitals.

The main strategy has been to establish health insurance purchasing cooperatives (HIPCs). These state-created HIPCs offer a standardized set of benefits (often publicly bid to private providers) to selected populations, usually state employees plus small business workers and the uninsured. Also, they are usually open to competitive purchase by groups, bigger businesses, and sometimes the general population. In this way they become statewide reforms.

Besides offering benefits and insurance, HICPs collect premiums, negotiate or set prices with providers, and provide competitive consumer data through cost and quality ratings comparisons. Thus they generally introduce true market forces and set tough standards of medical competition and access for private insurance, HMOs, and private providers (something lacking in the nonmarket aspects of medicine). Hawaii, Florida, Washington, California, and Minnesota have had varied forms of such purchasing and rating co-ops since the 1980s, and laws establishing them were implemented in Kentucky, Montana, Florida, New Jersey, and Maryland after 1993.

STATE REFORM OF MEDICAL MONOPOLISM

About ten states are also implementing laws to establish *pro-market reforms* and to regulate some of the more troublesome features of medical monopolism. Various laws regulate or negotiate hospital revenues or fees, give public notice of competitive fees and quality ratings for services, limit the financial awards in medical malpractice suits, regulate or eliminate unnecessary procedures, expand public and preventive health, expand the practice of alternative medical arts, expand medical practice in rural areas, and even ration the expenditure for near-death health care (Oregon) so as to transfer monies instead to preventive care. The conservatives and special interest groups have argued that all of these reforms are things that the national government should not regulate. However, increasing numbers of states are adopting such regulations to curtail exploding health costs and guarantee medical care for citizens. States with fairly stringent pro-market and anti-monopolism laws and programs include Maryland, New York and New Jersey (hospital revenue caps), Maine, Oregon, California, Minnesota, Montana, and Colorado (Council of State Governments 1994).

STATE GUARANTEES FOR UNIVERSAL COVERAGE

The most sweeping kind of state reform, which may be the trend of the future, is the *guarantee of universal insurance coverage and standard benefits* for either limited or broad segments of the population, usually through state-established managed care networks. The most notable states are Hawaii, which has extensive experience with this, and Washington, which established a sweeping comprehensive program in 1993.

The state that has the most experience in comprehensive health reform is Hawaii. In comparison with the other states, Hawaii has fewer infants die during their first year of life, longer life expectancy, less time spent in hospitals, and all with less money spent on medical care. This is the result of Hawaii's provision of near universal health insurance coverage, along with its emphasis on preventive, primary, and public health care. How has Hawaii done this?

Basically, Hawaii provides all residents with a universal insurance guarantee, through a combination of four strategies. First, Hawaii has a State Health Insurance Plan (SHIP) that covers the poor, defined as unemployed or workers not covered by employers, and which is in addition to Medicaid coverage for the extremely poor. Second, Hawaii's 1974 Prepaid Health Care Act *requires* all employers to provide health insurance for full-time workers, with employer and employee each paying 50 percent of the premiums. Hawaii is the only state with such a requirement. Third, the nearly universal coverage health insurance is *privately* provided through two big insurers covering more than 70 percent of the population—Blue Cross/Blue Shield's Hawaii Medical Service Association, and the giant HMO run by Kaiser Permanente, a traditional HMO with salaried physicians working in their health centers. Both insurers intensively practice managed care strategies. Also, the state has a vigorous health planning agency which controls excessive medical technology through a stringent certificate-of-need process that requires providers to justify big expenses on equipment. The result of all this is that less than 2 percent of the population lacks insurance coverage, and the coverages (except for the SHIP program for the poor) are quite generous, emphasizing preventive, primary, and specialist care with low deductibles.

What does Hawaii *not* do? First, it does not have a state-created health insurance purchasing cooperative—the two big private insurers do a fair job of managed and preventive care and offer consumer information on services—nor does it have a competitive "government insurance." Second, it does not directly regulate hospital revenues or doctor fees; it does so indirectly through the bargaining power of the two big insurers with their managed care strategies and through its state planning of hospital capital improvements. Third, it does not have laws that directly regulate medical monopolism or strengthen alternative medicine, since the excesses of monopolism are somewhat alleviated by the rigorous managed care practices of the two big insurers. Considerable cost shifting in hospitals apparently still takes place, since Medicare and Medicaid do not pay the entire costs of services billed even by the relatively less expensive Hawaii providers, and medical services are still unavailable in some of the more remote locations (*Consumer Reports*, September 1992, p. 590).

The state of Washington has captured national attention by passing a comprehensive 1993 law which establishes the nation's only other managed care-universal coverage system. The plan relies on employer–employee 50 percent split contributions, plus tobacco and alcohol taxes. Three competitive forms of insurance coverage have been created: (1) certified health plans, which are private insurance plans that meet state requirements for coverages and benefits; (2) health insurance purchasing cooperatives, to be formed by governments or other nonprofit groups; and (3) an expanded state employee system that functions as a competitive "big brother" HIPC.

The Washington state reform is notable because its mandated, comprehensive standard benefits package (which applies to all allowable insurance plans) pays for preventive and alternative medicine and also prescription drugs. It also calls for community rating of premium costs, and state regulation of physician fees, under a Health Care Access and Cost Commission. It does not significantly alter traditional long-term care for the elderly, however.

This program is remarkably similar to what the Clinton plan would have been if it had been passed by Congress. In essence, we can get some idea of what might have happened to health care under the Clinton plan by watching what does happen with Washington.

GOING CANADIAN: SINGLE-PAYER OR STATE GOVERNMENT INSURANCE

Only a few states, notably Vermont (1992) and Montana (1993), have come close to establishing single-payer or government-funded universal insurance plans. The laws in both states call for the state legislature to review and decide between a single-payer system versus a managed care, multiple private insurer system with health insurance purchasing co-ops as a base.

Single-payer plans (similar to that in Canada) establish government insurance systems or near-monopoly private bid winners, while limiting private insurance to old-age supplements, disability insurance, and other narrow markets.

Single-payer systems provide universal coverage to all. They control costs well for three reasons. First, they either negotiate or set budgets with hospitals, or they negotiate or set fee schedules with doctors (whether private or managed care), or they do both. This means they have the power to negotiate against *excessive* provider fees, essentially serving as a market force that counterbalances the near monopoly of traditional medicine. Second, single-payer systems eliminate cost shifting to businesses and consumers. Since single-payers cover everybody, there are no private payers on which to shift excessive costs. Third, single-payer systems avoid the tremendous overhead costs and administrative waste associated with private insurance and physician billing practices. Even studies of Medicare show it to have dramatically lower administrative costs (approximately 2 percent) than most private insurance companies (approximately 10 percent or more). Also, many studies show that in single-payer systems where the insurance is either a nonprofit government system (such as state worker and teacher nonprofit insurance funds) or near-monopoly private bid winners (such as Hawaii's two big private insurers) the scope and number of benefits are higher and the costs are lower. It is this power to set negotiated ceilings on private profits that allow costs to be contained so well in other countries even when medical practice is private.

There are additional public health advantages to single-payer systems. One is that planning agencies that grant certificates of need to operate new expensive equipment or services in hospitals or clinics usually have a greater capacity to control the geographic spread of medical facilities and practitioners and keep it even. This is the case because providers cannot reap huge profits by limiting themselves to rich urban or suburban areas. The result is that primary care and preventive medicine are evenly mixed with specialist care in more geographic areas, and so overall health is improved (consider Hawaii's public health record).

SUMMARY

While the national government has not yet managed to establish a meaningful policy of health care reform, most states seem to be moving toward doing the job themselves. The states are trying to tackle the problems of monopolism, arrest the medical cost explosions, and resolve the worsening problems of the uninsured and the decline of public health. To achieve these goals, most of the states are providing limited insurance coverage for poor or uninsured groups, some by expanding Medicaid programs, others by establishing state-created competitive insurance pools, with standard benefits for insurers to match, and still others through shared employer–employee contributions. Managed care strategies placed inside these various insurance schemes seem to be the current wave of reform.

A few states have extensive experience with more universal managed care systems provided through health insurance purchasing cooperatives or insurers that match state requirements or bids. This is probably the main wave of state reforms. It allows states to set the benefit requirements, and sets them up either as honest broker competitors or as regulatory managers of private insurance services to larger and larger segments of the population.

States are also going where no feds have gone before—in regulating the more dysfunctional aspects of medical monopolism and restoring market forces and cost restraints, thereby reversing some seventy years of near monopolism in medical arts and some thirty years of soaring medical costs. States have also moved boldly toward stronger measures of preventive medicine and public health, in an age of reluctance to do so in national policy. A few states are experimenting with broader guarantees of health care, mainly through universal insurance through managed care strategies. While no state has yet implemented a single-payer approach, Hawaii's two-payer system roughly approaches that system.

All these developments certainly are strong indicators of vitality in the American system of federalism. It underscores the shift of policy action to state and local governments while the national government has experienced political gridlock and relative policy inaction.

If current trends of state reform continue, the United States may arrive at a "fair" level of health reform by the turn of the century, perhaps in time to prevent medical costs from soaring past 25 percent of the gross economic product. The vitality of the states to reform health care should not be underestimated, and neither should the costs of delaying the reforms.

CHAPTER 10

*I*SSUES AND *E*THICS
AT THE *E*XTREMES OF *L*IFE

ABORTION AND EUTHANASIA

Our society is being compelled to search for answers in public policies to deal with circumstances of the very young and the very old. Uncertainty and contention permeate unresolved issues about ethics and rights at these extremes of life, especially the issues of abortion and euthanasia ("mercy killing").

Before the twentieth century, and in most respects before World War II, the circumstances of both young life and old life were not understood as having equal importance to those of mid-life adults—not in the marketplace, in politics, or in home life. The very young and very old were considered unproductive and under the control of those in the productive middle years, who were considered to have more rights. None of today's many early-life issues (abortion, birth control, prenatal care, child abuse, child sexual abuse) or late-life issues (euthanasia, right-to-die, retirement, long-term care of the elderly) were public issues in those times.

In those times young people were not much more than property under the near-total control of parents or, in their absence, the secular or religious authorities. In many ways those were not "the good old days." For instance, child labor was rampant and legal. Physical and sexual abuse at work, school, or in the home were at least as common, and certainly not for public discussion. Abortion was nearly universally banned by state law from the mid-1800s to the middle of this century, and women's rights to abortion and even the fetus itself were defined as being under the sole control of the state. As for the very old, they were largely left either to the care of whatever family existed or to religious charity. The aging had almost no opportunity for continued employment or self-support in the business world. Death itself was largely left to the processes of nature. The elderly were simply not a concern for government policy, support, or spending.

New Deal and postwar America, however, increasingly came to grapple with these issues, for a variety of political, technological, and social reasons. Today these issues spark vociferous and often unresolved public battles over political rights, public policies, and dignified equal treatment. The most contentious and difficult issues about the extremes of life are abortion and euthanasia. The main trends of public policies affecting these two issues are the subject of this chapter.

ABORTION: A NEVER-ENDING BATTLE

After 1821 various states began the first wave of legislative restrictions on abortions, mainly to guard against risky medical practices (Mohr 1978). By the end of the century, however, most states had laws that criminalized abortion. Abortion remained largely a criminal act through the mid-1900s and into the 1960s. In 1967 California legalized abortions, and by 1970 fourteen other states had also legalized abortion (Rubin 1987).

Some scholars have argued that most political strategies used by supporters and opponents in the abortion battle have stemmed from reactions to court decisions. Since the 1970s, however, both sides have developed tactics such as campaigns to defeat political candidates, protests modeled after civil rights marches, economic boycotts against states, and others. The issues surrounding abortion are laced heavily with political and religious values. Much of the abortion debate surrounds principles evoked in the Supreme Court's famous *Roe* v. *Wade* decision of 1973. Because of legal reasoning about political rights, medical knowledge of the viability of the fetus, and similar matters, the debate has been oversimplified and perhaps overdriven by these issues. The *Roe* decision established the principle that a woman has a right of privacy, a right derived either from the Ninth Amendment's guarantee of rights to the people or from the Fourteenth Amendment's equal protection of rights provision. The privacy right was interpreted in the *Roe* case as (1) allowing the woman to choose to have an abortion unrestricted until the end of the first trimester or three months of pregnancy; (2) conceding that the state or other parties may begin to have interests in protecting fetal life at the point of "viability," or the point at which a fetus can begin to survive on its own, assuming medical support; and (3) conceding that the third trimester tips the balance of decision and interest further in favor of the state or the fetus itself.

Much of this reasoning was predicated on medical testimony about the inability of the fetus to survive unaided at the earliest stage. The Court has been unwilling itself to define conception as the beginning of life or personhood, primarily for these (1973 era) medical reasons. However, opponents have argued that the sense of this argument recedes as increasing technology makes it more possible to support fetal life at earlier periods.

As anti-abortion strategists sought to counter this ruling in the 1970s and 1980s, they utilized several tactics, including lobbying and protests to establish restrictions by state laws or in medical practice and efforts to obtain court or legislative restrictions on abortion in the second and third trimesters (where Roe was weakest in granting women sole control). They also put pressure on Republican presidents to pack the Justice Department and federal appeals, district, and even Supreme Courts with appointees who were conservative in general and anti-abortion in particular, and filed cases in the federal courts, as the timing seemed right in the wake of these earlier efforts, to seek either the complete reversal of *Roe* or continued revisions imposed by the Courts or the states. The goal of these tactics was either directly or indirectly to render abortion less available to women, or to expand their sole right of choice to other parties, especially in the first and second trimesters.

These strategies of revision have worked fairly well, although slowly, since the late 1970s. But before we summarize where abortion policy and practice have headed since *Roe*, we must look more closely at the values or assumptions that underlie the debate about abortion. We will examine how the overall public debate was guided mainly by legal and philosophical reasoning in the federal courts, how abortion issues are actually more complex than they appear from what partisan factions put forth, and how we might interpret the directions of policy regulation of abortion today.

The debate about abortion involves many subtle and complex value assumptions. There are also many varieties of responses to the abortion issue, belying the idea that one must be either "pro-life" or "pro-choice." Public opinion has been about evenly divided on the questions since the early 1980s, no doubt because people themselves recognize that the issues are more complex than the way constitutional lawyers and the reacting antagonists have framed them.

With the entry of "values," the abortion debate was set up in the 1970s around the question of whether or not a woman had a proprietary constitutional right to abort (construed as privacy, involving medical decisions over her own medical future). The debate in the legal system initially tended to make point–counterpoint arguments around this collection of legal ideas, simply because those were the issues upon which constitutionality could be pursued. (In other words, did the existing Fourth, Fifth, Ninth, or Fourteenth Amendments provide room somewhere to create or deduce the existence of a zone of proprietary privacy that allows a pregnant woman to control the continuance of the pregnancy?) The precedence for this line of legal reasoning that defined the issues was established in *Griswold* v. *Connecticut* in 1965. In that famous case, the Court overturned a Connecticut anti-birth control law which had prevented married couples from buying and using contraceptives, on the basis that such a law had unconstitutionally intruded on the marital zone of privacy in sex and reproduction. Such a zone of right to privacy did not literally exist in the Constitution but had to be deduced from the Fourth, Ninth, and Fourteenth Amendments. If such a zone of privacy could be deduced as existing for sexual intercourse in the *Griswold* case, then similar reasoning could also find privacy for a woman's choice of abortion. To quote the Court's *Roe* decision:

> This right of privacy, whether it be founded in the Fourteenth Amendment's concept of personal liberty and restrictions upon state action, as we feel it is, or, as the District Court determined, in the Ninth Amendment's reservation of rights to the people, is broad enough to encompass a woman's decision whether or not to terminate her pregnancy.... We therefore conclude that the right of personal privacy includes the abortion decision, but that this right is not unqualified and must be considered against important state interests in regulation ... the Court has held that regulation limiting these rights may be justified only by a "compelling state interest," and that legislative enactments must be narrowly drawn to express only the legitimate state interests at stake.

From this language and reasoning, abortion issues in America at first tended to crystallize around legal jargon and a number of constitutional issues. These included privacy, right of reproductive choice, proprietary choice to abort (only the woman's choice), and state interest in intervention limited to the point after "viability."

As the Roe decision is worded, either the physician or the woman has sole control in the first trimester, and after that sole control slowly shifts to the state, at first only to protect the health of the mother, and then, in the final months—when the fetus can survive independently—to protect the potential of human life. The interests of all other parties are denied. As one party (the woman, in the first trimester) has sole control, other parties such as the fetus and fathers have zero control. This condition of extreme winning versus losing in equal measure is known as *zero sum* conditions. Regarding the time after the first trimester, the Court tried to strike a balance of interests between a woman's choice, a woman's health, and fetal viability. The *Roe* decision created an "open zone" of state interest in only the third trimester, or last three months of pregnancy. This constitutional reasoning early on held abortion as being about only some limited issues. And that situation set up an almost unresolvable collision between interests.

The explosive factor in *Roe*'s picture of the abortion issue was the concept that something as complex as abortion, which has the potential to affect various parties in myriad ways, can be defined as being the rightful choice of one party, without serious questions being raised. It was the *definition* of abortion as being one person's proprietary right in the early months of pregnancy that became so objectionable to opponents.

It is extremely important to see how the Court—in making the debate mainly about certain issues that lawyers could bring up as "tests of Constitutional rights," and in defining abortion as a "proprietary privacy right"—oversimplified the abortion issue and helped pave the way for the controversy that followed. See Box 10.1 for a discussion of how the Court established some of the issues.

10.1   HOW THE SUPREME COURT DEFINED KEY ISSUES IN ROE V. WADE 1973

How the Court interpreted the constitutional definition of "person" to exclude fetuses:

"... the appellee conceded on reargument that no case could be cited that holds that a fetus is a person within the meaning of the Fourteenth Amendment.... The Constitution does not define "person" in so many words ... in nearly all these instances (where the word person is mentioned) the use of the word is such that it has application only postnatally. None indicates, with any assurance, that it has any possible prenatal application."

How the Court at first claimed not to know when life begins:

"We need not resolve that difficult question of when life begins. When those trained in the respective disciplines of medicine, philosophy, and theology are unable to arrive at any consensus, the judiciary, at this point in the development of man's knowledge, is not in a position to speculate as to the answer.... In areas other than criminal abortion, the law has been reluctant to endorse any theory that life, as we recognize it, begins before live birth or to accord legal rights to the unborn except in narrowly defined situations and except when the rights are contingent upon live birth."

How the Court then used science to define when life begins:

"With respect to the State's important and legitimate interest in potential life, the "compelling" point is at viability. This is so because the fetus then presumably has the capability of meaningful life outside the mother's womb.... [the Court then goes on to pinpoint this as] ... the stage prior to approximately the end of the first trimester [when] the abortion decision and its effectuation must be left to the medical judgment of the pregnant woman's attending physician."

How the Court defined abortion as a proprietary privacy right of the woman, subject to eventual regulation:

"... it is reasonable and appropriate for a State to decide that at some point in time another interest, that of the health of the mother or that of potential human life, becomes significantly involved.... These interests are separate and distinct. Each grows in substantiality as the woman approaches term and, at a point during pregnancy, each becomes "compelling" ... [at this undefined point].... The woman's privacy is no longer sole, and any right of privacy she possesses must be measured accordingly."

How the Court defined the exceptions to regulate abortion, based on the trimesters of pregnancy:

"(A) For the stage prior to approximately the end of the first trimester, the abortion decision and its effectuation must be left to the medical judgment of the pregnant woman's attending physician.

(B) For the stage subsequent to approximately the end of the first trimester, the State, in promoting its interest in the health of the mother, may, if it chooses, regulate the abortion procedures in ways that are reasonably related to maternal health.

(C) For the stage subsequent to viability, the State in promoting its interest in the potentiality of human life may, if it chooses, regulate, and even proscribe abortion except where it is necessary, in appropriate medical judgment, for the preservation of the life or health of the mother."

Twenty years later we can be good "armchair quarterbacks." We can easily understand now that different segments of society have strong religious, cultural, ethnic, and political ideas about abortion. These groups rather naturally reacted strongly to the legalistically limited idea that one party or another has sole ownership and proprietary control in the early stages over something as controversial as abortion.

We will contrast this proprietary concept of abortion with the more realistic idea that abortion is a unique *balanced stakes* issue. In fact, both the states and the federal courts are redefining abortion today to this effect. Abortion is therefore probably more a *communitarian* than a *libertarian* issue, whereby one party may have stronger claims in some circumstances but many parties may claim interests. In this sense also, myriad parties will insist that the decision to abort could rarely be a proprietary right. It may be that the Courts and society are coming to view abortion as a complicated situation that may be best resolved on a case-by-case basis, with law serving to establish processes that grant negotiable rights to different claimants.

THE COURT'S ASSUMPTIONS OF ABORTION AS A PROPRIETARY RIGHT

In the initial *Roe* decision, when the Supreme Court made the abortion debate an issue about a woman's proprietary privacy right to choose, this view gave one party control over the outcomes of an act that can affect other parties with real or imagined interests. The idea of sole possession and control of a political right inevitably encounters serious constitutional, legal, and political resistance. The inherent weaknesses in this idea of sole possession of a political right opened the door to both the legal challenges to *Roe* and the vociferous social opposition that built up against it.

Scholars have argued that possibly what put *Roe* on somewhat weak constitutional ground is the fact that the right to privacy is not expressly mentioned in the Constitution. Rather, it has been *interpreted* from other rights. Some opponents of abortion have sought to reverse *Roe* by legal arguments, legislative revisions, and political pressures to appoint conservative judges to the courts precisely because they recognized that the idea of a privacy right is fluid and only indirectly constitutional and that it could be legally questioned on this basis by strict constructionist justices.

These anti-abortionists have found out, however, that legal conservatism is not easily predictable, and has numerous aspects. A Justice's social conservatism may not override his or her judicial conservatism, since "lawyers think mainly like lawyers." Strict legal constructionists may strictly interpret the Constitution and oppose *Roe* because they think it invents too much of a privacy right. But they may also be *more* devoted to legal precedent and thus be reluctant to change *Roe*. In this second way, Justices O'Connor, Kennedy, and Souter have turned out to be reluctant to overturn *Roe*.

But what really makes *Roe* so extraordinary is that *nowhere* in the Constitution does it grant people unlimited rights to *anything*. There is no such constitutional tradition. The Constitution seems always to qualify the rights of individuals with statements that allow the state to regulate rights when the state has a compelling interest. For instance, where the Constitution mentions a right to life, it does so in the context of the Fourteenth Amendment, which says that the state cannot deprive any person of life *without due process of law*. In other words, the Constitution does not say that the state must give all people an unlimited right to life (proprietary), but rather that any right to life that people have is subject to due process of law, which is what must be provided.

Generally speaking, therefore, it has never been constitutional or legal tradition to grant individuals political rights with *sole proprietorship* (total control over something as a possession or piece of property). Even such basic rights as speech, voting, protection from self-incrimination (and now dying— see the section on euthanasia) have been interpreted by the courts as having restrictions. Even the *Roe* decision itself enshrined the idea of the government's restricting the decision in the second and third trimesters. But by granting sole proprietorship to one party in the first trimester, the Court was to a considerable extent breaking with precedents. This action caused even stronger legal and public opposition, and it also opened the door for persuasive arguments for revising *Roe* in the 1980s.

Political opposition to the ruling was based on more than constitutional grounds or the idea that the woman would have sole control. Generally speaking, opposition built up over a large number of *values* about abortion, which are embedded in different religions, regional cultures, and even ethnic groups. These deeply revered values inevitably conflict with values enshrined in the legal decision.

For example, the Court said that *fetal viability* is defined by medical information about the survival potential of the fetus outside the womb. Using such medical information, the Court pictured the fetus as not viable at all in the first three months, so until then a woman is free to abort. Between three and six months the fetus is able to survive only with extreme assistance; it is only after six months that the fetus has a realistic probability of medically unassisted life. It is during the second and third trimesters, when the probability of life without medical assistance increases, that the Court has allowed states to regulate the abortion decision. By this medical reasoning, the Court avoided dealing with whether conception determines the beginning point of human life and therefore human rights.

A definition of life that relies on medical science may be satisfying to some, but large segments of society are motivated by religious values that define life as starting at conception, and no amount of legal or medical reasoning is going to prevail with those people whose world view is defined by religious authority. In fact, the Court eventually retreated from the viability definition of life in the *Webster* case, discussed in a later section.

The Catholic Church, the evangelical churches in America, including Baptists, and even such disparate religions as the Mormons and the Moslems have strong doctrinal views of life as irrevocably starting at the moment of conception. Historian J. D. Hunter (1991) has argued that groups holding such religious views encompass between 40 percent and 60 percent of the population. Such persons are motivated to a stronger or lesser extent by what Hunter calls the orthodox view of authority and values, which strongly influences them to adhere to the views of religious authorities. According to Hunter, the culture war in America is substantially increased by conflicts between these orthodox values versus political progressives and liberals, whose sources of authority are human rights philosophies rather than traditional religious authority or sacred texts (Hunter 1991).

CONFLICTING VALUES OF PRO-CHOICE VERSUS PRO-LIFE ADVOCATES

No doubt there are many reasons why the abortion debate became so intense, but two powerful and irreconcilable underlying political and cultural forces drove the conflict to ever higher levels. On the one side were two values enshrined in the *Roe* decision that appealed mainly to progressive and secular-thinking individuals and the pro-choice forces. They were the ideas that the federal courts found or created a proprietary, libertarian right for a woman to have an abortion (especially in the first trimester), and the scientific argument about medical viability not existing before the end of the second trimester. However, these forces were on a full-speed collision course with two opposing forces: orthodox religious values about the beginnings of human life and rights, and the constitutional view of political rights as nonproprietary and communitarian (balanced stakes), with the state as arbiter of interests.

Both pro-choice and pro-life advocates, then, have strongly held values about abortion, sex, and public policy. Through their tactics of appeal and rhetoric, the abortion debate becomes pitched to the more moderate general public as "pro-life" versus "pro-choice"; rights of the fetus versus rights of the woman; jars of fetuses versus bloody coat hangers" (Craig and O'Brien 1994, p. 47). Both value positions are in part contradictory, and sometimes self-defeating.

For instance, for most pro-choice advocates the right of *all* women to choose safe and legal abortion is essential to the well-being of many women's lives. Furthermore, the reproductive right is seen as the key that secures other freedoms against gender oppression. But ironically, by insisting on proprietary choice, pro-choice groups have produced some counterproductive tendencies. They have denied reproductive rights for men and thus created further disincentives for males to face up to sex role responsibilities. Even male feminists now question whether men have equal reproductive and child-rearing rights. (Women disproportionately enjoy legal control of abortion and custody and are achieving merited gains in child support.) Pro-choice advocates have also opened themselves to objections about the dehumanization of fetuses. And their disregard of other ethnic and cultural-religious views have alienated many women and men from the pro-choice and feminist movements (see several of these arguments as presented by the feminist Naomi Wolf 1993).

Pro-life advocates tend to believe irrevocably that fetuses are fully human and thus enjoy rights to life and choices equal to the mother's. Ironically, from the standpoint of the fetus, this idea may be more in line with the egalitarian tradition of liberal philosophy than with pro-choice views, which stress the welfare of the mother over that of the fetus. Also, pro-life advocates see sex and abortion primarily as acts with heavy community stakes and consequences. They tend to stress alternatives to abortion (adoption) and increasingly stress abortion prevention as essential to a "moral," pro-family society. But pro-life advocates tend to revere traditional white Anglo-Saxon Protestant roles for women: Their "pro-family" society requires the submission of a woman to her husband's authority; limits women's rights and equal participation in work, politics, and religion; and defines women's primary responsibilities as being to family and children. These beliefs in the submission of women to men and the denial of equal rights for women limit the appeal of the pro-life advocates, especially for more progressive groups such as liberal Protestants (Episcopalians, most Lutherans, and Methodists), many Midwesterners and non-Southerners, and highly educated people.

Ironically, pro-life advocates also tend to have counterproductive views that render them in fact merely pro-birth, *not* pro-child or pro-life. For instance, for conservative political reasons they generally do not favor public programs to enhance the lives of infants and children through measures such as preventive medicine and nutritional supplementation programs. Most "pro-life" advocates argue against birth control education, which could prevent many abortions as well as the contraction of AIDS. And they generally refuse to support state efforts to increase prenatal care or aid for pregnant women, which would help women to keep babies rather than abort them. They thus fight against preventive social policies that would help to reduce abortions, instead favoring government control of sex through restrictions of sex education and birth control, for example. These unrealistic desires to use law to regulate sex would probably work about as well to control sexual intercourse (and thus abortion) as did the useless attempts to ban liquor in the prohibition era in the 1920s.

The two big conflicts—between proprietary choice versus balanced stakes abortion rights and between viability versus conception as the beginning of fetal rights—are nearly irreconcilable. In general, the courts and the political forces have shifted slightly toward the *balanced stakes* position and somewhat away from the *Roe* proprietary rights position. This political battle will be discussed in the next section.

THE DRIFT TOWARD BALANCED STAKES ABORTION

THE POLITICAL BATTLE

Studies showed that the early opponents in the abortion battle tended to divide into camps of "traditional women" (unemployed homemakers, who had the time to be activists) versus "feminists." At first the anti-abortion movement was uncoordinated, small, and made up mainly of Roman Catholics. Activists sought state restrictions through legislation, which then became test cases in the federal courts against *Roe*. By the late 1970s anti-abortion coalitions had become large, their numbers increased partly by Southern evangelicals and Baptists. Anti-abortion demonstrations in Washington, D.C., grew from crowds of several hundreds to tens of thousands. Pro-choice forces were considerably larger and more effective until the late 1970s, when the numbers, tactics, and political intensity and rhetoric of both sides roughly equalized.

By the 1980s the political battle had taken on warlike tones. Senator James Buckley, a New York Republican, in 1974 proposed a constitutional amendment outlawing abortion, and it became the rallying ideal for the anti-abortion forces. By 1977 abortion opponents had won passage of restrictions on federal funding of abortions in Medicaid programs to cases of life-threatening pregnancies (the Hyde Amendment).

In 1982 and 1983, anti-abortion forces were following President Reagan's trumpet call for a constitutional amendment to outlaw abortion, but the U.S. Senate in both years voted against such amendments. They had won funding restrictions, but not an amendment to outlaw abortion. Opponents of abortion then approached the issue from different angles: increased demonstrations, and more challenges brought to the federal courts after state legislatures were persuaded to pass test-case restrictions. Finally, in 1985 President Reagan's secretary of health and human services, Dr. Otis Brown, slapped on regulations that ended funding to all organizations that provided counseling and abortion services under Title X of the Public Health Services law. For over twenty years family planning organizations had used federal funds to counsel women on abortion rights, referral, and services, among other things, but regulations enacted in 1988 specified organizations receiving such federal aid could no longer provide abortion counseling, make referrals, or engage in activities that referred to abortion as an option, including lobbying, disseminating materials, and the like. At this time nearly 90 percent of abortions were performed in clinics or family planning centers, so by denying this funding to such organizations the Reagan administration aimed not only to put these organizations out of business but also to take a giant chunk out of the nation's roughly 1.5 million abortions per year (nearly 30 percent of pregnancies). The Bush administration continued the restrictions, and continued Reagan's ban on federal scientists' using fetal tissue for research (see Craig and O'Brien 1993).

The fight over regulations took a swing away from funding restrictions in the Clinton administration, but at the same time many states refused to comply with Clinton's funding liberalization policies. In 1993 Congress, supported by President Clinton, passed a law amending the Hyde Amendment (which defines permissible uses of federal money for abortions), restoring Medicaid funding of abortions for low-income women but limiting it to pregnancies caused by rape or incest. But six states—Arkansas, South Dakota, Louisiana, Kentucky, Utah, and Oklahoma—refused to provide monies to women in such circumstances (*New York Times*, April 1, 1994). Federal officials maintained that 1979 and 1980 court cases require state Medicaid programs to pay for abortions for which federal money is made available, but state refusals to do so continue, and the issue remains in legal limbo as of 1995.

HOW STATES REGULATE ABORTION

Abortions became subject both to trickle-down revisions from federal policies (described above) and to trickle-sideways regulations developed by many states in the 1970s and 1980s, many of which were *not* reversed in federal courts.

Thirty-eight states adopted health regulations restricting abortions, most of them requiring abortions to be performed by licensed doctors in licensed clinics or hospitals. The goal in about half of these states was to restrict abortions—by making them expensive, for example, or subject to very high health standards including hospitalization requirements.

The federal courts became a battleground against many of these regulations, but many states simply ignored the courts. They refused to comply with court rulings overturning their laws, and some even extended their restrictions to banning abortions after the sixteenth to twenty-fourth week (Craig and O'Brien 1993, p. 80). The nonimplementation of legal abortion policies in the states and local areas became more the rule of the land than the exception in the 1980s. According to research by Craig and O'Brien (1993, p. 84), other state strategies included banning advertising for abortions (approximately a dozen states used this strategy, despite federal cases against this practice). Approximately nine states (Pennsylvania, Arizona, Arkansas, Illinois, Minnesota, North Dakota, Oklahoma, Utah, and Wyoming) still enforce laws requiring doctors to take steps to determine if fetuses are viable and to protect them, despite clear federal rulings against doing this.

An important result of these practices has been that in many states, especially outside of major urban areas, abortion has virtually disappeared, since doctors now commonly refuse to do the procedures for fear of political exposure and harassment leading to loss of income and for fear of their own safety. Abortion in America has become mainly a "big city" and "commuter shopping" procedure, where mainly richer women—who can afford the procedure and who can afford transportation to big cities to obtain the procedure, if necessary—get abortions.

THE PROBLEM OF SEMANTICS: RESTRICTION OR EXPANDED SHARED CHOICE?

The problem of using slanted terminology to describe abortion issues is a most difficult one. This is so because of the vast differences in values that persons bring to the abortion discussion. The politics of rhetoric are extremely powerful and subtle in this terminology. We need to spend some time getting away from slanted language before we can describe abortion policy change. The key question in describing abortion policies is which terminology to use. The key problem in thinking about abortion change is the paradoxes of meaning in different policy language.

Most analysts, including legal scholars but particularly pro-choice advocates, use the language of "choice" to describe the course of state and federal regulation of abortion. Using this terminology, most analysts and academics describe policy in terms of "restrictions placed on a woman's right of choice" by the government. Notice how the term *restriction* is used, rather than *revision* or even *expansion to other parties*. *Restriction* is the term most often used because of the zero-sum assumptions in the language of *Roe*, which establishes abortion as an issue of "which individual has proprietary rights."

But changes in abortion policies need not be understood as restrictions only. Changes can be more objectively understood as an *evolution toward shared and balanced stakes and rights*.

An example will make the language problem clear. I may call myself "restricted" if I cannot spend as much money as I used to on professional books and journals now that I am married and have children. However, I may instead recognize the legitimacy of the shared marital experience as a communitarian reality—that other parties have shared interests and stakes in my earnings that require me to partially surrender my sole proprietary control over spending, so that I get somewhat less money (not a total reduction to zero) for my priorities while others with shared stakes get slightly more for theirs. In the real world, then, I am living in a situation of "balanced interests and stakes" regardless of whether I wish to call it "restricted" or "shared." It is clearly more objective to call it "shared interests and stakes."

Language distortion slants the discussion even when one attempts to describe the course of change in abortion policies. For instance, the usual phrase used to characterize the revision of abortion rights is "restricting sole choice." But even this wording is semantically misleading because more often than not the real trend is to expand shared choice to several more parties.

Another political problem with using the term *restriction* to describe the changes in abortion policies is that it locks the discussion of abortion in the realm of somebody's proprietary right, a zero-sum picture of abortion which may well have been the original *Roe* point of view. But the more accurate view is that the courts have been rereading the meaning of abortion under *Roe* for over twenty years, not merely restricting it.

Language distortion likewise occurs—and can have serious consequences—when opponents of abortion use terms like "murder" and "holocaust" to describe abortion policies in America. Such incendiary rhetoric probably helps lead to violence, such as the bombing of abortion clinics and physical attacks on and even murder of doctors who perform abortions.

SHARED STAKES ABORTION RIGHTS IN THE FEDERAL COURTS

We can see how federal court rulings themselves evolved from the proprietary rights view of abortion toward a view that grants balanced and shared stakes and interests.

A key turning point in the Supreme Court's view of abortion came in the *Webster* v. *Reproductive Health Services* case in 1989. In this case Chief Justice Rehnquist wrote the Court's opinion (speaking for only three justices on this issue) that the trimester idea of balancing the interests of women seeking abortions against those of the states was highly questionable and should be rejected. A 1976 Missouri law had assumed fetal viability to be possible at twenty weeks (i.e., after the first trimester) and required doctors to prove with tests that the fetus was not viable prior to performing an abortion. The Supreme Court upheld the constitutionality of the key parts of the Missouri law which (1) decreed that life begins at conception and that unborn children have protectable interests in life, health, and well-being (apparently by casting doubt on the trimester interpretation of life), and (2) required a doctor to disprove a fetus's viability as early as twenty weeks before being able to abort.

With *Webster* the Court did not overturn a woman's right to choose abortion entirely in the first trimester, but in the split decision (five justices in favor, versus four) the Court declared that states had considerable powers to define abortion interests as being shared by several parties as early as the twentieth week of pregnancy. Furthermore, it moved the "state interest" into the first trimester. Chief Justice Rehnquist even wrote in the official opinion that the trimester idea should be rejected: "We do not see why the State's interest in protecting potential human life should come into existence only at the point of viability, and that there should therefore be a rigid line allowing state regulation after viability but prohibiting it before viability."

What this ruling did was essentially open the door to the idea that the fetus could be declared as having potential human life and therefore rights to life. This was not the first time that the Court had ruled that other parties had rights and stakes in abortion, but it was clearly the strongest move to *balance* rights among several parties—the woman, the state, and the fetus.

Having considerably revised the idea about viability and abortion interests, the Court in *Planned Parenthood* v. *Casey* (1992) went on to say that states were clearly allowed to place qualifications on abortion (in the first trimester) if the qualifications "do not have the effect of placing a substantial obstacle in the path of a woman seeking an abortion of a nonviable fetus." Such qualifications will apparently be decided on a case-by-case basis.

But the general trend has been for the Court to recognize other stakes and interests in abortion, in addition to the fetus's right to potential life. The Court has expanded parents' rights to be notified of or give consent to their child's decision to have an abortion (as long as an alternative of judicial consent is allowed) in test cases of laws in Michigan, Nebraska, South Carolina, and Maryland. It has granted states' rights to not provide funding for all abortions, especially publicly funded ones. It has granted states the right to require written consent, abortion counseling, and short "time-out" delays of abortion (Akron 1983; fetal development counseling in Pennsylvania; *Planned Parenthood* v. *Casey* 1992). After such counseling, women must wait twenty-four hours before the procedure. By 1994 Pennsylvania, Michigan, North Dakota, and Ohio had enacted similar laws and practices.

The Court has refused, however, to expand a share in abortion rights to certain parties. It has consistently turned down any right of the husband of an adult woman to be notified. It has also turned away laws that require hospitalization for abortion, and laws that require a doctor to "do everything" to keep a viable or potentially viable fetus alive. As was previously stated, however, several states refuse to comply with rulings and still enforce such laws.

SUMMARY: THE EVOLUTION OF SHARED ABORTION INTERESTS IN FEDERALISM

The federal and state courts have slowly evolved an interpretation of abortion that recognizes a certain amount of balanced, shared stakes and interests. In fact, the courts have redefined abortion rights on a case-by-case basis, and not always consistently. Abortion is now seen as an act in which several parties have a shifting mix of balanced, shared stakes and interests, while at the same time the courts have retained the idea that the woman, at least in the first trimester, has a predominant measure of legal sole control.

At the same time, there is a street-level reality to the practice of abortion in the federal system, which goes beyond laws and courts. States have *practiced* abortion regulation on a wide-ranging continuum. Some states stick rather closely to the new constitutional interpretation, others increasingly are moving through balanced stakes territory. Still others, especially Utah and Louisiana, have practices and policies that have the effect of socially ostracizing and nearly abolishing the practice of abortion even in the first trimester (a true expression of restriction, except from the standpoint of the fetus).

There is some regionalism in this pattern. Many Midwestern and Western states, and virtually all Southern and border states, practice restriction (or, if you wish, pro-fetus protective regulation). An extreme case is Utah, which passed a law in 1991 that makes the performance of an abortion a third-class felony, with a fine of $4,500 and up to five years in jail. Coastal and Northeastern states tend to retain practices that adhere more closely to federal court redefinitions of abortion as a "shared stakes and interests" realm, giving women substantial rights to abortion in the first trimester (Alaska, California, Connecticut, Hawaii, Maine, Maryland, New York, Vermont, and Washington state).

EUTHANASIA: CHOOSING HOW AND WHEN TO LEAVE

For millions of years people near death have been choosing to pass on in their own ways. In ancient times perhaps the younger people honored their elders' wishes by allowing them to walk off into the forest, or they left them behind to die a death in whatever their version of "honor" or necessity was.

Journalists and social scientists are "discovering" this phenomenon today as the *right to die* (when it is self-directed) or *euthanasia* (when others act for terminal and oppressed incompetents). There has been almost no research by political or policy scientists into the actual practice of induced or allowed dying in doctor–patient, family, or hospital settings. There is only a little research beyond what journalists, ethicists, or law scholars know. The small amount of political science research is highly legalistic and mainly examines state policies, laws, court cases, ethics papers, or the adoption of such by state governments (Glick 1994; Hoefler 1994).

There are many possible reasons why political scientists have stayed away from researching death settings. For one, hospitals and doctors for many reasons exclude researchers from intimate medical situations, generally practicing a rigid silence about such matters. Also, political scientists may have viewed hospitals as private settings to be studied by ethicists, economists, and social scientists and therefore not of political interest. Political science studies also have looked merely at official and visible legal policies or ethics statements because death practices seem to have come by way of judicial decisions or legislative acts. The ethical and constitutional law fields that dominate the studies tend to favor library work and the easier and cheaper computer-based manipulations of data from libraries or the internet. Few field-trained policy analysts or social scientists spend the time needed—and for medical protocol reasons will not be allowed—in sensitive, difficult-to-access situations when death comes knocking. Yet more such field and personal interview research is needed to find out what is *actually practiced* by patients, doctors, families, and hospitals (Kelner, Bourgeault, and Wahl 1994). All of the above and more explains why there is too little known about but lots of attention given to the new right-to-die.

Despite the gaps in knowledge about what happens in practice, the right-to-die movement swept through the medical community and state courts and legislatures like a prairie fire storm in the 1980s and 1990s. Talk show commentators had yet another heyday issue.

BEGINNINGS OF THE MODERN RIGHT TO DIE

Henry Glick (1994) argues that there was no legislative or appellate judicial policy regarding individuals' right to end life-prolonging medical treatment before 1976 and the famous Karen Ann Quinlan case. Karen was a young New Jersey woman who suffered respiratory failure and brain damage but not death, seemingly destined forever to be on a respirator in a vegetative state with no hope of recovery. Karen had left no written directives. Her parents and family pressed physicians to withdraw life support (but not intravenous food and water), and the New Jersey Supreme Court used an interpretation of the right to privacy and the right of parents to act as guardians to order the respirator removed (she lived for ten more years on intravenous feedings). This case established the right of surrogates or family to request withdrawal of support for vegetative patients. Similarly, in a federal case from Missouri (Cruzan 1990) the Court suggested that various forms of evidence of a patient's wishes could constitutionally be used by surrogates to withdraw supports for irreversibly vegetative persons. While the Court approved Missouri's law, which then required advance written instructions to withdraw treatment, it also provided this guideline and did not overturn other state policies.

CURRENT STATUS OF THE RIGHT TO DIE

This course of reform proceeded for more than two decades, with most changes coming in the mid-1980s and again in the early 1990s. State legislatures were more reluctant to liberalize rules, while state courts were more lenient (Glick 1994, p. 214). By the mid-1980s more than twenty states had adopted living-will laws or power-of-attorney style advance directives that allow treatments to be withdrawn from the terminally or irreversibly ill and that grant a surrogate person the right to order this withdrawal on the basis of prewritten patient instructions or other clear evidence of such intent. By 1994, forty-five states plus the District of Columbia had implemented living-will laws, while twenty-nine states plus the District of Columbia also had power-of-attorney/medical-surrogate regulations.

The medical and ethical communities rushed fairly quickly to put the stamp of approval on right-to-die provisions (Bok 1994). Even Congress acted in 1990 with the Patient Self-Determination Act, which requires hospitals or other providers who use Medicaid or Medicare monies to inform new patients of their opportunity to provide advance directives about their deaths.

By the mid-1990s both the U.S. Supreme Court and the vast majority of states generally allowed both written and oral expressions of a patient's wishes, and even permitted surrogates, such as family or friends, to act on behalf of patients who could not express wishes. States now permit as a constitutional right (1) the withdrawal of *all* treatment, including food and water for terminally ill and permanently vegetative patients, and (2) recognized suicide and physician-assisted mercy killings for vegetative conditions. State rulings allow these rights when a variety of advance directions exist (proxies, durable power of attorney, living wills), or even when no wishes are known by advance directives. The policy leaders of innovation between 1976 and 1987 were a combination of state court rulings in only seven states—New Jersey (Quinlan case, 1976), Massachusetts, Illinois, California, New York, Florida, and Minnesota.

By 1994 one federal court had ruled that the right to give directives for suicide is a constitutional right of privacy (similar to the privacy right of abortion) for informed, competent, terminally ill adults, including the right to have physician-assisted suicide (*Compassion in Dying* v. *Washington State*, May 1994).

Actually, as we shall argue, these practices were fairly common behind closed doors in medicine for years (if not always). The law mainly codified and perhaps accelerated these practices.

WHAT IS DEATH WITH DIGNITY? THE SHADOWY PRACTICE OF RIGHT TO DIE

Most discussion about right to die or euthanasia seems to lock on to the issues as a question of whether life should be continued by heroic medical intervention or whether the individual has a right to die in a dignified manner. This is the individualized version of the ethics issue (Anderson and Caddell 1993; Hall 1994).

This way of thinking about the issues is controversial and involves competing ideals about the individual's life. For instance, is there a right to privacy that allows individuals to control their own medical treatment? Should medical science prolong life? Should doctors have power to control the decision, withhold information from the family or the patient? Do doctors act strictly out of noble motives to continue life, or do they also have some less than noble motives? Do they justify crisis-level medical interventions only with "we can do it, let's go" attitudes in justifiable cases? Or are they reacting to situations with mixed motives, such as fear of lawsuits? Do they believe too much in their own heroic rescue skills? Do they engage in subtle rationalizations that cause them to devote less effort for patients who are uninsured, poor, medically passive, chronically self-neglectful (drinkers and smokers), or even minorities? And do they exert more effort for rich, well-insured, high-status, medically and legally aggressive patients? In other words, do doctors and hospitals ration medicine in critical near-death situations according to their own personal attitudes?

CASE STUDIES OF NEAR-DEATH CHOICES

Since research on these vital and sensitive issues has been almost nonexistent because of the medical community's code of silence, it is not possible to provide quantitative estimates of these problems. However, the examination of composite cases from real situations (based on our personal interviews of medical professionals) at least allows us to explain some of the ethical issues as they are actually being faced in practice. These cases illustrate the two main pictures or forms of ethics problems.

The first (and usual) picture of the ethics of near death, described above, sees ethics as if the issues were solely about the right to die or control a dignified death. This idea focuses on the individual and ignores the costs or consequences for society, for groups, and for the medical system.

The second and less-appreciated picture of ethics poses questions in a different way: What do these supposedly individual decisions mean for the rest of us? Who pays for these decisions? Do some benefit more than others? Are some being rationed by reality to die more quickly or to get less care?

The medical society has organized itself and defined ethics in such a way that professionals can avoid frank interviews (Hastings Center Guidelines 1987; Appleton Consensus guidelines 1989), so quantifiable estimates of these social problems may never be obtained through easy but obtrusive research methods such as big surveys. But case studies based on interviews *can* show the consequences of some real-world practice for individual ethics problems, and can suggest how bigger social problems emerge from the right-to-die and euthanasia situations.

What we will see is that ethics problems are not controlled by the vague provisions of the new right-to-die laws. Instead, right-to-die situations are affected more by the interplay of values between patients and doctors in individual cases, which show only partial patterns.

Decisions (especially by doctors) may be guided partly by an eye to legal consequences, but decisions really happen more on the basis of other values and dynamics. The cases will show how right-to-die and euthanasia are more affected by such issues as these: Is the patient young and therefore seen as deserving of all-out efforts? Is the patient middle age, and is he or she covered by private insurance? Is the patient suffering from self-induced problems? Has she or he shown efforts to recover from self-abusive habits? What is the patient's attitude about lawyers (lawsuits)? About fighting for life? What are the family's attitudes on these issues? Is the patient old and near terminal? Is the individual poor, without private coverage, or without an assertive family? Is the patient rich and well insured? Did the person leave directives, or are medically assertive family members involved?

These are the likely controlling values in near-death choices when *ethics are seen as being about an individual's control of his or her own death*. The controlling values bear only some resemblance to the more sterile requirements of law, hospital policy, and the like, although laws do signal and accelerate what's acceptable and control the worst abuses. But when the *ethics in right to die are seen as having big social consequences*, then attention is paid more to whether there may be significant consequences for different groups that result from collective individual decisions.

Our cases suggest that the near-death choices, and the related costs and burdens, fall rather differently depending on young versus old, rich and insured versus poor and uninsured, medically assertive versus medically passive, family assertiveness versus no family assertiveness, and possibly member of majority group versus member of minority group. Some individuals get more rights or different results than others, and society pays the costs and bears the burdens in different ways. This complexity raises major social and ethics questions about the true effects of the new right-to-die reforms.

MEDICAL INTERVENTION VERSUS THE RIGHT TO DIE

Case 1: What Values Play Out for a Very Young Patient with an Almost Hopeless Ailment?

Infant Sally was twenty-two months old, born with a severe major organ birth defect. She was covered by her father's work-provided medical insurance. When the parents asked the doctors what to do, the doctors told them that "statistically speaking" her chances were only slightly better for survival past one year of life with the organ transplant than without the organ transplant. The parents, like most people, knew nothing about organ transplants, what the experience would mean for the child, what rehabilitation was like, and so on. They just wanted their daughter to live. (Important here are the parents' values, and how the doctor explains or pictures the situation.) The parents went with the doctors' advice that Sally's chances for survival would be slightly improved with the transplant.

Extreme efforts were made to remedy Sally's birth defect. It was a truly heart-rending situation. Sally received a major organ transplant by age one. The transplant operation itself traumatized her severely. She required rehabilitation efforts, which were obviously extremely painful for her. Sally was also constantly receiving anti-organ rejection drugs, which further affected her health and awareness. Of course she was frequently hospitalized and plugged into equipment, without much chance to be held by her parents. Eventually her body rejected the new organ, and Baby Sally died a little past twenty-two months. The parents indicated they "really had no idea" what the baby would have to go through to get her statistically slightly better chance of survival.

The Issues   Many excruciating issues come into play here. In almost all cases involving infants or young children, strenuous and persistent efforts to extend life are made. The families typically have little knowledge of what it means to turn over a helpless patient to "the system." They just want their baby to live, or to get the best medical care. In the process, family members pay truly gargantuan emotional and financial costs. The tremendous financial costs are almost always passed on to consumers and society, since even the best insurance leaves big uncovered costs, often which families can't or won't entirely pay. In the process, entire families are often bankrupted, especially the many uninsured. Are such efforts really worthwhile? Are we trapped into all-out efforts by our sympathies for the young and our hopes for their futures? If we didn't have third-party payment insurance, would some of us make different choices? Should we at least have parents and families of young patients tell their stories so we all can be better prepared? Given the huge costs of intervention, perhaps a good public choice is to have large sums diverted more fruitfully to prenatal and infant care programs that could reduce the number of delicate-health newborns and avoid some of such terribly costly choices.

Case 2: What Values Play Out for an Uninsured Young Adult Crash Victim?   A few weeks after his high school graduation a star athlete crashed his car into a pole at high speed after having drunk several beers. The other passengers were not seriously injured, but the young athlete was rendered extremely brain-damaged. He lay comatose for several months, with all efforts made at resuscitating him. His chances for regaining consciousness were considered virtually nil, since brain scans showed a large amount of damage. Even if he were to regain consciousness, unanimous medical opinion was that he would never regain even basic language skills, much less motor skills, and would require permanent institutionalization. The youth's parents were working class with no health coverage. At tens of thousands of dollars a month on life support the medical bills threatened to bankrupt the family, leaving them with giant debts and the possibility that their son would be on life support, paid for by Medicaid, for life. Yet the family strenuously argued and the doctors agreed that efforts should be made to continue life support in hopes that he might regain consciousness. The youth lived for nine months, with health indicators gradually deteriorating. The family eventually agreed to withdraw heart-lung machines, and the youth died shortly thereafter.

The Issues   In this case the fact that the family had no insurance coverage made no difference. Instead, the fact that the patient was a vigorous youth who once held much promise was the deciding factor for heroic intervention despite a very bleak prognosis. The diagnosis would normally impel the doctors to recommend the earlier cessation of life support. If the patient were not a youth, support might have ceased on the basis of medical opinion and family concurrence in the first few weeks, rather than months later. In this case the hospital absorbed the cost difference, which amounted to several hundreds of thousands of dollars. And in such high-cost deaths, hospitals have no choice but to pass the huge costs on to the consumer through higher service fees. The hard issues of whether life support should be continued are similar to those in the infant case, and almost as difficult.

However, we should remember that the youth was an adult, and he was driving drunk. Since drunk driving was the cause, the better public choice probably is to spend more on drunk driver prevention and education programs to reduce such deaths. It may be wise to *require* all high school students to visit hospitals and see such cases and hear testimonials about them to help prevent such tragedies.

Case 3: What Values Play Out for an Uninsured Midlife Patient with a Self-Inflicted Ailment? A middle-aged white male, who smoked and drank heavily for years, had no serious liver damage but his lungs were entirely shot. He had no private insurance. He was now on Medicaid, and because of his condition he had been disabled for years, unable to do any work. In fact, *fifteen years* of tax-paid medical support from Medicaid and Medicare had been given to this patient. Doctors said his lungs had deteriorated to the point that he was a candidate for lung transplants. Lung transplants are among the most expensive of medical procedures, because of the cost of the new lungs, the procedure, the required medical support and anti-rejection drugs, and the extensive follow-up care. The patient was very positive in attitude, desired the procedure, and had avid support from family and friends. From a medical point of view, the patient had a slightly better than 50 percent chance of surviving the procedure, although the situation was complicated by the surgically related risks of stress on other weakened organs.

The Issues This case illustrates a big syndrome in America that might be called the choice to have a Golden Coffin Deluxe Death. In America, people can choose to have a million-dollar death, with procedures that extend life for only a short period, or procedures that they may not even survive. Furthermore, people can choose to do this—despite their own past habits of self-abuse that led to the condition—and "bill all of us."

A useful analogy is this: Would you agree that we should let cocaine users use cocaine until it destroyed their health, and then allow them to have the rest of us pay for their medical treatment for fifteen or twenty years? And then should we pay for a million-dollar procedure of their choice that extends their life a few more months? This *is* what we essentially do in thousands of cases a year.

This case shows the major conflicts between personal medical ethics versus social ethics and costs. What is strange is that the *medical social ethics problems* are not well recognized by medical professionals as being at issue, since both medical ethicists and law tend to define ethics as being only about individualized morality (Hall 1994). As you can see, it is just not that simple.

What values should we prioritize in deciding whether to support such an individual's medical costs? Are the important ethical issues, as law and practice now say, that we let the individual or doctor choose all efforts at all costs? Individuals in fact get better possibilities of doctor support if, like this man, they have a positive attitude and supportive family and friends. Should we always support them as well?

Is it ethical for us to support people who are in this situation because of long-term self-abusive habits, and for their bills to be paid either by taxpayers or through costs passed on to other hospital patients? Or should individuals who have created health problems by excessive smoking, drinking, or drug abuse take sole responsibility for their own actions? Is there no such thing as responsibility for your own actions? Should they be able to choose expensive medical procedures and have others pay for them when they have made these lifestyle choices? Also, in cases that require many years of support, there is really no important difference between (1) paying someone else's costs through tax-paid programs from the beginning and (2) paying someone else's costs through higher hospital and doctor fees and (if the person has private insurance) higher insurance premiums. Either way, we all pay.

AN EVALUATION OF THE ISSUES IN CASES 1, 2, AND 3

How would we make rules allowing support for some but not for others? For instance, is it "moral" to help the young but cut off the old? The usual controlling factor in such medical ethics decisions gives priority to the "young, with potential" (see cases 1 and 2). But is this really a good moral priority? Didn't the young athlete in case 2 put more lives in danger by drinking and driving than the smoker in case 3, who never directly endangered other people? Would it be more ethical to cut off from Golden Coffin decisions those who endanger others' lives directly or substantially?

Medical professionals we interviewed (see Appendix B) indicated that in some cases professionals more actively promote care and options than in others, in spite of whatever the laws specify. Current medical practice in the vast majority of death choice cases seems to favor aid and options for the young versus the old, and for those who wish to fight for life over those who don't. Many doctors also more actively seek options when individuals are not continuing in self-abuse of health, such as if they stop smoking. On the other hand, very few decisions to withhold or advocate all-out care are said to be made solely in favor of the insured (rich) versus the uninsured (poor).

In other words, medical practice already uses a balance of ethics to help decide individual cases, only partly informed by the laws. Practice is beginning to factor in the ethics of social costs and personal accountability. These two elements are probably worthy of more serious attention in law and by ethicists. They certainly are costly. We may not be able to afford to continue granting all aid and choices or defining "ethics" as individual morality while remaining blind to medical costs and personal accountability. In this area, law and ethics seem to be lagging behind medical practice—perhaps they always have been.

ACTIVE EUTHANASIA VERSUS THE RIGHT TO LIVE

Case 4: What Values Play Out for an Elderly, Terminally Ill, Barely Competent Patient Who Is Suffering?   A seventy-year-old female had cancer that had spread from the lungs to the spine. Her prognosis was quite hopeless, and the main problem from her view was the extreme pain. Morphine was being used, but the difficult problem was this: An increased morphine dosage might kill the patient (who was not far from death anyway), but not increasing the morphine would leave the patient in excruciating pain for probably weeks longer.

The levels of morphine that might be sufficient to put the pain at bearable levels might, in the opinion of the pulmonary doctors, be just enough to reduce lung functioning and breathing below the point where the patient could live. On the other hand, the cancer doctors feared that with the current level of pain, her prospects for living much longer were extremely low. What was the meaning of simply extending life just to go through a "tunnel of pain"?

The family was not told directly what the extra morphine might do, although they and the patient were aware of the risks without this direct communication. The patient finally firmly requested extra morphine, and without actually saying that it could lead to a quick death, the patient said goodbye to her family. The doctors took that as a signal (also without directly telling all that the dosage could lead to a quick death) and they complied with the patient's wishes. They administered the extra morphine, and the patient died very shortly thereafter.

The Issues   We will examine this case in detail because of the complex and controversial issues surrounding euthanasia in America, and because it disproves the common misconception that assisted mercy killing does not happen in the United States. As this case shows, it does happen, sometimes in veiled ways, with considerable humanity and respect for patient and family needs on the part of doctors, even though such medically led death is virtually illegal in state laws (though the trend is to make exceptions).

This case involved administering a pain-killer in a dosage that was known to result in death, and doing so without explicit proof of the patient's having full and direct knowledge of the result, while complying with the patient's wishes to relieve pain. It *is* a form of active euthanasia that most legalistic analysts of ethics have insisted does not exist in the United States, because it is not legal and is culturally taboo.

Rosemarie Tong (1993), for example, tries to distinguish between *nonvoluntary* active euthanasia (where physicians, family, or friends decide to end the lives of incompetent patients in enormous pain) and *involuntary* active euthanasia (where physicians, family, or friends end the lives of competent or incompetent patients who do or would not wish to be killed). She argues that both forms, which are legal and fairly common in the Netherlands, do not yet take place in the United States. Tong summarizes euthanasia policy in the Netherlands:

> ... physicians who adhere to three important court-recognized and state-endorsed conditions are, in practice, not subject to criminal sanctions: (1) The patient's request must be voluntary in the sense of persistent, conscious, and freely made; (2) the patient's suffering must be *unbearable* in the sense of being beyond recovery or amelioration; and (3) the patient's physicians must *consult* with a colleague about both (1) and (2). Only after all these conditions are met may the physician take steps to actively end the patient's life.

Tong contrasts this system with that in the United States, where these things allegedly do not happen. But they do happen. And such distinctions are nearly useless in complicated, real-life cases.

In case 4 the patient was allowed to die with assistance and test 1 was not met: The request was not persistent or direct; instead it occurred from one indirect signal of "goodbye" to family without explicit words such as "I know it will kill me, but ..."). The case apparently did not meet test 3 either: The doctors could not have discussed the patient's request since the patient made no direct request. Instead, all the parties were using indirect signals and cryptic language about *pain relief*. The patient, the doctors, and the family made a mutual decision by deciding not to talk explicitly about death. This indirect signaling and nonexplicit language possibly was to allow choice while also avoiding difficult issues and perhaps legal complications.

This example may be typical. Professionals, patients, and families can substitute "signal language"to avoid direct talk and legal requirements. This "decision making by clues' is useful in the current shaky legal environment. It is difficult to determine who was more "active" and who was more "passive" and what was or wasn't "voluntary" in such cases. And for several reasons, professionals want it that way.

HOW DOCTORS JUSTIFY ASSISTED DEATHS

Many and perhaps most physicians have respect for the family and/or patient choice, hoping to do the right thing for people and follow their requests while also hoping that few cases will be spoken about in public. This kind of gray area of active mercy killing takes place regularly in America, but determining how much is difficult because getting the doctors to say so is difficult.

In some cases doctors, family, or friends merely take signals from patients—and patients do give signals. They don't need to be so clearly competent nor specify what they want in writing, as legal analysis would lead one to believe. The real patterns of the decision to die or commit euthanasia in America are difficult to determine, since such decisions take place behind walls of silence—codified as ethics in the doctor–patient relationship or in client–patient privilege.

Law and public understanding belatedly follow the hidden practices. State laws and court rulings come to codify existing practices when those practices become widespread enough so that one or more rise up to become controversial media and legal issues. Then law or court cases simply open up and accelerate what is already being done.

In short, active euthanasia already occurs in the United States in ways that would not meet the legal requirements even of the Netherlands.

ARE DEATH CHOICES OFFERED DIFFERENTLY FOR DIFFERENT SOCIAL OR OTHER GROUPS?

Even more shadowy is the possibility that socioeconomic factors play a part in determining who gets what kinds of treatment in right-to-die situations. Medical sociologists and advocates for minorities and the poor have made compelling presentations about institutionalized racism and anti-poor tendencies in medical services, probably including right-to-die choices. In institutionalized discrimination, organizational systems and not necessarily individuals have incentives to discriminate.

Cases 5 and 6: What Values Play Out in Treatment of Racial Minorities and the Poor? Two elderly lymphatic cancer patients were poor, covered only by Medicare and potentially Medicaid. Both showed up with very late stages of identical cancer at the emergency room of a hospital. One patient was white, the other black. But in other respects they were similar patients. The black patient was admitted by the ER physician and referred to an on-call physician for advice. The patient and his family were advised that there was nothing that could be done and that the patient and family should prepare for death and grieving. The condition of the patient was in fact that the cancer was so far advanced that no reasonable chance of recovery was possible. The white patient, however, in virtually the same condition and with the same bleak prospects, was advised by a different on-call physician to take treatments and was admitted to intensive care and given several weeks of futile treatments. Both died within several months.

The Issues What possibilities exist to explain the different treatments? And what does the explanation mean socially and in the ethics of choice about death?

Both patients showed up at emergency rooms, so they had essentially similar admission environments. Emergency rooms are different from private-pay and even general hospital admission situations in several ways. Emergency room professionals are typically salaried, so they might have less economic incentive to decide in favor of trying all options. They tend to identify more with cost-control motives than would fee-based physicians, since they are more directly hospital employees. For the same reasons, they have less financial motivation to order up unnecessary diagnostics. Also, they work on a crisis, often rapid-fire basis, so they would presumably admit and refer cases more as neutral or even purely diagnostic cases rather than as potential clients.

Some studies show that the poor, both minority and white, tend to go to emergency rooms for heroic aid even for severe conditions like cancer. They tend not to go early in the course of a disease to specialists and private physicians; they have no insurance and these practitioners are more expensive and tend to take only richer patients with private insurance.

So since the two cases were medically similar, the admission settings were the same and presumably relatively neutral, and neither patient had the prospect of private insurance coverage, the only difference to explain the differential treatment appears to be race—the white person got treatment and the black person was told there was no hope.

Even though these are only two cases, the similarities *suggest* there may be institutionalized racism—that poor, uncovered minorities get less right to choose in right-to-death cases. However, the situation may not be this simple, for there are other unknown factors (and maybe unstudiable factors, given the codes of silence). Furthermore, the ethical implications are not so moralistically clear, as we shall see.

For instance, although the emergency room setting was the same, with similar decision-related incentives, the major difference was in the advice from the two different on-call physicians who the physicians were referred to by the emergency room physicians. The advice may have been different for several reasons. Perhaps different physicians have different perceptions and diagnostic talents, or perhaps the physicians had different attitudes about race and poor people. Also, the advice may have been different because one patient or family showed or signaled stronger attitudes about fighting cancer. Patient attitude has a big influence on physician recommendations. All the physicians we interviewed said that most doctors take their cues *primarily* from the attitudes of patients themselves or family members on whether to order up more procedures. Cancer physicians have learned that positive attitudes do enhance the patient's prospects for survival. Also, it is ethically (and perhaps legally) difficult for doctors to ignore such patient attitudes and expressed wishes for aid. In these two cases it is not known whether different physicians, patient attitudes, or minor differences in the stage of the disease might explain the difference in treatments.

We might be able to find out if race discrimination makes a difference in near-death choices through long-term studies, controlling for race, physicians, and patient–family attitudes. But such studies are scarce. These two cases only suggest, however, that race distinctions may come into play in getting different advice and treatment in nearly futile death-choice situations.

But we must also consider other ethical issues here. It may be true that the poor and uncovered, especially if they are minorities, tend to get less advice about options. But even if it is true, the medically and socially relevant issues about near-futile death choices for *everyone* (poor, rich, white, minority) are still not clear-cut.

For instance, are the rich, insured, and white better off or more dignified because they may find themselves plugged into machines or exposed to intrusive and perhaps extremely painful treatments such as chemotherapy, only because options are requested and can be paid for? Do painful and expensive treatments mean a better-quality life? Do the rich and covered really get to "choose" in such situations? Recall that the parents of the infant in case 1 felt they were placed in a tornado of "choices" once they had turned themselves over to the doctors. Is this really "being given choices"?

Are so-called informed, aggressive rich people who desire such treatments for themselves and for family members really more informed or smarter than poor, so-called uneducated people? Or do the latter group face death more realistically, with less denial and immeasurably less expense and possibly less pain? Who really is more enlightened?

And which advice is "discrimination" and which is "exploitation"? Is it discrimination that sends the poor home to face death and that does not bankrupt the families? Or is it exploitation that gives the rich (often false) hope, charges them hundreds of thousands of dollars, and passes the expense on to both the families and outside consumers through higher medical costs and insurance premiums?

We don't really know the degree to which the poor and minorities may be denied life-saving treatments that could extend life in near-death cases. And this is probably not the important issue. Rather, the poor and minorities are probably discriminated against more by the lack of spending on public health and the lack of universal coverage which might move them into care earlier and reduce chronic and deteriorative deaths. In this sense, they are not so much discriminated against in near-death cases as they are discriminated against by public policies that make their death rates much higher than those of the white, rich, and insured populations.

POLICY SOLUTIONS FOR EUTHANASIA AND ABORTION DILEMMAS

Four public policy choices seem to offer benefits in resolving the sticky issues and perhaps reducing the excessive costs of medical death choices. First, we could spend more in the federal system on preventive health and anti-substance abuse education programs (which already receive some emphasis).

Second, we could experiment more with establishing patient rights ethics and arbitration committees in hospitals and nursing homes or nonprofit community agencies—composed of doctors, social workers, and other counselors— which could help patients and families deal with these issues. Third, states could establish family ethics courts with counseling services—similar to divorce or youth services courts—to deal with euthanasia and perhaps abortion-related issues for families. The fourth possibility is that eventually we may be forced into the rationing of care and spending, especially for the self-abusive but also for the hopelessly ill elderly (see the Oregon rationing of Medicare services and spending, Chapter 9).

≋≋ CHAPTER **11**

How to Fit the Puzzle Pieces Together

RETHINKING FEASIBLE SOLUTIONS

Several basic premises have guided the writing of this book. The first is that the issues that public policy is called upon to resolve are vexing and have no easy solutions. Perhaps this is one of the reasons for the current widespread cynicism about government in the United States. People expect governments to resolve the most difficult issues, including problems the private sector flees from, or even contributes to (see Goodsell 1983). Taking Baby Catherine as our example (Chapter 1), if the health care debate has taught us anything, it has demonstrated that the issue of how to provide health care for all Americans, or even the most vulnerable ones, is not easy to resolve.

A second assumption of this book is that there *are* solutions. A third is that the policy system is complex, but describable. It only seems to be a jumble of puzzle pieces that do not fit together. This perception also fuels the cynicism characteristic of this time and perpetuates the powerful myth of government failure.

One reason issues seem intractable and the policy system seems a puzzle is found in the ways we have looked at policy. Traditional policy analysis has taken small pieces of the governmental systems and analyzed them in depth. While that approach has yielded much that is helpful, few attempts have been made to put all these studies together into an overall picture of the policy system. Parts of the system, such as the policies of Congress, the Courts, or the states can be seen clearly as separate pieces, viewed close up, but the pieces do not fit together to form a clear "big picture."

We have taken a holistic approach to the policy system—its history, problems, and solutions. We have tried to unravel the policy system and to identify feasible solutions to problems. We now seek to explain the coherence of the policy system, to sum up its record of solutions and trends, and to look for avenues of effective democratic options. The puzzle pieces can be fit together.

In order to fit the pieces into the policy puzzle, we need to address several important questions in this chapter. First, where is the American policy system at the beginning of the twenty-first century? To answer this, we will look at the viability of the major components of the American policy system. Second, how did we get to where we are? What factors and trends explain the condition of the American policy system at this turn of the century? Third and most important, how can solutions—from abroad, from new and local forms of volunteerism, and from the record of state and local governments in the United States—feed the effort to find solutions to America's critical problems? We believe one of the major reasons for social disinformation and the myopia of policy analysis is a provincialism that concentrates our attention on the national political scene, without focusing on what is being practiced by ordinary reformers, state and local governments, and other countries. Policy analysts in general and the media in particular have focused too much on the national scene. State and local reformers and governments are often the "physicians" and the "laboratories of democracy" and much can be learned from their experience. The search for answers to these three questions will also lead us to several ways to renew and extend the democratic character and control of the policy system.

THE STATE OF THE SYSTEM AT THE BEGINNING OF THE TWENTY-FIRST CENTURY

The theme of Chapter 2 was that Americans live too much in the present moment and are not informed of the successes and failures of the policy system in the past. Even a superficial review of policy history makes clear an important point: Change, often significant, occurs in the policy system. Changes in recent years have resulted in a new map of policy responsibility in the federal system (see Chapter 2), a map on which considerable responsibility has shifted to the state level. This raises an important question: What is the condition of the major components of the policy system? Can these components fulfill the responsibilities that the new map has placed on them? A review of the policy record indicates that the *national* government is in a period of relative policy failure while the state and local governments are in a period of relative policy success.

THE NATIONAL GOVERNMENT: POLICY GRIDLOCK AND RELATIVE FAILURE

Before we review the evidence to demonstrate that the national government is in a period of relative policy failure, we need to emphasize the word *relative*. As we suggested in the chapter on education policy, the myth of total failure is at best exaggerated. More likely, the myth that governments are total failures is a political tool used by many individuals and groups as a strategy to gain power. "Running against Washington" has been an effective campaign strategy at least since the mid-1970s. Also, the Washington-focused media have a tendency to magnify the myth of total failure. Repetition of the myth, as John Schwarz has shown, has turned the false image of government failure into an accepted doctrine (Schwarz 1988). The myth of government failure may also be somewhat of a self-fulfilling prophesy, one to which the national government is especially vulnerable. In essence, as people began to believe the myth of failure, the government became less able to accomplish its responsibilities. A brief review of the record will help to explain the relative failure of the national government in the present era.

NATIONAL ENVIRONMENTAL POLICY

The government's record in environmental policy is one of modest success in some areas, serious failures in some, and irresponsible neglect in others. The enactment of policy is an area of modest success, if success is measured by the number of bills and regulations that have been passed. The 1970s was marked by a parabolic increase in environmental legislation passed by the Congress. However, that modest success is dimmed by a number of realities, the most important of which is the nature of that legislation. A careful examination reveals that in many instances Congress was acting in response to strong pressures from environmentally conscious groups without a serious intent to establish policy that could be implemented (Wells 1986). In some instances legislative draftsmanship was so poor (such as the Superfund) that it would have been difficult even for well-meaning administrators to implement it. In others, Congress took the high road, apparently to ward off political pressures, and left implementation to the states (examples are the Clean Air Act, the Clean Water Act, and the Resource Conservation and Recovery Act, which established policy for chemical hazardous waste). The states were left to muddle through on the basis of an institutional strategy ill defined by the Congress, and they were given more specific direction only through regulations established over time by the EPA. Often the EPA was slow in developing the regulations necessary for implementation, and it sometimes neglected to develop regulations altogether. From a national perspective, then, environmental policy is seen as a flurry of bills and laws, most of which either were poorly drafted or passed the difficult work of implementing on to the states. It is hard to avoid the conclusion that in many cases environmental policy at the national level was a massive exercise in ducking the responsibility to act.

The national government did retain responsibility for environmental programs in some areas. Here the myth of failure is not exaggerated. The government's failure to substantially carry out the Superfund legislation is legendary in the 1980s for its ineptness, political cronyism, and outright scandal. Few programs in the nation's history stand as such bleak examples of the conversion of a public interest into private gain. During the 1980s only 14 of the 1,100 sites on the National Priority List were cleaned up, while billions of dollars committed to the effort were diverted to the coffers of private contractors.

The main program for which the national government retained exclusive responsibility is high-level nuclear waste. In spite of the enormity of the nuclear waste problem, the government has been unable to find and establish a depository site. Two decades of effort have finally resulted in the selection of a site—Yucca Flats, Nevada. Ironically, one of the most important factors in this selection was the fact that the national government owns approximately 90 percent of the land in the county in which the site is located. Nuclear waste continues to accumulate in various commercial sites around the country and in Hanford (Washington) and the Savannah River site in South Carolina, the repositories for military waste. The nation's nuclear waste program resembles more closely a junkyard dumping system than a formal plan based on intelligent use of the best available technology.

A brighter picture exists in the control of air pollution and water pollution, where national government efforts have achieved modest successes. Since these two programs are based in the partial preemption strategy, whereby Congress establishes general policy to be implemented by the states, it is difficult to sort out the relative contributions of the nation versus the states. It has often been alleged that joint responsibility in environmental matters allows administrators at both levels to pass off responsibility for program failures to each other. But the opposite is also true: It is difficult to determine which level should be given the credit for program success. However, the national government has been vigorous in reducing the levels of pollution from municipal waste water discharge. Certainly, the national government has been willing to put its money where its policy was, providing localities with generous grants for the construction of waste water treatment plants.

Also, the American record in reducing oxygen-demanding wastes resulting from municipal pollution sources compares very favorably with the record of other industrialized countries. The Organization for Economic Cooperation and Development, a multinational body established by treaty in 1960, which monitors the quality of the environment in member countries, found that surface water quality in the United States has improved as much as or more than in other member nations (primarily European) (OECD 1991, p. 60). The most important reason for the improvement is the construction of municipal waste water treatment facilities, largely with money provided by the national government. However, this modest success is tainted somewhat by the lack of progress in reducing nonpoint source pollution (such as feed lot runoff), hot spots in the nation's surface waters, and the pollution of groundwater (such as from septic tanks).

Most indicators suggest also that the nation's air quality is improving modestly (World Resources Institute 1993, p. 602). In regard to the role of the national government, it is important to note that much of the improvement was measured at the end of the 1980s following a period of national gridlock on clean air. That gridlock suggests that much if not most of the air quality improvement can be credited to the state and local governments. The Clean Air Act Amendment of 1991, however, indicates that the national legislative gridlock has been broken. It has the potential of being one of the most significant pieces of environmental legislation passed by the U.S. Congress.

The overall environmental record of the national government is best expressed by analysts from other countries. A comprehensive evaluation of the global environment was made by the World Resources Institute in cooperation with the U.N. Environment Programme and the U.N. Development Programme. In the somewhat constrained language of diplomacy, the report summarized the American record this way:

> The United States could markedly improve its efficiency in using energy and other natural resources and, at the same time, reduce local and regional pollution, avoid waste, and lower its contribution to the threat of global warming ... these steps need not carry heavy economic penalties and could indeed improve the country's economic competitiveness. (World Resources Institute 1992, p. 27)

That the United States has not taken the steps to increase efficiency in the use of energy and natural resources and reduce pollution, particularly when some of those steps would increase the nation's competitive posture in the global economy, is the best measure of the relative failure of the national government to establish and implement environmental policy.

NATIONAL EDUCATION POLICY

Evaluating the national government's role in education is made difficult by the tradition of local control of the public school system. Washington policy actors often point to this fact and argue that there is little the national government can do about elementary and secondary education problems. This posturing overlooks a very important point: Much of the ballyhoo over education reform during the last several decades has originated in Washington. Washington centered education policy has a long record of relative failure. The current issue of education choice is a good example.

As the experience in other countries demonstrates, the important issues of educational choice are in curriculum content—what program of study the student will pursue, and who will define the curriculum to be pursued. But Washington-focused politics has defined "education choice" almost exclusively as being about vouchers. Vouchers, if enacted into law, would give parents "coupons" to partially pay for any schools they choose, including private schools. Supporters of this voucher system emphasize that it would allow children to avoid the "problems of public schools"—usually characterized as safety and ineffective teachers. But this choice would also allow parents to give their children a narrow education, avoiding the social integration that only public schools are legally required to pursue. Thus parents could also be choosing to have their children avoid multi-ethnic histories, contact with groups other than their own, racial integration and sensitivity, and scientific and cultural training not colored by sectarian religious interpretations. In short, vouchers may increase the choices of mobility and curriculum, but it also encourages social divisiveness, sectarian training, or even social prejudices.

More important, the voucher issue diverts attention away from the more critical choice issues, namely, what the student should study and who should decide what the student studies. These issues have been condensed, avoided, and weakened in Washington to the narrow voucher issues of "can we switch schools" and "who will pay." The narrow debate about vouchers certainly shows how a broad public interest issue (what do our schools and students need) can be narrowly defined as being about the potential of private gain for small numbers of people in American society. The fact that Washington policy officials trumpet and simplify education issues—some of which seem to be motivated by private gain—while at the same time proclaiming that they are powerless to do anything about education is an indication of the relative failure of the national government in education policy.

The mid-1990s also saw a resurgence of the effort to add an amendment to the Constitution to permit prayer in the public schools. Following the Republican party's 1994 success in gaining a slim control of both houses of Congress, the new speaker of the House of Representatives, Newt Gingrich, placed the goal of a school prayer amendment high on his policy agenda. Some commentators suggested that he gave it higher priority than the "Contract" he and other Republicans had unilaterally made with the American people.

The school prayer amendment issue is a clear example of the cultural reaction syndrome in public problems. Fundamentalist Protestants were not only reacting in the 1980s against the 1963 Supreme Court case (*Engle* v. *Vitale*) that barred official school prayer as a violation of the First Amendment's ban on state-sponsored religion. In a deeper way they were also reacting against the growing religious and social diversity of America and the preferences of different groups. The more extreme fundamentalists see this diversity as an "us versus them" conflict, with "them" having led America into a "dire decline of civilization and morals" (These words taken from a 700 Club television broadcast, January 16, 1995, and from a paid newspaper ad in *USA Today*, January 18, 1995). The more extreme fundamentalists are seeking through the school prayer amendment to impose their religious priorities through the compulsory mechanism of the public schools. Even if the merits of the case for or against a school prayer amendment were laid aside, the strong push to place the issue on the policy agenda suggests the relative failure of the national policy system to resolve critical issues. After two hundred years of experience with the First Amendment, the system has been unable to resolve this school prayer issue. Like the general issue of school reform, prayer in the public schools seems to recycle through our politics again and again.

NATIONAL ECONOMIC POLICY

Economic policy is perhaps the best arena to assess the performance of national policy, reflecting as it does a combination of modest successes and abject failures. In at least one important respect the policy system took a step backward after having taken two steps forward. As John Schwarz has demonstrated, America's hidden success from 1960 through the mid-1970s was a reduction in the number of poor. The percentage of Americans in poverty declined from 16 percent in 1960 to about 8 percent in 1976 (Schwarz 1988:24). While some commentators claimed that this decline in poverty was traceable to the general economic growth in the period, Schwarz presents a convincing and statistically valid argument that anti-poverty public assistance programs were the more significant factors. In the 1980s the decline bottomed out and there began an increase in the number and percentages of poor.

Coinciding with an increase in the number of poor was an erosion of the economic well-being of the middle class. A comparative review of the United States, Canada, and several European countries in the 1970s and 1980s expressed the economic trends this way:

> The United States experienced steadier growth and lower unemployment than most European countries in the 1980s, yet the percentage of low-income households was nearly double that of the continental European countries by mid-decade." (World Resources Institute 1993, p. 19)

When analyzed over the period 1970–1990, the inflation-adjusted mean income of the bottom one-fifth of U.S. families declined from $10,176 in 1970 to $9,833 in 1990. The mean income of the top 5 percent rose from $116,555 in 1970 to $148,124 in 1990 (Census Bureau 1991, p. 2202). Since the late 1970s the United States has seen the rich become richer, while the middle class has lost ground measured by relative shares of income or wealth, and the poor have lost ground measured by median family income or percentage shares of wealth. (See Figure 3.2 on page 51 in Chapter 3).

Meanwhile national budget policy is in a shambles. For nearly two decades since 1980 political candidates have been running on balanced budget and debt reduction platforms. To say that neither has happened is probably to belabor the obvious. From 1980 to 1990 the cumulative historical total national debt rose from approximately $800 billion to approximately $4 trillion. The annual national debt quadrupled in less than a decade also ($67 billion to $250 billion). During the Reagan presidency more dollars were added to the national debt than were added in all the presidencies from George Washington through Jimmy Carter. The budget was not balanced either. In 1980 the budget deficit, which is the difference between what the national government received in revenue and what it spends, was approximately $66 billion. By the end of the decade annual budget deficits in excess of $200 billion were the norm. One of the great ironies of the American political system is the fact that as the political rhetoric of fiscal responsibility intensified, the budget deficit and consequently the national debt increased also.

The national policy system has been a relative failure in other areas of economic policy also. First, in spite of the fact that Ronald Reagan defined his economic policy in industrial policy language, the national government has been unable to develop a coherent and effective industrial policy. American economic policy relies on the triple pillars of monetary, fiscal, and regulatory policy, a somewhat truncated combination that seems lacking in a global economy. For instance, in contrast to the United States, most industrial nations' governments are strong users of business–government cooperation in industrial policy. Governments may become big investors in target and growth segments of their private economies or may use other means of government–business cooperation to stimulate exports. They also selectively protect domestic industries from excessive foreign penetration into home markets while prodding those industries to modernize and stay at home rather than seeking cheaper labor elsewhere (see Reich 1987). The United States relies little on such methods.

Second, the national policy system is a relative failure in coordinating economic development policy with environmental policy. Multinational analysts generally conclude that the United States could achieve a much cleaner environment at the same time that it improves the efficiency of its economic system. In other words, wastes that pollute the environment are the result of inefficiencies in the economic process. Herein lies another paradox of the American policy system. While on the one hand we pride ourselves on the efficiency of the economy and the commitment to improving efficiency, on the other hand we refuse to address one of the more important areas of inefficiency—wastes that pollute the environment.

A third region where the national government has generally failed in economic policy is in finding a balance between policies that can at the same time increase free trade; stimulate domestic corporate and big business capital investment, research, and development; and resolve labor policy needs. Some of the bleaker areas of failure can be quickly summarized. In labor policy the government has not been successful in arresting the slow net decline since the 1970s in family income and wages and especially for the middle classes and poor. We also have not been able to slow the shift to temporary and part-time labor, the decrease of leisure time, the erosion of benefit packages, and especially the rise of health care costs. In the industrial and business sectors the national government generally failed over the past twenty years to alleviate the problems of excessive mergers, downsizing (laying off large portions of middle management as well as wage laborers), excessively high corporate debt, and especially the balance of foreign trade and the erosion and migration of the industrial base to foreign countries.

The picture brightens with the modest progress that has been achieved from Bush through Clinton in international economic trade policies. The system has moved from an almost exclusive reliance before Bush on tariffs, currency and foreign investments as the instruments of international economic policy, to the current broader set of policy instruments. The most important of those newer instruments is participation in free trade associations such as GATT and NAFTA. The 1994 Miami conference of the heads of states in North and South America was an important step toward the largest free trade zone in the world. Aside from free trade zones, however, the United States has not yet developed a comprehensive international economic policy.

THE SPREAD OF SOLUTIONS ACROSS LEVELS OF THE FEDERAL SYSTEM

Policies can spread from one level to another in the federal system and become either regional or national in scope. (There is a notable but still small body of studies of policy diffusion across intergovernmental lines. See Wells and Hamilton 1990, Chapter 10; Peterson and Rom 1990; Schneider and Jacoby 1993). The relative failure to act by one level of the federal system can stimulate reforms to start from another level and then spread to all levels. For example, economic development policy drifted to the states in the 1980s because the national government failed to act. Similarly, states are reforming the health care system in the 1990s because the national government has failed to act.

Policies can also diffuse from local to local levels, or even from region to region. Private persons or professionals acting outside existing laws can cause change to spread around the federal system despite the absence of laws or court decisions. In this case, practices developed in private settings eventually force policymakers to catch up by enacting laws that codify these existing solutions. An example is the growing practice of euthanasia in the United States, which has been more widespread than law and courts permit but which law and courts are now acknowledging.

Policies can also spread inside the federal system as a result of higher- or lower-level officials' actions (not failure to act) that stimulate copycat policies and legal tests of the constitutionality of such policies. Both copycatting and court suits can set off waves of new practices in still other levels. An example of this pattern has been the change in abortion practices, led mainly by decisions in the courts and legislatures. Thus abortion practices have not followed the same course of intergovernmental policy change as euthanasia practices, yet both changes occurred through spreading among the levels of the federal system.

We show next how changes in abortion and euthanasia practices are different examples of *privately* versus *officially* stimulated patterns, respectively, that spread around the federal system but not because some government failed to act. Later we will show how health care reform started as a part of state and local policies because the feds did fail to act.

ABORTION AND EUTHANASIA SOLUTIONS

Private individuals or medical professionals acting independently at the state and local levels have produced the realities of abortion and euthanasia practices in the United States, but in two very different ways. First, while abortion is practiced less and while more parties are involved in the decision, euthanasia has become more common. Second, after the gate of federal policy opened and the courts defined abortion as an act in which several parties could have a voice, practices and policies changed at state and local levels. The opposite direction was taken with euthanasia. After the practice of euthanasia became common enough among doctors to become an issue of medical ethics commissions, hospital administrators, and then state lawmakers and courts, and then officials codified the practice into law and set policy guidelines to reflect the most careful practices. In the former case, law and regulation were guiding reality; in the latter case they were catching up to it.

Across the land legal abortion is disappearing, except in urban areas. Abortions may be temporarily on the rise in big cities—among rich and poor alike—due to the disappearance of abortion in rural areas and in anticipation of restrictions by Congress after the Republican majority called for restrictions in 1995. But the practices of limiting abortion or requiring joint decisions, as well as the controversy surrounding abortion and the resulting risks for doctors who perform abortions, has led many doctors to avoid the procedure, especially in rural areas and in the less populated, less urbanized states, particularly in the Midwest, the West, and the South. Doctors don't consider the financial and safety risks worth taking, and are restricted by community pressures—which may take the form of protests, harassment, and/or violence—in many locations. As a result, abortion is quickly becoming a big city or "commuter shopping" phenomenon, available mainly to wealthier women. It may not be widely recognized that in the less urbanized states in the South, the Border states, and the West, such as Alabama, Kentucky, and Nebraska, medical abortions are now unavailable, except in the biggest cities.

States are increasingly taking legal steps to modify the abortion decision or extend it to encompass new factors and additional parties. Many states are moving toward informed consent laws, especially for minors. States still require doctors to determine if fetuses are viable and, if so, to protect them, provided the woman's health is not threatened and the state has defined fetal life as a right to be protected. The legal rights to abortions are not pursued outside of big cities, since doctors or hospitals in these less populated areas refuse the procedure. Some states require abortions to be performed by licensed doctors, or at least in licensed settings, a further disincentive. And a few states, such as Louisiana and Utah, have actually criminalized the practice.

Euthanasia, however, is becoming more widespread. It is more institutionalized in the sense that, unlike abortion, its practice relies more on the joint decisions of doctors and family, as informed by ethics committees in the care settings.

Today the Supreme Court and the states generally permit written and oral expressions of a patient's wishes, and even permit surrogates to act to terminate life for patients who cannot express wishes. If such permissions or surrogates are in place, all treatment can be withheld, including food and water for terminal and permanently vegetative patients. Such "legal suicide" and physician-assisted mercy killings for vegetative conditions are increasingly common. The federal courts have ruled that a person has a constitutional right of privacy to have physician-assisted suicide, something doctors were practicing anyway and that will now likely be accelerated.

STATE AND LOCAL GOVERNMENTS: POLICY MOMENTUM AND RELATIVE SUCCESS

State and local governments are important policy units in the American federal system. It is difficult to explain why state and local governments get so little attention from the Washington-focused media. Jeffrey Henig's idea that the activities of state and local governments are by and large mundane helps explain the neglect (Henig 1985, p. 4). State and local governments deliver services that seem commonplace. There is not much glamour in putting a policeman on patrol.

But, as Henig emphasizes, being mundane does not mean being unimportant. The numerous policies adopted and implemented by state and local governments touch the lives of Americans most directly and personally. (See Table 2.3 on page 39 in Chapter 2).

State and local governments today are in a cycle of policy momentum, that is, policy activity and innovation have increased through volunteerism and official government actions. Several factors have contributed to this policy momentum. While policy gridlock characterizes the national government, there is more life below.

State and local governments are also in a period of relative policy success. Of course, they are not successful in everything they do. And it is still easy to find examples of buffoonery and scandal at the state and local levels (Henry 1987, p. 1). The experience within and between the states varies widely. In the environmental area the intergovernmental record of states and regions is spotty, and the same uneven results are true for most policies (see Chapter 4), both interstate and within states. There are programs that states perform well, and programs that states perform poorly. For example, there are big in-state differences in elementary schools, universities, law enforcement, child abuse prevention, child support collection, nursing homes, and vocational job train-ing. The shortage of careful comparative studies makes it hard to compare state and local policy performance.

One of the major points of emphasis in this book is that the American pol-icy system would be well served by increased attention to state and local pol-icy results. When the American policy record is viewed from the bottom up rather than from the Washington-centered bias, what is most impressive is the considerable success of state and local reformers and governments. We will now illustrate this view by a summary of state and local performance in the four remaining policy areas discussed in the policy chapters.

STATE AND LOCAL ENVIRONMENTAL POLICY

Environmental policy has seen at least the beginnings of comparative state studies (Kamlet 1979; Wells 1982; Lester, Franke, Bowman, and Kraemer 1983; Herzik 1992). A consistent finding has been the increased importance of envi-ronmental action by the states. In hazardous waste policy Herzik found that states are diverging from the federal model in several ways (Herzik 1992, p. 1476). A number of states have even developed a "go it our own way" posture. An extreme example of this attitude is found in Indiana, where state officials have threatened to withdraw completely from the federally established pro-grams on solid waste disposal and water quality protection and substitute their own programs (Arrandale 1993, p. 70). But Arrandale also reports that at least half the states have threatened to return to the national government the power to implement the Safe Drinking Water Act, citing this as an indication of a dysfunctional federal–state relationship. The situation is "dysfunctional" only if it is viewed from a national perspective by those who favor more strict national regulation. The partial preemption strategy of setting national stan-dards and certifying state programs is not working effectively when viewed with centralist ideas from "above." But when the situation is viewed from the bottom up (a dualist or intergovernmental view), there is more optimism about room for real state vitality even to the point where some states are willing to take significant risks and independently implement programs. States are responding to national government policies with actions they prefer.

These developments mean that policy action has shifted to the states, which are now the focal points for environmental policy. The consequences of this shift for the United States are unclear. Some observers are pessimistic. Arrandale concludes that "it's also clear that turning programs back to EPA offers no long-term hope for dealing with pollution problems" (1993, p. 70). But others think it is equally clear that continuing the present policy of partial preemption with its complex interlevel relationships offers little long-term hope for dealing with environmental problems (Wells 1996). Yet policy activism at the state level is the basis for some optimism: "state governments have long histories of policy innovation, often working incrementally and in rough concert to overcome perceived complexity" (Herzik 1992, p. 147).

There are several areas where the action of state and local governments tackle real environmental problems. One is the states' waste reduction strategy of recycling. While the national government pursues a hazard reduction strategy that virtually ignores the volumes of waste produced, states (and locals) have enacted hundreds of waste reduction policies in recent years. These programs range from encouraging voluntary participation in recycling to mandating recycling for local governments (Florida, North Carolina, Oregon, and Washington) to mandating citizen participation in recycling programs (Connecticut, New Jersey, New York, Pennsylvania, and Rhode Island). These are measures that the national government would do well to copy.

Other actions that state and local governments are taking are the comprehensive plans to ensure environmental quality. The Clean Air Plan of the South Coast Air Quality Management District, developed to serve the needs of the Los Angeles metropolitan area, is a good example of this type of comprehensive planning. The plan calls for 120 initiatives to be implemented in three stages. The first stage, to begin in 1994 and to be implemented over five years, relies on existing technology that is both cost effective and efficient. Strategies include flexible work hours to reduce freeway congestion, encouraging the use of mass transit through parking lot fees, and more effective controls on point sources of pollution such as outdoor barbecues, dry cleaning establishments, restaurants, and bakeries. The second phase, to be implemented by the year 2000, requires significant technological advances. This phase involves a state mandate for clean fuel vehicles. In the Los Angeles plan both buses and fleet vehicles (car pools, etc.) would be required to convert from gas or diesel to methanol, propane, butane, electricity, or compressed natural gas. Small engine equipment, such as lawn mowers, would also be required to convert to clean fuels or adopt features that would reduce emissions. The third stage, to be implemented by 2007, requires major technological breakthroughs.

Some of the advances incorporated in this plan are within the range of the expected. For example, the use of photovoltaic cells as a source of electric energy certainly is a probability by the year 2007. Others, such as superconducting magnets to power mass transit system vehicles, may require longer development periods. What is significant about stages 2 and 3 is that they encourage if not mandate technological development. They are innovative examples of technology-forcing strategies—useful demonstrations for other government policymakers.

STATE AND LOCAL EDUCATION POLICY

Acquiring a balanced view of the effectiveness of state and local policy actions in education is difficult because of the pervasive myth of failure (see Chapter

8). This myth of educational failure is at best exaggerated, and at worst it is a strategy cynically used in the never-ending process of gaining political power. There are millions of Americans who can read, but publicizing them does not win votes. The truth is that adequate standards for evaluating educational achievement have not been developed. Without a methodology to measure achievement, it is not possible, except by crude and inadequate measures such as per pupil expenditure or SAT scores, to determine how well state and local governments are doing with regard to educational achievement.

However, several important things need to be said about state and local educational policy activity. First, there is certainly a lot of it. There is a tornado of education reform activity in both states and localities. The range of innovations and modifications of existing practice is almost endless. Attempts to track policy activity, such as represented by the Digest of Educational Statistics, falls short. If the level of activity is taken as an indicator of reform success, then state and local policy systems are most assuredly successful in education policy.

The recent activity has resulted in profound changes in the American educational system. The model for public school organization until the 1950s was the neighborhood school. Today the model is the comprehensive school virtually unrelated to an identifiable neighborhood. The struggle to get technical schools accepted as a part of the educational system started with Eisenhower and centered in the Nixon presidency, and they are now the norm in all parts of the nation. Curriculum and pedagogical changes also have been numerous in the nation's schools in the last three decades. In spite of the public perception that the "educational establishment" is an unwieldy behemoth, extensive and significant change has in fact occurred. The problem is that we cannot determine whether or not those changes have brought about higher levels of educational achievement.

Yet there are numerous success stories in education. While no adequate inventory is kept of these, successes are found in inner-city schools, in education–business partnerships of various kinds, in literacy programs, in computer applications in instruction, and in many other areas. Focusing on specific cases of success would bring a fresh breeze of reality against the exaggerated and self-defeating myth of government failure.

All of this reinforces a primary point about public policy. The concepts, the assumptions, and the values that guide how one looks at any phenomenon determines at least in part what one concludes and recommends. A critical need in education policy is to develop an adequate and functional perspective that lays to rest the myth of failure, at least until standards and methodologies have been developed that demonstrate the degree to which the system has failed. American education has not clearly failed. Rather, when looked at from a policy perspective that recognizes the incredible diversity of American cultures, myths, regionalism, and policy history, American education adjusts to those diverse pressures. Since at least the early 1980s the American elementary and secondary educational systems have experienced a period of relative renewal and success.

STATE AND LOCAL ECONOMIC POLICY

Economic policy is another area of almost endless activity at the state and local levels. States are vigorously pursuing economic development policies while the national government is turning away from new macromanagement economic policies. We described the major state economic policies in Chapter 7. The question here is whether those policies have been successful.

It is important to recognize the basic change that occurred in state and local economic policies beginning in the 1980s. Prior to that time, state and local policies were based largely in supply-side strategies (Eisinger 1988). Supply-side strategies are designed to lure mobile capital to a particular area and include such devices as tax breaks, tax incentives, enterprise zones, site development, and the like. In the 1980s both a quantitative and qualitative shift occurred in state policy. First, state and local governments became more active in economic policy (Fosler 1988; Eisinger 1988; Schneider 1989). Also, states began to pursue different kinds of policies, policies that Eisinger labeled demand-side strategies. Demand-side strategies attempt to cultivate new markets and industries and stimulate capital formation, through such policies as venture capital programs, assistance to small business, innovation centers, and centers for the diffusion of high technology.

Studies of the two general strategies of economic development suggest that supply-side strategies do not work and demand-side strategies do. Case studies of supply side strategies (such as lower taxes) in seven states concluded that such policies at best had only a marginal effect on economic growth (Fosler 1988). Eisinger agrees, finding that "location incentives are ineffective as devices for the generation of new jobs and investment ..." and that overall "supply-side initiatives are at best seen principally as the exercise of symbolic politics in the effort to fashion a hospitable business climate" (1988, p. 337). On the other hand, careful studies have found that demand-side strategies have been effective in creating new jobs and stimulating economic growth (Eisinger 1988; Brace and Mucciaroni 1990). Brace and Mucciaroni conclude:

> The results reported here make clear that states have come to play a much larger role in managing their economies. States are acting more and ... matter economically when ... not overwhelmed by enormous external forces.... Ironically, as economic intervention has fallen from favor at the national level, there is increasing evidence of its efficacy at the state level. (1990, p. 166)

The entrepreneurial state government, apparently, is experiencing success.

STATES TAKING THE DRIVER'S SEAT IN HEALTH CARE REFORM

The states have taken over the leadership in the reform of health care systems, particularly following the failure of the national government to pass a health care act in 1994. Our review showed that the two most notable state reforms are probably those of Hawaii and Washington, with the Florida "pay-or-play" reforms and several other states' purchasing cooperatives as the models of the developing wave of state reforms.

Since the mid-1980s states have slowly moved toward laws that regulate some of the troublesome features of medical monopolism, attempting to restore market mechanisms to insurance and health markets. These laws give public notice of competitive fees, establish quality ratings for services, limit medical malpractice suits, variously regulate hospital revenues or fees, and expand public and preventive health. This older and probably weaker wave of reform continues, but the main method of state reform now is to use managed care, mainly through bids to HMOs or preferred provider organizations, or to create state insurance pools. Most states are experimenting with limited population insurance and care guarantees, by which care is provided by these new pooled or bidded providers or insurance plans.

The strongest move by states is the establishment of health insurance purchasing cooperatives (HIPCs), which guarantee a standardized set of benefits to compete with private insurance and private medical professionals. At first the HIPCs are offered to selected groups and later they are opened up to competitive purchase by the general population, becoming statewide reforms. Oregon, California, Minnesota, and Kentucky are among the states that have established such HIPCs. Some states add to this a requirement of "pay or play," which prods employers to provide (and usually split the costs for) insurance. Employers must provide split-cost insurance for workers by a deadline (play) or they must then be taken into the new state-created pool and pay for one of its plans (pay). All these state-created ideas, along with consumer reforms, are probably the wave of the future in health care.

WHY THE SHIFT FROM THE NATIONAL LEVEL: GRIDLOCK VERSUS ACTIVISM

The above summary of the state of the American policy system near the start of the twenty-first century suggests that an important shift has happened in the dynamics of American federalism. The 1960s and 1970s were characterized by policy activism at the national level. State and local governments were derided, and some observers even predicted that states would become field districts of the national government (for a review and a careful debunking of such myths see Anton 1982). Such observations failed to appreciate the dynamic character of the American federal system. The system has arrived at a phase that is characterized by policy gridlock and relative failure at the national level, and policy momentum and relative success at the subnational level. How did the American policy system get to where it is?

The relative failure is explainable in large part by the concept of gridlock. However, in both the popular press and policy analysis, gridlock is often seen as a partisan phenomenon or a standoff between the President and Congress. In this picture Congress is unable to function effectively because of conflict along party lines or with the President. It is important to understand, though, that the national political system actually manifests a much larger gridlock. The national government achieves policy successes in spite of the forces of gridlock in politics. To the extent that there is gridlock, it occurs substantially as a result of severe external political conflicts that get mirrored in government.

National political gridlock manifests itself across the entire decision-making process. Because of gridlock in the issue formation stage, there is no consensus about national health care amid the flood of opposing interest groups, and vouchers and school prayer, rather than curriculum choice, are the center of educational issues. Because of gridlock at the policy enactment stage as institutions struggle to pass laws or as they conflict with one another, national environmental laws and budget resolutions often are poorly drawn or largely symbolic in nature. Because of gridlock at the implementation stage where interest groups struggle against regulatory agencies attempting to follow laws, much of the Great Society legislation and civil rights enforcement has never been completely put into effect. And because of gridlock at the social reaction or feedback stage, the national system has been recycling over and over again for two hundred years the issues of prayer in the public schools, and no clear national resolution of abortion rights exists. So if gridlock is understood only as a result of partisan politics or the inability of the President and Congress to get along, then the real social roots of the national policy system's problems go unnoticed. Gridlock is a pervasive phenomenon of "two steps forward, one step backward" across time and all phases of the national political system. Gridlock, conflict, and inaction are probably *less* severe inside courts and bureaucracies, which are a little more independent of public conflicts and forces.

THE FACTORS PRODUCING NATIONAL POLICY GRIDLOCK

There are a number of factors that contribute to the pervasive national gridlock. We examine the four that are most important.

The Diversified Society and the WASP Reaction   The first factor is the changing demographic makeup of the American population. To put it simply, the white Anglo-Saxon Protestants, the fabled WASPs of American society, are no longer the majority demographic group in the nation. In fact, they are a minority, especially WASP males. At no more than 110 million in a nation of 270 million, WASPS are approximately 44 percent of the population, and 54 million WASP males (49 percent of the 110 million) are just less than 20 percent of all Americans. Females, non-European, and non-white peoples, and non-Protestant and non-Christian religions have increased significantly in recent decades and are now the majority, and ultimately are capable of exercising their majority influence in American society. (See Figures 3.1a and 3.1b on page 42, and Figure 3.1c on page 43 in Chapter 3.)

This extremely important change in the population has helped stimulate what we called (in Chapter 2) the cultural action-reaction syndrome. WASPS are reacting against the erosion of their numerical dominance and their traditional control of culture, politics, and economics with higher voting levels, new powerful grass-roots lobby groups, and proposals designed to protect their historically favored interests and status. In counter-reaction, non-WASPS are abstaining from voting or are constantly shifting their party allegiances, often in record numbers.

With only 36 percent of the population voting in the 1994 midterm elections (the lowest general turnout since 1950, but the highest Republican and WASP turnout), this syndrome of social group conflict is illustrated. Whereas WASP voters were only 12 percent of the 47 percent of eligible adults who voted in the Congressional elections of 1988, they were up to 33 percent of the mere 36 percent of eligible adults who voted in 1994. Clearly this does not constitute a "majority" of the voters. In 1994 the vast majority of eligible voters stayed away from the polls, a record 64 percent. In short, while WASPs are a decreasing minority in the total population, the WASP voters are a growing significant minority (33 percent) of the overall declining minority of voters (36 percent) who bother to vote at all. But they are the stronger and growing part. They realize they are the part that makes the difference, but they mistakenly think of themselves as being the majority of the people. Nearly all analysis of the 1994 election points to the flight of white males to the Republican party as being (especially in the South) the most important factor in Republican control of Congress for the first time in over forty years. And it demonstrated that in such low turnout elections, the WASPs' bloc vote *can* be decisive.

The current high turnout of WASPs and other Republicans was apparently in reaction to the 1992 elections, when a high turnout of non-whites and non-WASPs resulted in the Clinton administration's initial policies favoring those constituencies, which angered the WASPs.

Several scholars had previously seen this trend of social diversity-and-conflict politics coming. In the mid-1980s Kenneth Dolbeare (1986) especially had predicted that the 1990s would feature such an action–reaction struggle between a populism of the left versus one of the right, some of it with roots in ethnic and class conflicts over a relatively shrinking economy. We may be seeing a struggle between alienated demographic and religious groups and economic classes, as well as splits between regions of the country, as the 1992 versus 1994 elections tend to suggest.

The main features of this "culture war" (Hunter 1991) are based on religious, social, and regional splits, which have helped produce the national-level gridlock. These features seem to be as follows: Middle- and lower-income and suburban whites, especially males and particularly fundamentalist Christians in the South (and Mormons in the West), roughly align on one side and are turning to the populism of the Republican right. Meanwhile, the nonwhite and lower-income groups, the non-Christians, and especially the political liberals on both coasts are either turning to the populism of the left, going independent, or staying home in record numbers (as in 1994).

The cultural reaction syndrome of WASPs reacting against the growing diversity has produced policy proposals and activities on three fronts. The most important are the so-called *social backlash* proposals currently being considered at the Washington level. These proposals have as their purpose scaling back the gains of females, minorities, and the poor that have occurred over the last several decades. The most important of these backlash proposals are designed to retreat from affirmative action programs, to reduce welfare programs for the poor, to enforce child support provisions more actively, to take pregnant teenagers off AFDC, to eliminate government assistance to aliens, to reduce or eliminate plans similar to Clinton's comprehensive health care plan, and to modify the new anti-crime law, including increasing the number of death penalty offenses.

A second group of proposals emphasize economic policies traditionally favored by the WASPs. Among the most important of these are middle-class tax cuts, increased military spending, the balanced budget amendment, limits in liability laws, and measures purporting to create jobs such as reduction in the capital gains tax for the wealthy and subsidies for small business.

The final group of proposals flowing from the cultural WASP reaction syndrome are to increase active national government involvement in moral regulation. A striking early feature of this was the Reagan administration's commitment to *increase* national involvement in the regulation of morality at the same time that it was supposed to *decrease* involvement in other areas of American society. This position has been revived, with calls for a school prayer amendment, federal legislation on abortion and teenage pregnancy, limitations or elimination of the Public Broadcasting System and its television programs, reduced funding for the National Endowment for the Arts, and renewed activism for "values education" in schools.

All of this mainly WASP agenda, however, faces the meatgrinder of an increasingly non-WASP, diverse society with many veto points in the federalist system. Historically, the countervailing power of other groups has meant that no single group has been able to carry the day in Washington with its agenda. Rather than breaking the gridlock, the new slim Republican control of Congress, based largely on voting of WASPS versus big nonvoting majorities, could activate the sleeping opposing groups and thus contribute to even more social conflict and policy gridlock at the national level. Certainly, conflict between the many social groups that constitute the diverse U.S. population has been a major factor in policy gridlock in the past, notably the resistance to civil rights reforms in the 1950s and 1960s.

The Rise of the Losing Classes   A second major factor that has produced policy gridlock in national politics is an economic one. The American economy presents an anomaly that is puzzling when viewed on the basis of traditional economic dogma. On the one hand, the evidence from the period 1992–1994 suggests a robust, healthy economy. Total economic growth has been at about 4 percent, the annual inflation rate has been a mild 2.8 percent, the annual unemployment rate has averaged about 5.8 percent, and factories have been operating at a half-century high of 84.6 percent of capacity. On the other hand, the sense that Americans have of their economic well-being and their confidence in their own economic futures is low and shaky. Polling data, for the first time since World War II, record a decline in people's economic life expectations. And their uncertainty and anxiety grow the further they are asked to look into the future (Uchitelle 1994, p. 5). This uneasiness emerges as a generalized anxiety: Americans gulp diet pills because of their obesity and worry about whether or not they will have a meal tomorrow.

We believe this situation is explainable in large part by what Uchitelle labeled the "rise of the losing class." Robert Reich, secretary of labor in the Clinton administration, defined this group as "consisting of millions of Americans who no longer can count on having their jobs next year, or next month, and whose wages have stagnated or lost ground to inflation" (Uchitelle 1994).

Middle- and working-class Americans have real reasons for these worries. First, structural changes in the American economy and increasing international competition have meant a change in employment patterns. These changes are captured in the word *downsizing* as many companies automate or adopt efficiency measures to produce more with a smaller labor force. Employees who lose jobs by downsizing not only are unskilled and blue-collar workers, but also are found all across the corporate ladder and cut across the entire economic and education spectrum. The survey data also seem to indicate that most employees view downsizing as a permanent feature of the American economy. So the question always haunting the American worker is: Whose job is next?

The second characteristic of the "losing class" is that their wages have either been stagnant or actually lost ground to inflation. Wage performance combined with government tax and subsidy policy has significantly shifted wealth since the 1980s. Figure 3.2 on page 51 in Chapter 3 details how the rich became wealthier, the middle class either held or lost ground, and the poor are worse off since 1980. Ironically, in the early 1980s the conservative writer

Charles Murray wrote a book entitled *Losing Ground* with the inaccurate central thesis that America's poverty programs were counterproductive for the *poor*. There is a strong belief among the middle class, and some evidence supporting it, that it is *they* who are losing ground, and this belief fuels much of the economic uncertainty that is pervasive among Americans (see Philips 1992).

Current public opinion arising from the anxiety about economics also helps explain policy gridlock. In the past, when there were recessions or layoffs, workers who were hurt tended to blame the individual company and its management. This is no longer the case. There now seems to be a forgiving attitude toward management and a fatalistic attitude toward the economic forces that make companies downsize. Voter anger and frustration are instead directed either at the government or at groups marginal to the employment picture, namely foreign immigrants and the poor. Florence Skelly of the Daniel Yankelovich Group survey organization, referring to this effect in the 1994 elections, said:

> You would think that in a free enterprise system, there would be more criticisms of its warts. Instead, we say that government should be run more like a business. And we deal with the boss by ousting the congressman. (Uchitelle 1994, p. 1)

As we suggested in Chapter 2, Americans are responding to the changes associated with modernization with highly irrational and contradictory behavior. On the one hand, as a result of growing conservative sentiment Americans are increasingly limiting an already weak power of government to regulate the economy; on the other hand, they angrily blame government for not fixing the economy. The myth of failure reinforces the belief that government is the culprit in the nation's economic woes. Yet the denigration and weakening of the national government certainly reduces its ability to take effective actions.

The Disinformation System   The third factor increasing national ineffectiveness and policy gridlock is the disinformation system and the dumbing down of American political rhetoric. The disinformation system has a pervasive array of various propagandistic methods, such as partial truths and distortions, to influence public opinion and public policy. We suggest that you carefully study Table 3.1 on pages 46–47 in Chapter 3, a summary of how one can identify statistical disinformation and counteract its influence.

One of the important results of the disinformation system is what we call the dumbing down of political rhetoric. By this we mean that public issues are discussed in a very shallow and often emotional and biased way. It is a serious public problem that issues are not given the careful, intelligent examination that the solution to critical problems requires.

It is easy to succumb to a conspiracy theory viewpoint and blame the disinformation system on conniving politicians who want to exercise political power. Of course, there are politicians who make maximum use of the disinformation system. But we would emphasize a more basic factor in the pervasiveness of the disinformation system: *A society under stress tends to hype up issues while dumbing them down.* Such a society tends to look for a clear enemy to blame. When that enemy is identified, the society tends to overemphasize that enemy's contribution to the problem. The discussion becomes couched in simplistic terms in the search for easy answers and quick fixes. In this way, myths and ideologies become stronger in times of stress.

The best illustration of these tendencies is the anger and frustration that Americans currently direct at government or public agencies for various economic problems. To be sure, the American economy is under stress—a stress based primarily in structural changes in the economy and the emergence of the world economy. Those who exploit the disinformation system find the government to be a convenient enemy to target, exaggerating the powerful myth of government failure. Government is demonized as its role in the economy is exaggerated. The diagnoses of the problems of the economy whether of the populist left or right, are dumbed down to the simplistic assertion that it is all government's fault. Solutions are dumbed down to the proposal that what is needed is to get government *out* of the economy or to put more of it *in*. Such simplistic intonements are far from a basis for effective action on America's critical problems.

The Objective/Achievement Gap   A fourth major factor contributing to national policy gridlock is the objective/achievement gap. That is, there is a gap between what policy actors define as their objectives and what they actually achieve by their actions. Like gridlock, the objective/achievement gap occurs across the policy spectrum. It occurs in lawmaking, which has become largely symbolic, as in environmental legislation. It occurs in the budgetary process: Congress authorizes more money for programs than it appropriates, a symbol of action created by Congress largely to divert interest groups, who believe they have won in the authorization when in fact no money can be spent until it is appropriated. The objective/achievement gap appears also in the regulatory agencies, where rule-making authority granted by the Congress is not exercised or is delayed until its exercise is meaningless. And it occurs at the field level, where programs established by Congress or by regulatory agencies are implemented on a selective basis or even not at all.

In a sense, the objective/achievement gap is both a symptom and a cause of the relative failure of the national government since the late 1970s. The gap breeds societal conflict, which in turn breeds cynicism and attempts to weaken government, which then produces real failure. An important point to emphasize again is that this vicious cycle pervades mainly the *national* government. While Americans tend to hold the Congress in particularly low esteem, it would not be enough for only the Congress to get its act together. If the gap remains obvious to enough of the public, the entire policy process in Washington will tend to stay mired in the vicious cycle of exaggerated expectations, cynicism, and failure.

FACTORS PRODUCING THE NEW SUCCESS OF STATES AND LOCALS

By contrast, subnational governments are in a period of relative policy success. State and local governments have considerable abilities to adapt, but how Montana adapts to changing circumstances may not be the same as how Massachusetts adapts. Three factors best explain the new success of states.

Pragmatism   First, state and local policy actors seem to be more pragmatic than their more ideological national counterparts. The pragmatism of subnational governments was seen as far back as the 1930s in their response to the problems created by the Great Depression. As a congressional study from the period found, cities almost immediately assumed a prominent role in the implementation of New Deal legislation. While ideological battles raged at the national level, locals were carrying out relief measures, undertaking the construction or repair of the municipal physical plant, and otherwise acting to meet real needs (National Resources Committee 1939, p. 61).

A more recent study of housing confirms the tradition of pragmatism of local policy actors: "Left to their own devices, local governments get things done faster than Washington, even when difficult choices must be made" (Wrightson 1986, p. 272). An interesting feature of the locals' capacity to get things done is the fact that they often modify national objectives to suit local preferences, a process known as the localization of national policy objectives (Hamilton and Wells 1990, p. 163).

Stimulation by National Failure   A second overlooked force in the relative success of states and locals is that failure at one level of the federal system tends to stimulate action at other levels. A number of studies, many of which we have cited in this book, concluded that the relative failure of the national government in specific policy areas stimulated action at the state and local levels. The 1980s offer good examples as subnational governments moved to fill the gaps left by the retreat of the national government from a number of policy areas, such as environmental programs, housing, aid to the poor, jobless and youth, economic development and health care reforms. Thus if one level in the federal system does not address problems effectively, then other levels tend to become active.

A New Trend of Social Activism and Voluntarism   A third force in the relative policy success of state and local governments is the most encouraging one. There seems to be a strong new social activism at the local level which gets little national press or even academic attention.

While Americans are disdaining welfare, understood as the national government's response to poverty, they are showing strong local concern for the poor and disadvantaged. We referred earlier to strong American support for the quality of the environment as well. As a candidate for president, George

Bush accurately sensed this renewed social activism and the fact that it was largely local and voluntaristic in nature. However, rather than defining the true richness of the mosaic of voluntarism, he reduced it to a simplified political slogan in his famous phrase "a thousand points of light."

The new wave of state and local social activism President Bush sensed has produced a significant wave of reforms and also a new style of organization in the American policy system. The best term for these new organizations and reforms is third-sector services organizations. Third-sector services are largely voluntary, mainly nonprofit and private organizations that take on a quasi-public character and tackle severely neglected public problems. An extremely wide range of such organizations have formed in most localities since the late 1970s. They include hospices; soup kitchens; safe houses for abused children and battered spouses; literacy action groups; home health care and centers for the elderly; mental, marital, and family counseling centers; and the like. The range of their scope and purposes covers the full spectrum of needs within American communities.

Third-sector service organizations are different from the civic associations and voluntary organizations of the past. They have a quasi-public nature in that they often work in concert with subnational governments, receive and spend grant funds, and often actually implement the program, as with safe houses for abused children. These organizations have become major actors in the American policy system. They demonstrate the pragmatism of states and locals, often enabling state people to accomplish objectives that are neglected by governments or that seem to contradict local ideology. Thus we find what on the surface seems to be a contradiction: Organizations vigorously pursue activist social reform in all areas, even where conservative sentiment is high or where government activism is limited or disdained.

This renewed social activism is a start on the road to the recovery of the democratic community. It also has great potential as a lesson for the national policy system. We turn, then, to the experience of subnational governments in the American system and to the experience of other countries for important lessons for the American national policy system.

IMPORTANT LESSONS FROM OUR FRIENDS: THE RECOVERY OF DEMOCRATIC COMMUNITY

Myths are powerful ideas about how things are or should be. These powerful ideas influence how individuals act. Myths can be right or wrong, productive or counterproductive, malicious, kind, or benign in their effects. We have suggested, particularly in Chapter 2, that the best test of the effect of myths is the crucible of experience. Thus we believe in nations learning from each other's policy systems. Were it not for American provincialism, the experience of other countries could inform policy action in this country in many ways. And were it not for the myopia of analysis from a focus on Washington, the experience of subnational governments could inform the national government in this period of gridlock. In our view, the best way for a system to cycle through a government failure mode and transform itself is to be receptive to lessons learned in other systems.

Aristotle defined politics as the art of living together in community. The history of nations has been checkered in realizing this art of living together in community. The United States is in a cycle where many individuals are questioning the capacity of the national government to deal effectively with the critical choices that face our nation as a community. Here is one of the most important lessons that can be learned from the experiences of other nations: The most critical failure for the nation would be the breakdown of democratic community and control of the policy system. Such a breakdown of democratic sentiment and control of policy would mean that the system has moved from a cycle of relative failure toward a period of total failure. The soul of the American policy system is democratic community and control.

Therefore, what key lessons can we learn from other systems and from our own state and local reformers that have the potential to stem the tide of loss of confidence in government? Studies of the region of Emila-Romagna in Italy and of the U.S. city of Tupelo in Mississippi contain some of the most important lessons. Robert Putnam, in a study of Emila-Romagna entitled *Democracy and Civic Community*, found that effective governments, healthy economies, confidence in public institutions, and even personal happiness all flowed from strong civic involvement (Putnam 1992). Indicators of strong civic involvement are such things as participation in civic clubs, reading newspapers, voting, belonging to sports clubs, debating important decisions in civil and objective ways, and rolling up one's sleeves and working to solve community problems. Putnam argued that this effect was so strong that if you could tell him how many choral societies a community had a hundred years ago he could tell you how long it would take you to get a telephone call answered at a local public bureau. In short, when there is a history of strong civic involvement and moral recommitment, then citizens face problems honestly, resolve differences between them, make the critical choices required to solve problems, and work together to implement those solutions effectively.

The city of Tupelo in Mississippi is an excellent demonstration of this point in the United States. Until the 1940s Tupelo was the poorest city in the poorest region of the nation's poorest state. In the 1990s Tupelo was aptly described as a "miracle of rural development" (Bishop 1994, p. 10). The major factor in that transformation was strong civic involvement on the part of Tupelo's citizens. Rather than looking to external sources of assistance, Tupelo created rural development councils, built a rural hospital and a cooperative cotton gin, paved the roads into town, integrated its schools without the parallel development of all-white academies, and established a wide-ranging community development corporation. Its community activity has not stopped. In the last several years it has built a free health clinic, established a symphony orchestra (the smallest town in America to have one), and created a volunteer bank. This civic involvement seems to flow from a belief the people have in their ability to solve critical problems facing the community (Bishop 1994).

There has been a serious erosion of ethical and civic identity and involvement in the United States. Many civic organizations and most churches have lost membership since the 1970s. The organizations that have been most successful in gaining membership are those that can be joined by mail. Civic involvement seems to have deteriorated to the level of passive commitment. Newspaper readership is at a low for the modern period. The percentage of Americans who vote is down. Much of the civic discourse has degenerated to personal attacks and crass disinformation. All of this has had its effect on the American policy system. Bishop described this effect:

> There is a price to pay for this dissolution of civic society. The most obvious is that Americans have become an angry lot. We have lost faith in our economy, in our government, in every public institution ... the culprit is everywhere. (1994, p.12)

The prescription against the dissolution of civic society is the recovery of the sense of civic and spiritual obligation.

The sense of civic obligation can be nurtured by the realization that politics and caring work horizontally in society, not vertically. Since the 1950s the American policy system has turned this fact upside down. We have made politics function vertically, from Washington down, and in the process have transformed citizens into the clients of government. We need to recapture Aristotle's view that politics is the art of living together in community. We need to be realistic and understand that as an art, politics is a messy affair, certainly messier than the technical processes of the modern period. But while messy, politics is coherent, understandable, and amenable to the accomplishment of common objectives.

The American nation, as a subcommunity in the larger world community, faces some critical choices as it approaches the twenty-first century. The ultimate dumbing down of political rhetoric in the United States would be the widespread acceptance of the myth that the American system does not allow the people to govern themselves. Americans are close to that point with the widespread loss of confidence in governing structures and personalities and a disinformation system that exploits the loss of confidence and thereby nurtures it. The American people need to appreciate the strengths of their increasing diversity and recapture a belief in their basic institutions if they are to possess the ability to solve problems. A renewed vision of community and of our ability to solve problems can become the keys to effective solutions and to a politics more amenable to democracy.

 APPENDIX **A**

TECHNICAL DISTINCTIONS
OF REGIONS

Our breakdown of seven regions is informed by the literature of cultural geographers such as White, Foscue, and McKnight (1985) and Zelinksky (1980), as well as by Garreau's views (1980). But our views are more than adaptations of the pictures created by these individuals. For instance, our description of seven regions differs markedly from and does not follow Garreau's breakdown of "nine nations of North America" (although we do cite his term *Ecotopia* for the far west coast). Also, we present political dynamics in ways not mentioned by the cultural geographers. Our views are distillations and theoretical recombinations of the general political science and public policy literatures on differences in regions. In Chapter 4 we describe composite regional variations in politics, policies, cultures, and values in ways that the disparate literatures usually miss. Region is a neglected unit of analysis in political science, and especially in policy research.

We draw out regions in certain ways for certain reasons. In our description, cultural and historical zones do not neatly follow state boundaries, despite the legal and institutional importance of legal boundaries. For instance, we divide northwest Missouri from the Border states region and place it more in the Midwest. We also take the unusual step of placing the extreme southern parts of Illinois and Indiana in the Border States region. Basically, these areas make up a zone where the cultural and historical influence of the South fades out slowly as one moves north and west. The northeast region of Missouri, for instance, was settled mainly by post-Civil War immigrants from northern Europe who came to the Midwest and established an agricultural and industrial economy focused around the Kansas City-to-Chicago axis. Northwest Missouri was a springboard for overland wagon routes to the West, serving as both a clearinghouse for and recipient of these immigrants.

In the Border States, the northern immigrants concentrated along the great rivers of the Ohio and Mississippi, establishing water trade and commercial and industrial developments. Southern commercial and cultural development and plantation or slave interests were a minority presence in these river regions. Northern immigration and northern influences extended southward from the rivers for approximately one hundred miles, after which point northern influences weakened as southern influences became more predominant—as in south central Missouri and Kentucky, for instance. Thus, the real border between the Midwest and the more southern Border States slants upward, slightly to the north of those rivers, where the northern influences become much more dominant.

State borders do not neatly divide the West from the Midwest, either. Immigrants' cultural and linguistic differences tended to cut off the eastern parts of the plains states from the western parts. The West itself fades out into the western coastal zone that Garreau calls Ecotopia, at a point slightly west of the spine of the mountains as they move north into Canada.

Finally, our description covers the differences between the northern parts of the West and the more hispanic Southwest, as well as northern Yankees versus southern Yankees in the New England zone. But our description stops short of dividing the regions in half. It is simply a matter of estimation that the differences that delineate the South from the Border states and the industrial Northeast are greater than the distinctions inside the West and New England.

 APPENDIX **B**

A RESEARCH NOTE
ON THE EUTHANASIA CASE STUDIES

The case studies on the medical practices of euthanasia (in Chapter 10) are based on confidential interviews with five physicians and several other medical professionals in hospitals in the middle regions of the South. Our research goal was to obtain accurate information about the veiled practices of euthanasia—information that can be gained only from personal and strictly confidential interviews.

The details of some of the case studies represent individual cases with a number of circumstances altered to protect confidentiality; in other cases the details represent the combined factors of several typical cases that were similar in nature (also to protect confidentiality). Legal confidentiality is so highly protected in medical practice that it renders social science research on euthanasia exceedingly difficult, to say the least (see Chapter 10). Nevertheless, our dissatisfaction with the legalistic tone and character of the vast majority of published research on euthanasia led us to seek non-intrusive, confidential interviews so as to be better able to describe the implementation of euthanasia as it is actually practiced.

Because the walls of professional silence that have been built around the issue of euthanasia are extremely difficult to penetrate, it is a moot point to observe that more systematic research needs to be carried out on this topic—research that renders statistical generalization possible. Our research is useful because it contrasts the public and professional literature's commentary on euthanasia—which seems to be almost naively guided by the recitation of legal case principles—with the exceedingly ambiguous, ethically complex, and nearly invisible implementation of euthanasia as it is in fact practiced. Also, through these cases, we seek to raise issues of social ethics regarding euthanasia—issues that are not usually raised (see Chapter 10).

≈≈ BIBLIOGRAPHY

Aaron, Henry (1991). *Serious and Unstable Condition: Financing America's Health Care*. Washington, D.C.: Brookings Institution.

ACIR (1984). *Regulatory Federalism: Policy, Process, Impact, and Reform*. Washington, D.C.: U.S. Government Printing Office.

Adams, Don (1988). "Extending the Education Planning Discourse." *Comparative Education Review* 32: 400–415.

Ahmed, Yusef J., Salah El Serafez, and Ernst Lufts, eds. (1989). *Environmental Accounting for Sustainable Development*. Washington, D.C.: The World Bank.

Allison, Graham (1971). *Essence of Decision: Explaining the Cuban Missile Crisis*. Boston: Little Brown.

American Education Research Association (1985). *Standards for Educational and Psychological Testing*. Washington, D.C.: American Psychological Association.

Anderson, James E., David W. Brady, and Charles Bullock (1983). *Public Policy in the Eighties*. Monterey, CA: Brooks Cole Publishing Co.

Anderson, James G., and David P. Caddell (1993). "Attitudes of Medical Professionals toward Euthanasia." *Social Science and Medicine* 37, no. 1 (July), 105–115.

Anderson, Odin (1989). *The Health Services Continuum in Democratic States*. Ann Arbor, MI: Health Administration Press.

Arrandale, Tom (1993). "Environmental Giveback Fever: Will There Be an Epidemic?" *Governing*, November 1993, p. 70.

Astrup, R. E. (1992). "Charter Schools: A Dissenting Voice." *Education Week*, September 23, 1992, p. 29.

Atkinson, Michael M. (1988). Book review of Peter Leslie (1987). *Federal, State, and National Economies*, University of Toronto Press. In *Canadian Journal of Political Science* 21 (June), pp. 377–378.

_____. (1989). "Strong States and Weak States: Sectoral Policy Networks in Advanced Capitalist Economies." *British Journal of Political Science* 19 (January), 47–67.

Bacharach, Peter, and Morton S. Baratz (1970). *Poverty*. New York: Holt, Rinehart and Winston.

Baldwin, Stephen E. (1993). "Choosing from an Expanded Menu." *Journal of Policy Analysis and Management* 12, no.1, 200–202.

Barnard, Chester (1938). *The Functions of the Executive*. Cambridge, MA: Harvard University Press.

Bauman, Harold (1992). "Verging on National Health Insurance since 1910." In Robert P. Huefner and Margaret P. Battin, eds., *Changing to National Health Care: Ethics in a Changing World*. Salt Lake City: University of Utah Press, pp. 29–50.

Beard, Charles A. (1941). *An Economic Interpretation of the Constitution of the United States*. New York: Macmillan.

Beckhart, Benjamin H. (1972). *Federal Reserve System*. New York: Columbia University Press.

Berlant, Jeffrey L. (1975). *Profession and Monopoly: A Study of Medicine in the United States and Great Britain*. Los Angeles: University of California Press.

Bestor, Arthur (1953). *Educational Wastelands*. Urbana: University of Illinois Press.

Bishop, Bob (1994). "No Santa Claus in Appalachia." *Appalachian Heritage* 22, no. 4, 4–12.

Blendon, R., and K. Donelon (1990). "The Public and the Emerging Debate over National Health Insurance." *New England Journal of Medicine* 323, no. 3, 208–212.

Bok, Sissela (1994). "Voluntary Euthanasia: Private and Public Imperatives." *The Hastings Center Report* 24, no. 3 (May–June), 19–21.

Brace, Paul, and Gary Mucciaroni (1990). "The American States and the

Shifting Locus of Positive Economic Intervention." *Policy Studies Review* 10, no. 1, 151–173.

Brown, William (1990). "Europe's Forests Fall to Acid Rain." *New Scientist,* December 5, p. 11.

Bureau of the Census, U.S. Department of Commerce (1989). "Projections of the Population of the United States by Age, Sex, and Race: 1988–2080." Current Population Reports, Series P-25, no. 1018. Washington, D.C.: U.S. Government Printing Office.

Burner, Sally T., Danile Waldo, and David McKusick (1992). "National Health Expenditures Projections through 2030." *Health Care Financing Review* 14, no. 1, 1–29.

Busch, John C., and Richard M. Jaeger (1989). "Policy and Educational Standards." *Administrator's Handbook* 33, no. 6, 1–4.

Bynum, W. F., and Roy Porter, eds. (1993). *The Companion Encyclopedia of the History of Medicine,* 2 vol. New York: Routledge, Chapman and Hall.

Calleo, David P. (1992). *The Bankrupting of America: How the Federal Budget Is Impoverishing the Nation.* New York: William Morrow.

Cassedy, James H. (1991). *Medicine in America: A Short History.* Baltimore: John Hopkins University Press.

Census Bureau (1991). *Current Population Reports.* Series P-650, no. 174. Washington, D.C.: U.S. Government Printing Office.

Chafe, William H. (1991). *The Unfinished Journey: America since World War II,* 2nd ed. New York: Oxford University Press.

Chubb, John, and Terry Moe (1990). *Politics, Markets, and America's Schools.* Washington, D.C.: Brookings Institution.

Citron, C. H. (1985). "An Overview of Legal Issues in Teacher Quality." *Journal of Law and Education* 14, no. 3, 277–307.

Cochran, Clarke E., et al. (1990). *American Public Policy: An Introduction.* New York: St. Martin's Press.

Cohen, Benjamin (1978). *Organizing the World's Money: The Political Economy of International Monetary Relations.* London: Macmillan.

Cohen, Stephen D. (1988). *The Making of U.S. International Monetary Policy,* 3rd ed. New York: Praeger.

Colella, Cynthia Cates (1986). "The Supreme Court and Intergovernmental Relations." In Robert J. Dilger, ed., *American Intergovernmental Relations Today.* Englewood Cliffs, NJ: Prentice Hall.

Congressional Budget Office (1993). "Managed Competition and Its Potential to Reduce Health Spending." Washington, D.C.: U.S. Government Printing Office, May.

_____ (1994). "An Analysis of the Administration's Health Proposal." Washington, D.C.: U.S. Government Printing Office, February.

Consumer Reports (1992a). "Wasted Health Care Dollars," July, pp. 82–94.

_____ (1992b). "Are HMOs the Answer?" August, pp. 519–531.

Cooter, R., ed. (1988). *Studies in the History of Alternative Medicine*. New York: St. Martin's Press.

Council of State Governments States Information Center (1994). "Health Care Reform Initiatives in the States," May 1.

Craig, Barbara Hinkson, and David M. O'Brien (1993). *Abortion and American Politics*. Chatham, NJ: Chatham House.

Cuban, L. (1990). "Reforming Again, Again, and Again." *Educational Research* 19, no. 1, 3–13.

Dale, Edwin L., Jr. (1970). "When Will It Be Safe to Balance the Budget?" In Harold Wolozin, *American Fiscal and Monetary Policy*. New York: Quadrangle Books.

Deleu, Nancy, George Greenberg, and Kraig Kinchen (1992). "A Layman's Guide to the U.S. Health Care System: Special Report." *Health Care Finance Review* 14, no. 1, 151–169.

Denhardt, Robert B., and William H. Stewart (1992). *Executive Leadership in the Public Service*. Tuscaloosa: University of Alabama Press.

Department of Labor (1991). *What Work Requires of Schools: A SCANS Report for America 2000*. Washington, D.C.: Department of Labor.

Devlin, John (1991). "Privacy and Abortion Rights under the Louisiana State Constitution." *Louisiana Law Review* 52: 685–732.

Dietz, Thomas M., and Robert W. Rycroft (1987). *The Risk Professionals*. New York: Russell Sage Foundation.

DiIulio, Jr., and Richard P. Nathan, eds. (1994). *Making Health Reform Work: The View from the States*. Washington, D.C.: Brookings Institution.

Dolbeare, Kenneth (1986). *Democracy at Risk: The Politics of Economic Renewal*. Chatham, NJ: Chatham House.

Dorsset, Lyle W. (1977). *Franklin Roosevelt and the City Bosses*. Port Washington, NY: Kennikat Press.

Dresang, Dennis L., and James J. Gosling (1989). *Politics, Policy, and Management in the American States.* White Plains, NY: Longman.

Dubnick, Melvin J., and Barbara A. Bardes (1983). *Thinking About Public Policy: A Problem-Solving Approach.* New York: Wiley.

Dunlap, Riley E. and Angela G. Mertig, eds. *American Environmentalism.* Philadelphia: Taylor and Francis.

Dye, Thomas (1986). *Who's Running America? The Conservative Years.* Englewood Cliffs, NJ: Prentice Hall.

_____ (1987). *Understanding Public Policy,* 6th ed. Englewood Cliffs, NJ: Prentice Hall.

ECE (1984). *Report of the Seminar on Low-Waste Technology.* Geneva: U.N. Economic Commission for Europe.

Eisinger, Peter K. (1988). *The Rise of the Entrepreneurial State.* Madison: University of Wisconsin Press.

Elazar, Daniel (1962). *The American Partnership.* Chicago: University of Chicago Press.

_____ (1964). *American Federalism: A View from the States.* New York: Thomas Y. Crowell.

Ellwood, P. M., A. Enthoven, and L. Etheredge (1992). "The Jackson Hole Initiatives for a 21st Century American Health Care System." *Health Economics* 1: 149–168.

Evans, M. Stanton (1994). "Why There Is a Health Care Crisis." *Consumers Research,* June 1994, pp. 10–36

Farrand, Max, ed. (1966). *The Records of the Constitutional Convention of 1787.* New Haven, CT: Yale University Press.

Fein, Rashi (1994). "The Politics of Health Reform." *Dissent,* Winter 1994, pp. 43–51.

Fine, Sidney (1956). *Laissez Faire and the General-Welfare State.* Ann Arbor: University of Michigan Press.

Fosler, R. Scott, ed. (1988). *The New Economic Role of American States: Strategies in a Competitive World Economy.* New York: Oxford University Press.

Fox, Daniel M. (1993). "The Medical Institutions and the State." In W. F. Bynum and Roy Porter, eds. (1993), The Companion Encyclopedia of the History of Medicine. New York: Routledge, Chapman and Hall, pp. 1204–1330.

Frankfurter, Felix (1961). *Mr. Justice Holmes and the Supreme Court.* Cambridge, MA: Harvard University Press.

Freidson, Eliot (1970). *The Profession of Medicine.* New York: Dodd and Mead.

Fries, James F., C. Everett Koop, et al. (1993). "Reducing Health Care Costs by Reducing the Need and Demand for Medical Services." *New England Journal of Medicine* 329, no. 5 (July), 321–326.

Friedman, Milton, and Walter Heller (1969). *Monetary vs. Fiscal Policy.* New York: W. W. Norton.

Garreau, Joel (1992). *The Nine Nations of North America.* New York: Avon.

Gelfand, Toby (1993). "The History of the Medical Profession." In W. F. Bynum and Roy Porter, eds. (1993), The Companion Encyclopedia of the History of Medicine. New York: Routledge, Chapman and Hall, pp. 1119–1150.

General Accounting Office (1989). *Export of Unregistered Pesticides Is Not Adequately Monitored by EPA.* Washington, D.C.: U.S. Government Printing Office.

Gersten, Larry N. (1983). *Making Public Policy: From Conflict to Resolution.* Glenview, IL: Scott, Foresman.

Gevitz, Norman (1982). *The DOs: Osteopathic Medicine in America.* Baltimore: Johns Hopkins University Press. On chiropractors versus the American Medical Association, see pp. 291–297.

_____, ed. (1988). *Other Healers: Unorthodox Medicine in America.* Baltimore: Johns Hopkins University Press.

Glick, Henry R. (1994). "The Impact of Permissive Judicial Policies: The U.S. Supreme Court and the Right to Die." *Political Research Quarterly* 47, no. 1 (March), 207–223.

Goldwin, Robert A., and William A. Schambia, eds. (1982). *How Capitalistic Is the Constitution?* Washington, D.C.: American Enterprise Institute.

Goodsell, Charles (1983). *The Case for Bureaucracy.* Chatham, NJ: Chatham House.

Gowland, David H. (1983). *International Economics.* Totowa, NJ: Barnes and Noble.

Graetz, Michael, and James Tobin (1994). "Players and Payers." *New York Times,* June 12, 1994.

Graig, Laurence A. (1993). *Health of Nations: An International Perspective on U.S. Health Care Reform,* 2nd. ed. Washington, D.C.: Congressional Quarterly Inc.

Greider, William (1987). *Secrets of the Temple. How the Federal Reserve Runs the Country.* New York: Touchstone.

Grodzins, Morton (1966). *The American System: A New View of Government in the United States*. Chicago: Rand McNally.

Group Health Association of America (1995). Associated Press headline news story, January 4.

Hacker, Louis M. (1970). *The Course of American Economic Growth and Development*. New York: John Wiley.

Hall, Robert T. (1994). "Final Act: Sorting out the Ethics of Physician-Assisted Suicide." *The Humanist* 54, no. 6 (November–December), 10–15.

Hamilton, Christopher, and Donald T. Wells (1990). *Federalism, Power, and Political Economy: A New Theory of Federalism's Impact on American Life*. Englewood Cliffs, NJ: Prentice Hall.

Hansen, Susan B. (1984). "The Effects of State Industrial Policies on Economic Growth." Paper presented at the annual American Political Science Association meeting, Washington, D.C.

_____ (1986). "State Perspectives on Economic Development: Priorities and Outcomes." Paper presented at the annual Midwestern Political Science Association meeting, Chicago.

_____ (1992). "Shifting the Burden: The Struggle over Growth and Corporate Taxation." Multiple book review in *The Journal of Politics* 54, no. 4, (November), 1192–1194.

Harrigan, John J. (1988). *Political Change in the Metropolis*, 5th ed. New York: Harper College.

Hays, Samuel P. (1991). "Three Decades of Environmental Politics: The Historical Context." In Michael J. Lacey, ed., *Government and Environmental Politics*. Washington, D.C.: Woodrow Wilson Center.

Heck, Ronald H. (1992). "Systems Dynamics and Chicago School Reform: A Model for Redefining Who Governs." *Administrator's Notebook* 35, no. 4, 1–6.

Heclo, Hugh, Arnold J. Heidenheimer, and Carolyn T. Adams (1983). *Comparative Public Policy*. New York: St. Martin's Press.

Hedlund, Ronald, and H. Paul Friesma (1972). "Representatives' Perceptions on Constituency Opinion." *Journal of Politics* 34: 730–752.

Henig, Jeffrey (1985). *Public Policy and Federalism*. New York: St. Martin's Press.

Henry, Nicholas (1987). *Governing at the Grassroots: State and Local Politics*. Englewood Cliffs, NJ: Prentice Hall.

Herzik, Eric B. (1992). "The Development of Hazardous Waste Management as a State Policy Concern." *Policy Studies Review* 11, no. 1, 141–148.

Hoefler, James M. (1994). "Diffusion and Diversity: Federalism and the Right to Die in the Fifty States." *Publius* 24, no. 3 (Summer), 153–171.

Honsang, Joanna Boddens (1992). "Trade with Endangered Species." In *Green Globe Yearbook 1992*. New York: Oxford University Press.

Horowitz, Morton J. (1977). *The Transformation of American Law, 1790–1860*. Cambridge, MA: Harvard University Press.

Hunter, James Davison (1991). *Culture Wars: The Struggle to Define America*. New York: Basic Books.

Hurrell, Andrew, and Benedict Kingsbury (1992). *The International Politics of the Environment*. Oxford: Oxford University Press.

Irving, Patricia, ed. (1991). *Acid Deposition: State of Science and Technology: Summary Report of the United States National Acid Precipitation Assessment Program*. Washington, D.C.: U.S. Government Printing Office.

Jasinowski, Merry, and Sharon Canner (1989). *Meeting the Health Care Crisis*. National Association of Manufacturers.

Jewson, N. K. (1976). "Disappearance of the Sick-Man from Medical Cosmologies: 1770 to 1870." *Sociology* 10: 225–244.

Johnson, Chalmers (1984). *The Industrial Policy Debate*. San Francisco: ICS Press.

Jones, Charles O. (1970). *An Introduction to the Study of Public Policy*. Belmont, CA: Wadsworth.

Kamlet, Kenneth S. (1979). *Toxic Substances Programs in U.S. States and Territories: How Well Do They Work*. Washington, D.C.: National Wildlife Federation.

Kegley, Charles W., Jr., and Eugene R. Wittkopf (1989). *American Foreign Policy*. New York: St. Martin's Press.

Kelly, Michael (1993). "David Gergen, Master of the Game: How Image Became the Sacred Faith of Washington, and How This Insider's Insider Became Its High Priest." *New York Times Magazine*, October 31, pp. 64–96.

Kelner, Merrijoy J., Ivy L. Bourgeault, and Judith A. Wahl (1994). "Regulation and Legislation of the Dying Process: View of Health Care Professionals." *Death Studies* 18, no. 2 (March–April), 167–182.

Kenski, Henry C. (1990). *Saving the Hidden Treasure: The Evolution of Groundwater Policy*. Claremont, CA: Regina Books.

Keohane, Robert O., Jr., and Joseph Nye (1977). *Interdependence*. New York: Harper College.

Key, V. O., Jr. (1949). *Southern Politics*. New York: Vintage Books.

Kimmel, Lewis H. (1959). *Federal Judges and Fiscal Policy 1789–1958.* Washington, D.C.: The Brookings Institution.

King, Laurestan R. (1986). "Anticipatory Policy and Marine Resources." *Policy Studies Review* 6, no.2, 302–309.

Koop, C. Everett (1995). "A Personal Role in Health Care." *The American Journal of Public Health* 85, no. 6 (June), 759–761.

Kotlikoff, Laurence J. (1987). "Budget Deficits, Stripped of Illusions." *Wall Street Journal*, November 4, p. 6.

Lamb, David (1994). *A Sense of Place: Listening to Americans.* New York: Times Books.

Larkin, Gerald (1993). "The Emergence of Para-Medical Professions." In W. F. Bynum and Roy Porter, eds., *The Companion Encyclopedia of the History of Medicine.* New York: Routledge, Chapman and Hall, pp. 1329–1349.

Lester, James P., James L. Franke, Ann Bowman, and Kenneth W. Kraemer (1983). "Hazardous Waste Politics and Public Policy: A Comparative State Analysis." *Western Political Quarterly.* vol. 36. no. 2, 257–285.

Levit, K. R., and C. A. Cowan (1991). "Businesses, Households, and Governments: Health Care Costs, 1990." *Health Care Finance Review* 13, no. 2 (Winter), 83–93.

Levit, Katharine R., Gary Olin, and Suzanne Letsch (1992). "Americans' Health Insurance Coverage, 1980–1991." *Health Care Financing Review* 14, no. 1, 31–50.

Lewin-VHI, Inc. (December 1993). *The Financial Impact of the Health Security Act.* Fairfax, VA: Lewis-VHI.

Lifton, David S. (1980). *Best Evidence: Disguise and Deception in the Assassination of John F. Kennedy.* New York: Macmillan.

Lockard, Duane (1957). *The Politics of State and Local Government.* New York: Macmillan.

Lowi, Theodore (1969). *The End of Liberalism.* New York: W.W. Norton.

Lowrance, William W. (1976). *Of Acceptable Risk.* Los Altos, CA: William Kaufman.

Lynn, Frances M. (1986). "The Interplay of Science and Values in Assessing and Regulating Environmental Risks." *Science, Technology, and Human Values* 11, no. 2, 40–50.

Lynn, Laurence E. (1987). *Managing Public Policy.* Boston: Little Brown.

Maddox, William S., and Stuart A. Lilie (1984). *Beyond Liberal and Conservative: Reassessing the Political Spectrum.* Washington, D.C.: Cato Institute.

Magaziner, I. (1990). *America's Choice: High Skills or Low Wages*. Rochester, NY: National Center on Education and the Economy.

Maggs, Christopher (1993). "A General History of Nursing: 1800 to 1900." In W. F. Bynum and Roy Porter, eds., *The Companion Encyclopedia of the History of Medicine*. New York: Routledge, Chapman and Hall, pp. 1309–1328.

Mahtesian, Charles (1994). "The Precarious Politics of Privatizing Schools." *Governing*, June, pp. 46–51.

Makhijani, Arjun, Amanda Bickel, and Annie Makhijani (1990). "Beyond the Montreal Protocol: Still Working on the Ozone Hole." *Technology Review*, May/June, pp. 52–59.

Manning, Bayliss (1977). "The Congress, the Executive, and Intermestic Affairs." *Foreign Affairs* 55: 306–324.

March, James G., and Johan P. Olsen (1984). "The New Institutionalism: Organizational Factors in Political Life." *American Political Science Review* 78: 734–749.

Markusen, Ann (1987). *Regions: The Economies and Politics of Territory*. Totown, NJ: Roman and Littlefield.

Marland, Sidney P., Jr. (1972). "The Condition of Education in the Nation." *American Education* 7, no. 3, 2–9.

McDonald, Forrest (1982). "The Constitution and Hamiltonian Capitalism." In Robert A. Goldwin and William A. Schambra, eds., *How Capitalistic Is the Constitution?* Washington, D.C.: American Enterprise Institute for Public Policy Research.

Meier, Kenneth J. (1993). *Politics and the Bureaucracy*, 3rd ed. Monterey, CA: Brooks-Cole Publishers.

Melton, William C. (1985). *Inside the Fed: Making Monetary Policy*. Homewood, IL: Dow Jones–Irwin.

Mercer, Robert (Chair of Goodyear Tire and Rubber) (1989). Comments to the Conference Board. "A Harder Look at Health Care Costs." *Conference Board Research Report* no. 910, New York.

Mintzer, Irving M., and Alan S. Miller (1992). "Stratospheric Ozone Depletion: Can We Save the Sky?" In Helge Bergesen, Magnar Norderhaug, and Georg Parman, *Green Globe Yearbook* 1992. Oxford: Oxford University Press.

Mohr, James C. (1978). *Abortion in America: the Origins and Evolution of National Policy, 1800 to 1900*. New York: Oxford University Press.

Moon, William Least Heat (1992). *Prairy Erth*. Boston: Houghton-Mifflin.

Murray, Charles (1984). *Losing Ground: American Social Policy 1950–1980.* New York: Basic Books.

National Academy of Sciences (1991). *Policy Implications of Global Warming.* Washington, D.C.: National Academy Press.

National Center for Children in Poverty (1995). Associated Press headline news story, January 30.

National Commission on Excellence in Education (1983). *A Nation at Risk.* Washington, D.C.: Superintendent of Documents.

National Research Council (1984). *Toxicity Testing: Strategies to Determine Need and Priorities.* Washington, D.C.: National Academy Press.

National Resources Committee (1939). *Urban Government,* vol. 1, part II. Washington, D.C.: U.S. Government Printing Office.

Nelson, Michael, ed. (1985). *The Election of 1984.* Washington, D.C.: Congressional Quarterly Press.

OECD (1985). *The State of the Environment.* Washington, D.C.: Organization for Economic Cooperation and Development.

_____ (1988). *The State of the Environment.* Washington, D.C.: Organization for Economic Cooperation and Development.

_____ (1991). *The State of the Environment.* Paris: Organization for Economic Cooperation and Development.

Office of Science and Technology (1988). *State Technology Programs in the United States.* Minneapolis: Minnesota Department of Trade.

Ohanian, Susan (1987). "Japanese Education in America?" *Education Digest* 53, no. 1, 10–14.

Palumbo, Dennis, and Donald J. Calista (1990). *Implementation and the Policy Process: Opening Up the Black Box.* Westport, CT: Greenwood Press.

Parenti, Michael (1986). *Inventing Reality: The Politics of the Mass Media.* New York: St. Martin's Press.

_____ (1994). *Land of Idols: Political Mythology in America.* New York: St. Martin's Press.

_____ (1987). *Democracy for the Few,* 5th ed. New York: St. Martin's Press.

_____ (1991). *Make Believe Media: The Politics of Entertainment.* New York: St. Martin's Press.

Pareto, Vilfredo (1971). *Manual of Political Economy.* Trans. Ann S. Schwier. New York: A. M. Kelly.

Peters, B. Guy (1986). *American Public Policy: Promise and Performance*. Chatham, NJ: Chatham House Publishers.

Peterson, Paul E., Barry Rabe, and Kenneth Wong (1987). *When Federalism Works*. Washington, D.C.: Brookings Institution.

Phillips, Kevin (1994). *Boiling Point*. New York: Harper Perennial.

Piasecki, Bruce, and Gary Davis (1990). *America's Future in Toxic Waste Management: Lessons from Europe*. New York: Quorum Books.

Pizzo, Stephen, Mary Fricker, and Paul Muolo (1989). *Inside Job: The Looting of America's Savings and Loans*. New York: McGraw-Hill.

Plank, David N., and Don Adams (1989). "Death, Taxes, and School Reform: Educational Policy Change in Comparative Perspective." *Administrator's Notebook* 33, no. 1, 1–4.

Porter, Dorothy (1993). "Public Health." In W. F. Bynum and Roy Porter, eds. *The Companion Encyclopedia of the History of Medicine*. New York: Routledge, Chapman and Hall, pp. 1231–1260.

Pressman, Jeffrey L., and Aaron Wildavsky (1973). *Implementation*. Berkeley: University of California Press.

Putnam, Robert (1992). *Democracy and Civic Community: Tradition and Change in an Italian Community*. Princeton, NJ: Princeton University Press.

Rabinovitz, F. (1985). "Handling Hazardous Waste." In J. Kirlin and D. Winkler, eds., *California Policy Choices*, vol. 2. Sacramento: University of Southern California School of Public Affairs.

Rawls, John (1971). *A Theory Of Justice*. Cambridge, MA: Harvard University Press.

Reed, John Shelton (1972). *The Enduring South: Subcultural Persistence in Mass Society*. Lexington, MA: Lexington Books.

Reich, Robert B. (1987). *Tales of a New America: The Anxious Liberal's Guide to the Future*. New York: Random House.

Repetto, Robert (1986). *World Enough and Time*. New Haven, CT: Yale University Press.

Robinson, J. C. (1988). "Hospital Quality Competition and the Economics of Imperfect Information." *Milbank Quarterly* 66, no. 3, 465–481.

Roemer, Milton I. (1993a). "Internationalism, Medicine, and Public Health." In W. F. Bynum and Roy Porter, eds., *The Companion Encyclopedia of the History of Medicine*. New York: Routledge, Chapman and Hall, pp. 1417–1435.

_____ (1993b). "National Health Systems Throughout the World: Lessons for Health Systems Reforms in the United States." *American Behavioral Scientist* 36, no. 6 (July) 694–708.

Rose, Richard (1993). *Lesson Drawing in Public Policy.* Chatham, NJ: Chatham House Publishers.

Rosenberg, Charles E. (1983). *The Structure of American Medical Practice: 1875–1941.* Philadelphia: University of Pennsylvania Press.

_____ (1987). *The Care of Strangers: The Rise of the American Hospital System.* New York: Basic Books.

Rosenburg, N., W. Easterling, P. Crosson, and J. Darmstadter, eds. (1989). *Greenhouse Warming: Abatement and Adaptation.* Washington, D.C.: Resources for the Future.

Rovner, Julie (1992). "Prescription Drug Prices." *Congressional Quarterly Researcher,* July 17, 1992, pp. 599–613.

Rubin, Eva R. (1987). *Abortion, Politics, and the Courts: Roe v. Wade and Its Aftermath.* Westport, CT: Greenwood Press.

Rushefsky, Mark E. (1990). *Public Policy in the United States: Toward the 21st Century.* California: Wadsworth, Brooks-Cole.

Sadik, Nafis (1988). *The State of World Population.* New York: World Population Fund.

Samet, Jonathan M., and John D. Spengler (1991). *Indoor Air Pollution: A Health Perspective.* Baltimore: Johns Hopkins University Press.

Schattschneider, E. E. (1942). *Party Government.* New York: Farrar and Rinehart.

Schieber, G. J. Poullier, and L. M. Greenwald (1991). "Health Care Systems in Twenty-Four Countries." *Health Affairs* 10, no. 3 (Fall), 22–38.

Schmandt, Jurgen, Judith Clarkson, and Hilliard Roderick, eds. (1988). *Acid Rain and Friendly Neighbors: The Policy Dispute between Canada and the United States.* Durham, NC: Duke University Press.

Schneider, Mark (1989). *The Competitive City: The Political Economy of Suburbia.* Pittsburgh: University of Pittsburgh Press.

Schwarz, John E. (1988). *America's Hidden Success: A Reassessment of Public Policy from Kennedy to Reagan.* New York: W. W. Norton.

Selznick, Philip (1949). *TVA and the Grass Roots.* Berkeley: University of California Press.

Sharkansky, Ira (1970). *Regionalism in American Politics.* Indianapolis: Bobbs-Merrill.

Shimahara, Nobuo K. (1986). "Japanese Educational Reform in the 1980s." *Issues in Education* 4: 85–100.

Shorter, Edward (1993). "The History of the Doctor-Patient Relationship." In W. F. Bynum and Roy Porter, eds., *The Companion Encyclopedia of the History of Medicine*. New York: Routledge, Chapman and Hall, pp. 783–800.

Simon, Herbert A. (1947). *Administrative Behavior, or, a Study of Decision-Making Processes in Administrative Organizations*. New York: Macmillan.

Smith, J. B., and D. A. Tirpack, eds. (1989). *The Potential Effects of Global Warming in the United States*. Washington, D.C.: The Environmental Protection Agency.

Spring, Joel (1976). *The Sorting Machine*. New York: David McKay.

Starr, Paul (1982). *The Social Transformation of American Medicine*. New York: Basic Books.

Steelman, Lala Carr, and Brian Powell (1985). "Appraising the Implications of the SAT for Educational Policy." *Phi Delta Kappan* 66, no. 4, 1–6.

Stone, Deborah (1988). *Policy, Paradox, and Political Reason*. New York: Harper College.

Thurow, Lester (1984). "The Ultimate Keynesian." *Newsweek*, January 23, p. 49.

Tong, Rosemarie (1993). "Euthanasia in the 1990s: Dying a Good Death." *Current*, no. 354 (July–August), pp. 27–34.

Tribe, Laurence H. (1990). *Abortion: The Clash of Absolutes*. New York: Norton.

Tyack, David, Michael Kirst, and Elisabeth Hansot (1980). "Educational Reform: Retrospect and Prospect." *Teachers College Record* 32, 251–265.

Uchitelle, Louis (1994). "The Rise of the Losing Class." *The New York Times*, November 20, Section 4, pp. 1, 5.

U.N. Environment Programme (1988). *Assessment of Urban Air Quality*. London: United Nations.

U.S. Congressional Research Service (1988). "Health Insurance and the Uninsured." Washington D.C.: U.S. Government Printing Office, May.

U.S. Department of Education (1992). *Digest of Educational Statistics*. Washington, D.C.: National Center for Educational Statistics.

U.S. Senate (1991). *Policy Implications of Greenhouse Warming*. Hearings, Committee on Commerce, Science, and Transportation, 102nd Cong., 1st sess. Washington, D.C.: U.S. Government Printing Office.

Vernon, Raymond, and Debora L. Spar (1989). *Beyond Globalism: Remaking American Foreign Policy.* New York: Free Press.

Wahlke, John, Heinz Eulau, William Buchanan, and LeRoy C. Ferguson (1962). *The Legislative System.* New York: John Wiley.

Waldman, Steve, and Bob Cohn (1994). "Heath Care Reform: The Lost Chance." *Newsweek,* September 19, pp. 29–32.

Walker, Charles A., LeRoy Gould, and Edward J. Woodhouse (1983). *Too Hot to Handle: Social and Policy Issues in the Management of Radioactive Wastes.* New Haven, CT: Yale University Press.

Wells, Donald T. (1982). "Site Control of Hazardous Waste Facilities." *Policy Studies Review* 1, no. 4, 728–735.

_____ (1986). "Statutory and Structural Determinants of State Response in Hazardous Waste Policy." Paper delivered at the Western Social Science Association. Reno, Nevada, April.

_____ (1996). *Environmental Policy: A Global Perspective for the Twenty-First Century.* Englewood Cliffs, NJ: Prentice Hall.

White, Langdon, Edwin J. Foscue, and Tom L. McKnight (1985). *Regional Geography of Anglo-America,* 6th ed. Englewood Cliffs, NJ: Prentice Hall.

Williams, Scott, and Mark Buechler (1993). "Charter Schools." *Policy Bulletin.* Indiana Education Policy Center, January, pp. 1–7.

Wilson, James Q. (1989). *Bureaucracy: What Government Agencies Do and Why They Do It.* New York: Basic Books.

Wolinsky, Howard, and Tom Brune (1994). *The Serpent on the Staff: The Unhealthy Politics of the American Medical Association.* New York: Jeremy Tarcher.

Woodward, C. Van (1966). *The Strange Career of Jim Crow.* New York: Oxford University Press.

Wooley, John T. (1984). *Monetary Politics. The Federal Reserve and the Politics of Monetary Policy.* Cambridge: Cambridge University Press.

World Resources Institute (1993). *World Resources 1992–1993: A Guide to the Global Environment.* New York: Oxford University Press.

Wrightson, Margaret (1986). "Interlocal Cooperation and Urban Problems: Lessons for the New Federalism." *Urban Affairs Quarterly* 22, no. 2, 261–275.

Wyatt Company (1994). "The Health Security Act—An Assessment." Washington, D.C.: The Wyatt Co.

Zeigler, Harmon, and Michael Baer (1969). *Lobbying: Interaction, and Influence in American State Legislatures.* Belmont, CA: Wadsworth.

Zelinsky, William (1992). *The Cultural Geography of the United States*, rev. ed. Englewood Cliffs, NJ: Prentice Hall.

≋ *INDEX*

A

Abbington School District
    v. *Schempp*, 188
Accumulation theory, 41
Action channels, 89
Administrative discretion, 99
Allopaths, 236
Aristotle, 176, 303
At-large election, 94

B

Banking Act of 1935, 158
Board of Governors, Fed, 158–159
Brown v. *Board of Education*, 82
Budget and Accounting Act
    of 1921, 153
Budget and Impoundment Control Act
    of 1974, 153
Budget uncontrollables, 151
Business climate, 174
Business Roundtable, 36

C

Charter school, 196–197
Civic obligation, 304
Clean Air Act, 131–132, 281
Clean Air Act Amendments of 1990:
    ozone-depletion provisions, 117
    policy strategy, 122
    deadlock on air quality, 130
    provisions, 132
    significance, 283
Clean technology (*see* low waste tech-
    nology)
Clean Water Act, 133, 281
Compassion in Dying
    v. *Washington State*, 267
Competency-based education, 195
Comprehensive Environmental
    Response, Compensation,
    and Liability Act , 135
Conservatives, 52, 62
Contextualism, 86
Convention, 129
Convention on International Trade

in Endangered Species of Wild
 Fauna and Flora, 131
Cooptation, 87
Cultural reaction syndrome:
 definition, 25–26
 policy effects, 33–34
Cultural war, 35, 297

D

Declaration, 129
Democracy, 16, 159
Development bonds, 168
Direct federalism, 109
Disciplined intelligence model, 186
Discount rate, 160–161
Disinformation Society, 44
Distributive justice, 16
District election, 94
Downsizing,, 298
Drug Price Competition Act, 240

E

Effectiveness, 18
Efficiency, 17
Elastic currency, 157–158
Elite theory, 19
Employment Act of 1946, 156
Engel v. *Vitali*, 188, 284
Equality, 17
Equity, 16–17
Everson v. *Board of Education*, 188
Executive Order 8802, 30–31

F

Federal Food and Drug Act, 124
Federal funds market, 161–162
Federal Insecticide, Fungicide,
 and Rodenticide Act, 134
Federal Mining Act of 1872, 138–139

Federal Open Market Committee, 160
Federal Reserve Act of 1913, 158
Federal Reserve System, 158–159
Federalist policy cultures:
 definition, 49
 description, 65–68
Fetal viability, 257
Food, Drug, and Cosmetic Act, 240
Free trade zones, 287
Frost belt, 68

G

General circulation models, 119
Globalization of the environment, 114
Goldin Coffin Syndrome, 213, 271
Gramm-Rudman-Hollings Emergency
 Deficit Reduction and Balanced
 Budget Act, 153–154
Grace Commission, 154
Grass roots volunteerism, 72
Great Lakes Water Quality
 Agreement, 131
Greenhouse gases, 117–118
Gridlock, 96, 295
Griswold v. *Connecticut*, 253
Gross national product, 50, 178
Groundwater, 126–127
Guild and competitive market
 model, 206

H

Hamilton, Alexander, 67, 146, 157
Hawaii State Health Insurance
 Plan, 247–248
Hawkins v. *Shaw*, 108
Hazard, 113
Hazard-reduction strategy, 123
Health insurance purchasing
 cooperatives, 246, 294
Health maintenance
 organizations, 225–226

Higher Education Facilities Act, 188
Hill Burton Hospital
     Construction Act, 32, 239
Homeopath, 236
Housing and Community
     Development Act, 104
Hyperpluralism, 13, 96
Hyde Amendment, 260–261

I

Individual mandate proposals, 223
Inflation, 163
Information age, 43
Information pollution, 44
Innovative leadership pattern, 27
Intergovernmental Panel
     on Climate Change:
     recommendations, 119–120
     model for other policy
          areas, 140–141
Intermestic affairs, 10
International Convention for the
     Prevention of Pollution
     from Ships, 130
International Monetary Fund, 160
Interstate compacts, 107
Interstate Highway Trust
     Fund, 32–33
Institutionalism, 86–87
Irradiation, 125
Iron triangles, 89
Isolationism, 54–55

J

Jefferson, Thomas, 60, 67, 146, 181
Jim Crow laws, 83

K

Keynesianism, 162–164

L

Laissez-faire, 146
Lemon v. *Kurtzman*, 189–190
Liberals, 62–63
Libertarians, 63
Living-will laws, 266
London Accord:
     provisions, 129–130
     model for cooperation, 142
London Dumping Convention, 130
Low Level Radioactive Waste
     Act, 136
Low-waste technology, 123

M

Madison, James, 65–66, 108, 145
Marginal definition of the law, 100
Marketable emission credits:
     definition, 122
     strategy, 132
MARPOL, 130
McCullom v. *Board
     of Education*, 188–189
Medicaid, 2, 211, 222, 244–245
Medicare, 213, 215
Member banks, 158
Military-industrial complex, 31
Mixed market model, 206
Modernization/disaster syndrome:
     definition, 26–27
     policy effects, 33
Montreal Protocol on Substances
     that Deplete the Ozone Layer:
     provisions, 129
     model for cooperation, 142
Multiple expansion of bank
     deposits, 161

N

NASQUAN stations, 127

National ambient air quality standards, 132
National Council for the Accreditation of Teacher Education, 192
National Defense Education Act, 186
National pollutant discharge elimination system, 133
National Teachers Examination, 192–193
New Deal:
    origins, 22
    policy effects, 28–30
    regulation of industry, 36
Nondecision:
    definition, 7
    on local governments, 107
Nuclear Waste Policy Act, 135–136

O

Ownership managed care, 226
Open market transactions, 159–160

P

Packaged disinformation, 43–44
Par banking,, 157
Pareto theorem, 176
Patient Self Determination Act, 267
"Pay or play" incentives, 246
Planned Parenthood v. Casey, 264
Pluralism, 19
Pluralistic elitism, 20
Policy culture, 40, 48–49
Policy myths, 40, 48
Policy stalemate, 13
Political ideologues, 48–49
Populists, 52, 63
Privatization:
    in education, 183–184
    evaluation of, 191–192
Protocol, 129

Public choice, 86
Public interest, 16
Public interest groups, 107
Public service model, 206
Pure Food and Drug Act, 240
Public Health Services Law, Title X, 261

R

Range war, 75
Rawls, John, 176–177
Reaganomics (see supply side economics)
Recession, 163
Regional policy cultures, 49
Regional seas program, 130–131
Regulatory federalism, 105
Renaissance cities, 71
Representation, 18, 93
Reserve requirement, 161
Resource Conservation and Recovery Act:
    administrative discretion, 99
    provisions, 134–135
    as legislation, 281
Revenue Enhancement Act, 166
Right of privacy, 253–254
Risk, 113
Rodriquez v. the San Antonio Special District, 191
Roe v. Wade:
    federalist culture roots, 103
    content of the ruling, 252–254
Rust belt, 68

S

Safe Drinking Water Act, 133
Scholastic Aptitude Test, 199
Separation of powers:
    effects on federalism, 66
    definition, 92

policy impacts, 92–93
Serrano v. *Priest*, 190
Single-payer insurance plans, 248–249
Social backlash, 297
Social insurance model, 206
Socialized medicine (*see* public
    service model)
Special district governments, 190
Stagflation, 165
Stakeholder interests, 117
Structural functional theory, 85–86
Subnational policy momentum:
    definition, 14
    reasons for occurrence, 36–37
    policy effects, 38–39
Sun belt, 68
Superfund, 135
Supply side economics, 151, 162–165
Sustainable economic growth, 178

T

Tax increment financing, 169–170
Technology-forcing standards, 133, 291
TennCare program, 245
Third party managed care, 226
Third party payment system, 213
Third sector service organizations, 302
Tilton v. *Richardson*, 188
Toxic Substances Control Act, 134

Trace gases, 117
Treaty, 129
Trenton v. *New Jersey*, 107–108

U

Unexpected consequences, 9
Uniform state laws, 107
Uranium Mine Tailings Radiation
    Control Act, 137
Urban enterprise zones, 169

V

Vocational schools, 187
Voucher, 183, 283–284

W

Waste reduction strategy, 123
Webster v. *Reproductive Health
    Services*, 258, 263–264

Y

Yankee political culture, 69–70